*Tradition
and
Contemporary
Experience*

Tradition
and
Contemporary
Experience

ESSAYS ON JEWISH THOUGHT AND LIFE

Edited by ALFRED JOSPE

Published by SCHOCKEN BOOKS *for*
B'nai B'rith Hillel Foundations, Inc.

To Miriam, John, Eytan, and all members
of their generation, in the hope that the
insights that can be derived from our
people's collective experience will help
illumine and inform their own lives.

Acknowledgments

SEVERAL ESSAYS in this volume, originally presented as lectures before university students under the auspices of the B'nai B'rith Hillel Foundations, have previously appeared in print. Permission to reprint all or part of the following essays (in some cases revised or enlarged) is gratefully acknowledged:

WILL HERBERG, "Judaism as Personal Decision," *Conservative Judaism,* vol. 22, no. 4, Summer 1968.

RICHARD ISRAEL, "Jewish Tradition and Political Action," *Jewish Frontier,* January 1966.

ALFRED JOSPE, "The Jewish Image of the Jew: On the Meaning of Jewish Distinctiveness," *Great Jewish Ideas,* ed. by Abraham E. Millgram, B'nai B'rith Great Jewish Book Series, vol. 5, Washington, D.C., 1964.

———— "The Three-Fold Rebellion: Some Observations on Israel Today," *Jewish Heritage,* vol. 3, no. 4, Spring 1961.

MILTON KONVITZ, "Change and Tradition in American Judaism: A Letter to David Daiches" (originally entitled "A Letter to David Daiches: Change and Tradition in American Judaism"), *Commentary,* vol. 11, no. 5, May 1951. Reprinted from *Commentary,* by permission; copyright © 1951 by The American Jewish Committee.

MAURICE B. PEKARSKY, "The American Jewish Community— What Lies Ahead?" *The Legacy of Maurice Pekarsky,* ed. by Alfred Jospe, Chicago, 1965.

JAKOB J. PETUCHOWSKI, "Some Criteria for Modern Jewish Observance," chap. 14 of *Heirs of the Pharisees,* © 1970 by Basic Books, Inc., Publishers, New York.

Contents

PART ONE: ON BEING A JEW TODAY

ACKNOWLEDGEMENTS   vi

INTRODUCTION   1

1. *Freedom and Identity: The Challenge of Modernity*   7
   BENJAMIN M. KAHN

2. *Change and Tradition in Modern Judaism: A Letter to David Daiches*   20
   MILTON R. KONVITZ

PART TWO: ASPECTS OF THE JEWISH HERITAGE

3. *On the Meaning of Jewish Culture in Our Time*   35
   ALFRED JOSPE

4. *A Faith for Moderns: Three Views*
   The Nature of Religious Faith   51
   HENRY A. FISCHEL
   The Meaning of God for the Contemporary Jew   62
   MORDECAI M. KAPLAN
   Judaism as Personal Decision   77
   WILL HERBERG

5. *Between God and Man: The Meaning of Revelation for the Contemporary Jew*   91
   LOU H. SILBERMAN

vii

6. *The Jewish Image of Man and Its Relevance for Today*   112
   MANFRED VOGEL

7. *The Jewish Image of the Jew: On the Meaning of
   Jewish Distinctiveness*   126
   ALFRED JOSPE

8. *Judaism as a Source of Personal Values*
   A Liberal View   151
   MAURICE L. ZIGMOND
   A Traditional View   164
   NORMAN E. FRIMER

9. *Judaism as a Source of Social Values*
   Transient Isms and Abiding Values   176
   ARTHUR J. LELYVELD
   Jewish Tradition and Political Action   189
   RICHARD J. ISRAEL

PART THREE: THE EXPERIENCE OF TRADITION

10. *A Modern Approach to the Bible*   207
    ROBERT GORDIS

11. *The Way of the Law*
    Law and Observance in Jewish Experience   221
    ERNST SIMON
    Some Criteria for Modern Jewish Observance   239
    JAKOB J. PETUCHOWSKI
    Jewish Law and the Ways of Judaism in Our Time   249
    IRA EISENSTEIN
    Law as Living Discipline: The Sabbath as Paradigm   257
    NORMAN E. FRIMER

12. *On the Meaning of Prayer*   269
    ERNST SIMON

PART FOUR: OF AMERICAN JEWS AND WORLD JEWRY

13. *The American Jewish Community—What Lies Ahead?*   283
    MAURICE B. PEKARSKY

Contents

14. *The Threefold Rebellion: Some Reflections
    on Israel Today*   293
    ALFRED JOSPE
15. *Challenges to the Jewish People in Our Time*   311
    AVRAHAM HARMAN

*PART FIVE: THE JEWISH INTELLECTUAL
AND THE JEWISH COMMUNITY*

16. *Jewish Tradition and the Educated Jew*   325
    MILTON HIMMELFARB
17. *The Jewish Intellectual, the University, and the Jewish
    Community*   336
    MILTON R. KONVITZ
18. *Leadership and the Jewish Community*   348
    BENJAMIN M. KAHN

    NOTES   359

    CONTRIBUTORS   371

*Tradition
and
Contemporary
Experience*

INTRODUCTION

Of Tradition and Contemporary Experience

AMONG THE fundamental questions confronting Jews in our time is whether and under what conditions Jewish survival is possible in a free society. In past centuries, Jews had to battle for the right to be equal, to be *like* all other people, to gain full acceptance as citizens whose inalienable rights as human beings were assured and respected. Our struggle today is for the right to be different, to be *unlike* other people, to be ourselves, to retain and maintain our Jewish distinctiveness.

The predicament of the Jew in the western world actually goes deeper. The question is no longer whether he has the right to be different. He has the right not only *de jure* but, by and large, also *de facto*. He is free to be or not to be a Jew. He asks different questions: Granted that I have the right to be different—what is the meaning of this difference? How can I, as a modern man, be truly Jewish? What is there that is distinctive and meaningful in Judaism that can still speak to my deepest needs as a human being in this world and at this time? What is the nature of Jewish tradition, and what, if anything, does it still have to say to me that is relevant to my problems and may help me understand what I am and who I am, and what I am to do with my life? For Jews are ultimately groping for what every human being seeks and needs—a meaningful identity, a clear and satisfying image of himself, a sense of at-homeness in the world he inhabits. But to find his identity, man needs a threefold sense of at-homeness—

1

a sense of at-homeness in the universe, a sense of at-homeness with his fellowman, and a sense of at-homeness with himself.

It is interesting to note, and it may be significant, that three of the most influential minds of the modern world to have dealt with these three fundamental needs were either Jews or Jews by origin: Albert Einstein, who sought to illumine and clarify man's understanding of the universe; Karl Marx, who attempted to formulate what he considered to be the ultimate principle governing man's relationship with his fellowmen; and Sigmund Freud, who explored the depth of man's subconscious drives and their impact upon his self-image and behavior.

All three men were related to the Jewish group at least by origin, yet none felt that the Judaism he knew—or what he knew of Judaism—provided an answer to his questions or could be a reservoir of insight and value for his ultimate orientation. Similarly, many contemporary Jews feel that the major affirmations of their tradition cannot be reconciled with modern thought and culture, and that Judaism does not speak pertinently to the contemporary human situation. Is Judaism's time therefore past? Is there nothing that Judaism can offer to satisfy modern man's hunger for identity, purpose, and a sense of at-homeness in the world?

The predicament of the modern Jew seems to be the feeling that he is confronted by an either/or proposition: either to choose Judaism at the expense of the world, or the world at the expense of Judaism.

But are these the only possible alternatives? Are we limited to a choice *between* Judaism and the world? Or is it not also possible to live a meaningful and creative Jewish life as a Jew *in* the world? In order to find an answer to these questions, many issues have to be resolved. What is the nature of Jewish tradition, and how much of this tradition is valid in the modern world? Should we maintain our heritage untouched as a whole? If not, what parts are indispensable to Jewish living and for what reasons? What does Jewish tradition say about God, man, and the meaning of Jewish existence that is or can be relevant to modern man? What are the purpose and function of Jewish "law," and what is its relationship to the ways of Judaism in our time? Can the Jew live a full Jewish life only in the State of Israel today, or is it possible to live creatively as a Jew outside Israel? In sum, to what extent and in what ways can Jewish tradition still be relevant as idea and contemporary experience to the American Jew and, especially, to the questioning mind in the university community? These are among the central questions to which this volume seeks to address itself. The essays it contains were selected from a wealth of manuscripts or transcriptions of lectures and papers presented over a number of years before university students in B'nai B'rith Hillel Foundations or under Hillel auspices in the United States. Several considerations guided the selection of the material. Jewish educators on and off campus have long and keenly felt the need for a publication which, in one handy volume, would present informed discussions of a number of fundamental themes of Jewish life. There is an equally great need to bring together statements reflecting the often widely differing dominant views on the same theme that coexist in the Jewish community. But above all, the various papers were selected because we feel they pose trenchant questions or present articulate and challenging statements of personal conviction about the pertinence of fundamental aspects of the Jewish tradition for modern man and the Jewish person in our time.

The readings in this volume are not meant to be a substitute for the study of the classical Jewish sources themselves. There is no substitute for the study of the sources (most of which are readily accessible in the original or in English translation). The essays are meant to illustrate and elucidate what a number of contemporary Jewish scholars, educators, and observers of Jewish life consider to be the meaning and relevance of the Jewish tradition in the light of contemporary knowledge and experience.

Their views are published as a resource for reading, study, and discussion on the university campus as well as in the general community, in the hope that this volume will stimulate the further exploration of some fundamental themes of Jewish thought and life and thus contribute to a deepened understanding of the relevance of Jewish tradition as idea and contemporary experience.

ALFRED JOSPE

Washington, D.C.

Part One

ON BEING A JEW
TODAY

BENJAMIN M. KAHN

1. Freedom and Identity: The Challenge of Modernity

HISTORY IS REPLETE with statements asserting or forecasting the disappearance of the Jewish people.

After Mesha, the King of Moab, had won a great victory over Ahab, the King of Israel, twenty-eight centuries ago, he inscribed on a tablet known as the Moabite Stone the words, "And I destroyed Israel with an everlasting destruction." Were it not for the Moabite Stone, discovered in Palestine in 1868, and an occasional reference in the Bible, the name of Mesha of Moab might not be remembered in our day.

In the ancient Forum of Rome there stands a monumental arch that Titus built after the destruction of the Second Temple in order to commemorate his victory over Jewish Palestine and mark the end of the Jewish people. In the nineteen centuries since then, no Jew, whatever his country of origin, had ever walked under it —until 1945, when the Palestinian Jewish Brigade, having participated in the liberation of Rome, marched through the arch in triumphal procession.

In 1898, Pobiedonostzev, head of the Holy Synod of Russia, received a Jewish delegation and forecast the end of Jewish life in Russia with the following words: "One-third will die, one-third will leave the country, and the rest will be completely absorbed."

More recently, Arnold Toynbee wrote a series of monumental volumes in which he devoted some very uncomplimentary pages to the Jewish people, calling it a "fossil," an epithet which he subsequently retracted when the fossil reared up on its hind legs and kicked a mighty kick.

These are dramatic illustrations which seem to point to a mystique in Jewish history, a built-in assurance of Jewish survival. Despite repeated declarations and assumptions that the existence of the Jewish people had come to an end, it continued to exist, defying prophecies of doom, insuperable obstacles, and fatal cataclysms. It would seem that, should the earth be submerged under another Great Flood, the Jewish people would learn to live under water!

I

The physical survival of the Jewish people is, however, not the central Jewish problem of our time, at least not in the western world. Our fundamental problem is the quality of Jewish life—the goals and the meaningfulness of Jewish existence. These are, in turn, conditioned by the understanding Jews can achieve of the significance of the Jewish tradition and its relevance to modern life and to their own existence.

To achieve this understanding is among the most crucial tasks of our time, in which, as many people feel, tradition is challenged by modernity and the past is considered incapable of illuminating the predicaments of the present. Interestingly enough, the Hebrew language does not recognize such a distinction between "past" and "present"—it does not possess a genuine *present* tense. Life and experience are continually in process. By the time we become aware of a given moment, it is no longer in the present but in the past. Process and time presuppose change; change, in turn, is a reaction to the problem of existence, to the challenges of circumstance.

Jews have had to face the challenge of "modernity" many times in their long history. This is no contradiction in terms, for every successive generation has to face the challenge of its own modernity. Three thousand years ago, when Joshua led the Hebrew tribes into Palestine, the Israelites, desert-oriented, nomadic, suddenly came face to face with the relatively advanced civilization of the Canaanites, a civilization that was agricultural and urbane, modern for its time. The Hebrew tribes met their challenge of modernity by assimilating into their developing Jewish tradition the best of the ideas and practices of the peoples of ancient Canaan—by transmuting, for instance, the Canaanite polytheistic and idolatrous agricultural celebrations into God-centered, ethically oriented pilgrimage festivals.

Over a thousand years later, when Greek culture challenged Judaism in the Hellenistic world, Philo, the Alexandrian Jewish philosopher, attempted to meet the modern challenge of his time by an allegorical interpretation of biblical tradition in which he sought to reconcile what seemed to him to be a clash between it and the sophisticated religious philosophy of the Greeks.

Still another thousand years later, we find an example *par excellence* of this confrontation in Maimonides, who essayed the reconciliation of faith and reason, of Judaism and Aristotelianism.

In *Past and Present,* a study of Maimonides, Israel Friedlaender wrote:

> The problem that faced Maimonides—the reconciliation of Judaism with non-Jewish culture—renews itself with every generation, and never more persistently than today when the visible barriers between the Jewish and the non-Jewish environment have been raised. The example of Maimonides teaches that Judaism has nothing to fear from other cultures. The ideas of the twentieth century are not more opposed to the Judaism of today than the Aristotelian conceptions were to the Judaism of the twelfth century. Still they were accepted and absorbed by the doctrine of Judaism.[1]

Each generation of our ancestors had to face and resolve its own challenge of modernity. The question is whether the challenge confronting our generation is different from earlier experiences in our history. Is it different in scope or nature? Is it more decisive or more critical than those with which Joshua, Philo, Maimonides, and their respective contemporaries had to wrestle?

These questions merit an affirmative answer: the challenge of the twentieth century, though it has aspects in common with its predecessors, is different, for it possesses two characteristics which are *sui generis.*

The first is that the twentieth-century challenge of modernity is directed not only at the Jew but at mankind as a whole.

The second is that the problems of modern Jewish life that resulted from the shock of the Jew's initial confrontation with modern civilization have created conflicts of adjustment with which he did not have to deal in previous generations. Today's challenge is the result of the very freedom which contemporary Jewry has achieved.

II

Freedom creates problems and challenges for those who live under it. In a democratic society, the individual is subject to many more strains than he is in a totalitarian society, as he is continually faced with the obligation to make choices, to exercise his will, and to help determine his own destiny, as far as it is possible.

Those of us who were Hillel directors at the end of World War II remember the painful problems of adjustment with which a considerable number of veterans had to cope when they returned to the campus. Many of them decided to leave the universities again in order to reenlist in the Armed Forces. Having been cogs in a system for five or more years, with virtually every moment scheduled for them by others, they felt overwhelmed by the necessity of having to make their own daily decisions in the free climate of the university. Erich Fromm described the same phenomenon in his *Escape From Freedom,* in which he analyzed the syndrome of people who turned to totalitarian systems as a refuge from the complexities of decision which freedom requires.[2]

The Pentateuch presents what may be the most dramatic illustration of the predicament of freedom when it describes the fate of the slave who refused the offer of freedom by his master and whose earlobe was punctured as a sign to all that he had chosen to reject man's God-given right to be free. American history knows a parallel—the story of numerous Negroes during the Civil War who insisted on remaining slaves rather than go out as free men into an uncertain and unfamiliar world.

Paradoxically, the history of modern times has demonstrated that freedom has in large measure been accompanied by man's alienation from the moral certainties of the ancient tradition, from his fellowman, and thus from himself. Two of Kafka's books, *The Trial* and *The Castle,* both allegories of alienation and of receding certainty, are striking literary illustrations of this phenomenon. "The quest for identity is the malaise of our times," wrote Dr. Allen Wheelis, a San Francisco psychoanalyst, in *The Quest for Identity*.[3] This book was not, but could have been, written by a Jew seeking to describe the problem of the Jew in modern times— his search for identity, his quest for a self-definition.

> Identity is a coherent sense of self. It depends upon the awareness that one's endeavors and one's life make sense, that they are meaningful in the context in which life is lived. It depends also upon stable values, and upon the conviction that one's actions and values are harmoniously related. It is a sense of wholeness, of integration, of knowing what is right and what is wrong and of being able to choose.

The writings of Jewish intellectuals alienated from their tradition and the Jewish people are explicable in the light of this thesis.

The loss of "a coherent sense of self" also seems to be the problem of the adolescent and young adult today. We no longer have an easy and effective answer to his quest for an understanding of the meaning of life. The truths of previous generations no longer speak to the contemporary generation. We seem to have lost our continuity with the past. In the modern home, there is no room for family portraits, certainly not of ancestors. Nor can we predict to what degree our children will inherit the values to which we subscribe. In the midst of the greatest freedom man has ever enjoyed, he has not been able to sustain and retain the traditional values of religion, ethics, and society. Nor has he been able to replace them once they were lost. The democratic tradition is more than simply a political or economic order: it is man-centered. It has meaning and permanence only when it is based on moral principles and founded on faith in the essential dignity and sacredness of the human personality. When these undergird-ings of democracy begin to collapse, what will take their place? "The democratic tradition," wrote John Dewey in *Freedom and Culture,* "call it dream or call it penetrating vision, was so closely allied with beliefs about human nature and about the moral ends which political institutions should serve, that a rude shock occurs when these affiliations break down. Is there anything to take their place, anything that will give the kind of support they once gave?" [4]

A similar picture is drawn by Professor Edmond Cahn:

> It is unnecessary to rehearse here all the influences that have made for moral confusion in our times. . . . A society changing at an unprecedented pace has simply brushed away the inhibitions of the past. In their place, there seem to be only doubts—not merely the healthy doubts of a critical examination but the sickening and panicky doubts that come when one's bearings fade out of view.[5]

A final example: the Theater of the Absurd emerged from a belief that the human condition is absurd and that man, no longer able to accept the certainties of faith, religion, and tradition, has failed to replace them with convictions that make his life and that of society meaningful and worthwhile.

These are reflections of the general condition of our time. The moral precepts and faiths of previous generations no longer seem relevant to a rapidly changing world. Alienation is, of course, not a specifically Jewish response to the confusions of our world. There are vast numbers of people of all religious backgrounds whose relationship with their past and with society has been shattered. The rejection of religion in general, like the rejection of Judaism in particular, is a symptom of the repudiation of inherited values which characterizes our time and which becomes ever more serious as the chasm between generations grows deeper. There has been a massive hemorrhage of faith in the meaningfulness of life, illustrated by the negativism and nihilism which dominate much of contemporary philosophical thought. Man no longer conceives of himself as "slightly lower than the angels." He has lost faith in himself, in man.

III

The Jew shares the challenge of this development with every other human being. He has, however, his own peculiar configuration of historical circumstances which has made his particular situation even more difficult and complex. Modernity began for the Jew five centuries later than for the rest of the western world. The emancipation catapulted him from a parochial, closed, isolated world of his own—an *imperium in imperio*—into a strange and alien world of scientific progress, philosophical rationalism, urbane culture, and sophisticated music and art. He was unprepared for what turned out to be a radical and revolutionary transformation of his entire way of life, an almost incomprehensible threat to the ideas, practices, and institutions which for generations he had considered sacred.

Jewish reaction to the dawn of freedom manifested itself in various ways. In eighteenth- and nineteenth-century western Europe, the reactions found expression, among other things, in the growth of Jewish rationalism, the teachings of Moses Mendelssohn, the *Wissenschaft des Judentums,* and the birth of Reform Judaism. These trends and movements were groping attempts to bridge the gap between the theological and social structure of the ghetto and the exciting and colorful new world of science, literature, and art. In this conflict, thousands of Jews were lost to Judaism.

Jewish reaction in eastern Europe was different. The irresistible pressures of severe social and economic restrictions compelled the Jewish masses to build inwardly in order to armor themselves against the onslaught of the world. In the eighteenth century, they developed Messianic doctrines and mystical philosophies to shelter themselves from the harshness of reality. With the approach of the nineteenth century, they began to move into new areas of thought which were essentially nonreligious. The "enlightened ones" of the Haskalah period viewed the Hebrew language no longer as the "sacred tongue" of the past but as the secular language of a living people. Their scholarly and literary endeavors were concentrated on disciplines and areas which were divorced from the religious tradition. Spurred by the growing nationalism of Europe, they wove the fabric of Zionist ideology and spearheaded the Zionist movement, substituting national ideas and aspirations for reliance on religious faith and the traditional doctrine that national redemption must await the coming of the Messiah. Their thoughts and actions reflected their conviction that, in eastern Europe, second-class citizenship for the Jew was a permanent status and that the rebirth of Jewish culture and the Jewish people would be possible only in their own homeland.

Yet, despite these preliminary efforts at adjustment to the modern world—rationalism, the science of Judaism, and Reform Judaism in western Europe; mysticism, Haskalah, and Zionism in eastern Europe—the Jew still was unable to prepare himself adequately for what turned out to be a radical and revolutionary transformation of his entire outlook and way of life.

This transformation was the result of a rivalry of forces which emerged within Jewish life. As Jews secured greater freedom, acquired citizenship rights, and began to live in closer physical contact with their neighbors, their loss of identity grew in inverse ratio to their achievement of freedom. As their old beliefs were called into question, Jews were deeply afflicted with a sense of discontinuity with the past. As science and rationalism began to challenge the validity of their accepted faith, their traditional beliefs in God, Messiah, and revelation were shaken, with the consequent loss of a sense of inner security.

The meaning and implications of this process of alienation are strikingly portrayed in an essay by Ahad Ha'am entitled "Slavery in Freedom." [6] Ahad Ha'am wrote this essay in 1891. It could have been written yesterday, in the United States or in any country of the western world in which Jews reside. Ahad Ha'am, with uncommon insight tempered by love for his people and enriched by Zionist aspirations, grapples with this very problem. He describes the problem of the Jew who appears to live in freedom and to enjoy complete human rights, but has lost a sense of security as a Jew and a sense of relationship to his people. Despite his apparent freedom, he is a slave intellectually and morally. Ahad Ha'am, writing from Russia, which he describes as a "scene of degradation, ignorance and poverty," looks across the borders to France where there are Jewish professors, Jewish officers,

Jewish politicians, but where, despite these achievements, there is spiritual slavery because Jews hesitate to proclaim their closeness with each other, their yearning for Zion, their self-acceptance. He concluded, "The spiritual freedom which I enjoy, scoff who will, I would not exchange or barter for all the emancipation in the world."

Ahad Ha'am could have looked farther than France, across the ocean to the New World. He could have pointed to Bernard Berenson, the great art critic who, in his *Rumor and Reflection,* described how he had to repudiate his Jewish loyalties in order to acquire the culture of the gentile world.[7] He forecast the strange drama of Jewish intellectuals who, when anti-Semitism began to decline in the last decade of the nineteenth century, found themselves rootless and homeless to a greater degree than ever before; having identified their Jewishness with persecution and not with freedom, they were unable to replace antidefamation with affirmative motivation.

IV

Goethe once said that the greatest evil that can befall a man is that he shall come to think ill of himself. This, precisely, was the result of the dislocation and disorganization of Jewish life in its transition from medieval to modern times.

A story by the Yiddish writer I. L. Peretz illustrates this process or erosion. Peretz, born in Poland in 1852, was himself a product as well as a victim of the process of emancipation. He, too, was alienated from Judaism, but he found his way back through Jewish literature and through his identification with the Jewish masses of eastern Europe.

His writings contain a masterful short story, "Four Generations, Four Wills." [8] These four testaments are a poignant and dramatic illustration of the progressive disintegration of values which accompanied the process of emancipation.

The first will is simple, no more than ten lines of text, written by a traditional Jew of the pre-emancipation era. He bequeaths his books to his children and asks that they use the funds they will inherit from him to continue to maintain the synagogue and other Jewish institutions. And he blesses them in the name of God.

The second will is written by the son of this patriarch. He expresses the hope that his children will read the books or, failing this, at least present them to a good library. The financial inheritance, he hopes, will be properly invested and utilized, and it is his wish that his children continue their membership in the Jewish community.

The grandson writes the third testament. He is a "modern man," only loosely attached to the things the patriarch had held dear. It is a typical will of materialist man, with many a "to wit" and "whereas." "The funds I bequeath are to be held in escrow and in trust and properly used for the education of any children and the ultimate establishment of trust funds."

The final will is that of the great-grandson of the old Jew who had written with such love of Jewish books and learning, who had been devoted to the synagogue, and who had considered money primarily a means of support of Jewish institutions and education. The will is written in a garret by a man who pathetically declares, "I have all this money—yet I have no one to give it to, no one to share it with, no meaning in my life, no roots, no past, no present, no future." And after signing the will, he ends his existence by his own hand.

Four wills, four paragraphs, some longer, some shorter—yet they constitute a capsule history of what has happened to the Jewish people, to Jewish identity, to Jewish institutions, since the beginning of the emancipation. Our generation has inherited the backlash of the winds which blew down the walls of the ghetto and swept the Jews unprepared and ill equipped into the main stream of modern civilization.

This development has not been restricted to Europe. In the past fifty years of American Jewish history, there has been a discontinuity between generations, in which each new generation has failed to speak the language of the preceding generation. The story of acculturation and adjustment of the first, second, third, and now fourth generations of American Jews is too well known to merit repetition here. However, the same trend can be observed even in Israel. It is illustrated by a dialogue which, according to newspaper reports, took place there between Hayyim Hazaz and David Ben-Gurion.

Hazaz, one of Israel's distinguished writers, had delivered a public address on what he described as the "general spirit of nihilism" creeping into Israeli society. Ben-Gurion, at that time still the prime minister of Israel, took exception to Hazaz' thesis. Hazaz responded by challenging the prime minister to a public debate of the issue, and the two men sat down together in the presence of an illustrious gathering of Israelis to discuss what both felt was a basic question affecting the future of Israel. For Hazaz, "the trouble with Israeli youth is that it has cut itself off from the past; and this past includes the world of the ghetto." Ben-Gurion, on the other hand, questioned the validity of the ghetto experience. For him the centuries of Jewish Diaspora existence were secondary, if not unimportant, in the light of the new State and its *de novo* accomplishments. This dialogue was important, not only because of the two personalities involved, but because it posed the very question with which we are dealing: How can Jewish identity be achieved in Israel or anywhere else? How and to what extent, if at all, is the past involved in creating a present identity?

V

In the past decades, several new factors have had an affirmative effect on Jewish identity—factors which have given a new dimension to the meaning of freedom as something far more significant than the mere absence of physical and economic restraint. The shattering tragedy of the loss of six million Jews has radically affected the attitude of numerous Jews who had hitherto felt little kinship with the Jewish people. Many of them have begun to think of themselves at least nominally as Jews, even though they still may have to acquire a meaningful sense of Jewish identity. Among the young, the recollection of the Holocaust has generated a determination so to act that "it will never happen again."

Second, there is a new climate in America that enables the Jew to identify himself naturally as a Jew and that encourages him to undergird his nominal self-identification with knowledge and an understanding of its meaning. By and large, American Jews are no longer trying to hide their identity or to escape from their Jewishness. They are seeking answers, meaningful and compelling answers, to the fundamental questions confronting Jews as individuals and Judaism as a tradition. They may yet be on the verge of active involvement in their people's history, in the living experience of every generation of Jews.

Above all, the establishment of the State of Israel and the courage and self-sacrifice of its creators and defenders have given the Jew a new self-respect and strengthened his will to live as a Jew. The American poet Karl Shapiro illustrates the impact of Israel's existence on the American Jew. After being for years far from Jewish ideas and institutions, he was so deeply affected by the establishment of the State of Israel that he wrote in a moving poem, entitled "Israel,"

> When I see the name of Israel high in print
> The fences crumble in my flesh; I sink
> Deep in a Western chair and rest my soul.
> I look the stranger clear to the blue depths
> Of his unclouded eye. I say my name
> Aloud for the first time unconsciously.[9]

VI

These trends and factors have created the setting in which it is possible for us to move ahead in our task to meet the challenge of modernity head-on and to seek to achieve our full Jewish identity under freedom. If we succeed, it may well be because of the efforts and orientation of the younger generation. For it is a generation which, born in freedom, is not self-conscious about its Jewishness. Probing the meaning of freedom, it is initiating the search for Jewish knowledge and involvement. These are the cornerstones of the structure of Jewish life. Potentially, this is the generation of which David Frishman speaks in his poem "The Messiah," where he pictures the Messiah chained to the throne of God. Bitterly frustrated over his inability to descend to earth to help man free himself, he cries, "How long?" The closing words of the poem give the answer. The Messiah will come

> When there will arise a new generation,
> A generation that will understand the meaning of
>   redemption,
> A generation that will arise to be redeemed.[10]

MILTON R. KONVITZ

2. Change and Tradition in American Judaism: A Letter to David Daiches

DEAR DAVID DAICHES,

Had your article in the February 1951 *Commentary* been only an exposition and defense of agnosticism, it would have awakened in me echoes of Thomas Huxley and Bertrand Russell, but I would not have felt myself personally involved. Your article, however, because it is your "personal view" of American Judaism, has started up in me reverberations from some of the deepest layers of my mind; I find myself profoundly and inextricably involved. For you and I have had pretty much the same upbringing, experiences, and education. My father, too, as you know, was a distinguished Orthodox rabbi who enjoyed the respect and confidence of both Jew and Christian; my education, too, was in several cultures, sacred and profane; my career, too, has brought me, in my vocation as a teacher, to an American university campus. However, though I accept some of the incidental things you say in your article, if your fundamental assertions are right, then I have been misliving my life; I have gained from my background, experiences, and education only a bushel of tares, while you possess the wheat. I feel myself, therefore, personally challenged.

Cutting away some of the underbrush, I find that our differences arise from our different attitudes toward tradition, particularly as to the function of tradition in Judaism. Our differences here are over fundamentals.

One extreme view of tradition may be characterized as the Platonic view. Plato held that the good is what preserves, that evil is what changes. Change leads away from what is perfect, the Form or the Idea; change tends toward the imperfect, evil. Any change whatever, Plato says in the *Laws,* "is the gravest of all the treacherous dangers that can befall a thing—whether it is now a change of season, or of wind, or of the diet of the body, or of the character of the soul." This statement, he says, applies to everything except to what is evil. Again in the *Laws* he says: "The lawgiver must continue by hook or by crook a method which ensures for his state that the whole soul of every citizen will resist, from reverence and fear, changing any of the things that are established of old." In the *Philebus* Plato says: "The men of old . . . were better than we are now, and . . . lived nearer to the gods. . . ."

An opposite extreme view of tradition may be characterized as the Emersonian view. If a man claims to know and speak of God, says Emerson in his essay "Self-Reliance," and yet

> carries you backward to the phraseology of some old mouldered nation in another country, in another world, believe him not. . . . Is the parent better than the child into whom he has cast his ripened being? Whence then this worship of the past? . . . When we have new perception, we shall gladly disburden the memory of its hoarded treasures as old rubbish. . . . This one fact the world hates, that the soul *becomes;* for that forever degrades the past. . . . Say to them: "O father, O mother, O brother, O friend, I have lived with you after appearances hitherto. Henceforward I am the truth's. Be it known unto you that henceforth I obey no laws less than the eternal law. . . . I appeal from your customs. I must be myself. I cannot break myself any longer for you, or you."

Emerson, who knew his Plato, was here, I believe, answering him by substituting one extreme view for another. Plato was on a quest for certainty, Emerson was on a quest for change. Plato identified the good with being; Emerson identified the good with becoming.

If one is offered a choice between these two extremes, a person with a warm attachment to life and experience must do what Emerson counseled: break with the past completely, tell the dead to bury the dead, kiss one's parents good-bye and turn one's face in the direction of the future and the unknown.

In a way, David, it seems that this is what you have done. The Orthodox Judaism of your father was, you say, "the real thing." Judaism is that religion which you associate with your father—"the full historical Judaism with its richness, its ceremonial, its discipline, and its strange beauty." When you think of Judaism, you are a Platonist and would put a curse on anyone who removes his father's landmark. Judaism is a perfect Form or Idea; it is unchanging; any change is a step toward imperfection: "The men of old . . . were better than we are now, and . . . lived nearer to the gods." If Jews wish to continue as Jews, they should go back to your father's *shul,* his way of life, and his ways of looking at life and the world.

But you yourself, David, because of your intelligence and spirit, find your father's ways and views no longer congenial or acceptable. You, therefore, feel that you must break with the past completely, and so you go over to Emerson's side. For you, there can be no worship of the past. You say to your father: "O father, henceforward I am the truth's." You have made the leap from Jew to humanist, from Judaism to humanism, from the dead past to the live present and future, from being to becoming.

If Judaism is something that is finished, completed, a Form that will not reflect anything that is alive and throbbing today and this minute, how could one blame you? If Judaism is only a mummified corpse, what could you personally do with it except hack it to pieces, free yourself from it, and run outdoors for a bit of fresh air and sunshine?

In a way, however, your position is extremely equivocal. You still want the cake, but only for *others to eat.* Identifying Judaism with your father's *shul* and home, you want others to sustain it for "its richness, its ceremonial, its discipline, and its strange beauty." For others, Judaism is a Platonic Form, perfect in its being. But not for you. For yourself, you are on an Emersonian quest of becoming; you shatter the past, you have disburdened your memory of its hoarded treasure as so much old rubbish.

Now I say, David, if the choice were only between Plato and Emerson, I would be on your and Emerson's side. But you have narrowed the possible choices to two impossible extremes.

There is a third way. It is the way of all that is best in Judaism.

For a description of this third way I shall go to T. S. Eliot's essay "Tradition and the Individual Talent"—and I go to him rather than to, say, Solomon Schechter, because his discussion will bring home to you the fact that you have treated tradition in Judaism differently from the way you would treat tradition in English literature or culture, for I believe you share the views Eliot expresses in this essay.

Tradition, says Eliot, cannot be inherited as a dead weight—the way a son inherits his father's house or his books. The inheritance of tradition involves a number of things. First of all, it involves the historical sense. This sense involves a perception, "not only of the pastness of the past, but of its presence." The historical sense "compels a man to write not merely with his own generation in his bones, but with a feeling that the whole of the literature of Europe from Homer and within it the whole of the literature of his own country has a simultaneous existence and composes a simultaneous order." This historical sense is "a sense of the timeless and of the temporal together." No writer or artist can be seen as standing alone. "His significance, his appreciation is the appreciation of his relation to the dead poets and artists. You cannot value him alone; you must set him, for contrast and comparison, among the dead."

This is only one side of a two-sided transaction. "The existing monuments form an ideal order among themselves, which is modified," says Eliot, "by the introduction of the new (really new) work of art among them. The existing order is complete before the new work arrives; for order to persist after the supervention of novelty, the whole existing order must be, if ever so slightly, altered; and so the relations, proportions, values of each work of art toward the whole are readjusted; and this is conformity between the old and the new." The past, then, "is altered by the present as much as the present is directed by the past."

In Judaism we find—at least I offer it as my personal view—both sides of the creative transaction described by Eliot. We have the historical sense, which gives to Jewish history a simultaneous existence and which composes of Jewish history a simultaneous order. Let me illustrate this point from the Passover Haggadah: "We were the slaves of Pharaoh in Egypt; and the Lord our God brought us forth from there with a mighty hand and an out-stretched arm. And if the Holy One, blessed be He, had not brought us forth from Egypt, then surely we, and our children, and our children's children, would be enslaved to Pharaoh in Egypt." We are taught that every Jew in every generation must think of himself as having gone forth from Egypt: "It was not only our forefathers that the Holy One, blessed be He, redeemed. Us, too, the living, He redeemed together with them. . . ." The past, then, changes the present: I, in 1951, an American, have been redeemed from slavery and Egypt. The past is significant to me not in its character of pastness but in its existential presentness.

And the past in Judaism is changed by the present. When Moses was shown the Torah as it was to be interpreted and ap-plied by Rabbi Akiba many centuries later, he looked at it in amazement and consternation, for he could not—the rabbis tell us—recognize in it the Torah that he transmitted to the Jews at Sinai. The Torah as it has passed through the alembic of the minds of the Prophets, of Maimonides, Saadyah Gaon, and of the thou-sands of rabbis of the Talmud and of the centuries since then, has undergone profound sea changes. "Turn it over, turn it over," we are told, "for everything is in it." Judaism can no more be re-duced to a number of dogmas and practices, or even, as you seem to intimate, to monotheism, humanism, and a sense of righteous-ness, than English poetry can be reduced to a textbook of abstract generalizations.

In Judaism, then, the past is altered by the present, and the present is altered by the past. Had you considered Judaism in this light, you could not then have permitted yourself to identify Ju-daism with your father's beliefs and practices. To freeze Judaism into any form is to give substance to Toynbee's charge that Judaism is a fossil; for it means identifying Judaism with the past as utter and dead pastness; it means inheriting Judaism from one's father as one inherits one's father's house or books. There is only one thing to do with one's father, as John Bright has said, and that is: to stand upon his shoulders—and to see farther. For a child to carry his father upon *his* shoulders is to identify his father with obsolescence and to invite nihilism.

Let me for a moment look at this matter from another point of view. It seems to me that an identification of Judaism with the *shul* and the forms of observance of one's father lays one open to the charge of idolatry. "And thou shalt love the Lord thy God with all thy heart, and all thy soul, and all thy might." We have not been taught to love our synagogues, or our *kiddush* cups, or our Sabbaths and holy days, or our rabbis, or even the Bible or the Torah, with all our hearts, with all our souls, and all our might—but only God. (We are taught to honor our fathers and mothers; we are not taught to love them with all our hearts, with all our souls, and with all our might.) Holy places, holy days, holy books, and holy men are important, but their importance is of a secondary, relative, contingent nature. To identify Judaism with them is to confuse form with substance, shadow with reality. To worship the Bible is to practice bibliolatry—witness the Jewish judgment on the Karaites. To worship an infallible church or pope, or a Sanhedrin, or a land, or a book, is to love something other than God with all one's heart, all one's soul, and all one's might.

It was Cardinal Faulhaber, though it could have been a great rabbi, who said, "We cannot separate the Law of the Lord from the Lord of the Law." To give centrality in Judaism even to the Law of the Lord is to set up an idol. Only the Lord of the Law is entitled to centrality as an absolute.

This, incidentally, is one reason that I object to making the Law of the Lord the law of the State of Israel, for it means separation of the Law of the Lord from the Lord of the Law; it means the intervention of a policeman between Jew and God, and the displacement of God by the state. The intention of the rabbis is, of course, to enthrone God; but the effect is precisely the opposite. When you, David, say that the separation of church and state in Israel may be good Jeffersonian Americanism but is not good Judaism, you are again fossilizing Judaism, refusing to admit that the Judaism of thousands of years ago has been changed by the centuries and the many millions of Jews—and non-Jews, including Jefferson—who have lived and died since the destruction of the Temple.

It is in a nonidolatrous, Jewish spirit that we observe rites and ceremonies. "The commandments," said Rab, "were given to Israel only in order that men should be purified through them. For what can it matter to God whether a beast is slain at the throat or at the neck?" Even the Temple was used by our forefathers as an idol. "Trust ye not in lying words, saying: 'The temple of the Lord, the temple of the Lord, the temple of the Lord are these,'" said Jeremiah to them. "I will do unto the house, whereupon My name is called, wherein ye trust . . . as I have done to Shiloh." To call a place the temple of the Lord and to trust in it in such a way as to displace God is to engage an idol-worship. (We see here the essential reason that Jews find it impossible to reconcile themselves to a religion which says that the way to the Father is only through the Son—or through the Church; for this means the positing of an absolute besides God. The Jew, *per contra,* says: the way to the Father is through your heart and your deeds. Nor does he add: and through your father's synagogue and observances.)

I want to quote to you a Psalm which you know very well—Psalm 15:

> Lord, who shall sojourn in Thy tabernacle?
> Who shall dwell upon Thy mountain?
> He that walketh uprightly, and worketh
>   righteousness,
> And speaketh truth in his heart;
> That hath no slander upon his tongue,
> Nor doeth evil to his fellow,
> Nor taketh up a reproach against his
>   neighbor;
> In whose eyes a vile person is despised,
> But he honoureth them that fear the Lord;
> He that sweareth to his own hurt, and
>   changeth not;
> He that putteth not out his money on
>   interest,
> Nor taketh a bribe against the innocent.
> He that doeth these things shall never be
>   moved.

I quote this Psalm not so much for what is in it as for what is *not* in it. You will note there is not a word in it about the Temple, about forms of worship, not even a word about Jews or Judaism. And it was this Psalm which, according to the rabbis of the Talmud, summarized the 613 commandments. It was in the spirit of this Psalm (and such passages in the Bible are legion) that Saadyah Gaon said that he who observes the commandment regarding honest weights and measures may, for all we know, be as righteous as he who observes the ritual commandments; and that Rabbi Kook said that the *halutzim* in Palestine were earning great merits in the world to come by observing the commandment of *avoda* (labor). I cite these examples not to prove that deeds are more important than rituals, but only for the purpose of demonstrating that it is a falsification to give to rituals or to any institution or to any person or book a position of centrality in Judaism.

You, David, are no worshiper of ancestors, and no worshiper of idols. Your intelligence is free and brave, so you have shattered the image of Judaism which you had projected upon the image of your father; and by shattering one, you have shattered both. But you were wrong in the beginning when you identified Judaism with your father's loyalties and practices. Had you climbed up to your father's shoulders, you would have seen farther—you would have seen yourself as changed by him—and as changing him. From the standpoint of a tradition that is not inherited as a dead weight but that is alive and creative, it may be said that even as he is the child of the man, the child is also the father of the man. Piety, said Santayana, is loyalty to the sources of our being. This is the piety that characterizes the direction of sentiment from son to father. But this is only half the story. The other half is the piety which characterizes the direction of sentiment from father to son. Either half alone is impiety; the two taken together give us a tradition in which the present is enriched by the past and the past is enriched by the present, thus saving us from nihilism as well as from idolatry.

Seen this way, Judaism is no hindrance to humanism. On the contrary, it affords one a stance from which one can say with Terence: *Homo sum; humani nihil a me alienum puto.* Jews and Christians have been great humanists without feeling that either their religion or their humanism was compromised. A proper perspective makes possible a perception of the timeless and the temporal together, and of man and God together. When a man knows with Saadyah Gaon that God is "the God of all mankind," and that "the worth of each man and his lot are equally precious before Him," and with Ben Azzai that the verse in Genesis, "This is the book of the generations of Adam," is the greatest principle in the Torah, then nothing human—not even agnosticism, David—can be alien to him. Judaism, as thus conceived, stands committed to all that is open and free and is the enemy of all that is closed and restricted. If you will say that this is not the Judaism of your father and mine, but a Jeffersonian Judaism, I will answer that I am not at all sure that they were not Jeffersonian Jews. Though at times they felt themselves possessed by God, they never acted as if God were possessed by them.

You are inclined, David, it seems to me, to seek a simple solution—total Orthodoxy or total assimilation—to a problem that is very complex. Let me try to make my meaning clear by a brief comparison between your father's experiences as rabbi in Edinburgh and my father's experiences as rabbi in Newark, New Jersey.

When your father came to Edinburgh in 1919, he found four hundred Jewish families and two Orthodox congregations. The call to your father came from congregations acting jointly. After some years and much effort, your father succeeded in bringing together the two congregations, forming a new, united synagogue.

When my father came to Newark in 1924, the synagogue that called him had a membership of some four hundred families. Newark then had an estimated Jewish population of between sixty and seventy thousand (many thousands have since moved to satellite towns). There was no census of congregations, but I venture to say that there were no fewer than thirty or forty Orthodox congregations, besides a Reform temple and two Conservative congregations. In addition to my father, there were only two or three other Orthodox rabbis with *smicha,* that is, properly ordained. But there were in addition many fakers—I use the term advisedly —who professed to be rabbis: former Hebrew teachers, *shammosim* (sextons), *chazanim* (cantors), and *shochtim* (ritual slaughterers), a despicable crew of "reverends" who were perpetually covetous of money and publicity. They were a stinking abomination to both God and man. Yet these fake rabbis had congregations, performed all the functions of rabbis, buried the dead, and flattered the living. They were constantly tempted to make a racket of *kashrut*. This was not very difficult in a city where there were, I would say, between 125 and 150 butchers and many poultry markets that catered to the Jewish trade.

It was not long before my father and his colleagues found themselves in a life-and-death struggle. I am not exaggerating. If I were to disclose the facts, our antidefamationists would charge me with contributing to anti-Semitism! (The record, however, of the kosher poultry racket of New York City, in which the union of *shochtim* played a prominent role, may be found in the proceedings of the New York State courts.) That episode in my father's life is one which I find extremely painful to recall; for at least a decade my father had no sense of personal security, and no inner or outer peace.

Now I submit to you, David, that it is not helpful to judge the anarchic complexity of Jewish life in Newark (or Chicago, or Philadelphia, or San Francisco) by the relatively idyllic simplicity of Jewish life in Edinburgh. Going home from Edinburgh to Newark is like going from Walden Pond to Boston—or from Selborne to London. There is, as Mr. Justice Brandeis said, the curse of bigness. It is not merely that with bigness a small problem becomes a big problem; bigness and smallness may be incommensurable.

Please note that what I am talking about is the large-scale *hefkerut,* the utter disorder that one can find in a large Orthodox community in the United States, a state of affairs that exists among American Jews who profess to adhere to your father's *shul* and to his religious values. Orthodoxy, then, is no guarantee against vulgarity, corruption, and even plain criminality. To say to American Jews (of whom some four million are said to live in cities with a Jewish population of ten thousand or more) that they should be Orthodox or assimilate, and to say this in a context which implies that Orthodoxy will shield them from evils which you associate with non-Orthodox Judaism, is, I fear, to hold out illusory hopes. The evils we see around us are not due to the fact that some Jews are non-Orthodox.

Let me be clear on this point: Just as I am not attempting to whitewash Reform and Conservative Jews, so I am not attempting to blacken the repute of Orthodox Jews. My intent is only to caution against the prescription of a cure that is irrelevant to the malady. Just as it does not follow, I believe, from what you have said, that Jews should not be or become Reform or Conservative, so it does not follow from what I have said that Jews should not be or become Orthodox. The decision regarding religious commitment should be made only on the basis of religious faith and belief as to what best ministers to the individual's deepest personal needs.

But you, David, seem to be advising American Jews to base their decision regarding personal religious commitment on institutional behavior; that is, on observation of the way in which congregations and rabbis behave. You ask them, in effect, to choose their religion on sociological rather than religious considerations. The moral import of your approach can tend only further to eat away the foundations of Judaism. If followed, your approach would, in the long run, contribute to a deepened vulgarization and a more widespread shallowness, so that ultimately we would all become hollow men. In a word, you tell us to be or become Orthodox, but for the wrong reasons—reasons which, if taken seriously, would cause Judaism to crumble. It would be both dry and empty.

There is, of course, much that is wrong, and even rotten, in American Jewish life. But this is equally true of American life in general (as it is true also of British, French, Asian life, and of every man's life, wherever his local habitation and whatever his name). Yet we do not, by any means, despair of American life. Why, then, should we despair of Jewish life in America? If we are not better than others, are we worse? Amos, Hosea, Jeremiah, and Ezekiel saw no less evil in their own days, yet they were prophets of hope as well as prophets of doom. Their mission was to call for and promise a renewal. American Jews today, as Jews everywhere and at all times, prefer the lesser to the greater good, see the better but follow the worse. There is so much good that must be done and so much evil that is being done that one wishes to cry out, "But yet the pity of it . . . !"

One is torn between pity and anger—at oneself as well as at others; but Judaism is committed to both anger and pity. For just as pity alone may weaken the will so that it becomes tolerant of evil, so anger alone may destroy the world—with all the good that is in it and all its promise of good for the future. It is not only Judaism but sanity that compels us to stake all we have on the good, and on the future—eschatological or natural. Judaism will yet flourish, even in America—perhaps especially in America. There is much vexation of spirit, and that which is wanting cannot be numbered. Yet the crooked *can* and *will* be made straight.

Part Two

ASPECTS OF THE
JEWISH HERITAGE

ALFRED JOSPE

3. On the Meaning of Jewish Culture in Our Time

To INQUIRE ABOUT the "meaning" of a culture seems to be a futile enterprise. One can ask, What is culture? One can describe the culture of a group and study its moods, trends, and expressions. One can dissect and examine it as a sociologist, musicologist, historian, philosopher, or archeologist. But to ask, What is the meaning of a culture? is in itself a meaningless question. Culture basically has no meaning. It is the manifestation of a people's life process. The culture of a group is its way of living— the language it speaks, its tools and industries, the social and educational institutions it creates, the literature that reflects its values, gropings, and experiences, the art and music that manifest its particular "style" and sense of harmony.

Only in the Jewish group is this question asked. And the fact that Jews frequently ask, What is the meaning of Jewish culture? is a symptom of the identity crisis of many modern Jews. We are self-conscious about our identity. We want to be convinced not only that it is natural to live as Jews but that Judaism is something good and worthwhile. We are told or exhorted that Judaism should mean something to us, but we are groping around for what this meaning might be. Jewish identity is replaced by a discussion of the advantages or disadvantages of Jewish identity.

The predicament of numerous modern Jews manifests itself essentially in this search for a self-definition. They seek a verbal definition precisely because they lack the definition that springs from a satisfying experience of their Jewishness. The Judaism they know, or, to be more precise, what they know of Judaism, frequently has little or no relevance to their thinking and needs. Especially for many young Jewish writers, thinkers, and academicians, Judaism, if defined in religious terms, is an offense to reason and contrary to the evidence of verifiable knowledge. Though they are often responsive to Israel's human needs, they feel that Zionism requires identification with the evils of a nationalism which has been and continues to be the curse of the world. Jewish observance and practices are the meaningless relics of an antiquated past that has no claim upon them. To speak of Jewish culture is nonsense; our culture is American. Nor can they find their place in the synagogue, because they feel it is full of mediocrity and dominated by the personal ambitions and social values of the inhabitants of the "golden ghetto."

This feeling of irrelevance is among the dominant factors which have created the enormous abyss separating some of our best young minds from Jewish life and the Jewish community. Some of our most sensitive and perceptive young Jewish men and women, on the college campus as well as in the community, feel they have no home in the Jewish mansion. What they know of the Jewish heritage fails to illumine their understanding of themselves as Jews and of the predicaments of life.

The corrosive acids of ignorance and alienation have eaten deeply into Jewish self-affirmation. But is it true that Judaism, Jewish culture, has nothing significant and distinctive to contribute to our search for personal significance and to our quest for an understanding of man's life and the world?

I

Some years ago, I had a chance to visit the British Museum in London for the first time. To wander through its halls is an exciting and unforgettable experience. There you find examples of virtually everything men have been creating for more than fifty centuries—the compact art of Egypt and her tombs and monuments to death; the polished sculptures of Rome and Greece and their rows of graceful columns; the stone filigree patterns of Indian temple buildings; the icons and mosaics of Byzantium; the delicate fragility of old Chinese porcelain; the finely crafted figurines of pre-Colombian goldsmiths. The products of the artistic genius of all peoples are exhibited in these halls.

But what about the Jews?

A small room on the second floor contains several glass cases. One of them holds some chipped clay tablets—several of the so-called Tel el Amarna letters. Unearthed in Egypt about eighty years ago, they are the remnants of the archives of an Egyptian ruler who reigned about 1400 B.C.E., and tell of the invasion of Palestine by a Semitic tribe from the other side of the Jordan. A document of Jewish history. A second case contains an open book, a copy of the Bible, written by hand centuries before the invention of the printing press. It is probably one of the oldest Bible manuscripts in existence. That seems to be all we have to show. The primary product of Jewish creativity that seems to merit public exhibition is a book.

Archeologists who have conducted excavations in the Near East have indeed been disappointed by the paucity of the remains of ancient Hebrew culture they were able to unearth.[1] Not that their efforts were completely fruitless. They found a variety of scrolls, coins, *menorot* and spice boxes; and they uncovered some superbly constructed ancient synagogues, ornamented with figures and a variety of iconic symbols. Moreover, general research has revealed that Jews in ancient times showed superior craftsmanship in the production of pottery, ceramics, jewelry, and especially of gold-inlaid goblets and other types of glassware.[2]

Nevertheless, these achievements pale into insignificance if we compare them with the creations of other peoples of antiquity. Nor does Jewish artistic creativity in later centuries seem to have been much more impressive. For centuries, the painters and sculptors who turned to the Hebrew Bible as a source of thematic inspiration were Christians, not Jews. Jewish folk and synagogue music has been, until recently, largely dominated by the modes and melodies of the people among whom the Jews have lived— Oriental, eastern European, Germanic. And, until a few decades ago, the synagogues erected in Europe and America were designed mostly by non-Jews and in styles which ranged from Egyptian and

Moorish patterns to Greek, Romanesque, and Renaissance designs.

Therefore, it was easy for some scholars or artists to characterize the ancient Hebrews as a group of uncivilized nomads, unresponsive to the beauties of nature and culture. Friedrich Delitzsch, the German anti-Semite, devoted an entire book to an attempt to demonstrate not only that biblical thought and law had been stolen from the Babylonians but that the Jews could not have developed an art and culture of their own because "they had a defective sense of color and form." [3] This biological defect accounted for their abstinence from painting and for the promulgation of the commandment to make no graven images. They feared and therefore outlawed the image because they possessed no artistic imagination or talent, a conviction shared by Richard Wagner, who said that "Jews have never given evidence of aesthetic intuition." [4]

Adolph Lods, a more objective scholar, contests the notion that the Jewish rejection of the image represents a defect in the biological endowment of the Jew. He views the Jewish refusal to make images as a symptom of an inherent conservatism. In its earliest period, the Jewish people did not know sculpture at all; in later periods priests and people alike tried to preserve the habits of the earlier days in order to safeguard their identity in widely differing places and circumstances. "To cling to old ways became a sign of the national longing and the guarantee of its ultimate fulfillment." [5]

That social conditions, political pressures, and the desire to avoid contamination by contact with alien values or customs may have contributed substantially to the Jewish "fear of the image" hardly requires discussion. Nevertheless, theories of this kind fail to explain why it is a book that has become the primary symbol and vehicle of Jewish self-expression. I consider it likely that the symbol of Jewish creativity is a book because *the primary medium of Jewish self-expression has been the word.* In contrast to the cultures of other peoples, the dominant medium through which the Jewish cultural impulse seems to have sought and found expression has not been tactile, tangible matter—marble, steel, wood, color—but the word.

II

The Bible itself supports this view. It candidly reports the fact that even the sanctuary, Solomon's Temple, had to be built not by Jews but by foreign architects and craftsmen. For, as Solomon told King Hiram of Tyre, "There is none among us who has the skill to hew timber like the Phoenicians." [6]

Yet against this lack of competence in dealing with the elements of space, the Bible records a constant emphasis on the aural dimension, the acoustic element, the voice that speaks—and speaks, of course, in words.[7] According to Martin Buber, the Jews were not a people of the "eye and imitation," they were the people of the "ear and obedience." [8] For Professor Hans Kohn "the Jew did not see so much as he heard." His organ of perception was the ear, in contradistinction to the ancient Greeks, who were the people of the spatial and plastic sense and who, in Jakob Burckhardt's phrase, were the "eye of the world." [9] To the ancient Jew, God was a voice. Biblically understood, He manifested Himself in call and command, not in image. Commandments are not looked at but heard—and obeyed or disobeyed.[10] Moses pleads with God for permission to see Him face to face in order to be reassured in his faith. But God cannot be seen; Moses can only hear His presence, listen to His voice, hear His commandment. Again and again throughout the Bible sounds the command, "Hear." Elijah discovers God in the still, small voice. It is the voice and the word that guide the leaders from Moses to the Prophets. The word has been the medium through which the Jew has sought to express his thoughts and feelings about God, man, and the world.

At the same time, the Jew was not indifferent to physical beauty. He "prized it no matter where it was found and praised it even when it was put to uses of which he heartily disapproved." [11] Though Jews rarely attempted to reproduce the glories of nature on canvas, they described them in word pictures unmatched in the way they sketched the universe in a few bold touches and strokes. Nor were they insensitive to woman's charm and loveliness, if we are to judge their sentiments by the tribute they paid to her in the Song of Songs. Even the rabbis of the Talmud—often scorned as dry legalists and reputedly impervious to anything but their books —were not unresponsive to a woman's beauty. As Solomon Goldman, himself a master of the word, pointed out in his *Book of Books:*

> In a spirit of adoration, untouched by prudery or concupiscence, they scanned the secrets of her charm, contemplating the suppleness of her body, the damask smoothness of her skin, the swanlike stateliness of her neck, the arched beauty of her brow, the rich luster of her hair, the mellow azure of her eyes, the lusty redness of her lips, the melodious sweetness of her voice, the graceful lightness of her gait, and limning with utmost delicacy the glory of her breasts whose development they compared with three stages in the growth of a fruit: its budding, the formation of its calyx, and its ripening. They were bold enough, these Pharisees and Talmudists, to make the attractiveness of woman actually the concern of God, and fanciful enough to imagine Him adorning and plaiting Eve's hair before bringing her to Adam, or dropping cosmetic compounds from heaven, together with the manna, for her especial benefit.[12]

Cultural creativity manifests itself not only in the production of *objets d'art.* There are other media of creativity, among them language, the word. This probably is what Bialik meant when he said that the word is a "revealment of the spirit." [13] It is man's instrument of *Sinngebung,* the vehicle he has created to name the nameless, render reality intelligible, classify impressions and observations, describe experiences, and articulate the meaning he ascribes to them. It is through the medium of the word that he communicates with others and transcends his existential loneliness.

Nevertheless, there are other media. There are moments in man's life when words are not enough and language is inadequate to express what wells up from his innermost being. Man's life encompasses more than what can be disclosed by words. Life frequently transcends verbalization. There are times when man strains against the chains imposed by words,[14] when he needs other media of expression, a language without words, the language of "songs, tears, and laughter." [15] It releases what is pent up within him—his loves and his rejections, his heartbreaks and his joys, his rebellions as well as his passionate affirmation of life.

Jews, too, have found release in languages without words. They have sung; they have wept; they have laughed at themselves and the world. They have used the languages of dance and music in temple cult and worship. When they muted their harps at the waters of Babylon, they demonstrated by this very act of self-denial the vital role of song and music in their lives. Even today, they glorify the Creator of the world in the ecstasy of the Hasidic *niggun,* pray with swaying bodies, carry the Torah scrolls in joyful dance around the synagogue on *Simhat Torah,* and express the fullness of their hearts in the songs and dances of modern Israel.

Still, our major vehicle of self-expression has been the word. Our music, with some exceptions, has until recently been primarily vocal, not instrumental.[16] Our emotions have rarely found expression in symphonies or paintings but in prayer, *piyyut,* or moral exhortation. And our laughter has in the main been the humor of the word, the barb of the intellect, often dueling with itself and the world.

I am not glorifying the absence of a concern with the visual arts in Jewish culture. Ernst Simon rightly points out that it represents an *aesthetic deficit* in Jewish life.[17] I admire the sophisticated perfection that graces the hills of Rome and Athens. I have often found myself wishing that the harshness of the Judean hills were softened by similarly graceful products of Jewish creativity. The "aesthetic deficit" is regrettable. I wish it did not exist. But the fact remains that the Jew has expressed himself mainly through the word. Whether embodied in prophecy or philosophy, in *Halakhah* or *Aggadah,* in prayer or religious poetry, in folk tale or moral tract, the word has been his primary instrument in attempting to penetrate and respond to the mystery of life and man's place in the world.

III

But questions remain. I have emphasized the role of the word in Jewish culture. But is an emphasis on the word, spoken or written, something uniquely or characteristically Jewish? I said that our greatest cultural treasure is a book. But do not other peoples also have a vast literature that articulates their creative impulses?

Most peoples have created a national literature, and this literature, as all other manifestations of culture, is the image of a people's soul. Yet there is a profound difference between the Bible and other literatures. As Ludwig Lewisohn put it in his thoughtful book, *The American Jew:* "Every Frenchman finds his soul mirrored in and symbolized by Racine. Every Englishman by Shakespeare. . . . The great and representative books of other peoples are works of literature. The great and representative book of the Jewish people is not *literature* but Scripture." [18] Literature speaks of people; Scripture speaks to people. Literature describes man as he is; Scripture sets before man what he ought to become. Literature depicts; Scripture demands, summons, and sets goals for human life.

Here emerges a second characteristic of Jewish culture: *The primary concern of Jewish culture is man's moral posture.* More precisely, Jewish culture seeks to reflect Judaism's fundamental conviction that man's essential humanity expresses itself in his morality.

According to Immanuel Kant, man's creative efforts are embodied in his quest for the true, the good, and the beautiful. Judaism, however, has consistently subordinated all other aspects to the quest for the good. And it has done this for several reasons.

Throughout Jewish history, Jewish thought has shown a profound distrust of matter. Pitirim Sorokin diagnosed the disease of our time as an overemphasis on sensate, material culture; and he defined "sensate" culture as predicated on the principle that true reality and values are sensory. Only what we see, hear, smell, touch, or perceive through our sense organs is real and has value.[19] Hence our distrust of ideas, our rejection of the importance of the ideational, our glorification of technical progress and material culture above everything else.

Mr. Sorokin's protest against sensate culture is not new. Judaism has voiced it since antiquity. The Jew was rarely satisfied with the things that can be seen or felt or heard or touched or analyzed in the glass tubes of the laboratory. He wanted to grasp the invisible behind the visible, the idea behind the phenomenon, the whole behind the parts, the law behind the sequence of facts, the meaning and purpose beneath the surface, the reason why things are the way they are. Unlike the Greeks, he never accepted "matter" as final. "Through the diversity of life and the eternal flux of things, he sought out the underlying unity of reality and attempted to discover the invisible links of interrelatedness" of all phenomena.[20]

For this reason, the ancient Jews not only distrusted "matter," they also distrusted the plastic arts. They saw people take wood or silver or gold and fashion statues out of it. They saw these people take the work of their own hands and worship it as a god.

The Jew recoiled from the thought that people could take something they themselves had made, their own handiwork, and worship it as a god, addressing themselves to a lifeless thing and fixing their hopes on it. A symbol is precisely what it means—a symbol. It represents an idea or points to a reality. But the symbol can never become the idea or reality behind it. The Jew realized early that even the most beautiful image cannot be a substitute for God. God's infinity can be neither captured nor represented in man's finite handiwork. The seeker for truth cannot be satisfied with an aesthetic experience wrenched from eternity. The sculptor can imitate life. He can interpret life. But he cannot create life. He can approximate but not equate. He can hew a face or body out of marble, but he cannot infuse it with breath.[21] And it was with man's "breath," with his existence, with the meaning of his life and the mystery of being, that the Jewish spirit concerned itself.

The worship of a symbol is idolatry. Where form, rather than the reality it symbolizes, is worshiped, there is idolatry. Where men worship the gods they make rather than the God who made them, there is idolatry. Therefore the sweeping injunctions of the Bible against the making of images. Therefore the invectives of the Prophets against the folly of bowing down before images of wood and stone.[22] Therefore the derision and scorn which the Psalmist heaps upon the stupidity of the idolater:

> Their idols are silver and gold,
> The work of men's hands.
> They have mouths, but they speak not;
> Eyes have they, but they see not;
> They have ears, but they hear not;
> Noses have they, but they smell not.[23]

Moreover, their revulsion against idolatry was fortified by the immoral practices commonly associated with idolatry among the peoples of antiquity. The human sacrifices, phallus worship, ritual prostitution, and necromancy associated with the ancient Canaanite cults were for the Jews just as much a moral abomination as they were an intellectual aberration. And what they knew of Greek art and its influence on people did not tempt them to change their views. As the artists portrayed him, Zeus remained a seducer to the end;[24] the seductive Aphrodite was anything but an advocate of chastity; the jealous Hera drove a man mad and made him slay his children; the alluring Calypso complained that she could not take mortals openly as her bedfellows; and Dionysus was worshiped with orgiastic rites. Whatever concern with beauty may have motivated the artist, the people looking at the statues of the gods found them to be not solely an aesthetic experience but frequently also a suggestive model and erotic stimulant.

But the Jews distrusted the plastic arts not merely because they sought, or were admonished, to guard themselves against the idolatrous and immoral practices of the people with whom they had contact. They distrusted them for still another reason. A work of art has finality. It always remains what it is. Once the artist has given his painting or statue the final touch, the art object is completed and removed from the impact of life and change. "Eternity becomes fixed in one moment, and the moment is arrested in eternal immutability."[25] This is what Schopenhauer meant when he said that "art is always at its goal," and what Lewis Mumford implied in his penetrating statement that "art is life arrested." Nothing is left for man but to behold the beauty of the object, to admire its perfection, to contemplate its meaning. This indeed was the Greek concept of man's role and destiny, *ataraxia*—the unperturbed contemplation of perfection.[26]

In Judaism, energy replaces contemplation. *Solu solu panu darekh,* says the Prophet, "make a path, clear the way." [27] Man's life is under command to work and create. Nothing living is ever at its goal. Life arrested is death. Life is not being but becoming; it is to be viewed not as something completed but as something yet to be completed. Man's role and destiny do not lie in the contemplation of static perfection—which exists only in the perfection of death—but in his unceasing efforts to complete himself and the world [28]—the moral transformation of reality.

An objection could be raised at this point. Granted that the Jewish stance is to reject the finality of matter and the immutability that seems inherent in the completed work of art. But does not Jewish tradition, more than any other tradition, also claim that there is something which is final and immutable—namely, the *word?* Has not Judaism deliberately frozen its own development by insisting that every single word of Scripture is derived from God, and thus unchangeable?

That every syllable of Scripture is of divine origin is indeed axiomatic in Jewish tradition. Traditional Judaism therefore ascribes finality to the biblical word. Yet the freezing of the word has not arrested the development of Jewish thought and life. In Judaism the word has no magic power, as it has in ancient mythology. It is but the gate to God. Man's unending task is to seek out the meaning and will that are revealed by, or concealed behind, the word. The word may be frozen, unchangeable, as is every word as soon as it has been uttered. Its meaning is not. It has new meaning for every new generation. To the faithful, the Bible has always contained the word of God, which persists for all ages. However, in Leo Baeck's words,

> Each age must search in it what is most relevant and peculiar to itself. Each generation heard in the Bible's words its own wishes, hopes and thoughts, each individual his heart's desire. . . . With each conquest of human thought the Bible took on a different meaning. There are characteristic differences between a Philo, an Akiba, a Maimonides, a Mendelssohn. They read the same book, and yet in many ways it was a different book to each of them. It is not a heritage to be accepted passively but rather a heritage that has to be won through study.[29]

Jewish tradition demands that every new generation turn every word until it will reveal the living God behind it.[30] The text may be fixed; but it has new meaning for each new generation of seekers.

IV

The fabric of Jewish culture is woven out of these strands: the fact that classical Jewish literature is essentially Scripture; a concern with meaning and purpose behind the visible reality; a distrust of the plastic arts directed not merely against the danger of their abuse in idolatrous practices but against their claim to finality; a protest against that which claims to be perfect and complete; a view of man's life as a response to the command to work for the completion of himself and the world. Hence, Jewish culture embodies a special "value stance" [31] concerning man, his role in the world, and the goals he should seek. This value stance points to a third dimension which characterizes Jewish culture: if the primary medium of Jewish self-expression is the word, and the primary concern of Jewish culture is man's moral conduct and creativity, *the foundation of Jewish culture is the Jewish concept of life.*

Different cultures generate different philosophies of life. For the Stoic, ancient and modern alike, man is a citizen of two worlds. One is the world of his wishes, desires, and aspirations; the other is the world in which the merciless law of nature rules. The tragedy of man's existence is that the abyss between these two worlds can never be bridged. Reality takes no cognizance of man's desires. It will always frustrate his hopes. Man is a powerless atom pushed around by the irresistible forces of nature. All he can do is to submit to his fate in resignation. Thus the Stoic insists that man's supreme virtue is indifference to life. Do not give in to any emotions about the unavoidable pains and tragedies of life. Disregard your feelings and emotions, pain and pleasure alike. A mature person is affected by neither joy nor grief.

Marxism has generated a philosophy of life and society which is not fatalistic like the Stoic's but mechanistic. It does not preach the inevitability of the natural process; it preaches the inevitability of the historical process. It does not blame nature for the ills of mankind. It blames the institutions of society for betraying man's rightful hopes and claims. Thus, the commissar in Arthur Koestler's *The Yogi and the Commissar* can assert that the ills of humanity can be cured, but only by change from without, by the radical reorganization of our system of production and distribution of goods.

A similar mechanistic approach can occasionally be found in the insistence of some sociologists, psychologists, and social workers on the determinative inevitability of the social process: a person's environment is the dominant factor in determining the development of his personality structure and values. The antisocial habits of a young person are the direct result of the fact that he grew up in slums. Social ills are bound to disappear if society provides sufficient resources to change a person's or group's environment.

That external conditions and a person's environment affect his development and values profoundly is beyond argument. Nevertheless, the valid aspects of such theories must not be used to obscure the fact that man is not only the victim, the product, of slums; it is also man who creates them and permits them to exist. The root of man's lust for power and of his often cruel actions and self-righteous judgments of his fellows lies in himself, not in some social or economic system. Man can create, use, or refashion political or economic institutions to harness, deflect, or suppress human egotism. But it is man himself who creates the institutions, and his drives and imperfections are reflected in their structure and the use he makes of them. Can we therefore have a reconstructed society as long as we do not have reconstructed human beings? If the building blocks are rotten, how can we expect to erect a stable structure?

If the Marxist preaches the inevitability of the historical process and the behaviorist proclaims the inevitability of the social process, the Epicurean of all generations, like the Stoic, bases his philosophy of life on the inevitability of the natural process. Human life is but the nightmare interlude between two nothings, the nothing that was and the nothing that will be. Man is asked neither whether he wants to live nor whether he wants to die. Born by chance, he eats and drinks and sleeps and sweats and procreates and dies. There is no escape from death. Life has neither meaning nor purpose. Therefore the Epicurean preaches a cynical and hedonistic fatalism. No opportunity for self-indulgence and self-gratification should be wasted. Drain the cup of life to its very dregs. Taste life's fullness before you disappear into the nothingness from which you sprang and to which you will return.

These philosophies have exerted a powerful influence upon millions. An even more powerful philosophy of life that has dominated our world since antiquity is what T. H. Huxley defined as the "gladiatorial theory of existence" [32]—the old yet ever new "tooth and claw" ethic. Already promulgated by the ancient Greeks who said *ho polemos pater panton,* "war is the father of all things," it was resurrected in the Nietzschean concept of the superman and in his disciples' concept of a superrace or superstate. Every man for himself in the struggle for existence. The strongest will triumph in the unceasing battle for survival.

It is only a minor variant of this ancient theme that Maurice Samuel introduces when he describes the philosophy of the "gentleman" that dominates the western world. The old concepts of combat, conflict, and competition remain unchanged but are tempered by the spirit of "cricket"—a sense of honor and respect for the rules of the game as expressed, for instance, in Newbolt's poem:

> To love the game beyond the prize,
> To honor, while you strike him down,
> The foe that comes with fearless eyes.

Life is fighting under the motto, "a good clean fight, no hitting below the belt, may the best man win—and no hard feelings." [33]

The mainstream of Jewish thought has persistently rejected these philosophies of life. Unlike the Stoic, the Jew did not surrender to resignation. Aware that nature often masters man, he also knew that man can also master nature, and that his hopes are not always destined to frustration. Unlike the commissar, the Jew has not put his sole trust in a change of the structure of society as the key to man's redemption. He has always sensed that although institutions or economic systems shape man's attitudes, it is man himself who is the creator of his institutions. Unlike the Epicurean, the Jew has rarely surrendered to defeatism because of the evil and darkness that are part of the human condition. He has always known that, just as Moses was able to lead his people from Egypt to Sinai and to transform a gang of illiterate slaves into a people of God, man can grow and rise from the jungle and reach for the stars. Unlike Christianity, Judaism has not preached a redemption from this world but has stubbornly insisted on the possibility of redemption for this world. Therefore, we have not rejected life in all its manifestations but have always attempted to sanctify life, to render it significant, to infuse every action with meaning, purpose, and dignity—eating and drinking and labor and rest and procreation and fellowship and study and planting and harvesting alike, all with one ultimate purpose: to avoid cruelty, to diminish evil, and to enhance the fullness of every man's life. And unlike Huxley's gladiatorial man, we have become persuaded by our people's collective experiences that this goal can be reached only when people are governed not by the laws of competition but by the laws of cooperation and a spirit that seeks the rational reconciliation of differences.

V

These affirmations—negations at the same time—are the ingredients of the Jewish concept of life.

Sigmund Freud liked to define dreams as an extension of reality. As a Jew, I would define reality as an extension of the dream, of the vision. The Jew sees the world as it is. He sees reality and its darkness—the consuming evil that men have done and continue to do, the misery and pain they inflict upon one another. However, he neither negates reality nor surrenders to it. He seeks to transform reality. What is must be transformed into what ought to be. Jewish life at its best is therefore meant to be a value judgment, a protest, and a call to action. It is meant to be a value judgment on intolerance, bondage, and oppression, it is meant to be a protest against all that deems itself perfect. It is meant to be a protest against the evil conditions that rob man of his humanity. It is meant to be a call to action and the fellowship of sacrificial cooperation for the attainment of that outer and inner harmony by which alone men can live in dignity and fulfill their destiny.

Does Jewish culture have "meaning"? Jews have expressed their will to live in many forms. They build synagogues, write books, sing songs, dance dances, and design sophisticated products of arts and crafts. They have even developed the culinary aspects of culture. All these are legitimate expressions of Jewish life. But Jewish life itself is predicated on a spirit that defines the purposes and meaning of Jewish existence.

As a people we have not created distinctive architectural designs. But the challenge remains to design an enduring architecture of the human heart and mind. We have not enriched the treasures of the world by contributing significant paintings. But the challenge remains to carry in our hearts an image, the vision of the road that leads to God and man. We have produced few blueprints for palaces or cathedrals. But the challenge remains to design a blueprint for man's life in a truly human society. We have composed little music as yet, few melodies which merit performance in the concert halls of the world. But as Jews we continue to face the challenge to remain attuned to the melody which may yet help bring harmony to the hearts and minds of men.

4. A Faith for Moderns: Three Views

HENRY A. FISCHEL

The Nature of Religious Faith

WHAT WILL BE SAID in this paper is not a dogmatic statement nor above challenge. It represents a personal and critical attempt to define what religion can mean to modern man. It is an argument rather than a statement; a continuous argument with others but, no less, also with myself, in an attempt to clarify the nature and meaning of religious faith for a man in our time.

I

The term "religion" is derived from the Latin word *re-ligio*. *Ligio* means relationship, connection, as in the English words "ligament" or "league." The prefix *re-* in "religion" merely emphasizes this meaning, just as "re-assure" emphasizes the word "assure." Religion is therefore a strong connection of some kind, a relationship. For a relationship, two partners are necessary. Who are these two partners? Let us make our definition so broad that it includes all religion, that of the ancient Greeks as much as that of a Maimonides or an Einstein. The one partner, or, to choose a better analogy, the one pole of the magnetic field, is man in his imperfection, subject to birth and death, with his power for destruction, subject to his environment—man with his physical and psychological limitations as well as with his possibilities for good, but nevertheless a mixed creature and therefore finite, imperfect.

The other partner or pole is the perfect, the infinite, without

51

limitations of power and vision, of time and space, of intelligence and goodness. But does "it" exist? Is it a reality or merely a dream or figment of our imagination? After all, we are unable to perceive it with our sense perception, and it is our sense perception that we trust.

At this point, a note of warning must be sounded. Our brilliant critics of religion are astoundingly uncritical when it comes to understanding the everyday common sense on which they choose to base their views. Our everyday mind is amazingly primitive regarding the "reality" of the physical world. Competent scientists have repeatedly assured us that the objects of scientific investigation may not be real in the ordinary sense of the word but only a projection of our minds. Similarly, the phenomena of the physical world may appear in one way to man, who is equipped with a certain apparatus of apperception, but may appear as something entirely different, or perhaps even incomprehensible, to other beings. Reality is a more complicated matter than we imagine— if it is "matter" at all. Einstein, in a letter to his friend Viscount Samuel, restated a view first held by Kant, the eighteenth-century philosopher: "The 'real' is in no way immediately given to us. Given to us are merely the data of our consciousness."

In looking at the world, we apply an intellectual construction inherent in our minds—order, measure, time. We are therefore unable to perceive the world as it really is.

If these assertions are correct, we must redefine our ideas of matter and reality. Reality is a highly complicated, man-centered, and, in a sense, "spiritual" affair. Actually, we are resting our view of the universe, and, in a way, our daily actions, on a hypothesis. The risk involved may be the best we can do in our situation as human beings.

Religion is a similarly spiritual, similarly risk-involving relation. It is a relation to the world of perfection and permanence. The essence of this world may remain to finite man as incomprehensible as that of the physical world. The "leap," to use Kierkegaard's term, into this realm, the risk taken in confiding ourselves to it, is called faith. Faith is an adventure. It is an act of trust, a new perspective in looking at the universe, not dissimilar to that of the scientist, yet more complete, penetrating not only the physical world but also the realm of eternal values. Nevertheless, modern man seems predisposed to use only the perspective of the scientist and believes it enables him to master the totality of life.

Our view of the other pole of our magnetic field must similarly be clarified. Men have at all times felt that they are able to perceive this other pole, the perfect, the source of all being, God, or whatever name they may have given it. There has always been a strong human element in religious experience. Yet there has also always been something else that seems to break into human experience, something which cannot be explained away. To be sure, this "something" looked different in different ages. Primitive man recognized a multitude of superhuman powers or spirits, the ancient nations a dozen major gods, the Persians two divine powers—until finally, through the instrumentality of the Jewish people, this "something" was conceived as the all-powerful personal God, unifying the universe. But in all phases of this historical development, this superhuman power was felt as a reality. Logical considerations backed the validity of this experience. The attempt, for instance, to ascribe all existence to chance or coincidence, to the mechanical laws of an unfeeling nature or mute urges in the universe *(élan vital),* was to bring into the picture a vague new power that was less comprehensible than the god of the most extravagant mystic.

Religion thus is a relation between finite man and that infinite intelligent power called, in the western world, God. This power is, to a certain extent, beyond human comprehension. The decision to establish or to recognize this relationship between such unequal partners is called faith. In other words, faith is a man's courage to prove a hypothesis by the example and content of his life. Humanity has no other choice than between these two hypotheses: to see the world based on blind urges and mechanical laws, or permeated by meaning and divine planning. The religious genii of mankind and the truly pious may feel that they live in relationship *(religio)* with a reality and not merely with the object of a hypothesis. Logically speaking, however, and for any rational approach, the question concerning the existence of the "other pole" must be changed into a choice confronting every seeker for truth: the choice between the hyopthesis of mechanism and the hypothesis of meaningfulness and purposiveness.

The basic structure of religion may now be clear. But a puzzling problem remains: Why a plurality of religions? Why do religions differ in their teachings?

Scientists have often received a powerful impetus toward their outlook by an event of limited importance. Archimedes is supposed to have been greatly moved when he observed the rising water level in his bathtub, and the falling apple which so thoroughly impressed Newton has become proverbial. Similarly, the impetus toward discovering the other pole of religion has often been provoked by the experience of a partial aspect of spiritual life. The experience of a perfect act of kindness, the discovery of justice in history, the encounter with logical perfection in mathematics, the impact of "the starred heaven above me and conscience within me"—all these have stimulated individuals and nations to turn to the realm of perfection. Fashioned by this initial stimulus as well as the individual temperament and historical fate of each group, the relationship between man and God assumes a different character with every community of faith. Some —the mystics—subordinated themselves so fully to the overwhelming Thou of divine perfection that they effaced themselves completely; others waxed into poetical ecstasy, seeking to alleviate the suffering of their fellowmen or to find intellectual clarification of their experience in ardent thought. Still others, in search for even greater perfection, rebelled against what they found in either world—Prometheus, Jeremiah, the Berdichever Rebbe. All these different yet authentic approaches cause the variety of religious life.

Using another analogy, we could speak of groups and individuals trying to climb a steep mountain peak from different starting points. Each one will have different experiences and adventures on the way, a different view of the summit, a different incline. Each will have a different story to tell. An infant born to one of these parties will have to stay with his group—he has no choice. But the skill and the vantage-point already achieved by his group make this necessity meaningful and practical. In the same way, the religion into which we are born is the best or true one for us, just as other religions are true for others. Of course, we are speaking of the higher religions or, to remain within our analogy, of climbing parties who do not lose the vision of the summit and take the necessary precautions in their ascent.

The state of being moved and permanently elated through the discovery of this infinite power is usually called "salvation." Through the acceptance of his partnership, man has changed his life, has transcended his limits, has come in contact with a world of permanence and thus acquired certain features of immortality. The moments in which he is able to grasp its nearness, in which a communication from the divine pole to the human pole takes place, is commonly called "revelation."

At all times the religious genii of mankind have tried to probe further into their encounter and extract a directive or demand from it, a message useful and necessary for the human situation. When they put their interpretation, the message that they believed they heard, into writing, Holy Scriptures came into being. All scriptures, therefore, have a transitory element caused by the human limitations of the author. But they also contain a reflection of the glimpse which the author had of perfection.

II

But why not humanism? Why not a mixture of scientific method and respect for man, combined with self-criticism—but without God, without ritual and organized religion? Why not concentrate our efforts on that reality in which man and his reason are sovereign?

The religionist would answer that his and the humanist's perspectives are different. His experience of the power of what is eternal and perfect is so intense that he feels it everywhere, in deeds of kindness, in beauty, in serious effort, in constructiveness, in the smile of hope, in the courage to resist evil. He feels that the perfect and the imperfect interpenetrate and that the imperfect, without this pattern of the perfect, without its comfort and inspiration, would wander in the dark and ultimately fail. He feels that man without the vision of the perfect would be proud and arrogant or tragically desperate. He feels that any outlook which is based solely on man's sovereignty and power condemns us to living with a patchwork of thought and effort, a snail's perspective, and an image of man that leaves unused his greatest possibility: the attempt to look beyond his shadow.

The humanist can have little assurance that inner strife or cosmic catastrophe will not finally destroy the world. The religionist is not sure either, but his trust in the intelligence and goodness of the all-embracing divine power tells him that such a happening, as threatening and real as it may be, is ultimately destined to run counter to the nature of divine perfection. Thus he claims that man is not alone, and that he is part of an intelligent, intelligible, and constructive plan. The ways of divine perfection may be involved and tortuous, but there is no reason for despair. The humanist may show endurance in adversity, but his final posture must be either the resigned smile of the sage who knows that all is in vain, or the tragically gritted teeth of one who stands at the edge of a bottomless abyss.

Some people maintain another view which is not remote from the humanist position. They ask, Why do we need a personal God at all? Why not affirm a divine principle (deism), or a divine element inherent in all things (pantheism)? It is obvious that personality represents the highest level of existence known to us because it involves consciousness, memory, will power, sensitivity, freedom of decision. In the religious traditions of the West, God can thus not be conceived as being something less than man is. Of course, religion has always been aware of the danger of creating a god according to human patterns. God is infinitely more than "personality" in the human sense. The limits of human experience, however, are prescribed by the mind and language of man. Even if we knew more about God, we could say no more than we say today. The Talmud is aware of this predicament when it says, *dibbrah Torah bilshon b'nai adam,* "the Torah can only speak in human terms."

A final question: Why is every discussion of religion so complicated and involved? Should not religion be straightforward and simple? Unfortunately, only to the simple is religion simple. For most of us, it is the most complex of all human ventures because it refers the finite to the infinite, a process that is actually beyond the human possibility. This insight finds recognition in a Midrash in which God is an incomprehensible harmony of contradictions. He is both absolute Mercy and absolute Justice in creating and judging the world. He is sublime, yet close to the deprived and suffering. He is the source of both free will and necessity. Nicolaus Cusanus called Him the *coincidentia oppositorum,* the coinciding of all opposites. The nature of divine perfection is the real and only "mystery" in religion.

III

Does science challenge religion? Science describes what *is* and how it came into being (a quest that is a problem of science, not of religion). Science tries to establish the laws governing all phenomena, but it does not ask, as religion does, for the *meaning of the whole,* nor does it evaluate the whole.

Scientific observation, moreover, is detached, disinterested, in contrast to the religious attitude, which aims at the greatest attachment, be it gratitude or wonder, enthusiasm or the fight for justice. Unlike the scientist, who is and should be satisfied with analysis and experiment, and occasionally perhaps with the struggle for the acceptance of new insights, the religionist goes farther. To him, religion is not only knowledge but a transformation of his entire life. It is involvement in the ideas and ideals of his religion. The expert who analyzes the soil of Israel knows its chemical composition, but the pious Jew who, on his arrival, falls to the ground and kisses the soil of Israel, willing to dedicate his life to its redemption, knows more. According to Feuerbach, only the objects of passion are real. Passion, however, is transitory. Judaism has clearly recognized that religion must be a *lasting passion* which should transform man's entire life.

Lastly, science cannot arrive at ideals or values. Medicine, for instance, has developed the injection. But the decision whether to heal or massacre people with it lies outside the realm of medicine or science. Atomic power can be used for constructive purposes of still undetermined proportions or for destruction on an unparalleled scale. Physics does not indicate *what to do*. Here religion enters and proclaims the dignity and sanctity of all life, which it views as the image and reflection of the divine.

Hostility to religion is not confined to the natural sciences. The more recent social sciences share it. Although psychology frequently cooperates with religion in practice, psychologists will occasionally still assert that religion is based on human "complexes," on fear and guilt, and cannot lay claim to any truth beyond these. Yet such a view is blind to the fact that a truth can be hidden behind a complex.

Even if one knows what a lion is, temporary fear when confronting a lion unarmed is a legitimate feeling, shared by even the most daring psychologist. Guilt may be very real in the case of a guilty person. Creations may be fruitful even if born of mental difficulty. Koestler, in one of his novels, told the symbolic story of Thales, the ancient Greek thinker, who suffered from a "triangle" complex because he was in marital difficulties involving the fate of three persons. He finally took to drawing triangles wherever he went until one day, drawing his triangles in the sand on the beach, he discovered an important law of geometry. Was his discovery invalid because it was born of a complex, or is it a truth independent of his mental condition? Would he have been able to discover it without his handicap? Religion, fully aware of the human condition, claims similarly that behind our predisposition—behind our loneliness in the universe, our fear and guilt-feelings—a truth independent of our condition can be visualized.

More challenging than criticism is the endorsement which religion occasionally receives from anthropologists and sociologists when they "approve" of religion because it strengthens society or fills certain human needs. Here we see traces of an outdated utilitarianism which claims that what is useful is true or right. Yet although religion does frequently cement society and fulfills many useful functions, its usefulness does not constitute its claim to truth. Unlike magic, it was not created for the satisfaction of needs. Moses' struggle against idolatry, the prophetic fight against injustice, the rabbinic criticism of human nature, did not correspond to the tastes or demands of society. The self-sacrifice of our martyrs can hardly be termed "useful." Nor is it the task of religion to make man or society more peaceful at all costs. It is no sedative or laxative. It is far from the caricature which Marx drew of it when he called it an opiate for the people. True religion is, whenever necessary, militant, aggressive, critical. Inspired by the example and prototype of divine perfection, mature religion is a system of dynamic self-criticism, in which individual and society seek to eliminate all concealed self-interest in their midst regardless of "needs" and satisfactions—a process that is frequently as painful as it is in radical conflict with accepted views and norms.

IV

What, then, are the specific qualities which make Judaism a particular tradition within western religion?

The first principle that underlies all action and thought in Judaism is the idea of *berit,* of a covenant or alliance with the divine perfection, involving a specific group: the Jewish people. To be sure, Judaism asserts that other peoples have also heard God's voice and that the righteous of all nations have a share in salvation. The Jewish people, however, has a special task to fulfill in the historical process, through choice as much as through fate. Since Abraham and Mount Sinai, this partnership in God's plans has made the Jewish people a group pioneering in the jubilant discovery of divine perfection, transforming Israel into God's missionary to the nations, the prophet and servant and, frequently, the suffering servant, of the Lord.

The second principle of Judaism is *Torah,* law, the effort to make the Jewish people at all times conscious of the divine command and the necessity to express this consciousness in every person's actions regarding his food, business affairs, family life, and even his conversation. Jewish life is supposed to be a continuous religious service, testifying to the interdependence of these two worlds. Jewish law, in traditional Judaism, is not merely an aspect of our civilization, an instrument for survival, hygiene, and self-discipline but, above all, the drawing of the divine· perfection into the life of the Jew.

Judaism's third principle is that of *tzedek,* justice. The Jew is to imitate divine perfection in all his ways, doing justice to his fellowmen, to the animal, and to the inanimate object—even to God Himself. This active "fairness" is the substance of practical Judaism, in accordance with the pointed emphasis of the Torah— *tzedek tzedek tirdof,* "justice, justice shalt thou pursue." Isaiah knew that "Zion will be redeemed through righteousness, its inhabitants with justice"; and Hillel repeated a law of the Torah in his golden rule: "Thou shalt love thy neighbor, for he is like thyself." The principle of active and sensitive rightdoing (the word "righteousness" sounds pompous) is so important that it cannot be canceled even in emergencies or in order to achieve a vitally important objective—an interesting contrast to some systems which also promise an era of hope and happiness, to be achieved, however, through bribery, pressure, liquidation of the opposition, or war.

The principle of justice is so important that it is believed to be the greatest approximation to the realm of perfection which man can achieve. By justice or genuinely renewed effort in case of failure ("repentance"), man is redeemed and becomes part of the realm of perfection or, as others have it, immortal. In Judaism, the belief in the efficacy of human effort is so great that no intermediary is necessary to save man; no cosmic or other sacrifice, no particular act of God's grace or choice, no shedding of blood, actually or symbolically, is required. This direct interaction between the perfect and the imperfect reduced mythology in Judaism to a minimum and made it a highly *rational* religion. It is this factor which made Christianity unable to absorb Judaism or to exert a lasting influence upon it.

A fourth principle is *meshihut,* the Messianic idea. Judaism has always been sensitive to the stream of history. Unlike the far-eastern religions with their retreat from the world, and unlike cults which, considering the world beyond hope, made the salvation of the individual soul their preoccupation, Judaism saw in history the meeting place of finite and infinite. Understanding the voice of perfection, which is always audible, man can act in partnership with God. The world is left to his free will. It is therefore full of evil, yet, at the same time, full of potentialities for progress.

Injustice, wickedness, the sham and the false will be finally vanquished. Some measure of perfection and justice can materialize among men, although at enormous cost and often through testing the breaking point of the just. History will lead up to an age that will represent the closest possible approximation of the imperfect toward the perfect.

A messianic figure or age is clearly not expected to achieve "forgiveness" for man. The realignment, that new at-oneness with perfection that we call salvation or forgiveness, can at all times be achieved through repentance and renewed effort. It does not require a Messiah or Messianic age. The result of the Messianic age will be peace, goodness, and knowledge established on earth as firmly "as waters cover the sea." Here again, it is evident why Judaism did not follow its daughter religion in spite of much similarity in outlook.

It should by now be clear that the demands of Judaism cannot be ignored. Says the Psalmist: "Where can I flee from Thy presence?" Judaism is not an entity to be taken or left alone. After what has been said, Judaism must claim that in refusing it we would neglect our duty, overlook the most unusual partnership on earth, and cripple, at our own peril, great possibilities in us and in society. Religion must claim to be the most comprehensive attempt at understanding and perfecting the world. It must claim that without it we would resort to less potent, less constructive, less probable systems, less noble, less deep, less elating.

MORDECAI M. KAPLAN

The Meaning of God for the Contemporary Jew

WHAT GOD CAN or should mean to the contemporary
Jew can be answered only in the context of what being a Jew
means to him. Usually, the only meaning which being a Jew has
for him is the fact that he belongs to the Jewish people with its
three and a half millennia of eventful and influential evolving
religious civilization.

The idea of God which is embodied in this civilization must be
seen and understood in the light of three considerations. First, it
is integral to the history, culture, and way of life during each particular stage of the evolving religious civilization of the Jewish
people. Second, the idea of God has undergone development in
keeping with the evolution of this civilization. Third, the *modern*
idea of God must reflect the democratic and scientific character of
the only kind of Jewish civilization that can be viable in our day.

Several stages characterize the development of the idea of God
in Jewish experience. Past stages in this development were mythical, otherworldly, metaphysical and/or mystical. The present stage
is bound to be functional.

The mythical idea of God was thoroughly anthropomorphic.
God was known by the proper noun "YHWH." Man was conceived as having been created in the image of God. In the stories of
Genesis, God is said to have rested, to have walked in the Garden,
to have smelled the sweet savor of Noah's sacrifice. He was one
of the three strangers who accepted Abraham's hospitality. In
Exodus God appears as fire within a cloud and as a manlike being

62

"at whose feet there was the likeness of a sapphire." In I Samuel, His presence was believed to be associated with the ark carried into battle.

From about 300 B.C.E. God's main function is conceived as the power that dispenses justice—a function associated with the promise of reward or punishment in the world to come. During the Alexandrian era (100 B.C.E.–100 C.E.) God was conceived in metaphysical terms, and, since the Middle Ages (from about 1000 C.E.), also in mystical terms. At present, the term "God" is increasingly understood as a functional, not as a substantive, noun, thus denoting that power in the cosmos, including man, that makes for the salvation of men and nations.

Theoretically each of the stages in the development of the idea of God could have given rise to a different religion. Two factors precluded this development. One is the fact that the Jewish people constituted a continuum, which enabled it to reinterpret the idea of God whenever it had become obsolete and to formulate a new version or concept. The mythical idea was allegorized. Philo, during the first century B.C.E., reinterpreted it in metaphysical terms. So did Saadyah, Maimonides, and other philosophers during the Middle Ages. Moreover—and this is the second factor—every stage from the mythical to the otherworldly, metaphysical, and mystical has stressed the primacy of justice and loving-kindness as essential to man's fulfillment individually and collectively. This tendency is already evident in the story of Abraham and the three strangers, as told in Genesis.

I

If we want to get at the heart of the predicament in which religion finds itself today, we must realize that religion, in the western and near-eastern worlds, is based on supernaturalism. Supernaturalism, however, ignores what we know of human nature, of the physical world, and of the apotheosis of tradition. By conforming to a religious tradition that claimed to be based on a supernatural revelation, a person was assumed to become worthy of obtaining from God whatever worldly goods he needed for his well-being in this world, and to achieve whatever merit he required to attain eternal bliss in the hereafter. A religion like Buddhism, on the other hand, has sought to divert man altogether from the quest for worldly goods; it deprecates all human desire and considers Nirvana, nonexistence, to be man's ultimate destiny.

The traditional purposes of religion—well-being in this world, bliss in the hereafter, and the elimination of desire—can no longer be taken seriously as purposes of religion. Having discovered vast reservoirs of worldly power, man sees no reason that he should not avail himself of it. The nuclear energy resulting from the breakdown of matter itself has opened up virtually unlimited possibilities for increasing man's power. What men formerly believed the gods could do for them is nugatory as compared with what they can get nuclear energy to do for them.

Yet something unexpected has taken place. People failed to realize that their new power might constitute an *embarras de richesse* and become a terrifying menace to their survival. They failed to consider the possibility that they might not know how to control their vastly increased power. They saw no need for expanding the range of the moral law simultaneously with the expansion of their knowledge and power, in order to govern the vastly enlarged world in which they found themselves.

This failure to reckon with the need of bringing the accession of unlimited power under the control of moral or spiritual purpose and direction, had, according to F. S. C. Northrop, "the tragic effect of giving modern man powerful and even dangerous instruments, without at the same time educating him in the moral, legal and religious norms necessary to distinguish good from bad uses of these instruments." [1] Few if any such norms have been established either by traditional law, morals, or religion. Yet what is the purpose of religion if not to teach men "to distinguish the good from bad uses" of the instruments of power they have fashioned or discovered? Religion has failed in what should have been its main task—to inculcate a sense of horror for war as nothing less than murder on a mass scale. Instead of helping to control and direct the uses of power in the interests of peace, justice, and freedom, religion itself has been used in the interests of class and national domination.

II

To make the control and direction of the worldly powers the *primary* function of religion is a revolutionary undertaking. To give first priority to moral and spiritual values in the exercise of religion which is based on the belief in God, and to derive that belief not from tradition but from tested experience, presupposes nothing else than weaning away entire nations and great religious bodies from deeply rooted prejudices, age-old habits of thought, and formally set ways of human conduct.

It calls, in the first place, for a release from the authoritarianism and claim to infallibility which have always been regarded as indispensable to religion. In premodern society the pressure of tradition and the momentum of established social practice were irresistible in maintaining this authoritarianism and claim to infallibility. They could be felt in all areas of life, including personal habits, political views, economic practices, cultural trends, and social activities. One merely need recall the opposition and ridicule which the physician Semmelweis had to endure when he insisted that his fellow practitioners, after dissecting cadavers, should wash and sterilize their hands before proceeding to deliver babies. He discovered that their failure to follow this procedure had been the cause of the high mortality rate of mothers in the maternity ward of the hospital in which he served, and his discovery was received with ridicule and scorn by the other members of the medical staff. The compelling force of habit and routine in personal life is translated into duty and obedience in collective life. Collective habit that is transmitted from generation to generation tends to assume the form of infallible authority.

This process has operated even more strongly in religion, where the compelling authority and force of socially transmitted beliefs and practices were based on the claim that they had been revealed by God. However, as the individual emerged progressively from his social context and achieved human dignity based on the notion of every person's inalienable rights, men have gradually learned to free themselves from the authoritarian character of social custom or cultural tradition in their secular affairs. Only in the realm of religion is man still in bondage to dogmatism and authoritarianism.

There is only one way in which religion can be redeemed from such bondage. We must learn to trust the exploratory human mind in its search for that in human experience which is authentic. Man's ingenuity, culminating in the scientific and technological revolutions, has enabled him to penetrate and open up vast new secrets of nature. The human mind must now learn to apply itself to the problem of religion with all the zeal for truth of which it is capable, regardless of where it may lead. The problem of religion is the one important problem upon whose solution the future of the human race depends. It is essentially not a problem about God but about man. What God is for the purpose of religion is different from any of the purposes with which metaphysics or mysticism is concerned. The main question of religion is: *What shall man believe and do in order to experience that life, despite the evil and suffering which mar it, is extremely worthwhile? So worthwhile, indeed, that for its sake man should be and do the best of which he is capable and endure without bitterness or despair the worst that may befall him.*

III

The expectation that religion can undergo a genuine revival if the unfettered human mind were to apply itself to it with all the zeal, objectivity, and love of truth it displays in its scientific endeavors, is founded upon three considerations. First, it takes the intellect to give us authentic knowledge of reality, or at least of what comes closer to it than can be attained by any other means. Second, if the reality it reveals needs to be transformed so that man might cope with it, only the intellect can be of help to us in indicating what has to be done in order to achieve this transformation. Last, if the reality is such that nothing we can do is of any avail, only the intellect will save us from wasting our energies through engaging in futile endeavors, and teach us to live with the inevitable.

Religion, whether indigenous or derivative, would have been hopelessly sunk in superstition had not the human intellect—

timidly in the Middle Ages, more daringly in modern times—
entered its domain. Each of the three religions which claim to
have been revealed by God—Judaism, Christianity, and Islam—
produced theologians during the early Middle Ages who ventured
to express various opinions which deviated from their respective
traditions. It was at that time that the doctrine of revelation, with
its authoritarianism, ceased to monopolize religion. During the
Middle Ages, the doctrine of revelation had to share with the intellect the role of validating religious teaching and practice. The
theologians, however, deemed it necessary to establish and validate
the right of the intellect to break into what had been previously
regarded as a domain reserved solely for revelation. They maintained that God had made known His will both through the revealed word as laid down in tradition, and through the human
intellect. They added, however, that few men possessed the intellect that would qualify them to learn about the existence of God
and what He wanted men to do to merit His blessings. They felt
countless generations would have to pass before human beings
would acquire sufficient knowledge of God and His laws to achieve
salvation. Hence God revealed His will to Moses and the prophets
who, in turn, communicated it to the multitudes. A similar approach characterizes the development of Christian and Moslem
thought.

Later thinkers, however, began to question the historicity of the
theophanies as well as of the other miracles recorded in Scripture.
Most of them can no longer accept that there can be two sources
of truth and salvation—divine revelation and man's reason. The
intellect has assumed the right to pass on the validity of the teachings of religion, including the belief in God. Nevertheless, numerous theologians refuse to surrender a belief in supernaturalism—
in the possibility of the occasional suspension of the order of
nature. They continue to consider this belief as indispensable and
maintain that any religion that negates supernaturalism (in which
we may include otherworldliness) has no right to the name of
religion, and that its conception of God is nothing less than idolatrous. They still take the medieval theory of the twin sources
of our knowledge of God seriously. Even though they may no
longer subscribe to the theophanies of the Bible as literal fact, they

assume that the divine grace, which is experienced by the elect of God or in the moment of religious conversion, is indeed itself a supernatural event, a miracle. However, outside the limited group of professional theologians, most thinking men and women would gladly rely on man's intellect as the source of the belief in God and of whatever conception they should have of Him and of His will for man, provided man's intellect has something to say about God that is affirmative, verifiable, and illuminating.

There can be little doubt that the attempt of the intellect to retrieve the religions which mankind has been abandoning has so far been ineffective. As a result, the religious situation today is not different from the one described long ago by Feuerbach, and more recently also by William E. Hocking. Feuerbach wrote, "The faith of the modern world is only an ostensible faith, a faith that does not believe what it fancies that it believes, and is only undecided, pusillanimous unbelief;" [2] and Hocking summarized the contemporary religious situation as follows:

> When all religions are losing their hold on multitudes, no one can say that any of them is doing too well, through its human representatives, what a religion has to do for the soul of man! They are all wretched vessels. They are all wrapped in sanctimony, dusty-eyed with self-satisfaction, stiff-jointed with the rheum rust of their creedal conceits, so timorous under the whips of uniformity that only a few dare the perilous task of *thinking* and the complacency-disturbing task of trying the spirit of other faiths. They wear the aspect of senility while the world is crying to them to be young. Men are not unready for faith, even for concrete and particular faith, if they can find life in it. [3]

What mankind needs more than ever is not to arrive by some logical tour de force at the abstract proposition that there is a God, but to identify as divine, godly, or holy whatever impels and helps man individually and collectively to bring about a better and happier world, a world in which freedom, justice, and peace enable men and nations to fulfill their creative potentialities to the maximum.

IV

But why should this particular functioning of human nature in the individual and in society be defined or identified as divine, godly, or holy?

The identification is justified because people subconsciously implied it whenever they spoke of the "will" or "law" of God. To be sure, they did not consciously formulate their notion of God in this functional manner. Nevertheless, if we were to collect all statements about God expressed in the various religions, from the most primitive to the most advanced, we would inevitably arrive inductively as the proposition that the term "God" or its equivalent was always *associated* with whatever the authors of those statements regarded as the power that makes for a better and happier world and that renders life in this world worthwhile. Only a functionally empirical approach of this kind to the meaning of God makes sense.

Hence, one of the most important tasks to which the intellect must address itself is to define in specific terms what we are to understand by a better and happier world, and to spell out in specific political, economic, social, cultural, and spiritual terms how we are to bring it about.

The main function of religion should be to subordinate the secular powers—which are the objectives of the pleasure and prestige principles—to the power of the moral law. This function can be exercised only through the social order of some continuing group. In the hierarchy of powers—physical, mental, and spiritual —the existence of a social order presupposes the operation of all these powers. The social order of each nation, however, determines the kind of salvation its individual citizens are to strive for and the kind of international order mankind is to have, insofar as it determines the uses to which mind, life, and material energy are to be put. *It is, therefore, mainly in the social order of each nation that we should expect to behold the manifestation of Divinity.* Only in and through the politico-economic society to which a person belongs can he obtain the physical and mental resources which he needs to live, to achieve personal status, and to experience salvation or to render life worthwhile.

Unfortunately, few continuing groups are so constituted as to provide the means, guidance, and inspiration that are necessary for the salvation of their members. This difficulty is due mainly to social evils that are the product of the selfishness and narrow-mindedness of most members of any group, whether it be a tribe, nation, city-state, or church. Evils of this kind are, however, preventable, and their prevention should be the main business of religion. The elimination of social evils would enable those vital and mental powers to thrive which make life worthwhile and which can help to bring about the better and happier world known as the kingdom of God on earth.

Thus, from a purely intellectual standpoint, man is in need of experiencing salvation. Neither political nor economic or cultural institutions and activities can meet this need by themselves. To meet it is the specific function of religion. When religion speaks of salvation it means in essence the experience of the worthwhileness of life. When we analyze our personal experience of life's worthwhileness we find that it is invariably based on specific ethical experiences—moral responsibility, honesty, loyalty, love, service. If carefully pursued, this analysis reveals that the *source* of our ethical experiences is found in our willingness and ability to achieve self-fulfillment through reciprocity with others. This reciprocity in turn is an expression of a larger principle that operates in the cosmos in response to the demands of a cosmic force, the force that makes for creativity and interdependence in all things.

V

We may now ask: How can we formulate an intellectually justifiable cosmic conception of God?

In order to formulate such a conception we must first discard or reject the assumption that the idea of God transcends man's power to grasp it. That we cannot know what Divinity is apart from our idea of it should not be surprising. There is nothing we can possibly know apart from our idea of it. We are told, for instance, that matter is frozen energy. Yet how helpful is this definition to us? What do we really know about energy except the way it functions? As long as religion is alive, its adherents take for granted that God not only *can* but *must* be known in order to be worshiped in the proper spirit. Again and again the prophets denounced their contemporaries for not knowing God. Jeremiah states specifically what it means to know God (Jer. 9:22–23). Among the glories of the millennium, Isaiah promises that the entire earth will be filled with the knowledge of God (Isa. 11:9).

Second, as part of religion, the idea of God is the correlate of the idea of a better and happier world, or of the salvation of man. That does not mean that God, Divinity, is merely an idea. *Divinity is the creative, coordinating, integrative process of the universe, insofar as it makes for the salvation of man, both individual and social.* This process operates as the unifying tendency of electrons to combine into atoms, of atoms into molecules, of molecules into colloids, and, with the appearance of life, of all these units to combine into organisms. Thus far the process is "Nature." It becomes divine when mankind organizes itself into societies, just as the electric current turns into light when it passes through the substance that offers sufficient resistance to cause it to turn into light. Likewise it may be said that the cosmic process of interdependence and the tensions among individuals in a society give rise to an awareness of the creative process and of the conditions under which it operates or is hindered in its operation. Thus, Divinity is the power or process of interdependence and creativity that enables society to fulfill itself. The *idea* of God is the correlate of the *idea* of society as self-fulfilled. By the same token, the idea of Divinity is the correlate of the idea of the human person experiencing salvation.

To acquire the habit of using the term "God" as a correlate of salvation, it is well to think in such paired terms as parent-child, king-people, teacher-pupil, master-servant, employer-employee, etc. Each of the foregoing individual nouns necessarily refers to its correlate noun; it is meaningless without it. In the same way, the term "God," to the ancients, suggested "people." In the oft-repeated statement, "I shall be unto you a God and you shall be unto Me a people," the correlative use of the term "God" is unmistakable. God is not a God apart from a people any more than a parent is a parent apart from a child. God is the cosmic end of the relationship of which the other end is some group, a people.

If God is not an entity, but the process of interdependence and creativity that makes for salvation, the next question arises: What is at the other end of that relationship? The answer depends upon the degree to which we succeed in conceiving as process the individual person who, to the eye, appears as a static entity. A person is such by virtue of his social relationship to other persons. He exists in his relationships, not in the body which we see with our eyes. That means that even a person is not a distinct entity, but a process of interdependence and creativity. Even if we were to conceive God as a personal being, He would still have to be conceived not as an identifiable *entity,* but as the interdependence and creativity that render the social order of societies possible and through them the fulfillment of the lives of the individual persons. Hence, the term "God" is a correlate, in the sense that it refers to whatever in nature or in man enables man to achieve salvation or to improve the world.

Third, as a consequence of the foregoing, the cosmic approach to the meaning of God must start with the attempt to arrive at specific and workable ideas of how to eliminate preventable evils from the social order and from the character of the individual. The fact that those ideas are workable implies that reality is so conditioned as to render their objectives achievable. The fact that the cosmos is thus conditioned constitutes its *divine* character, its character as a mankind-redeeming and person-saving kind of reality. When Spinoza identified God with *substance,* and treated substance as synonymous with the whole of reality, he overshot the mark. He had to deny the reality of evil and to make salvation synonymous with Stoic resignation and intellectual passivity, a conception of salvation which is not calculated to make for social or world progress.

Revolutionary as this way of conceiving God may seem, the fact is that some of our medieval theologians adopted it. Maimonides stated that it is more correct to say of God that He is life than that He is living. In the Jewish liturgy God is addressed as "the life of the worlds" (this world and the next). Bernard of Clairvaux is quoted as having "argued earnestly that love is not an attribute but of the substance of the Deity." Among modern thinkers, Henry Nelson Wieman, who himself conceives of God as process, names Smuts, Hobhouse, Alfred North Whitehead, Michael Pupin, Samuel Alexander, Lloyd Morgan, and Hocking as taking the same view.[4] Godhood or Divinity as the cosmic process of interdependence and creativity can be identified only through the ethical values that are its manifestations. We therefore learn more about what God or Godhood should mean to us when we use those terms as predicates of sentences than when we use them as subjects. We learn more about God when we say love is divine than when we say God is love. *A veritable transformation takes place in our religious thinking when the adjectival or functional sense of Divinity replaces the substantive. Divinity becomes relevant to authentic experience and therefore takes on a definiteness which is accompanied by an awareness of authenticity.*

VI

Thus the tradition that "God created the world," though as a rule glibly stated, actually does not make sense to the average thinking person. One would hardly suggest that the teachings of religion are intended only for those of superior mind. If we are expected to believe that God created the world out of nothing—an idea we cannot force the mind to conceive or imagine—we might as well forbid the intellect to meddle with religion and be left without any criteria for distinguishing between truth and superstition in religion. The statement that God created the world should be interpreted to mean that the continuing process of creativity in the universe is a phase of its divinity or divine character. As creativity, creation is synonymous with evolution, which Spencer defines as the development from the simple to the complex. When we therefore speak of creativity as divine, we mean that evolution is a manifestation of the divine aspect of the world, insofar as it enables man to fulfill himself and to contribute his share toward the improvement of the life of mankind.

Psalm 19 offers another illustration of the advantage inherent in the adjectival or functional meaning of the concept of Divinity. Psalm 19 contains a number of verses about "the Law of the Lord" which describe it as "perfect, restoring the soul," as trustworthy, and "making wise the simple." If we adopt the principle of inverting traditional statements concerning God or anything pertaining to Him, so that the subjects can figure as predicates, those verses would read: "Whatever law is perfect, restores the soul, is trustworthy, and makes wise the simple is divine," in that it enables the individual to make life worthwhile, and the nations to bring about a better and happier world.

These illustrations point to an additional advantage of the adjectival or functional use of the term "Divinity" or "Godhood." It not only rescues these terms from their vagueness, which borders on meaninglessness, but it also indicates what can be done to save from our religious traditions whatever is worth saving. Tradition as such has an intrinsic value which we can ill afford to forgo. Tradition gives us a sense of continuity in time without which there can be no meaning to change, growth, progress, or history. *A tradition which has been outlived, but which is remembered and part of the living consciousness of a person or people, is essential to the human individual and to the individuality of a people.* It confers moral status and prestige upon the people, because a tradition is a record of some achievement. Having overcome some danger or evil is a creative achievement. That prestige is conferred upon the individual whom the people needs, when he responds to that need.

The proposed cosmic approach to the idea of God and the attempt to describe the meaning of God in terms of ethical experience are bound to overcome the chief aberration of religion in the past—that of giving worship precedence over righteousness. This aberration is an inevitable consequence of the conventional tendency to conceive God as a personal being. Given that conception of God, communion with Him must take on a form similar to that with one's fellowmen. When we ask a favor of a fellowman, especially if he is a superior person, we first address ourselves to him in a way that indicates that we take cognizance of his rank or standing. If, in addressing ourselves to God, we have some mind-picture of a person immeasurably magnified, the urge to take cognizance of His greatness becomes overwhelming, so much so that it pushes our responsibilities to our fellowmen into the background. The very fact that the Psalmist deems it necessary to stress on two different occasions that only "he who is clean of hands and pure of heart" (Ps. 15 and 24) is worthy of communing with God, shows that the prevailing tendency was to see no reason for making moral conduct a prerequisite to communion with God.

VII

At this point we find ourselves confronted with the usual objection: How can we pray to God, unless we think of Him as a personal being? The answer is that the method of communing with God, as a result of a changed conception of Him, must of necessity also undergo change. There was a time in Jewish religion, for example, when animal, meal, and incense offerings were regarded as indispensable to perfect communion with God. However, most modern Jews consider animal offerings an obsolete form of worship, because it does not harmonize with their idea of God. A parallel development has taken place among some liberal Christian sects with regard to the Mass. Hence we must expect that a depersonalized conception of God will give rise to a new form of communion with Him. It will consist of intellectual reflection on human experience seeking to identify those elements in it which are a manifestation of Divinity. In addition, whenever we commune with God, we should perform some action, or make some commitment leading to action, whose purpose it is to make life worthwhile.

The most significant conclusion which can perhaps be drawn from the proposed intellectual approach to the knowledge of God affects an issue that is frequently raised with regard to the relation of religion to ethics. It is contended that a person cannot be ethical without a grounding in religion. One has to believe in God as the Author of the moral law; otherwise, the moral law is only an expression of enlightened selfishness. Selfishness, however, tends to become pure and unadulterated because intellectual enlightenment is unreliable inasmuch as it lends itself to the uses of rationalization.

Yet the only way we can know God as the Power that makes for salvation is not through tradition, which claims supernatural revelation as its source, but through the experience which accompanies our own efforts to render life worthwhile. This experience, when made the object of reflection, yields a knowledge of Divinity or Godhood as that function of reality which makes of it a cosmos. In other words, we act justly and kindly toward one another not because we believe God commanded us to do so, even though we may think we do, but because it is in our nature as human beings to act thus. However, if we wish to act justly and kindly all the time, even when it is hard to do so, or when we are strongly tempted to act otherwise, we need religion, which is both collective and individual, in order to realize that justice and kindness have their roots in the world order, that is, in the Divinity of the universe.

WILL HERBERG

Judaism as Personal Decision

RELIGION, as I see it, is not merely a metaphysic of the universe, although a philosophical element enters into it; nor is religion simply an experience of the holy, although a mystical element enters into every valid religious experience. Religion is essentially a quality of existence. It is "man's life insofar as it is defined by supreme loyalty and devotion." This definition by Robert Calhoun indicates that religion is existence, and that the basic problem of religion is the basic problem of existence—the problem of ultimate allegiance and commitment.

The decision of faith, which everyone is obliged to make because he is a living human being, defines the nature and character of his existence. In nonhuman animals, life is the unfolding of the pattern of their nature. But man's nature is open, not closed. This fact constitutes his freedom, the freedom of his existence. Every vital decision of life contributes to the formation of his being, and the most crucial and vital decision of life is a decision of faith, which is the definition of existence.

Radical self-understanding is ultimately possible only in terms of faith, for it is only in terms of faith that our existence is defined. Therefore, it is only in terms of faith that we can really understand ourselves.

Religion is, thus, in the first place, commitment. What commitment means can be clarified by a distinction between two types of thinking that are characteristic of the human enterprise. One I call "objective" thinking, the other, "existential" thinking. There is a radical difference between the two, although they are naturally combined and fused in actual life. Objective thinking is the kind of thinking that has standing in philosophy and in the sciences. It is detached, disinterested thinking. It tries to eliminate the "personal equation," to use a term familiar in the methodology of science. It is thinking about something from the outside as an object. It is the thinking of a spectator—contemplative, speculative. It is "grandstand" thinking—the thinking about the game that is going on in the playing field from the point of view of the spectator in the grandstand. In this kind of objective thinking, truth is ready-made and external. It exists outside and independent of man; he has to conform to it as he thinks.

But there is another kind of thinking—the thinking not of the spectator in the grandstand watching the game, but of the player in the playing field who thinks about the game as he plays it. This kind of thinking is not detached; it is involved, "interested," caught up in, "engaged." Something of the thinker himself is at stake in what he is thinking about. It is thinking, not from the outside but in confrontation, in meeting, in encounter. Instead of being spectatorial, speculative, contemplative, it is active, the thinking of a participant. It is "the thinking of the existing subject about his existence as he exists his existence" (Kierkegaard). It is the thinking of the player in the playing field about the game in which he is engaged. In this kind of thinking, truth is not external or ready-made; it is personal, and it is "made true," at least in part, by commitment and action.

The objective type of thinking is relevant to science and speculative philosophy. But where human existence is concerned, only existential thinking would seem to be appropriate. Existential thinking is the thinking relevant to the problems of life, especially and preeminently to personal relations, ethics, and religion.

Religious faith is at bottom an act of commitment. It is staking one's life on truth to be "made true." The truth of faith is not a ready-made, external truth; it is a personal truth that has to be "verified" by commitment and action. It is a truth that demands the staking of one's life on the venture because the decision of faith is indeed the total determination of life. As Milton Steinberg once put it, "as a man thinks about ultimates, so he deals with immediates," including his own existence. Faith is essentially neither a state of mind, as the rationalists claim, nor a compendium of propositions about a divine metaphysics, nor a state of feeling, as the mystics would contend. Faith is a structure of being-in-action, because human being is itself essentially and inescapably being-in-action. Faith is thus a restructuring of existence, similar to a mass of iron filings that is restructured when a magnet is brought near: nothing new is added; the filings were there before; but everything is different.

I

The great question of human existence, whether it is asked or not, is, Who am I? Human life, in one form or another, is an attempt to define and answer this question. The answer for the Jew is, however, twofold: I am a human being, and I am a Jew. The problem of faith, from this point of view, is the problem of making sense of both parts of this answer. What do I mean when I say I am a *human being?* What are the implications of this assertion for my existence? And what do I mean when I say I am a *Jew?* Two levels of self-understanding and commitment are involved here. One is the ultimate determination of *personal* existence, which is defined in terms of *God*. The other is the ultimate determination of *Jewish* existence, which is defined in terms of Israel, the people Israel, the people of God.

The ultimate determination of personal existence requires a definition of what it means to be a person. What does it mean to be a self? H. Richard Niebuhr answers this question in a profound and classic manner: "To be a self is to have a god"— a god with a small *g.* Human existence, in contradistinction to nonhuman being, is ultimately god-related. It is intrinsically existence in terms of an ultimate concern—of that *by and for* which one lives—which is the god of one's existence. Human existence is self-transcending because the human condition is a condition of tension, of crisis, of anxiety. We live in two worlds: we are immersed in the context of nature yet somehow we transcend the dimensions of nature. Man is finite; but, alone of all finite beings, he *knows* he is finite. Therefore he can never rest easy in his finitude; he is ever striving to reach beyond it. Man is mortal; but, alone of all mortal beings, he *knows* he is mortal. Therefore he can never rest easy in his mortality; he is ever straining to overcome it. Man is a creature; but, alone of all creatures, he *knows* he is a creature. Therefore, he can never rest easy in his creatureliness; he is forever striving to raise himself above it. Man is the kind of being who cannot stay put, he cannot rest within his creaturely limitations. Human existence, when we attempt to live and understand it in merely human terms, is self-contradictory and self-destructive.

Certain situations in life serve to bring man's efforts in achieving autonomy to an abrupt and tragic halt. They are what Karl Jaspers calls fundamental "limit situations," situations which bring a man to a sudden awareness of his dependent and transient nature and make him conscious of the inadequacy of the empirical mode of existence and therefore of his ordination to transcendence. Freedom is such a limit situation: human existence is specifically existence in freedom; yet freedom meets its limit and crisis in the determinism of nature and thought. The moral sense is another limit situation: human existence is specifically existence in the moral dimension; but the moral sense meets its limit and crisis in the scientific picture of a universe drained of value. Still another limit situation is human effort: human existence is existence in action, yet the ongoing activity of human life meets its limit and crisis in the ambiguity and transitoriness of all human achievement. Man strives and works and builds; yet he knows, or should know, that everything is here today and gone tomorrow. The things we build are not the solid, everlasting structures we imagine them to be; they are sand castles on the beach, which the next wave of history may wipe out. The ultimate limit situation is life itself: life meets its limit and crisis in death. . . . Death, as someone has said, is the ultimate crisis in life.

Human existence conceived simply in its own terms comes up against these limit situations and necessarily reveals its own self-destructive logic. As a result, we experience that "lostness," that anxiety and insecurity that characterize human life. Man feels himself alone and homeless in the universe. He is forever teetering at the brink of an abyss of meaninglessness and nothingness—in A. E. Housman's phrase, "a stranger and afraid in a world I never made." Moreover, there is a restlessness in human existence that reflects the insatiability of the human spirit. Once you've got everything you want, you find that you don't want anything you've got. This restlessness and insatiability are a consequence of the freedom of the human spirit. Man is never content to rest in the limitations of his being. He is always striving to transcend himself —to relate himself to a larger whole beyond himself in which to ground his existence so as to give it meaning and security. This is what Richard Niebuhr means when he says that "to be a self is to have a god." To live a human life is to live in terms of a god —of something that is the object of one's supreme loyalty and devotion—that which gives content, meaning, and direction to life. Faith is a person's relation to his god. In this sense, every man has his god and his faith, whether he knows it or not, whether he wants to or not. The meaning of being human is to have a god, to live in faith.

The real problem, therefore, is not *whether* to have faith or not, *whether* to affirm a god or not. A man can no more escape having a god and living in faith than he can escape the necessity of eating or breathing. As Feodor Dostoevski said, "Man must worship something; if he does not worship God, he will worship an idol made of wood, or of gold, or of ideas." Thus, the real question is not *whether* faith, but what *kind* of faith, faith in *what*. Some faith for living there must be, and the kind of faith we live by defines the kind of life we lead.

The basic choice is startlingly simple. It is *God or an idol!* The choice is inescapable and all-important. It is a choice between some god with a small *g* and God with a capital *G*. We must have something ultimate, some object of supreme loyalty and devotion, to give content, meaning, direction, and value to life. This object of our supreme loyalty and devotion may be something of this world, something partial, relative, conditioned—some value, idea, person, power, movement, institution, or program—taken and exalted to ultimacy and absoluteness, made into the god of our existence. Or it may be the God who transcends and is beyond all things of the world. There is no other choice. To take something of this world and worship it as God: that is what the Bible and our religious tradition know as idolatry. The choice is between idolatry and God-centered faith.

These are the two roads. Where does each of them lead? What are the consequences of the choice?

The evil of idolatry is not due to the badness of the thing idolized. The things of the world are good things *in their place.* The evil of idolatry resides in the fact that a *partial* and *limited* good—and all goods of the world are merely partial and limited— is taken and exalted to absoluteness. It is the process of idolatriza- tion that does the mischief; it turns a partial good into a total evil. A story in the Mishnah illumines this insight. The Jewish elders in Rome were asked, "If your God has no pleasure in the wor- ship of idols, why does He not destroy them?" To which they replied, "If a man worshiped things of which the world had no need, God would make an end of them, but lo, they worship the sun and the moon and the stars and the planets, shall God destroy the world because of fools?" The things which are wor- shiped are good things; all things that God has created are good. The folly—which is not merely ignorance but a kind of perverse- ness—consists in elevating partial and relative goods to absolute- ness, that is, in worshiping them as if they were God.

The first consequence of idolatry is, therefore, *delusion.* This is what the Bible means when it says that idolatry is "vanity," fool- ishness. The man who makes something of this world his god is driven to distort the rest of reality to suit the demands of his idol. The structure of his existence is distorted because a partial view or value is made absolute. Something that is only part of reality is exalted into the be-all and end-all of life and is made the measure of all things.

A second consequence of idolatry is *enslavement.* Our religious tradition speaks of idolatry as "demonism." The implication is clear and compelling. The man who makes anything of this world his god makes it his master. This is true whether he worships his business, family, or nation, or some ideal or movement or social program. The moment he makes it his god—that for which, or by which, he lives—he exalts it beyond criticism or control: it be- comes his master and he becomes its slave. The truth of the biblical teaching about idolatry is abundantly verified in the experience of mankind.

A third consequence of idolatry is an ethic of *dehumanization*. If we take something of this world and make it our god, that something, precisely because it is something *in* and *of* the world, divides the human race into two parts—one part within the magic circle defined by the idol; the other, much larger part, without. A man, for example, who makes his family or his nation his god, divides mankind into two parts—those within his particular family or nation, who are fully human and entitled to be treated as human beings, and those outside the family or nation, who are not really human in the same sense and who are quite expendable where the interests of family or nation are concerned. Every idolatry involves a "segregationist" ethic of this kind, for it exalts something of this world and thus defines an "in-group" that, by its very nature, is held to be superior to the rest of the human race. Idolatry and dehumanizing ethics go hand in hand.

The consequences of a God-centered faith are radically different. Insofar as a man grounds his existence in God, he is protected against the delusion and distortion that come with idolatry. He will not permit himself to regard anything of this world with such utter devotion that he will make it an absolute to which all of reality must be twisted to conform. Nothing of this world can make absolute claims on him. God-centered faith thus makes for *realism*. But it is also a *liberating* faith. Our subjection to the God beyond is our charter of freedom in this world, for insofar as we are and remain loyal to the God beyond, we will reject the claims of anything in this world to absolute loyalty, to absolute devotion, to absolute allegiance, whether that claim be made on an economic, social, political, intellectual, or even spiritual level. Being the servant of God, man is free from subjection to mere man. A rabbinic saying illustrates this point to perfection. "Unto me are the children of Israel slaves," God is represented as saying in the Bible; to which the rabbis add, "therefore not slaves unto slaves." Thomas Jefferson applied this maxim to the realm of politics when he said that "Resistance to tyrants is obedience to God." The tyrant is one who claims for himself the absolute allegiance that is due to God alone. The tyrant may be a man or an institution, an organization, a system, or an idea. In every case, the man of God-centered faith will answer the demand for absolute, total devotion with a resolute *no*. He will not permit himself to be enslaved by anybody or anything of this world because the only master he acknowledges is God. He will deal with everything critically; he will see everything in its proper perspective; he will keep everything under control and not permit himself to be over-whelmed by the things of the world—which are all good things, but good things *in their place*. He will know how to keep them in their place.

God-centered faith is a liberating faith. It frees one for con-trolling and dealing with the things of the world. It is also a faith that makes for an ethic of human worth; indeed, only on the basis of such a faith can an ethic of human worth really be established. In every empirical respect—physical, biological, so-cial, psychological, even moral and spiritual—men are manifestly unequal. An ethic that sees men merely as natural beings is bound to declare that, while all men are human, some are more human than others. But the man of God-centered faith sees men not merely as natural organisms but as persons in their God-relation-ship. He therefore sees beyond all empirical inequalities and per-ceives something supremely significant in which all men are indeed alike—their God-relationship. The empirical inequalities among men do not disappear. They remain important, but they are overshadowed by the ultimate equality of all men in the face of a God who is transcendent and sovereign. Here, and here alone, we have the ground for an equalitarian ethic of human worth and dignity.

Idolatry makes for delusion, enslavement, a dehumanizing ethic. God-centered faith makes for realism, freedom, and an ethic of human worth and equality. But there is still a deeper level of comparison and contrast. Idolatry does not lead to any real self-transcendence. In idolatry, the self merely finds and worships itself writ large. It never gets beyond itself. Hence, there is no ultimate security at all. In God-centered faith, there is the possi-bility of genuine self-transcendence. In God-centered faith, we are offered a security beyond—and shattering—all earthly securities. It is the security of the "peace that passeth understanding," which is never the work of psychological techniques, but always the gift of God received in faith. As Augustine puts it, "For Thou hast made us for Thyself alone and our hearts are restless till they rest in Thee."

The decision for or against God is the primary decision of life. We have to make it by virtue of the fact that we are human beings. If we do not decide for God, it is not as if we "withheld judgment" and made no decision at all; if we do not decide for God, quite inevitably we decide for some idol, with all the consequences of idolatry.

The decision confronts us as a demand. The demand is given in the biblical injunction: "Choose you this day whom you will serve." Note the nature of this demand. It is not philosophical or mystical; it is a straight "political" demand or, rather, a straight "theo-political" demand. What is asked for is absolute loyalty and service to God, who is to be acknowledged as sovereign Lord and Master. And the authentic Jewish answer is the one Joshua gives: "As for me and my house, we will serve the Lord." To live an authentic human life means that we will serve the Lord. To live an authentic human life means that we ground our existence in the living God and thus stand protected by our faith from the demonic idolatries that beset us on all sides. That is what the decision of faith is—the choice of a God, the supreme venture of life.

The decision of faith, if it is genuine, is not merely, or even primarily, an intelligent decision. It is a decision that defines our life. Above all, it is a commitment of the whole person. It is a decision of faith in which one stakes one's life on a truth that one has to "make true" through commitment and action.

II

We define our humanity in terms of the god we worship and the truth we live by. What then does it mean to be a Jew? Again, I am not raising a question of objective research but of existence. When I ask the question, What does it mean to be a Jew? I am really asking the question, What does it mean *for me* to be a Jew?

It is easier to define what being a Jew is *not*. To be a Jew is not to be a member of a distinct and separate race. According to anthropologists, Jews are racially and ethnically one of the most mixed groups in the world. No definition in racial terms can serve to define them. Nor does being a Jew mean being a member of a distinct and separate nation—if we employ the word "nation" in the same way in which we speak of the English, French, or American nations. Nor is it possible to define Jewish existence in cultural terms. Aside from religion, there is no cultural character or trait that is unique and common to all Jews. Neither can Jewish existence be defined simply in terms of membership in a religious denomination. A man is a Baptist if he adheres to a Baptist church, affirms the basic Baptist beliefs, or does both. Many Jews in America adhere to no synagogue, hold no religious belief, and indeed call themselves atheists. Yet it would be a gross violation of the usage of the term to deny them the name of "Jew." In short, being a Jew is not like being a member of a race, nation, cultural group, or even of a religious denomination. Any attempt to define Jewishness in secular–empirical terms, on a level that makes no reference to one's relations to God, is futile. The well-known anthropologist Melville J. Herskovits, after a prolonged attempt to define the Jews exclusively in secular and empirical terms, finally comes to this conclusion:

> It is . . . apparent that it is neither race, nor such an aspect of physical type as nasality, nor a "Jewish look" that affords terms in which the question, "Who are the Jews" is to be answered. In like manner, language, culture, belief, all exhibit so great a range of variation that no definition cast in terms of these concepts can be more than partial. Yet the Jews do represent a historical continuum. . . . Is there any least common denominator other than the designation "Jew" that can be used to mark the historical *fait accompli* which the Jew, however he may be defined, seems to be? It is seriously to be questioned.

And when an anthropologist says, "It is seriously to be questioned," he means *no*.

The fact is that there is no way in which Jewishness can be

adequately defined or given positive content on a secular, empirical level. Therefore, Jews trying to understand their Jewishness in secular terms have regularly been driven to a negative conception of Jewishness. They view their Jewishness primarily as the result of an historical irrationality, anti-Semitism, which forced the label "Jew" on them. Being herded together, they will develop some common traits; basically, however, they have nothing in common except the label. Jews are Jews simply because they are treated—that is, mistreated—as Jews by the world. The world will not let them *not* be Jews, whatever that term may mean.

This view is inadequate, though it contains some truth. If it were true that Jewishness is nothing positive but simply a label signifying the way a Jew may be treated by the world, why should anyone want to remain a Jew or to retain for himself and his children a meaningless and onerous burden? Being a Jew in the world, at best, brings with it annoyances and handicaps; at worst, it can involve great perils. It may be difficult to throw off one's Jewishness; but to yield to difficulties without an effort to overcome them is an unworthy defeatism. If being a Jew means nothing but being branded as "Jew," it clearly is something to be discarded as quickly as possible. Such is the logic of secular Judaism, and many secular Jews have recognized it, much to their own perplexity. The secular Jew frequently wants to remain a Jew, yet is unable to understand or explain what it is he wants to remain, or why.

The meaning of Jewish existence can be affirmed and understood only in faith. Jewish existence is something unique; on this, the theologian and the sociologist, the Jew and the Christian, agree. Martin Buber, the Jewish philosopher, says that "the existence of Israel is something unique, unclassifiable; this name marks the community as one that cannot be grasped in the categories of sociology and ethnology," and Carl Mayer, the Christian sociologist, reiterates that "the Jewish people represents a sociologically unique phenomenon and defies all attempts at definition." This uniqueness makes no sense in secular–empirical terms; it is intelligible only in terms of faith. To quote Buber again, "We have but one way to apprehend this positive meaning of this negative phenomenon, the way of faith. From any viewpoint other than faith, our inability to fit into a category would be intolerable, something contrary to history, contrary to nature; but from the viewpoint of faith, our inability to fit into a category is the foundation and meaning of our existence."

I can answer the question, What does it mean to be a Jew? only in faith. Jewry—Israel collectively—can understand itself only in faith. The tradition of Israel, the ongoing tradition of self-understanding of Israel in relation to its God, has always defined Israel as a covenant folk—not as a race, nation, or culture group, but as a covenant folk. Israel is not a nation like other nations; it is not a nation at all. As Jewish teaching has always understood it, Israel is a people brought into being by God to serve Him as a kind of task force in the fulfillment of His purposes in history. Israel's special relation to God is defined and established in the covenant that binds it to God. Apart from the covenant and the vocation it implies, Israel is as nothing and Jewish existence a mere delusion. But in terms of the covenant and the vocation it implies, Jewish existence becomes supremely significant and meaningful to the Jew.

The vocation to which Israel is appointed by divine covenant is traditionally defined in the term *kiddush hashem*—"sanctification of the Name"—standing witness to the living God amid the idolatries of the world.

The world is idolatry-ridden and in rebellion against God; men are forever striving to throw off their allegiance to their rightful Lord, the living God. The vocation, the function of Jewry, is to remain loyal and to stand witness to its Lord and the Lord of all being amid this universal rebellion and disobedience: to say no to every idolatrous pretension; to reject every claim of an earthly power, whether person, institution, or idea, to finality and absolute devotion; to call men to knowledge and service of the living God, to whom alone absolute devotion is due. In word and deed, individually and corporately, in inner life and in outward action, "to give the world no rest so long as the world has not God" (Maritain). Such is the vocation of Israel. This conviction concerning Israel's nature and destiny is neither an empirical finding nor a sociological conclusion; it is a commitment of faith. When I say that Israel is a covenant folk, appointed for this vocation, I am not describing a scientific notion; no sociologist or anthropologist can confirm—or refute—the statement. What I am saying is that, from the standpoint of faith, I interpret my Jewish existence as covenant existence. I am engaging in existential, not objective, thinking. This conviction concerning Israel's nature and destiny, held in faith, illumines one's self-understanding as Jew as nothing else can, because every attempt to understand Jewishness apart from the standpoint of faith, apart from the covenant, ends in negativism and nihilism. It is impossible to understand Jewish existence positively on any other level.

This conviction held in faith affords an unshakable ground for Jewish existence and survival. Again, a basic choice is involved—a choice between covenant existence and some form of secular idolatry. The choice again is inescapable. It defines my existence as a Jew. The terms of the decision are either self-affirmation in faith as a Jew or self-surrender to some secular idolatry. No other alternative is possible. Even "conversion" to Christianity, if it is sincere in faith, implies prior self-affirmation as a Jew, as Franz Rosenzweig has pointed out.

The crux of decision is given in terms of demand and response. The demand is, "You shall be unto Me a kingdom of priests and a holy nation." The response determines whether my existence as a Jew shall be authentic or inauthentic. I can affirm my existence as a Jew in terms of covenant existence and thus make my Jewishness a source of meaning and power for life. Or I can attempt to deny and reject my covenant existence. In this case, my Jewishness becomes a curse and burden and a source of self-hatred, with its psychological and sociological consequences. We are, in a measure, free to choose, but we are not free *not* to choose. It is for each of us to decide; it is our fate that is at stake. And when we make the decision, it must be a genuine decision—a commitment of the whole person to a truth, which we are now ready to "make true" with our lives.

III

On both levels of faith, Judaism is decision and commitment. It is just as much decision and commitment on the corporate level of Israel as on the personal level of the affirmation of God. On both levels it involves an ultimate affirmation which is at once an ultimate allegiance and the staking of one's life on a truth that is nevertheless to be "made true" by commitment and action. On both levels, this personal commitment is both the ground of security and the illumination of existence.

But the two levels are essentially one. For the God of personal existence—*my* God—is the God of the covenant, the "God of our fathers." For the Jew, the decision for God is a decision for the covenant, and the decision for the covenant is a decision for God. The Jew finds the living God of faith in and through Israel, in and through the covenanted people of God, which has stood witness to God through the ages and which sees the meaning of its hard and perilous existence only in its world-challenging and world-transforming vocation.

LOU H. SILBERMAN

5. *Between God and Man: The Meaning of Revelation for the Contemporary Jew*

I CAN THINK of few words less congenial to our society than the term "revelation." Not that revelation is a loaded
word, from which sparks fly when it is mentioned. On the contrary. It is a very quiet and subdued word whose meaning tends
to be obscure, hazy, and unimportant to most people. It is
certainly not among the words that rouse the Jewish community.
Yet I believe it is important that we examine this somewhat foreign
word and confront its meaning here and now.

I

As a young boy, I had a chance to see the first version of
Cecil B. DeMille's "The Ten Commandments." It was shown
in a motion picture theater built like an Egyptian temple and hence
quite appropriate for the spectacle. I vividly recall the wonders
performed by Moses, Aaron, and the Egyptian magicians in
Pharaoh's court. I can still see the waters of the Red Sea, first
piled in two gelatinous walls as the Children of Israel marched
through, and then tumbling down on the chariots and horsemen
of Egypt. Above all, I remember how the Ten Commandments
flashed across the sky in some vast electric display as a heroic
Moses, long of lock and beard, chiseled them into the rock of
Sinai, and how at last the two tablets were riven from the living
stone by the finger of God in the form of a lightning bolt. Here

was revelation that was palpable, wonderful, easy to comprehend.

I suspect it is this kind of overblown neo-fundamentalist make-believe which comes to mind when we use or hear the word "revelation." But in a world of the atomic cloud and the hydrogen bomb, this meaning of the term receives little attention. Moses and Aaron may have outdone the magicians in Pharaoh's court, but modern man outdoes God Himself in the battle of electronic effects.

Whether we form our notion of revelation on the basis of Hollywood's overliteralism, in which the mystery of the meeting of God and man is spelled out in primer language bereft of depth and meaning, or ignore this concept as intellectually outdated and untenable, we render any understanding of the history of Israel impossible and transform Judaism from a living faith into a quasi-religious façade for ethnic survival.

Any attempt to understand the nature and meaning of revelation must start from the fact that even within the biblical tradition revelation is not necessarily tied to Sinai's public account.

In the pentateuchal narrative we read:

> And it came to pass on the third day, when it was morning, that there were thunders and lightnings and a thick cloud upon the mount, and the voice of a horn exceeding loud [*kol shofar hazak m'od*]; and all the people that were in the camp trembled.
>
> (Exod. 19:16)

And again:

> Now Mount Sinai was altogether on smoke, because the Lord descended upon it in fire; and the smoke thereof ascended as the smoke of a furnace, and the whole mount quaked greatly. And when the voice of the horn waxed louder and louder, Moses spoke, and God answered him by a voice.
>
> (Exod. 19:18–19)

Yet these external trappings of the Sinaitic revelation play little or no role in other portions of Scripture. They are apparently not seen as central to God's meeting with Israel. Thus we read in the familiar story of the Prophet Elijah:

> And, behold, the Lord passed by, and a great and terrible wind rent the mountains, and broke to pieces the rock before the Lord; but the Lord was not in the wind; and after the wind an earthquake; but the Lord was not in the earthquake; and after the earthquake a fire; but the Lord was not in the fire; and after the fire a voice of gentle quiet [*kol demamah dakah*].
>
> (I Kings 19:11 ff.)

The passage in I Kings may well be a comment on the narrative in Exodus seeking to define the voice (*kol*) with which God spoke to Moses as *kol demamah dakah,* "a voice of gentle quiet," in contrast to the *kol shofar hazak m'od,* "the voice of a horn exceeding loud." It also denies God's presence in the "great and terrible wind" as well as the fire and the earthquake which accompany the revelation at Sinai.

Here, the revelation is not bound up with external events. Amos suggests the naturalness of revelation when he locates his meeting with God not in some extraordinary and overwhelming experience but alongside common experiences of life:

> Do two walk together, without a common purpose?
> Does a lion roar in the forest, when there is no prey?
> Does a young lion give forth his voice, having captured nothing?
> Does a bird fall to earth, when no one snares it?
> Does the trap spring up from the earth, without asking anything?
> If the shofar sounds in the gate, do not the people tremble?
> If evil befall a city, shall not God have done it?
> The lion has roared, who does not fear?
> God has spoken, who will not prophesy?
>
> (Amos 3:3–8)

If the understanding of revelation even within the biblical tradition is not tied to a literal affirmation of Sinai's public account, the trend is even more clearly indicated in rabbinic thought, though there have been some scholars who have insisted upon burdening rabbinic thought with a thoroughgoing literalism. For example, Claude J. G. Montefiore, the distinguished liberal Jewish scholar, wrote:

> But . . . as the Rabbis often took all that is said about God in the Hebrew Bible very literally, and as they were so sadly fettered by the burden of regarding every biblical utterance as good and true and inspired, they seemed often to talk about God like so many big children. I do not think it is possible to regard all that they say as conscious "accommodation." These childishnesses are too constant and too simple for that, and in spite of the famous saying that "the Torah speaks in the language of men" the Rabbis seldom seem to hint that God cannot *really* be supposed to think and speak and act as they represent Him as thinking, speaking and acting.[1]

In other words, Montefiore is ascribing an unconditional fundamentalist attitude to rabbinic Judaism.

Yet this view of tradition is not in keeping with its real nature. Rabbinic Judaism in its earliest sources found such literalism unacceptable. The *Mekhilta,* in discussing the phrase (from Exod. 19) "and the smoke thereof ascended as the smoke of a furnace," says,

> One might think it was like an ordinary smoke, therefore it says "of a furnace." But if: "of a furnace," one might still think it was just like that of a furnace. It says, however [in Deut. 4:11], "And the mountain with fire unto the heart of heaven." Why then does it say "of a furnace"? That the ear might get it in accordance with its capacity of hearing.[2]

Immediately following this the verse from Amos is quoted: "The lion has roared, who does not fear? God has spoken, who will not prophesy?" The rabbis seem apprehensive about the comparison between the lion's roaring and God's speaking. Hence they ask,

> Who gave strength and force to the lion? Was it not He? But it is merely that we describe Him by figures known to us from His creations so that the ear may get it in accordance with its capacity of hearing.

In the words of a contemporary scholar, the rabbis operated on the premise that "comparison of anything about God to a phenomenon in the world . . . is not a true comparison. God is other." [3]

The rabbis clearly insist that scriptural language is our point of beginning. If we remain with its literalness, we fail to grasp its meaning—a point which is underscored by a comment of Hezekiah bar Hiyya:

> Blessed are the prophets who compare the Creator to His creation, the Planter to His planting, as in the verses:
> "For the Lord is a sun and shield."
>
> > (Ps. 84:12)
>
> "The Lion hath roared, who does not fear?
> The Lord God hath spoken, who will not prophesy?"
>
> > (Amos 3:8)
>
> "And His voice was like the voice of many waters."
>
> > (Ezek. 43:2)
>
> For they thus cause the ear to hear what it is able to hear and the eye to see what it is able to see.[4]

Rabbinic Judaism, even in its earliest stratum, is thus aware of the fundamental problem of revelation: Are a discussion and an understanding of revelation to be inextricably bound to a literalness close to the childishness of which Montefiore spoke, or are we free to move with responsibility beyond the surface of the text to implied meaning?

I am not suggesting that naïve literalism has never been a part of Jewish thinking. Jewish tradition is too long, broad, and deep to have avoided such an approach. Nor am I implying that the mode of understanding that I am emphasizing has always been dominant or normative in Jewish history. What I am claiming is that the problem we face in any attempt to understand revelation as we confront the Bible has never been irrelevant.

The Middle Ages and its philosophic tradition support this claim. As a Moslem thinker wrote a thousand years ago, "Moslems, Jews, Christians, Magians, they are all walking in error and darkness. There are only two kinds of people left in the world. The one group is intelligent but lacking in faith. The other has faith but is lacking in intelligence." It was to the reunion of intelligence and faith that medieval philosophy—Islamic, Christian, and

Jewish—devoted itself; and the meaning of revelation was one of its central themes.

Thus Maimonides, in his *Guide of the Perplexed,* went to considerable lengths to explain the literalness of the biblical account by introducing a distinction between Moses and the masses of the common people. According to Maimonides, it was Moses alone who could be said to have received the revelation at Sinai. Hence, revelation became a singular and special event, involving but one man. The people were excluded from the reality of revelation and experienced only its peripheral and external accompaniments. As Maimonides wrote:

> They saw the fire, they heard the sounds, which were those of thunder and lightning during a storm, and the loud sound of the shofar; . . . but the voice of the Lord, that is, the voice created for that purpose, which was understood to include the diverse commandments, was heard only once . . . when the people heard this voice their soul left them. . . . It must . . . be noticed that the people did not understand the voice in the same degree as Moses did.[5]

Maimonides' interpretation reflected his conviction that prophecy is a very special and unusual gift, the possession of a chosen few, belonging to them only as a gift of God's grace. The rest of mankind has its faith only at second hand and in an inferior form. God is near to only a few souls; for the masses, God is remote, and accessible only through the experience and endeavors of others.

Consequently, a literal understanding of revelation as described in the Bible was totally unacceptable to the philosopher. Nor was the rabbinic attempt to modify or mitigate the biblical account satisfactory. The conclusions and explanations of the rationalists were remote from the biblical text and from the rabbinic understanding of it.

Not all philosophers were, of course, rationalists, nor did all medieval thinkers follow the path of philosophy. Jewish mysticism represented an equally important trend among medieval Jewish thinkers. As Gershom Scholem pointed out in *Major*

Trends in Jewish Mysticism, "the characteristic feature of the mystical experience, the direct contact between the individual and God," gives all important religious conceptions, among them revelation, their characteristic tone and content:

> Revelation . . . is to the mystic not only a definite historical occurrence which, at a given moment in history, puts an end to any further direct relation between mankind and God. With no thought of denying Revelation as a fact of history, the mystic still conceives the source of religious knowledge and experience which bursts forth from his own heart as being of equal importance for the conception of religious truth. . . . To the mystic, the original act of Revelation to the community—the . . . public revelation of Mount Sinai . . . appears as something whose true meaning has yet to unfold itself. . . .[6]

According to the mystic, man not only faces "the living presence of God, the God of the Bible, the God who is good, wise, just, and merciful," but he must also recognize the hidden God who remains eternally unknowable in the depths of His own self. "The hidden God of whom nothing is known to us" and "the living God of religious experience and revelation" are one and the same. Hence, the major task of mysticism is the attempt to bridge the gap, to understand the way in which the hidden God has moved out of His hiddenness into creation and revelation. Much of Jewish mysticism is thus a continuing explanation of creation and revelation which—unlike their position in philosophy—are actually one and the same in mysticism.

The answers of earlier generations may, of course, not seem to be very meaningful to us. Yet they point up a significant fact. The situation in which a question is asked is highly relevant to the answer that is given to it. The meaning of the answer must therefore be understood and judged in the particular situation in which it was given, not in ours. Neither the internal interpretation of the Bible, nor the rabbinic, philosophic, or mystical reworkings of the biblical ideas can truly speak to our situation. They may provide us with insights and matter for thought, but they cannot serve as answers to *our* question about the meaning of revelation, though it is the same question previous generations asked.

For an answer which may conceivably address itself to our contemporary situation, we shall have to turn from tradition to contemporary thinkers.

The nineteenth century found the Jews of western Europe confronting the elaborate structure of German idealism as it had developed after Kant and had come to fullest expression in Hegel. In this new situation, the meaning of revelation underwent a radical revision. In the words of Emil Fackenheim, "Religion was no longer understood as the attempt of man to relate himself to a God outside himself. It was a self-transformation of finite into infinite spirit. . . ." It was something that happened *within,* not *between.*

The basic approach of the nineteenth century to the problem of revelation is clearly exhibited in the so-called "Pittsburgh Platform" adopted by a small group of Reform rabbis in 1885. The first article of this document is an unmistakable attempt to provide a new understanding of the meaning of revelation:

> We recognize in every religion an attempt to grasp the Infinite, and in every mode, source, or book of revelation held sacred in any religious system the consciousness of the indwelling of God in man. We hold that Judaism presents the highest conception of the God-idea as taught in our Holy Scriptures and developed and spiritualized by the Jewish teachers, in accordance with the moral and philosophical progress of their respective ages. We maintain that Judaism preserved and defended, midst continual struggles and trials and under enforced isolation, this God-idea as the central religious truth for the human race.[7]

The statement clearly defines religion in "within" rather than "between" terms. Man is subject, and out of man emerges the God concept. Revelation is an unfolding from within. "The Bible reflects the primitive ideas of its own age, and at times clothes its conception of divine providence and justice dealing with man in miraculous narratives." While this approach did what previous generations had done—transformed the literalness of the biblical narrative—it went beyond them in dissolving the historical. For previous generations something had happened between Israel and God, even though this *between* was not as described in the biblical narrative. Now something happened *within* Israel, out of which developed the idea, the God concept. The concreteness of history was transformed into the evolution of ideas.

This particular tendency also found expression in the *Guiding Principles* adopted by the Central Conference of American Rabbis at Columbus, Ohio, in 1937. The first article of Part I defines Judaism as "the historical religious experience of the Jewish people," while Article Four of the same part, dealing with Torah, states that "God reveals Himself not only in the majesty, beauty and orderliness of nature, but also in the vision and moral striving of the human spirit." Here is Immanuel Kant *redivivus*. Although the language seems to make God the subject of the verb "reveals," the real meaning of the sentence places man at the center. It is the "people of Israel, through its prophets and sages, who achieved unique insight in the realm of religious truth."

Here we are at the very heart of our problem. Like all preceding generations, we find it necessary to understand the meaning of revelation, which is at the heart of Judaism, in a fashion which will make it ours in our contemporary situation. Yet this is a task with which we are not—or not yet—grappling. There have been few substantial attempts to understand and articulate, in contemporary terms, the unmistakable intention of the tradition. The passages from the documents of Reform Judaism that I have quoted are not contemporary statements, although the latest was written in 1937. The Columbus statement "represents in large part the historicizing, psychologizing, sociologizing religionism that marked the twenties and thirties. It . . . was an end product, not a seminal document." Nothing that has happened since then would justify a different judgment. The philosophical world view that enabled the men of Pittsburgh to issue their statement has vanished. The ideology that motivated the Columbus statement has largely evaporated, and our words have lost their meaning.

I, for one, am not willing to see in Judaism the product of a unique genius in the sphere of religion inherent in the Jewish people. Very little in the contemporary state of Jewish existence leads me to affirm this genius, and little in the history of our people points to it. Judah Ha-Levi thought he could find a particular, biologically recessive quality in Israel, the quality of being the sensitive receptor of divine influence; but this quality is not the same thing as seeing Judaism as a product of the spirit of the Jewish people. Nor am I sure that the nineteenth- and early twentieth-century formulations represent a "progressive development in religion." Their chronological position is no guarantee of superiority or adequacy. They may be set side by side with, but not above, the chronologically earlier. They represent meaningful attempts to understand the situations whose trends they reflect. To give them more status than this is to transform them into dogmas.

Without a contemporary theological grasp, we are thus left with a DeMillian literalism, a vague sentimentalism, or, all too often, with nothing at all. And it is this nothing-at-all that is our problem today. What can we ourselves, in our particular situation, understand the meaning of our world to be? Put differently, what does this vast transition running through the centuries say to us? Rashi introduced his note on the biblical words "In the beginning God created," with the statement that, "This verse calls out, 'Understand Me!' " This is what our tradition says to us, too.

II

Thus far I have dealt with the event of Sinai as the crucial point in any attempt to understand the meaning of revelation. But nowhere in Jewish thought is Sinai the sum and substance of revelation. As Robert Gordis has shown, the talmudic concept of *Torah min ha-shamayim,* "Torah from heaven," revelation, is not synonymous with the more or less contemporary traditionalist–apologetic phrase, *Torah mi-Sinai,* "Torah from Sinai," which argues for the Mosaic authorship of the Pentateuch.[8] Jacob Petuchowski, along with Gordis, has argued that to confuse the two terms is to confuse a theological with a literary question. The theological question is, Is this God's revelation? Petuchowski rightly points out that "It becomes neither more nor less so the nearer it is placed in time to the age of Moses." [9] Or, as Gordis writes, "To build the sanctions of Judaism on the doctrine that the Five Books of Moses were completely written in their present form by the great liberator, is to prejudge a scientific question and to court disaster." He quotes Franz Rosenzweig's letter to Jakob Rosenheim, the Orthodox leader in Frankfurt: "Where we differ is our reluctance to draw from our belief in the holiness or uniqueness of the Torah and its character of revelation any conclusions as to its literary genesis and the philological value of the text as it has come down to us." [10] In other words, the question of revelation is not the question of the literary history of the documents that make up the collection we speak of as Torah, the Five Books of Moses, or Torah, the totality of the teaching that is the heritage of the people of Israel. Thus, to defend the crucial importance of revelation in Judaism is not to defend the Mosaic authorship or inerrancy of the texts as we have them. Our affirmation of revelation does not require such assertions. Vice versa, the affirmation of a critical approach that sees in the texts a long and involved oral and literary tradition does not require a denial of the theological concept of revelation.

Gordis mentions Kaufmann Kohler's statement that he lost his faith in traditional Judaism as expounded by his master, Samson Raphael Hirsch, when his study of Semitic languages demonstrated that Hebrew was not the oldest and original language of mankind, as his teacher had insisted. What is tragically sad about this statement is the implication that traditional Judaism as understood by Hirsch had to demand acquiescence to ideas about the origin and history of language and that the denial of those ideas was considered a denial of traditional Judaism.

This issue helps to clarify an important point. When I am speaking of the Word of God, I am not making a literary judgment about the text of the Bible. I am not claiming that the Masoretic text of the second Rabbinic Bible printed by the Christian printer Daniel Bomberg in Venice in 1521 is the Word of God. I am convinced that a critical approach to the text is an absolute necessity, that it yields many important insights, and that we ignore it only at our intellectual and spiritual peril. But I do not imply that this critical approach makes it impossible for these texts to be the Word of God.

Revelation, as indicated before, must be viewed as event, not as content. Revelation, traditionally, was something that happened *between* and not something that happened *within*. The *between* nature of revelation is defined by a Jewish thinker whose influence upon modern thought in many fields has been of greatest importance: Martin Buber.

For Buber there are two basic attitudes in which we exist, two ways of standing toward others, the I–It and the I–Thou relations. The former is our connection with things which we move about, manipulate, use. It is the everyday world in which we live, the world of business, science, politics, industry. The things we use in it are machines, buildings, goods, ideas, and—human beings. Our connection with them is always with what is used or thought of as a thing.

The other attitude is that of relation, of between, in which I do not *use* but *meet* another, whatever that "other" may be. I do not grasp hold of it, manipulate it, make it mine, but only face it and am faced by it in such a way that there is something between us. We stand independent but not isolated. We address one another; we say "Thou" to each other. We are person, one to the other. We do not have a different kind of attitude toward human beings than toward nonhumans. I–Thou and I–It represent two different stances, and that with which we are in connection or in relation is not limited by its nature but by the absence or presence of between-ness. A man may be a thing (and tragically, all too frequently is); an idea may be person, that to which I say "Thou," that with which I stand in relation.

For Buber this I–Thou relation is the primary state of man, from which he has time and again removed himself, yet toward which he time and again strives. We live in a world of I–It, the spread-out world of action, but on occasion find ourselves not in this manipulative world but in the world of meeting, relation, and love, when we stand fulfilled in the present moment and come to know the infinite love that is present and shines through all love, the love of God. We are transformed in this moment. Something has been added to our lives that was not there before. How it came to us we do not know; yet it is now ours.

Existence in between-ness is not a solitary and unusual aspect of life. It is that moment when we are in love, and it belongs to the whole range of life. The closing lines of *The Rose Tattoo*—

vengo, vengo, amore, "I come, I come, love!"—are the proclamation of relation, of I–Thou as the present moment of our human existence. Thus, between-ness is the moment in which I stand over against a person, bound in love. It is the moment in which I entirely proclaim the other and in which I am proclaimed by the other. Who I am is never more clearly stated than at this moment.

When we speak of revelation, we are referring to this between-ness, the relation of I–Thou. Revelation in the Bible is the encounter, in the seeming ordinariness of history, not of mere divine power, undifferentiated deity, but of just that to which we can, must, and do say "Thou." Revelation is the saying within the event, "Here am I," and man's response is, "Here am I." Thus, revelation in the Bible is not a one-time event. It is the ever-recurring event.

The twelfth chapter of Genesis may help clarify the meaning of this definition. The previous chapter, after describing the scattering of the nations, ends with a dull genealogy full of "begots." Then, without further ado, without thunder or lightning, in all naturalness and in the midst of life, the text continues, "The Lord said to Abram, 'Go forth from your native land and from your father's house to the land that I will show you.' " And a few verses later, "Abram went forth as the Lord had spoken to him." [11] The rabbinic commentators, overwhelmed by the suddenness of this passage, tried to fill in what had been left unsaid between the chapters. But their answers, often lovely and moving, cannot be ours. What we find in the biblical text is the moment of meeting when Abram, in the midst of the ordinariness of his life, found himself over against a real other. The shapeless divine power of his ancestral religion, concretized in the imagery of the Midrash in the clay statuettes his idol-making father produced for sale, fell away before the presence in his life of Him, of this One who, for Abraham, was absolutely trustworthy, who was the direction of this man's life from that moment on. This was revelation. The sudden knowledge had come to Abram that he had meaning, for he existed in the presence of One whom he trusted with the unquestioning love that is the heart of trust. Here is no special religious experience, no complex of feelings, but the straightforward experience of being called in love and responding in trust.

The twenty-ninth chapter of Genesis provides another illustration. Jacob is running for his life from Esau's angry vengeance. Jacob is by no means an exemplary character. Yet in a stony desert waste, in the midst of turmoil and fear, suddenly a voice enters into a life as desolate as the surrounding land: "I am the Lord, the God of your father Abraham, and the God of Isaac." [12] It was only a dream; yet it was more than a dream. It was meeting. Again there was that One who stood over against this Jacob so that the word that broke forth from his lips could only be: "Surely He is in this place; and I had not known it." Revelation was the coming of between-ness, the standing in relation with Him, with the One who was there even in desolation. Here was the One whom you trusted because His being there in your life, His letting Himself be known to you, was His love that defined you, that made you other than you had thought yourself to be.

Exodus 3 presents still another illustration (although here the element of external wonder makes its appearance for the first time). The shepherd Moses, tending his father-in-law's sheep, turns aside to "look at this marvelous sight; why is the bush not burnt?" and is met with "I am the God of your father, the God of Abraham, the God of Isaac, and the God of Jacob." [13] The refugee, the man without direction and history, now has the direction and has become heir of his history. He has been addressed, and he has responded. He who is there in a man's life, as He will be there —not summoned by priestly formulae, not tied down by the magic of cult, but in the unconstrained freedom of His own being—has in the sheer love of His being there called forth the trust that is the meaning of a man's life.

But the encounter of man and God is just the beginning. For it is not just this man in his individuality, in the privacy of his own existence, with which we must deal, but with the public events as well. They define the *am,* "the people," the community that exists because it is *im,* with Him who has made Himself known. Thus we must begin again, this time with a ragtail rabble of enslaved laborers called *ivrim,* "people at the edge," an ill-defined status in the ancient Semitic world, from whose midst Moses had emerged and to whom he now returned to tell them of the God of their fathers, the center of the past of which they were to be heirs. In the beginning, there is no "He who is present" to them; but then they are met by the One of whom they must acknowledge in the midst of the event, "He is here!" It is a pointing of the self in *emunah,* in "trustfulness," not toward a force or power but toward the One who addresses, who commands, who defines you because He is there. At this moment of standing in relation, the people of Israel came into being. The people is the creation of His self-disclosure. From now on, it is always defined in this relation. The love, which is the meaning of revelation, commands or demands *emunah,* "trust." The history of this people is its meeting in the flowing of events with him who is encountered in the event.

Yet *emunah* is not always present. This people had met Him in the hour of escape as they sloshed across the mud flats of the Sea of Reeds. They trusted His guidance as Abraham had trusted it centuries before. They had met Him when His *navi,* His spokes-man, had led them to the holy mountain and had there told them what was required of those who were with the Lord. They trusted Him when Moses had died and Joshua had taken his place. But now, in the land, they were not always sure. They were doubtful of His being there. The *baalim,* the "landlord deities," seemed to be in possession. They felt He could not be there when the battle was lost and the Philistines had captured the Ark on which He rode. They had forgotten that He would be there not as they wanted it but as He would be. Thus, time and again they fled the relation; they did not trust Him. And time and again prophets rose up to remind them that it was they who had absented themselves, not He; that He was as much present when the enemy was encamped about Jerusalem as when the land was at peace; and that He made Himself known and confronted them on the weary road to Baby-lon, rather than in the regal splendor of a petty dynast's court.

Revelation is the breaking of God's presence into the lives of men in history. It is not thinking about history and drawing philo-sophical or theological conclusions. It is being confronted by the One to whom you say "Thou" in the brokenness and incomplete-ness of existence. Its human counterpart is the response of trust to the love that is there. The history of Israel is the saving act of God that discloses man's meaning. It is public and, seen from the outside, it is almost commonplace:

> Are ye not as the children of the Ethiopians unto Me,
> O children of Israel? saith the Lord.
> Have I not brought up Israel out of the land of Egypt,
> And the Philistines from Caphtor, and Aram from Kir?
>   (Amos 9:7)

Yet, "You only have I known of all the families of the earth." He is the Lord of all history, but through *this* history, which is full of intimacy, He is made manifest as the sovereign ruler.

Here at least part of the meaning of revelation can be found. It escapes a literalism that ends in a materialistic portrayal and avoids a subjectivism that explains God as a concept created by the Jewish people but cannot provide a meaning for the Jewish people. God is met in event, in the concreteness of our existence. According to the order of service for the eve of Passover,

> In every generation one ought to look upon himself as though he had gone forth from Egypt. As it is said, And thou shalt tell thy son on that day, saying: This is on account of that which He did for me, when I went forth from Egypt. The Holy One blessed be He did not redeem our fathers only, but He redeemed *us* with them, as it is said: He brought *us* forth from thence, in order to bring *us* in, to give us the land which He had sworn unto our fathers.

We are called upon to encounter God in the event. The redemption from Egypt is a contemporaneous experience. The redeeming act of God is in *our* lives. In his novel, *For the Sake of Heaven,* Buber says that if the Seder could be celebrated as it should, that is, if we were actually facing God in history, the *geullah,* "redemption," would be here. Thus, to understand revelation as the encounter of God and man in the midst of history, as the coming-in of love and the response of trust, is, at least for me, the mode and manner of the contemporary Jew's understanding of the ultimate fact of his existence.

III

I have thus far discussed revelation in event, as the act of God. But what about revelation as word? What about the Bible? What is the relation of Torah to revelation?

The Bible text cannot be the revelation of God, if this term is taken to mean that the Five Books of Moses, for instance, are the inerrant word dictated by God to Moses atop Mount Sinai. The concept of "Torah from Sinai" is hardly sustainable in the light of contemporary scholarship, and it is irrelevant to our question. This does not, however, settle the question of "Torah from Heaven." I am insisting upon the reality and actuality of the encounter of God and man. But does my insistence on the reality of this encounter imply that some part of the Bible is in some way divine, in some sense the Word of God? If so, in what sense? Is the Bible in any way revelation?

I believe the Bible is the Word of God. However, this affirmation requires clarification.

In the first place, the Bible is the book of the acts of God. It is the recounting, through many lips, of those events in which these individuals and especially this people encountered God, and of the way, in trust or rebellion, in which they responded to the encounter. Its language, its literary usage, its structure, are of another time. It tells its story in its own way, in broad flowing narrative or high-flown rhetoric, in the terse shorthand of the legislator and judge. It reflects local pride, parochial prejudice, moral grandeur, prophetic insight, political perversity. It is entirely human, yet, paradoxically, entirely divine, for it proclaims over and over again the meeting of God and Israel. It is susceptible to critical analysis. The traditions woven together may be pointed to; the documents out of which it was composed can probably be discovered. Its parallels in the literature of other peoples may be indicated. Its legal forms may be explained on the basis of clay tablets found in cities far more ancient than Israel's settlement in Canaan, even earlier than the sojourn in Egypt, even antedating the wanderings of Abraham. Yet it is, or can be, the Word of God.

It is not the Word of God as it lies on the scholar's dissecting table. Nor is it the Word of God when it is read as the scientifically not always accurate account of the ancient Near East from about the twentieth to the second century B.C.E. It is not even the Word of God when it is read in more or less perfunctory fashion in church or synagogue. But it becomes the Word of God when the community to whom it is addressed hears it as the proclamation of God's saving action and love for His people whom He has called. It becomes the Word of God, His revelation, when we meet God in its recital. It is the Word of God when He who is present as He will be present is met by us in this book. There is no guarantee that He will be met there. He cannot be met, and it cannot reveal Him, if *we* are not there. There can be no betweenness, which is the heart of revelation, unless two stand over against each other. When we are not there, He, as it were, is not there, either.

Rosenzweig has indicated the promise and the danger in his commentary on a poem by Judah Ha-Levi, *Hinneni,* "Here am I."

In the Jewish community of a village in the southern part of the Black Forest there lived a dull-wit named Mendele, whom the congregation supported. One day while he was busily chopping wood near the small synagogue that stood on a high place close to a steep slope, a pair of boys spied him as they came down the mountain path. Full of fun, they called down, "Mendele!" He looked around but saw no one. A little while and again they called, "Mendele! Mendele!" He looked up, confused, but nothing was to be seen. Another wait and then, "Mendele! Mendele!" This time he threw down the axe, ran into the synagogue, mounted the platform from which the Torah is read, threw wide his arms, and cried out in Abraham's words, *Hinneni!* "Here am I!" Man is able to cry "Here am I," for these words echo back to him God's lips. It is this divine "Here am I" that is longed for, desired, sought after, pleaded for by the poem in the twenty-threefold repetition of the rhyme, until the twenty-fourth time the answer to the longing, the desire, the seeking, the pleading finally comes. But the answer is not merely longed for, desired, sought after, pleaded for. No, so utterly human must be the word to which the divine answer comes as a reply, that as in this poem there can be that moment when the answer is threatened: "Yet when I sorrow, my sorrow drive Thee off." The human heart has the inalienable right ever to deny the greatest truth of revelation, that sorrow is a gift of God. It has the right to deny this when, as always, it becomes a mere theological form, and to set in its place nature's ancient truth that sorrow is sorrow, nothing else. God replies only to the word that mounts up out of the abyss of all human powers, both slumbering and awake.[14]

IV

Does revelation still have meaning for the contemporary Jew? The question is real, no matter how fruitlessly we may deal with it. God meets us in the ordinariness of our lives. He reveals Himself in the moment of love as we stand face to face with those to whom we speak the living word "Thou." He meets us in the events of our life joined together as Israel, as the community called into being by His command. He meets us in the word that proclaims the meeting in history—in the Bible confronted as the place in which He reveals Himself. Here, standing in love, we hear ourselves called to meaning as the single one and as the community of Israel. God makes Himself known to us in both love and command. This fact indicates our responsibility. It calls for our response.

This is the pattern of our predicament. We are called; the very form and texture of our history show forth God Himself. We are called in our daily lives as we confront those who would be addressed as Thou, as person, not to be used but to be loved, and not to use, but to love us. We are called in that meeting by our God. But what is the demand? I can repeat Micah's words and say that God requires of me "to do justly, to love mercy, to walk humbly." But I can never know what "to do justly" with Him means, except when I stand in the place where this, just this, act of justice is required of me. I can never know where or when it will be required. It may be asked of me not in some public and grandiose way, but in the daily or weekly round of life, in the run-of-the-mill routine involvement with students and colleagues. It may be that the just act which is my responsibility and must be my response is called for in my reading of a term paper or the

checking of a quiz—in as little and as much as that. The responsibility laid upon us by the presence of God in our lives is at our
desks, at the counter, in the PTA meeting, behind the green
curtain of the voting machine, for here are the places in which
just doing is called for.

Nor is the love of *hesed,* the love of "mercy," something done
in abstraction. The commandment "thou shalt love thy neighbor"
speaks of the one who is near or next to you and who, standing
right before you in this moment, needs your love for the sake of
his very existence. Your neighbor is he who is there to be loved;
and you respond to God by being the person of *hesed* in that moment. This is not abstraction but reality. My neighbor is my wife,
my daughters, my friends, my colleagues. Employer, employee,
casual acquaintance, harassed community fund raiser, unhappy
teacher—the list can be extended endlessly—all of them stand in
need of us.

And when do I walk humbly with Him? In the very hour He
calls upon me to do justly and I am just, and when the *hesed* He
has bestowed upon me overflows into the lives of others. There is
not a single moment in which we are free from the responsibility
to respond to the call; and our response must be the act, the deed
of justice, love, and humility which that very moment asks of us.

We are called as individuals to respond. Otherwise we tragically
fail. But we are called not only in our singularity but also in the
union of our lives. For I am not I alone nor are you simply you.
We are the called community as well, the people of Him who calls.
That He has revealed Himself in our history, that millennia of our
story show Him forth, asks of us answers, imposes upon us responsibility, demands of us response.

In the long march of history, what have we been called to be?
Library shelves groan with their burden of answers. Sects and
sectarians quarrel with one another. Politicians, secular and theological, pass resolutions to set it straight. Yet the question remains.
For it is not answered in theory but in existence. We are called to
be what we are, "the People of Israel," the priestly kingdom, the
holy community, whose life must disclose to the peoples what it
means to be with God.

To be with God? But where or when? Again, not in abstraction but in life; to be with God just at that point where we are. If here, to show forth with every means the very wonder of our existence as Jews. To make the pattern of tradition vividly vibrant within our lives so that Sabbath and holy day, festival and fast, be not false fronts in which we have no belief, but disclosures of God's meaning in man's life. Not to shrug one's shoulders, not to refuse, but to show in home, office, factory, and store that this people has caught sight of how men must live, in love, to be truly men.

Though we have not yet done it, or not done it well enough, we must learn to discover for ourselves the scope of our tradition so that men, beholding what we have built, will praise not us but God who bade us build.

And our response will always have to be what the hour calls from us. To till the soil and live in such a way as shall make the peoples know that greed, enmity, self-seeking are not the ultimates of life. To face man's cruelty and inhumanity with the proclamation that God's kingdom is—nevertheless—real. No one knows or can foresee what the hour or place will ask of us, nor what our answer will be. But this is our responsibility. This is what we are.

V

Revelation, in Rashi's words, calls out, "Understand me!" The margin between failure and success in this venture is, paradoxically, both infinitely wide and infinitely narrow. Perhaps we do not understand the meaning of this changing word in the spread-out, precise way in which academicians like to mount their subjects. But I believe it is possible to learn through our patience and love as well as through the love of Him whose ways we seek, that He in His own way breaks into our single lives and into our lives as His people and makes Himself known in our deepest heart and mind.

MANFRED VOGEL

6. The Jewish Image of Man and Its Relevance for Today

WHAT IS THE image of man in Jewish tradition? What answers does Judaism give to the basic questions which inevitably arise regarding man? Who is man? Is he in essence spirit or body? Where is he coming from, and where is he going? What is he supposed to do with his life? Does his existence have meaning and worth? Is man intrinsically evil, or is he basically good and only corrupted by society? What is his relation to society?

These questions that man has persistently raised about himself constitute the basic concern of every religion. For religion speaks not to God's situation but to the situation of man. And the questions man asks about himself reflect the ultimate situation in which he finds himself. All else is contingent on the answers to these questions. Nothing makes sense unless man has a basic frame of orientation. The paramount task of religion is to provide this frame. And even though Judaism has not expressed itself doctrinally and systematically in theological formulation, and though its tradition reflects many nuances, Judaism offers a basic image of man which is definite and constant.

To examine this basic image is an undertaking that has a particular urgency in the modern world. The crisis which encompasses every facet of contemporary culture and life is at bottom the crisis of man. Who is man? is still the fundamental question, but the answer is not heard with a clear and unambiguous voice. The fierce and fearsome conflict between the various ideologies, religious and pseudoreligious, of our world is fundamentally the conflict between different answers to the question, Who is man? It is here that the battle lines are drawn and that the issues of man's future will be decided.

The Jewish view of man may have been promulgated long ago, but it speaks to man's present situation with the same force with which it was spoken at Mount Sinai. In these matters there is no obsolescence. The basic problem of Who is man? has not changed with time and the accumulation of new knowledge. In technology and science, the twentieth century is worlds apart from the biblical era. Yesterday's avant-garde ideas are today's obsolete fancies. The Bible, however, or, for that matter, the texts of any religious or philosophical tradition, are outside the passage of time. The Upanishads, the Bible, Plato's dialogues, are contemporaneous with every age regardless of the date of their composition. Two thousand years ago, man was confronted by the same mystery and challenge that confront him today. What changes and distinguishes one period from another is whether or not a period can accept an answer as the basic orientation of its existence, and what answer is accepted. An answer that is acceptable to the temper of one period may prove unacceptable to that of another.

This points to a basic difference between answers to scientific questions and answers to our questions about man. Questions about man are not scientific questions. They cannot be answered scientifically. Their truth is not objective and impersonal; it is subjective and existential. The answers cannot be deduced from empirical data, nor can their validity be tested in experiments. They can only be accepted or rejected. And what one person accepts as existentially valid may be rejected by someone else as meaningless.

This is what is meant when we say that these answers must be taken on trust. The risk is always present that the answers may be objectively false; yet we accept them on trust and hope they are true. For the believer, the truth of these answers will be decided only when the Messiah comes and ultimate questions will be settled. In the meantime, the only criterion at man's disposal is his authenticity to himself. Each person must decide for himself whether or not the answers speak to him meaningfully. Thus, it is not possible to "prove" the objective truth of the Jewish portrayal of man or to demonstrate its validity as against other portrayals. What can be done is to outline its basic features and delineate some of its implications.

I

The question Who is man? is short and succinct, yet it contains the most profound searchings and yearnings of the human spirit. And the answer that Judaism gives is equally short and succinct. Man is a creature created in God's image. The rest is commentary and explication.

The first thing to note about the statement that man is a created being who shares in the likeness of God is the paradox that it attributes to the being of man. It describes man as a creature, yet asserts that man partakes of the divine image, whose very essence is never to be a creature. Man belongs both to the natural and to the divine realms; more precisely, he belongs exclusively neither to the natural nor to the divine. Man thus appears to have a being which is suspended between two worlds, sharing in both yet never a full and exclusive citizen of either.

Does this mean, however, that there are ultimately only two distinct categories of being, the natural and the divine, and that the being of man is but a composite of these two elemental categories? Is man merely a derivative or combination which can be dissolved into its two primary constituents? If so, another question inevitably arises. Where, in which category, does the essence of man, his ultimate destiny, lie? Is man essentially divine, a creating spirit, although in his present existence he is fallen and thus limited by the natural and the material? Or does man essentially belong to the natural kingdom, although he possesses the peculiarity of consciousness and with it the ability of self-transcendence?

These age-old questions will become more familiar to us if we use terms such as "body and soul" or "matter and spirit." Granted that man is a composite of body and soul, wherein lies his essence and true self? Is he essentially matter or spirit? Plato answered that the true essence of man resides in his soul. But, alas, the soul of man is fallen and thus finds itself imprisoned within a body. The body is a mere prison which confines the soul. Man's true destiny is to escape the body and free the soul. The free, unfettered soul is man's true self.

A whole cluster of traditions—spiritualism, idealism, corporeal asceticism, Manicheism—which crisscross the length and breadth of the history of western culture emerges from Plato's view that man's true essence is his spirit and that his realization, therefore, calls for the negation of matter and all bodily concerns. But we also recall Aristotle's answer: man belongs essentially to the natural, material universe. His soul, or reason, is but a distinct attribute which his body evolved and by which he can be differentiated from the other members of the natural domain. True, man's soul and reason are the highest and noblest achievements of his evolution; nevertheless, they remain but aspects or attributes of his corporeal essence. From this view too, a whole cluster of traditions, such as naturalism, empiricism, materialism, has emerged, pervading the history of western culture.

Judaism—and Christianity as well, to the extent that it follows Judaism in this matter—represents a third position. For Judaism, the being of man is no longer a loose and dissoluble union of two primary categories of being, soul and body. Nor does the essence of man inhere either in a spirit imprisoned by matter or in matter evolving spiritual qualities. Through the union of body and soul a new independent and irreducible, *sui generis* category of being emerges which encompasses body and soul as one undifferentiated unit. Man's spirit is not an actual divine element residing in him. As an attribute of man's being, which is a created being, the spirit is itself also created.

Thus, the being of man forms a qualitatively distinct and irreducible category of being. Soul and body are inseparable aspects or predicates of this being. You cannot have one without the other and still have the being of man. Man's essence inheres equally in both. The moment we speak of the soul without the body or of the body without the soul, we no longer speak, not even potentially, of the human body and soul as they are understood in Judaism.

This equality, this inextricable unity of body and soul, is a fundamental tenet of Judaism. It underlies the whole of Jewish thought and law. The body no less than the spirit is the creation of God. Hence Judaism requires of the body just as much as it requires of the spirit that it bear witness to the glory of God. At the same time, it invests the body, no less than the spirit, with the sanctity and worth befitting the handiwork of God. The body's needs and functions are not base and despicable. Nothing could be farther from Judaism than the statement attributed to Epictetus that he was ashamed of his body. A Jew is called upon to worship God with every member of his body, each singing the praises of God's marvelous work. By the same token, he not only is forbidden to inflict on his body any form of molestation or deformity, but he is actually required to guard its health by proper nourishment and cleanliness. When the doctrine of resurrection was introduced into rabbinic Judaism and became part of the normative tradition, it was so formulated as to apply equally to soul and body. Although the notion of the resurrection of the body has been a source of severe intellectual difficulties in later generations, the tradition, with an unerring instinct, resisted any change and insisted that the doctrine applied equally to body and soul. Indeed, it had to, since man, according to Judaism, would cease to be man if one of these two aspects was missing. Man's body and soul are inseparable. Hence, man constitutes a third kind of being which is distinct from and irreducible to the other two kinds of being known to us, the being of nature and the being of God.

Consequently, any formulation which attempts to establish a continuum, partial or whole, between nature and man or between man and God must be rejected by Judaism. Judaism opposes pantheism, materialism, and idealism precisely because they violate the basic threefold distinction between the being of the world, of man, and of God by asserting, to a greater or lesser extent, a continuum between them. Pantheism eliminates man and the world as distinct beings. There is only one category of being—the being of God. The being of man and the being of the world are ultimately but manifestations of the divine being, the sole reality and being.

Materialism eliminates the threefold distinction in the opposite direction. It declares that the only being is the being of the material world; the being of man and the being of God are reduced to the being of matter. Both pantheism and materialism are monistic views which assert the ultimate reality of only one kind of being, absorbing the other two into the one. They express a total and comprehensive continuum which stands in radical opposition to Judaism.

In contrast to these views, idealism, in most though not all of its formulations, expresses a partial continuum. It distinguishes between the being of the world, on the one hand, and the being of man and God, on the other, but eliminates the distinction between the being of man and the being of God. A continuum is established between the being of God and the being of man, which in essence is reason or spirit. The being of man is eliminated, and we get a dualistic view with just two categories of being—the being of the material world and the being of the spiritual divine. Christianity could in many of its classical formulations ally itself with this kind of idealism. For Judaism, however, the distinction between God and man is basic and cannot be bridged under any circumstances. Consequently, Judaism must reject any attempt at man's apotheosis or God's humanization. The road of salvation in Judaism can never lead toward apotheosis.

II

The distinction between man, God, and the world does not, however, imply that interaction and communication among them are impossible. For Judaism, the interdependence and interaction of the world, man, and God are just as fundamental a tenet as is their separate reality. The basic Jewish understanding of reality is in terms of *relation* or *dialogue,* not of *isolation.* The essence of man, the world, and God lies not in their isolated and self-sufficient being but in their relation, which is all-pervasive. But what kind of relation is it which, according to Judaism, binds God, man, and the world together?

Let us remember that in the Jewish definition of man the verb "created" occupies a crucial position. God created the world and man. However, the relationship between God and man which is embodied in the act of creation is still impersonal and general. It is impersonal inasmuch as it is based on God's impersonal attri-

butes of glory and dominion. It is general inasmuch as it relates
God to the totality of created nature; man participates in this
relation only by virtue of the fact that his being is also a created
being. This relationship is now concretized and personalized in a
special relation which is established between God and man. It is
rooted not in creation but in what is really the fulfillment of creation, in historical revelation. Revelation can be defined as "fulfillment of creation" because the act of creation itself is already
an act of revelation. It is the act through which God's power and
dominion are ever-presently revealed. Indeed, this is the reason
for which Jewish thinkers often refer to creation as "continuous
revelation." This "continuous revelation" is now fulfilled in historical revelation when God, through His free gift of grace, chooses to
reveal Himself to the people of Israel at certain moments in their
history in order to communicate specifically to man that He, God,
is not only all-powerful and glorious but also compassionate, demanding, concerned, and loving.

In other words, God establishes a relation with man in which
both "partners" are conscious, personal beings. In this relationship, certain demands are placed on man, and certain promises are
offered in return. Through these demands man knows that God is
a personal being who is concerned with man. God's concern
originates in His love for man. This fact does not preclude the
possibility of God's anger and displeasure with man. God, indeed,
may also be an angry and punishing God. But the interplay between a forgiving and an exacting God is secondary to the fact
that, in both, God is revealed as a personal being who is concerned
with and aware of man.

The act of historical revelation completes the relationship between God and man by the act of creation. Whereas in creation
the relationship neither refers uniquely to man nor involves God
explicitly as a personal being, historical revelation establishes a
unique relation between man and a living, personal God.

It is only in this relation that man comes to know fully that he
is not alone and isolated but that there is an ultimate, supreme
consciousness which is always aware of him and continuously concerned with what he does. In the presence of this personal God
man can never be alone. As Rosenzweig pointed out, the major

achievement of Judaism was that it managed to overcome the isolation and loneliness of man in paganism. In paganism—and this applies to the various expressions of modern and contemporary paganism as much as it did to ancient, classical paganism—man, in the last analysis, is alone. Ultimately, there is no other being that is concerned with him. The ultimate for paganism is blind, impersonal fate.

The pervasive experience of modern man seems to be that he is alone. The technical advances of modernity have given man immense power but not companionship. To this extent Sartre has captured the authentic situation of modern man—he is alone. Whether man today accepts his situation heroically or stoically or tries frantically to escape it, his basic orientation shackles him to his tragic loneliness. The crowd, the multitude, the hectic involvement in activities, are but feeble reactions to his condition. In the midst of the many he remains alone—a tragic nonentity.

This sorrowful and pitiable image is, however, only one side of the coin of man's aloneness. The other side is the madness and irresponsibility to which aloneness tends to lead. There is no one to whom man is ultimately responsible for his actions. There is no standard, no demand for accountability to limit man's raving appetites and impulses. Brutal and impersonal power is the final judge and standard of man's actions. All is permitted as long as you have the power with which to back it up. Lonely man can be as tragic and pitiable as a driven leaf, but he can also be as terrifying in his cruelty as a ferocious beast.

Yet these psychological and political manifestations do not reveal the full depth of the predicament of aloneness. It is basically an ontological predicament. For the being of man is a being-for-someone. It needs continuous confirmation and recognition. The worst suffering man can inflict upon his fellowman is to ignore him. Man would rather be hated, maligned, and beaten than ignored. Even being hated denotes at least recognition and confirmation of one's being, and any kind of recognition is superior to indifference. Without the confirmation of our being we are nothing.

In the faith of Judaism, God, the ultimate personal being, is the "other" who confirms man's being. The man who lives in the faith of Judaism may suffer and be persecuted, but he is never alone. The believing Jew, therefore, never presents a tragic figure. In the midst of tribulations, his being and the meaning of his life are known and confirmed by God. This is the ultimate significance of the relation established by historical revelation. It confirms man's being and gives it meaning and value.

III

The relationship which creation and historical revelation establish is, however, not yet completely defined. It still is a one-way road leading from God to man, in which God gives and man is merely the recipient. True relationship must be a two-way street, a mutual give-and-take. The relationship, to be complete, requires that man contribute his share; he must actively respond.

One way of responding is vertical—the confessional prayer which man can address to God. But there is another way. Man can respond through his deeds and acts which are directed horizontally toward the world. In the Jewish scheme of things, man responds primarily in the second way. Man is to respond to God's act of revelation by his deeds toward the world. The world, although created by God, is not yet completed. It still stands in need of redemption. And man is called upon to respond to God's revelation by becoming God's partner in the work of redemption. He responds to God by the way he acts toward the world. Man's relation to God, first established by the act of creation and then specified by the act of revelation, is now fully consummated in the act of redemption.

But it is precisely in the task of redemption—final stage and pinnacle in the process of man's fulfillment—that man's transgression and evil manifest themselves. Evil exists or arises where man fails to respond to God—where he fails to carry out his task of sharing in the work of redeeming the world. Evil is thus a failure of will and decision. This failure, however, is not the inevitable consequence of the creaturely status of man's being. Man, admittedly, is a creature and consequently a limited being. This, however, is not the cause of his evil. Judaism utterly rejects the ontological view that evil is rooted in man's nature as a finite being, that as a finite being he is imperfect, and that, being imperfect, man cannot help but sin.

Judaism rejects this concept of "original sin." Man's finiteness and creatureliness are not the inescapable source of his transgressions. On the contrary, man is to live in accordance with his status as a creature. It is a constant reminder to him that he is dependent and that nothing is ultimately his by right. Whatever man has, be it his earthly properties, his talents, or even his very life, is ultimately not his own but merely entrusted to him for a given period of time.

Hence, evil arises not when he acts in accordance with his creatureliness but when he attempts to transcend it. It is when man forgets his status as a creature that he commits what to Judaism is the basic transgression and evil—the transgression of pride and rebellion against God. Only the awareness of his creatureliness keeps man within his proper bounds and restrains the Faustian urges that often culminate in inflicting cruelty and disaster upon mankind. It checks man's all too ready inclination toward arrogance and boastful pride, which can lead only to his self-destruction.

But if the creaturely aspect of man's being is not the source of his evil, we must seek its source in the other aspect of his being, the divine aspect. Judaism does, indeed, view the divine aspect of man as the source not only of his goodness but also of his potential downfall. The source of his spirituality and creativity can also be the source of his transgression and debasement.

To understand this seeming paradox, we must clarify what Judaism conceives to be the "divine aspect of man's being." In what way does man reflect the divine image? By possessing divine knowledge, divine power, or divine eternity? Surely not. These are attributes of perfection whose very essence is to transcend all finiteness, whereas man, as a created being, is neither perfect nor infinite. Judaism does not challenge this, yet it asserts that this created and, therefore, finite being is endowed with a will that is free. Man is a created being yet has the ability to choose and decide freely his course of action. And it is precisely in this ability that man reflects the divine image. For the unique aspect of the

Jewish conception of God lies not so much in His attributes of perfection, omniscience, and omnipotence, nor in His mathematical unity, but in His supreme will, which is completely free and unconstrained.

Man, as the possessor of free will, is therefore truly the bearer of the very essence of the divine image. It is here that his creativity and distinctiveness from the rest of creation reside. Indeed, it is only by ascribing free will to man that the scheme of relationships which underlies the Jewish view of reality is made possible. For there can be no true two-way relationship between God and man unless man is able to enter it by his own free will. The relationship has meaning and validity only because man is free to enter it.

But man's very freedom involves the danger that he may choose not to enter the relationship. If man is truly granted free will and choice of decision, this possibility will always exist. Man can choose to transgress and do evil by choosing not to respond. Evil is thus the consequence not of his inevitable creaturely being, but of his free will which is the reflection of the divine image in him. It is important to note, however, that Judaism affirms the *possibility* of man's transgression, but not its *necessity*. Man may, but need not, commit evil. The good and righteous act is an equally open and feasible alternative for man. Good and evil are both contingent on his free decision, and one is as real and imminent a possibility as the other.

Because of this view Judaism has often been described as an "optimistic" religion. This resignation is frequently used in a derogatory sense, especially at a time when pessimism is a mark of profundity. Judaism is said to be superficial in its optimism which, supposedly, fails to see the depth of human evil and man's utter incapacity to combat it, and which considers redemption an easy matter that is just around the corner. This view is utterly unjustified. Judaism is keenly aware of the frailty of man's good intentions and his great capacity for evil. It knows how difficult it is for man to do what is right and to live by it. It is fully cognizant of the other side of the coin—man's evil impulse. Judaism is anything but superficially optimistic about man's redemption. But neither is it utterly pessimistic and resigned, proclaiming that man is totally helpless and must await his redemption from above. Judaism knows the wickedness of man, but it also knows the good in him.

Thus, Judaism is optimistic, if optimism implies the faith in man's ability to choose the right and do the good. Judaism says not that it is easy, but that it is possible. And it can insist that it is possible because it has never despaired of man and creation. God created man and the world and, as God's creation, they are basically good. The story of the fall does not symbolize for Judaism the utter deprivation of man but the first in a long series of wrong decisions that man has made. It is the archetype of man's decision against God. But the possibility to choose the right was never foreclosed by it. As long as man is endowed with free will he continues to reflect the image of God, and the possibility of making the right decision remains open. Thus, man assumes an active role in the work of redemption. Much depends on what he does or does not do, for his actions leave their imprint on the destiny of the world. Judaism does not allow man to take what in the last analysis is the easy way out, and to say, "There is nothing I can do about it."

IV

Three important corollary views emerge from this position. First, in maintaining that man has free will, Judaism places the burden of responsibility squarely on man's shoulders. There can be no responsibility without free will. I cannot be held accountable for something I was constrained to do. Only if I am given the capacity to choose freely and determine my action can I be held responsible.

Second, only with responsibility comes human dignity. Without responsibility man is reduced to being a cog in a machine manipulated by outide forces. The inviolable dignity of every man, regardless of his talents or station of life, precisely because he is the bearer of responsibility and thus of the divine image, is perhaps the most important facet of Judaism's relevance for today. The annihilation of this elemental dignity is the most imminent danger, aside from total nuclear suicide, confronting man today. The drift of our contemporary secularized and technological society is toward inhuman and impersonal totalitarianism in which man is deprived of all dignity.

Third, it is only in this elemental dignity that the equality of all men is found. We know men are not equal when we judge them by any of the naturalistic criteria at our disposal. We are not equal in our talents, health, disposition, appearance. Here inequality reigns supreme. Indeed, some people consider death the great equalizer; only in death are we all equal. But we do not have to wait for death in order to realize our equality. It lies in the dignity that is invested in every human being by virtue of his ability to choose freely and thus to assume responsibility. We are equal because all men—from the bum in the Bowery to the great creative spirits of all ages—are bearers of the divine image. This fundamental equality in life transcends all inequalities that accompany man through life.

These three basic views are contingent on free will and can be maintained only if we assert that man is indeed endowed with free will. But the assertion that a created being has free will vis-à-vis God must lead to logical and theological difficulties. How can the will of a created being that is limited and determined, not itself be limited and determined? And how can one maintain an omnipotent and omniscient God and, at the same time, endow man with free will? Judaism, with a boldness of spirit that defies logical and theological niceties, has held fast to both. Everything is in God's power and knowledge, yet man is free to choose. Evidently, the intent of Judaism is not to offer a neat, objective, logically consistent, abstract and self-enclosed theological package, but to deal with the concrete, existential, human situation. This situation is paradoxical and full of tensions. Judaism is a way of life, not a system of thought. And here man is a created being, but he also mirrors the divine image. Man is determined and contingent, but he is also free to choose. Only by maintaining this tension is Judaism able to present us with its portrayal of man. The physiology of the human body works by maintaining an equilibrium of the tension between two opposites. The physiology of the human spirit may work in a similar way.

The faculty of the will is thus the locus of both man's transgression and his realization. Will expresses itself, however, in decision, and the matrix in which decision can be expressed and concretized is time and history. Consequently, man is viewed and understood in Judaism principally by means of the categories of time and history, not of nature. The Jewish portrayal of man is dynamic, not static. Man is placed in the movement of time. His life is seen as a drama of action whose center is the will. The will can decide, if only partially, the destiny of man, and the decision is made in time and history. Hence, the essence of man, its corruption and realization, is within history.

But true history is possible in terms of the group only and not in terms of the isolated individual. The primary unit, the carrier of history, is the community. The individual's destiny is immersed in and inextricably linked to the destiny of his community. Consequently, for any further understanding of man one must turn to the community of man. In our case we must turn to Judaism. The Jewish image of man must lead to and culminate in the Jewish image of the Jew, i.e., the image of man in the context of his community.

ALFRED JOSPE

7. The Jewish Image of the Jew: On the Meaning of Jewish Distinctiveness

WHETHER JUDAISM STILL represents a vital and distinctive orientation to life and the world and can still speak to the deepest needs of modern man is a question which has long troubled some of our best minds.

It troubled Franz Rosenzweig, one of the most creative and provocative Jewish thinkers of our time and the author of a profound book on Jewish theology, *The Star of Redemption.* The son of a wealthy businessman, brought up without any contact with Jewish values and experiences, in his youth concerned only with art and music, a first-rate Hegel scholar and historian, utterly disinterested in Jewish life and affairs—what made this man write a book on Jewish theology?

A letter he wrote to his parents in 1909 gives us a clue. One of his cousins had converted to Christianity. Rosenzweig's parents wrote their son how shocked they had been by their nephew's defection, which they considered a disgrace. Rosenzweig answered that he himself had advised this step. Hans, the cousin, had felt in need of a living religion, something which his parents had completely failed to give him. Under these circumstances, was it not better to acquire a religious identification belatedly than not at all? "Because I am hungry, must I, on principle, go on being hungry? Does principle satisfy a hunger? Can being nonreligious on principle satisfy a religious need?" Can a man who searches for abiding values and enduring loyalties be satisfied to be a Jew merely by the accident of birth, by carrying an empty label that is of use

126

only for legal purposes—for a marriage or death certificate? "Confronted with the choice between an empty purse and a handful of money, shall I choose the empty purse?" We are really Christians in nearly every respect; our country is Christian, as are our schools, the books we read, the entire culture which forms us. Judaism is a dead religion, unable to quench the thirst of the seeker after a living faith.[1]

Later, Rosenzweig was to discover the meaning of Jewish distinctiveness. But when he wrote this letter at the age of twenty-three, Judaism was theologically dead, irrelevant, meaningless to him.

I

Numerous persons have shared this feeling: Israel's time is past. There is nothing distinctive which it can still say to the Jew or the modern world.

Sidney Hook, the contemporary philosopher, reaches the same conclusion, not on theological but on sociological and philosophical grounds. As he sees it, Jews differ so completely in the articulation of their faith, background, history, ancestry, beliefs, culture, language, and political aspirations, that the quest for any formula to express what Jews may have in common is fruitless. Every criterion breaks down in the face of the multiplicity of facts concerning the beliefs and behavior of those who call themselves Jews or are so called by others. Hence, the only statement that can be made about a Jew is that he is "anyone who for any reason calls himself such or is called such in any community whose practices take note of the distinction." [2] Professor Hook realizes that the bond which, for him, unifies the Jewish group is merely something negative—the experience of prejudice and social exclusion which, he feels, is common to all Jews and sets them apart from others; but he denies that there is any other bond that holds Jews together. Judaism possesses no distinctive ideals, beliefs, or values which are generally accepted or can be described in positive terms.

This conclusion is shared by many other thinkers, among them the sociologist Melville Herskovits, who was the first to define the

Jew as "a person who calls himself a Jew or who is called Jewish by others"; [3] Jean-Paul Sartre, the French existentialist, who defines a Jew as "one whom other men consider a Jew"; and the poet Karl Shapiro, who, in the introduction to his *Poems of a Jew,* says that "no one has been able to define Jew," for "being a Jew is the consciousness of being a Jew, and the Jewish identity, with or without religion, with or without history, is the significant fact."

Even so deeply committed a Jew as the late Kurt Lewin, the social psychologist, felt that it was difficult, if not impossible, to find a convincing positive rationale for the continued existence of the Jewish group. He knew that categories such as religion, race, nation, or ethnic culture were inadequate to define the Jews. Surveying the sweep of Jewish experience, he found it was not easy to see "why such a group ought to be preserved as a separate unit, why it has not entirely given up its will to live, and why the nations have refused to grant the Jews a full assimilation." [4] Nevertheless, he recommended that the Jewish group accept the fact of its minority status and try to make the most of it. Even though Judaism may not possess distinctive theological or cultural values, there is psychological value in membership in the Jewish group. Every person must have a sense of belonging for the sake of his emotional well-being, and it is far better to be a member of a persecuted minority than to be a marginal man who is doubly uprooted. The best armor against prejudice is self-respect. Hence, the early development of a clear and positive feeling of belongingness to the Jewish group is one of the few effective programs that parents can pursue to help ensure the later happiness of their children.[5]

The difficulty is that Lewin's remedy is the very malaise from which Jews suffer. He counsels them to accept their membership in the Jewish group for the sake of emotional adjustment, when the very source of their trouble is their doubt whether membership in the Jewish group is spiritually meaningful and socially desirable. Lewin, too, is unable to offer a positive rationale for the maintenance of Jewish distinctiveness.

As one surveys the numerous attempts that have been made to define the meaning of Jewish existence, a striking fact emerges: the Jewish people has usually been an enigma to itself no less than to outsiders. To John, in the Fourth Gospel, the Jews are of the devil, while for the Talmud they are as indispensable to the survival of the world as the winds. To the late-nineteenth-century German historian Heinrich von Treitschke, most Jews were parasites, detrimental to Germany's national well-being, while for Judah Ha-Levi, the medieval Jewish poet, Israel was the heart of mankind by virtue of its special propensity for religious insight and experience.[6] To sociologist Max Weber, the Jews, because of their lack of power and persistent insecurity, had to be classified as a pariah group, while even so rational a thinker as the German Reform leader Abraham Geiger claimed that Jews have a special genius for religion.[7] To the poet Heinrich Heine, Judaism, as he once quipped with more bitterness than irony, was not a religion but a misfortune, while other Jews throughout the centuries have found strength in Isaiah's definition of the Jewish people as a light unto the nations and God's witness in an idolatrous world. To British historian Arnold Toynbee, the Jews are a fossilized relic of an ancient Syriac civilization, whereas to philosopher Alfred Whitehead the Jews are very much alive, and their survival is largely due to the fact that they are probably the ablest race in existence.[8]

The difficulty is compounded by the fact that the Jewish tradition itself does not offer a clear and unambiguous answer either. Judaism has never formulated an authoritative creed defining what one must believe in order to be accounted a Jew:

> There is no Jewish equivalent of the Nicene Creed, honored by Roman Catholics, the Apostles' Creed of the Episcopalians, the Westminster Confession of the Presbyterians, or the Augsburg Confession of the Lutherans. . . . The Talmud, whose interpretations and applications have shaped Jewish deeds and practices even more so than the Bible did, records the clashing views of differing schools and scholars, preserving minority opinions together with the binding majority dicta. Even the Thirteen Articles of Faith, drawn up by Maimonides in the 12th century, have not gained universal acceptance and approval. . . . Being the culture of a community rather than the creed of a church, Judaism never found it necessary to make uniformity of belief its central cohesion.[9]

II

Nevertheless, it is possible to trace the dominant features of the historic image Jews have had of themselves.

The Jewish image of the Jew is embodied in what has been called a "value stance," [10] a specific attitude toward life and the world. Man basically has only two possibilities of establishing a relationship to the world. He can accept or reject it. Both world views exist. One is embodied in the way of Judaism, the other in the way of an eastern religion, Buddhism.

Judaism, as Leo Baeck has pointed out, demands moral affirmation of man's relation to the world by will and deed, and declares the world to be the field of life's tasks. Buddhism denies this relation: man is to devote himself to self-meditation and negate his volition. The one is the expression of the command to work and create, the other of the need for rest. The one works for the kingdom of God in which all men may be included, the other leads to the desire to sink into nothingness and to find deliverance from the ego. The one calls for ascent, development, growth, the steady march toward the future; the other preaches return, cessation, a futureless existence in silence. Judaism, therefore, is ultimately the affirmation of an active, creative relationship to the world, Buddhism, the denial of such a relationship.[11]

But there are various ways in which life and the world can be affirmed. The Greeks, for instance, also affirmed them, but in a way wholly different from the Jews. Socrates accepted death even though he was innocent by his own definition of justice. He refused to escape when his friends wanted to make it possible because he accepted and affirmed the higher authority of the state. The state cannot exist when law is set aside. Defiance would result in chaos.[12]

Compare Socrates' attitude with that of the Prophet Nathan, who castigates David's defiance of justice in his affair with Bathsheba; with Elijah, who denounces Ahab for his murder of Nabot; with Isaiah's denunciation of the religious and political leaders of Jerusalem because of their corruption; with Jeremiah's fearless and flaming indictment of the religious hypocrisy and moral depravity of his generation and its government. The Greek thinker gives passive assent to the existing social order even though it may be evil. The Jewish prophet challenges the social order precisely because it is evil. For the one, government imposes laws which cannot be challenged. For the other, government itself stands under the judgment of the law and must, if necessary, be challenged in God's name. One is the teacher who wishes to influence man's minds and thoughts, the other the firebrand, the prophet who wants to redeem the social order. For the one, the highest virtue is that man think correctly: the intellectual apperception of reality. For the other, the highest virtue is that man act correctly: the moral penetration of reality.

For this reason, the value stance of Judaism also differs profoundly from the world view of Christianity, which insists that the highest virtue is that man believe correctly. Habakkuk's saying (2:4), which Paul quotes in the first chapter of his Letter to the Romans, became the cornerstone of the new religion: "The just shall live by His faith." The difference between Judaism and Christianity emerges from their different views of the nature of man. For Christianity, man is sinful from birth, incorrigible; no matter how hard he may try, he cannot overcome sin and achieve salvation through his own efforts. For Judaism, man can and does sin, but must not. Created in the image of God, he has the capacity for growth, love, and compassion, for doing what is right and good. Therefore, Christianity insists that, though deeds are important, the indispensable condition of salvation is faith in Jesus as the Christ; that ultimately nothing has to be done, nothing to be fulfilled; that after the works are done, salvation is achieved not by the merit of one's deeds but by the acceptance, in faith, of the officially formulated correct form of belief. Judaism proclaims that ultimately it is man's acts which matter and not his notions or thoughts, which may well be erroneous or mistaken. God's nature and thoughts are beyond human grasp, but His commandments are "neither hidden nor far off."

While Christianity offers the promise of man's redemption from this world of sin through his faith, Judaism urges the redemption of this world from sin through man's actions.

III

The Jewish value stance toward life and the world provides the frame for the picture. The details of the picture reveal the image Jews have had of themselves as Jews.

This image has several dominant features. One is what is usually called the doctrine of Israel's "election" or, to use the more widely known phrase, the concept of the "chosen people." This concept permeates much of Jewish literature and thought. We encounter it in our folklore, prayers, and liturgy. Even though Moses Maimonides, the medieval Jewish philosopher, did not include it in his Thirteen Articles of Faith, the concept of election has always been deeply embedded in the Jewish consciousness. When a male Jew is called to the Torah, he recites the traditional blessing, *asher bahar banu mikol ha'amim,* praising God "Who has chosen us from among all other nations." When Jews recite their daily morning prayer, they say the benediction, *shelo assani goy,* thanking God "that He has not made [us] gentiles." When they read the Torah, they encounter passages singling them out as God's treasured people:

> You have affirmed this day that the Lord is your God, that you will walk in His ways, that you will observe His laws and commandments and norms, and that you will obey Him. And the Lord has affirmed this day that you are, as He promised you, His treasured people which shall observe all His commandments, and that He will set you, in fame and renown and glory, high above all the nations that He has made; and that you shall be, as He promised, a holy people to the Lord your God.
>
> (Deut. 26:17–19)

When Jews pronounce the benediction over the Sabbath wine, they declare that God has chosen and sanctified Jews from among all other peoples in the same way in which He has distinguished between Sabbath and weekday. And when they make *havdalah* on Saturday nights, they recite the traditional *ha-mavdil,* glorifying God for setting Jews apart from all other peoples just as He set apart the sacred from the profane, and light from darkness.

Few of Judaism's teachings have been so misunderstood as the concept of the "chosen people." Some thinkers and critics have called it a moral outrage and a typical example of the scandalous arrogance of the Jewish people.[13] George Bernard Shaw compared it to the *Herrenvolk* concept of the Nazis and castigated the Jews for the arrogance of their claim to racial superiority. H. G. Wells considered the concept a hindrance to world unity. Protestant theologians continue to describe the God of Judaism as a tribal deity interested only in protecting his own people and not as a God who is concerned with the whole of mankind. Avowed anti-Semites cite this idea to prove that there is a Jewish conspiracy to dominate the Christian world.

The concept has also been rejected by Jewish thinkers, among them especially Mordecai Kaplan and other members of the Reconstructionist movement, who consider it an anachronism, a concept belonging to a thought-world of the past which is incompatible with the equality and dignity of all men and the demands of democracy. For Kaplan, the arrogant assumption by any individual or group that it is the chosen and indispensable vehicle of God's grace to others is utterly untenable for modern man.[14]

Nearly two hundred years before Kaplan, similar doubts and reservations had been voiced by Moses Mendelssohn, who firmly believed that, if a knowledge of truth was indispensable to the achievement of human happiness, truth had to be accessible to all people alike without distinction of race, creed, social status, or origin. It was inconceivable to him that a good God could capriciously have revealed His truth only to a part of mankind and left the rest of mankind without revelation and, therefore, without the means of achieving happiness. No religion, not even his own Judaism, could be the sole instrument through which God reveals His truth. Truth is indivisible. It belongs to all men. No religion has the right to claim that it possesses for all time, or even for a limited period, special revelations, even if they imply special responsibilities.[15]

Mendelssohn's and Kaplan's egalitarian critique is appealing, especially if one considers the pernicious policies which have been propagated in the same of "chosenness," whether among the ancient Greeks, some of whose leading thinkers did not hesitate to designate all non-Greek peoples as *barbaroi*, "barbarians," [16] or wherever claims of racial superiority have corroded a society.

Yet election has never implied such a claim in the classical Jewish tradition. How, then, did this tradition understand the meaning of election?

For the biblical mind, election is a historical fact. The Jewish people is not merely one of many peoples; it was selected by God as His peculiar treasure. Israel's place and role in the world are part of a divine plan which manifested itself first in the early days of the world's existence, when the Creator of the universe bestowed His blessings upon the patriarchs as reward for their faithfulness and love and promised that their children and all future generations would continue to receive His blessings because of "the merits of their fathers."

Centuries later, at a particular time in the cosmic drama and a particular place, Sinai, God revealed Himself anew when He made His will known to the entire Jewish people. His will is embodied in a particular document, the Torah. This reveals not only the law which is to govern man's life but also the instrument which God has chosen to make His will known to the rest of the world. This instrument is the people known as Israel. Israel is God's chosen people.

The rabbis and thinkers of the past were, of course, not unaware of the difficulties surrounding the concept of election. They were troubled by the same question which troubles many contemporary Jews: Why should God have singled out one particular people, the Jews, for His purposes? Maimonides and others with him felt that all that can be said in response to this question is that God so willed it. It is impossible for us to understand why God should have revealed His will to one particular nation and not also to others. The fact is, however, that He did. Man can do nothing but acknowledge this fact, for man is not God and cannot hope to fathom the secrets of divine Providence. [17]

Other scholars and thinkers attempted to find positive reasons for Israel's claim to election. Two diametrically opposed streams of thought and argument emerged. For some rabbis, the people of Israel merited and continues to merit election because of its special service and faithfulness to God. Jews were the first ones to proclaim God as the Supreme King at the shores of the Red Sea (Exod. 15:18). They were the only ones who were willing and prepared to accept the yoke of God's kingdom at Mount Sinai when all other nations refused God's gift of the Torah.[18] Their special faithfulness merits their special relationship with God.

But just as much or more emphasis is placed by Jewish tradition on the opposite point of view: that God chose the Jews for reasons of His own; that election is not based on merit but represents an act of grace on God's part; that His love for Israel is not given as a reward but offered freely despite His people's shortcomings. Quoting Hosea, "I will love them freely" (14:5), the Midrash conceives of God as saying, "My soul volunteered to love them though they are not worthy of it." And the Tanna of the school of Elijah proclaims:

> Blessed be He who chose Israel from among all the nations and made them verily His own and called them children and servants unto His name . . . and all this because of the love with which He rejoiced in them.[19]

Whatever "reasons" could be found—whether the traditional Jew felt he was chosen because of some special merit of his own or on his father's part or because of God's freely offered though unmerited love, or whether he could find no ultimate justification for this claim—he firmly believed that the Jewish people had been singled out by Providence to receive God's law and to serve as the faithful guardian of the divine will and message until all men would accept them.

In the mainstream of traditional thought, election has thus been seen as an objective, supernatural fact. It is precisely at this point, however, that the two fundamental positions emerge which have polarized the Jewish community in modern times. The traditionalist continues to insist that Jewish existence derives its meaning and distinctiveness from a supernatural act of God, who singled out the Jewish people for a special role in the cosmic drama. Some nontraditional contemporary Jewish thinkers share this view, among them Will Herberg, who defines election as "God's act of creating and maintaining Israel for His purposes in history," [20] and Professor Emil Fackenheim, who feels that "a Jew is anyone who by his descent is subject to Jewish fate, the covenant—whether he responds to Jewish fate with Jewish faith does not affect, though it is related to, his Jewishness." [21]

Religiously liberal Jews, on the other hand, frequently have intellectual and moral doubts about the proposition that the meaning and distinctiveness of Jewish existence are rooted in an act of supernatural revelation. For many liberal Jews, the Bible is not God's anthropology but man's theology—the record not of God's search for man but of man's search for God. Hence Jewish distinctiveness is found in the value stance and life style which reflect and embody the collective experiences, insights, and aspirations of the Jewish people through the ages.

The two positions are so strongly polarized that the gap separating them seems unbridgeable. Yet, though they start from opposite ends in their thinking about the ontological origin and character of Jewish distinctiveness, they seem remarkably close in their thinking about its nature and implications. Both insist that the concept of the chosen people in Jewish tradition has never been and is not exclusivist and does not imply the rejection of the rest of mankind as inferior. Even though the Jews claimed a monopoly of God's revelation, they never claimed to be superior to the rest of mankind by reason of birth, blood, or race. Anyone can become a Jew by embracing Judaism. A person who converts to Judaism becomes a *ben Avraham,* a "son of Abraham," by entering into Abraham's covenant. Rabbi Meir said that Adam had been created from dust which had been collected from all corners of the earth so that no nation could claim the distinction of being better or having cradled mankind. Some of the greatest rabbis are said to have been descended from converts to Judaism. Indeed, according to Jewish tradition, King David, from whose house the Messiah would come, was a direct descendant of Ruth, the Moabite.

Judaism clearly acknowledges that men can be blessed with salvation even though they are outside the Sinaitic covenant. A special calling is demanded, but no exclusiveness of salvation is proclaimed. Traditional Judaism insists that "the righteous of all nations have a share in the world to come" [22] and that man should first lead a good life and then ask God for religious truth.[23] As Morris Joseph puts it, "Israel's election does not give him a monopoly of the divine love." [24] For Judaism, all human beings are God's children and have an equal claim upon His care and solicitude. The divine test of a man's worth is not his theology or descent, but his life.

In the same way, the protection of the law was extended to every inhabitant of the country, Jew and non-Jew alike. In the words of Numbers, "Ye shall have one statute both for the stranger and for him that is born in the land." Jews have always been particularly sensitive to these problems, for, as the Bible and Jewish observances constantly remind them, they themselves had been strangers in Egypt, and the memory of that experience had burned itself into their consciousness. Because they knew what oppression of minorities meant and what it could do to the soul of the oppressed, they hated oppression and wanted to make sure they would never succumb to its practice.

What the concept of election has meant in Jewish life, in positive terms, is illustrated by a story of the rabbis. The ancient rabbis once asked, Why did God choose Israel? Because all other nations refused to accept the Torah. Originally, God had offered it to all nations of the world. But the children of Esau rejected it because they could not reconcile themselves to the commandment "Thou shalt not kill." The Moabites declined the offer because they felt they could not accept the commandment "Thou shalt not commit adultery." The Ishmaelites refused because they could not square their habits with the commandment "Thou shalt not steal." All of them rejected the Torah; only Israel was prepared to accept it. (A good many Jews have regretted this fact ever since.)

Disregard the theological language. The story makes a crucial point. Think of ancient Israel—an insignificant little people in the vast spaces of the Near East. It could have been like all other peoples of the area, content to live in some forgotten corner of the world, working, procreating, building houses, plowing fields, struggling to wrest a living from nature, and gradually fading away from the arena of history.

And yet, in this very people, there suddenly blazed forth the conviction that it is not enough just to exist, to live, but that man must live for something, and that, therefore, this people is different from the peoples in whose midst it had been living; that there is something that gives meaning to its life, in which it finds itself and through which it becomes articulate about the meaning and purpose of its existence. For the first time in the history of mankind, *national difference* becomes transformed into *moral and spiritual distinctiveness*.[25]

Here we can grasp the full meaning of "election." It means the awareness of this distinctiveness and of its supreme significance irrespective of our views regarding its ontic character. It means the conviction that there is something—an idea, a moral imperative, an ultimate truth—for whose sake it is supremely important to stand apart, to be singled out, to stand separated from the old, the customary, the commonplace.

There can be three kinds of separation. You can separate yourself from the world by withdrawing into your home. You can lock the door, pull the shades, and retreat into your private world, where the anxieties, concerns, demands, and claims of the day cannot follow you. You lock yourself in to keep the world out.

Separation can also be enforced. In a prison, the doors are locked behind you. You are shut out from the world, forcibly isolated from it.

But there is a third kind of separation—a separation in which we set ourselves apart from the world for the sake of the world, indeed, for the sake of life itself. When we get hold of an idea which we want to share with others; when a conviction seizes us that there is a truth which is important not only for us but for others; when we begin to feel that it is our task to witness to the importance of this truth and have it become a compelling force in the lives of others—then we separate ourselves from the world for the sake of the world. Everyone who possesses a truth—or believes he possesses a truth—experiences it as a peculiar possession which separates him from other men, and he becomes conscious of the fact that, for the sake of this truth, he may have to stand in the world yet against it, opposing it in order to help change it.

This sense of purpose and mission moved the prophets to their words and deeds. It was the motive force in the life of Gandhi. It started Martin Luther King on his road from Montgomery to Memphis. It impelled the *Bilu* and the *halutzim* to push ahead against a hostile environment. It is born of the consciousness that you have to stand for something greater than yourself, whether it be a concern for the aged bereft of proper care, the Negro bereft of hope, the child denied grass, space, and air, the adult denied dignity and privacy, the eye starved for beauty, a society deprived of justice, a world bereft of hope and peace. It involves a readiness to suffer personal hardship and privation for the sake of the task, a stubborn affirmation of the rightness of one's cause even in the face of rejection and persecution.

It is in the idea of his "election" that the Jew has thus become conscious and articulate about what he conceives his task and role to be. He becomes conscious that he possesses a truth that separates him from others. And he declares that this difference between him and the others is not only justified but is something valuable and important—a truth (whether discovered by him or disclosed to him) which he possesses but which addresses itself to all of mankind. Hence, election is the living certainty of a religious community that it possesses a truth which distinguishes it from all other peoples or nations and is a unique and vital possession that gives its existence a sense of purpose and direction.

IV

This truth which distinguishes the Jew from all other peoples is embodied in the concept of the "covenant," the second feature in the image which Jews have of themselves as Jews.

The Hebrew term for covenant is *berit,* a covenant or agree-This acceptance implies two fundamental notions. First, the agree-ment between God and Israel by which Israel accepted the Torah. ment between God and Israel is bilateral. If God selected Israel, Israel consented to be elected. If God chose Israel, Israel, in turn, chose God. As Zangwill once put it, a chosen people is at bottom a choosing people.

Second, if the concept of *election* signifies the consciousness that the Jew possesses a truth which sets him apart from others, the concept of the *covenant* signifies the consciousness of what that truth is. It is Torah. It is the Law of Sinai. It is the acceptance and affirmation of God's design for man's life, the consciousness of what God demands of man—of what man must do to make His truth alive regardless of the hardships or obligations it may entail. The covenant is man's response, *hinneni*—"Here I am"—to the voice that calls; it is the acceptance of the obligation inherent in election. In Franz Rosenzweig's formulation, it is "the Law whereby divine election is turned into human electing, and the passive state of a people being chosen and set apart is changed into the activity, on the people's side, of doing the deed which sets it apart." [26]

The concept of the covenant has numerous connotations in Jewish tradition and literature. After the Flood, God enters into a compact with mankind through Noah, in which God pledges that He will never again destroy the human race, and man in turn pledges to abide by the fundamental moral laws in dealing with his fellowmen. The term is used again when God enters into a covenant with Abraham, and calls upon him to train his descendants to keep the ways of the Lord, while God pledges Himself to bless Abraham and his descendants and to multiply their seed.

The Prophet Hosea defines the covenant as an act of love between God and Israel, symbolizing their bond of partnership, in which man is given a share in the never-ending process of creation and the redemption of mankind through love and faithfulness:

> I shall betroth thee unto Me forever.
> I shall betroth thee unto Me with right and
>   justice, with love and mercy.
> I shall betroth thee unto Me in truth, and
>   thou shalt know the Lord.
>   (Hosea 2:21–22)

The most significant expression of the covenant idea, however, can be found in Exodus:

Now then, if you will obey My voice and keep My covenant, then ye shall be a peculiar treasure unto Me above all other people. For all the earth is Mine. And ye shall be unto Me a kingdom of priests and a holy nation.

(Exod. 19:5–6)

These two verses point to the two major convictions embodied in the covenant relationship between God and Israel. One is the profound and basic Jewish belief that the earth is the Lord's. He had promised the land to their forefathers; He had liberated the people from Egyptian bondage; He had guided them through the perils of the wilderness until they reached the land He had promised them. But the land itself belongs to God. He has given it to the people in fulfillment of His part of the covenant. But Israel can never claim absolute possession of it. That possession depends on the faithfulness with which it fulfills its part of the covenantal relationship.

And the obligation which God has set before Israel in the covenant is defined in the task to become "a kingdom of priests and a holy nation." Election is not a divine favor extended to a people, but a task imposed upon it. It does not bestow privileges; it demands service. It is not a prerogative but an ethical charge, not a claim but an obligation, not a divine title for rights but a divine mandate for duties. The obligation is to live in accordance with the word and spirit of Sinai, to serve God in thought and act, to sanctify life and render it significant, to avoid cruelty, diminish evil, and purify man's hands and heart. Election means to become the prophet and if necessary the suffering servant of the Lord, to be heir to and perpetuator of the spirit of the men who entered the arena of history not as soldiers, statesmen, or builders of empires, but as prophets of the ideal society, as the legislators of the priestly and sanctified life, as the visionaries of justice and human reconciliation, as the challengers of evil and the singers of hope, as rebels against paganism and cruelty, as the supreme architects of the religious life.

More, not less, is expected of Israel by virtue of the covenant. People who are ignorant of God and His will, men who have never been taught what truth and justice are, may be forgiven impiety and sin. But Jews cannot be forgiven so easily—Israel has a special commitment to God. When Israel fails, it commits a *hillul hashem,* a desecration of the divine name. Failure to live up to the ideal will be punished. Hence the Prophet Amos warns the people in God's name, "Only you have I known of all the families of the earth. Therefore I will visit upon you all your iniquities" (Amos 3:2).

The Jewish people understood and defined their experiences in terms of this covenant relationship. Faithfulness was rewarded, defection punished. Therefore, even the destruction of the Temple, the people's exile and suffering, the persecutions and expulsions of the Middle Ages, could not shatter the image Jews had of themselves. Destruction and exile were a national disaster but not completely unforeseen. They were part of the divine plan, foretold in the admonitions of the prophets. They were the punishment that was bound to come upon those who had violated the covenant and strayed from the path of God. Severance from the land did not imply severance from God. More specifically, severance from the land was dispersion in space, but not severance in time, a break in the continuity of the covenantal relationship with God. The Jew felt he was persecuted not because God had abandoned or rejected him, as the victorious nations of the world claimed; God still loved him but wanted to chastise him into obedience and return. He suffered because he was not equal to his moral task. In the words of the prayer book, "because of our sins were we exiled from our land." Other people sinned too, and would receive their punishment in due time. Israel, however, was the covenant people of whom God expected more than of others. Suffering was defined as punishment, and punishment in turn was a call to duty. Exile was God's call to return to the faithfulness inherent in Israel's role as the chosen people. The acceptance of punishment opened the gate to redemption and return to the land.

But suffering was, for the Jew, not only a judgment on himself but also a judgment on the world. It was not only a punishment for sin, a proof of his own shortcomings and imperfections; it was also a sign that the world itself was still unredeemed, that evil was still rampant, that God's community of love and peace was still unrealized and would remain unrealized as long as the peoples of the world continued to reject the God who had made man, and served the gods they had fashioned for themselves. The Jew began to realize that those who do not suffer are not always innocent, that worldly success or failures are not the ultimate measure of things, that a man or nation which disavows the use of power is almost certain to be worsted in the pressures of life, that might is not necessarily right, and that suffering is not necessarily evidence of divine rejection but the price one may have to pay for loyalty to ideals in an unredeemed world. As Yannai, an early medieval Hebrew poet, put it:

> Not everyone who is loved is loved;
> Not everyone who is hated is hated;
> Some are hated below, and loved above . . .
> Hated we are for You we love, O Holy One! [27]

Israel's unbroken love of God, the Jew's dedicated fulfillment of his responsibilities under the covenant—this was the only road that would ultimately lead to the redemption of man and the social order. The suffering of the Jew was the constant reminder that man's work was not yet completed and, therefore, a call to all men no less than to the Jewish people to resume their never-ending task to do God's will, to banish evil and realize the good.

V

The conception of life as a moral task and as an unremitting quest for perfection is the third and perhaps most characteristic feature of the Jewish image of the Jew. It finds its highest expression in the concept of the Messiah.

Jewish messianic thinking is rooted in one of man's profoundest needs and concerns, his concern with the future. We know what was. We know what is (or think we do). But who can know what will be tomorrow? We hunger for certainty. We want knowledge of that which is to come. But it is in the nature of things that there cannot be any such certainty and knowledge.

For this reason some nations of antiquity, living through eras of crisis and catastrophe, despaired of the future and turned their vision to the past. The present was chaotic, the future dark.

Therefore, they yearned for a renewal of the past that they felt was the embodiment of all goodness and happiness. Hesiod and Ovid, for instance, in their descriptions of the five successive ages and races of man, began with the Golden Age, when men lived happily and painlessly on the fruits of the untilled soil, passing away in dreamless sleep to become the guardian angels of the world. They ended with the Iron Age, the most degenerate of all, in which the authors themselves lived. The past was good, perfect, and ideal. The present was evil, the future dark and foreboding.

In contrast to these attitudes, the Jew did not try to evade the problem posed by the future. He never placed perfection in the past but projected it into the future. Of course, the Bible starts with perfection: the first man, Adam, must necessarily have been happy and perfect until his fall. Yet this idea has never played a significant part in Jewish thought. What is important is not man's descent but his ascent, not his past but his future. Jewish thinking looks for happiness, virtue, and perfection, not to a past Golden Age, but to the future, to "the end of days," a favorite phrase of the prophets.

This projection of perfection into the future is an integral part of Jewish thinking. It has been called the most striking and characteristic feature of the religion of Israel. It is an affirmation of trust and faith that man's efforts will ultimately not be in vain. It originated in the Bible, whose pages constantly echo this challenge to work for human perfection until it will ultimately be established on earth. This trend in Jewish thinking can be summarized in a single phrase—messianic thinking.

Messianic thinking in Jewish tradition is composed of numerous sub-themes and differing views. Some ancient rabbis declare that the Messiah is the son of Joseph; others maintain he is a scion of the house of David. Some assert he is a divine being, others that he is fully human. Some traditions insist that the Messiah will arrive when men repent and the world becomes good enough to warrant his coming. Others hold the opposite view: he will come only when the world will be so wicked and degenerate as to make his coming necessary. Some proclaim that his coming is a historic possibility, others that it is apocalyptic—the announcement of an event beyond time, signifying ultimate judgment when historical time will have ended. Some say he will come in response to and as a result of man's unceasing efforts in faithfulness, others insist that he will come as a free and perhaps even unmerited gift of God's freely given grace and love.

Yet behind these multiple nuances, two dominant views of the Messiah emerge, frequently in dialectical tension, in Jewish tradition. The one has come to be called the *man,* the personal Messiah. The other is called the *time,* or the messianic era. The one is a man, the other an age. The one is a son of the house of David, the other an epoch in the history of Israel and the world. The one is a Jew, the other a time yet to come.

The concept of a personal Messiah has its inception in the historical experiences of the Jewish people and the dreary political conditions in ancient Israel. The patriarchs had had to leave their native countries and wander in foreign lands. Then followed the Egyptian slavery with its memories of oppression. And even after the people had entered the Promised Land, they were not secure. They suffered the humiliation of frequent defeats and ultimately the loss of national independence.

It was only natural that a people with such a past and present should long for a future in which there would be an end to suffering, for a political redeemer who would unite the people and establish a strong nation able to withstand all enemies.

It was only in the reign of David that the popular longing for such a redeemer was satisfied. Under David's leadership, the people grew powerful, establishing a kingdom that reached from the borders of Egypt to the gates of Damascus. The glory of this kingdom and of the man who had wrought this miracle caught the imagination of the masses. David became the ideal Jewish king, the great national hero and redeemer. He had inaugurated a state of national glory. People hoped it would last forever—a hope that was strengthened by Nathan's prophecy that the throne of David would be established forever.

It was at this time that the messianic ideal took shape in the minds of the Jewish people. In its inception, the Messiah was a political, a national, ideal. He was the person who would bring relief from oppression, end the nation's disunity and insecurity, and establish a stable national government that would last forever.

But the Messiah was conceived not merely as a political liberator; he would also bring about the spiritual regeneration of the people. This is the second ingredient of the messianic concept. While the Messiah was originally a national savior, a compensatory ideal conceived in times of national distress, a symbol of the indomitable will of the people to survive, he now began to personify the spiritual values and religious ideals to which the people of God should be dedicated. Gradually, the Messiah was conceived not only as the king but as the ideal king, the perfect ruler who would establish not only a stable government but one based on righeousness and justice.

This hope runs through the fabric of all the prophetic books and the Psalms. But it was Isaiah who crystallized it when he spoke of a new king who, endowed with the divine spirit, would arise from the house of David to establish peace and equity in the land, who would usher in the time when tyranny and violence would no longer be practiced on God's holy mountain and when the land would be full of the knowledge of God as the waters cover the earth (Isa. 11:9).

The messianic idea, at this stage of its development, was still particularistic. When the prophets spoke of the Messiah king, they meant a king who was to rule over Israel. When they spoke of the need for justice and perfection, they did not envision a utopian world-state based on justice and perfection. They demanded that the people of Israel practice justice in the land of Israel. The Messiah was still a national concept. He was the redeemer of Israel, not the redeemer of the world.

The development of the messianic concept could not, however, stop at this point. This is the third and most important stage in the development of Jewish messianic thinking. The prophets had proclaimed the one God who created man and the world and who demands righteousness. But if there is only one God, can He be merely the God of one people, of Israel? Is He not also the God of all peoples, of mankind? The prophets had preached that Israel had been appointed by God to practice righteousness, set an example of life in holiness, stamp out evil, establish the good society. But should evil not be eradicated and righteousness be practiced wherever men live? The prophets had proclaimed the moral law.

But is there one moral code for one people and different moral codes for other peoples? The moral law is universal law. Justice and righteousness are indivisible. God's demands are directed alike toward all men.

It is in this thought that Jewish messianic thinking finds its consummation. Driven by its own inner logic, it widens into genuine universalism. It is at this point that the concept of mankind emerges for the first time in Jewish and, indeed, in western thought. If there is one God who created the world and fashioned man in His image, all men are His children. If there is one God, there must be one mankind. And if there is one mankind, there can be only one truth, one justice, and one religion, to which not merely Israel but all men are called and which cannot find its historic fulfillment until all men are united in it.

Thus, the messianic concept receives an entirely new direction. Deutero-Isaiah, Micah, and other prophets no longer speak of the personal Messiah of the house of David, the individual who will become king and establish a reign of righteousness and peace for Zion. They speak of the new life which is to arise upon earth. The concept of the *one man* retreats behind the concept of the *one time*. The personal Messiah gives way to the "days of the Messiah," in which universal peace and brotherhood will be established and all mankind will be united in the service of the one God.

VI

The people of Israel, however, has a special task in helping to fashion the messianic age. Having conceived of the one God for the one mankind, Israel has as its mission to be the bearer and guardian of this truth until it will be accepted by all the nations of the earth.

I, the Lord, have called thee in righteousness, and will hold thine hand and will keep thee for a covenant of the people, for a light of the nations, to open the blind eyes, to bring out the prisoners from the prisons, and them that sit in darkness out of the prison house.

(Isa. 42:6–7)

Thus the prophets proclaim that Israel itself has a messianic role in world history. They speak *to* Israel, but they speak *of* the world and the nations. Israel is to be the servant of the Lord. As God's servant, Israel will suffer and will be persecuted because injustice, oppression, and evil will continue to exist. But Israel's suffering will not be meaningless or in vain. By its very existence, Israel will be the symbol of protest—against oppression, injustice, idolatry, darkness, and evil. Ultimately, the time will come when Israel will be vindicated, when its trials will be rewarded, when the world will know that "from the rising of the sun and from the west there is none beside Me," when men will mend their ways and a new heaven and earth will be established—a day when "the Lord shall be king over all the earth," when "the Lord shall be one and His name be one" for all the peoples (Zech. 14:9).

VII

Jewish messianic thinking, thus defined, has a number of fundamental implications.

First, the concept of a universal God is inseparably associated with the concept of a universal religion. If the God of Israel is the God of all nations, the faith of Israel must ultimately become the faith of all nations. God desires the homage of all men. Prophetic Judaism envisions the ultimate universal acceptance of Israel's universal God.

There is a radical difference between this prophetic notion and the kind of interfaith statements which are in vogue in many parts of the world in our time. The prophets do not say that all religions are more or less the same and that the differences between them do not matter because "we all worship the same God though we approach Him in different ways." They do not claim, as Count Zinzendorff, founder of the Moravian Brethren Congregation, did two centuries ago, that all religions are only *tropes,* variants, of the one central kernel which all have in common. They do not argue, as Lessing did in his parable of the three rings, that the sons of the king should respect each other and live in peace with one another because none of them can be sure who has received the genuine ring. They do not assert, as Rosenzweig did, that both Judaism and Christianity are equally authentic ways to God, the one leading through the son to the Father, the other leading directly to the Father. And they certainly are diametrically opposed to that popular kind of contemporary interfaith religion which proclaims that one religion is just as good as the other and that Christianity is the best religion for the Christian while Judaism is the best religion for the Jew. Contrary to all these approaches, the prophets, and especially Deutero-Isaiah, confidently express the hope that the time will come when Judaism will have become the religion of all nations.

Second, the Messianic Age will not come solely through the grace of God; it requires the labors of man. It does not signify an announcement of an apocalyptic breakthrough of God into history, the expectation of something which will ultimately descend to the earth from some other world. It will have to be merited, earned, achieved by man, whose action brings the passion of messianic fulfillment into the here and now. Messianic thinking demands courageous engagement in the historical process, even when it is most threatening, not withdrawal from it because it is threatening or has become unbearable. It arises, in Leo Baeck's words, out of the very depths of the significance of life: it is the demand and the certainty of that which every person and every generation must do so that God's will, and through it man's life, be fulfilled.

Consequently—this is the third implication—the Messianic Age is of this world, not of a world to come. It is a historic task and possibility, not an eschatological expectation. It is to happen here on earth and not in apocalyptical times, after the end of time. It is the great goal toward which mankind must work and move here in this world of time and space.

Fourth, messianic thinking implies that man is not merely an object of history. He is also the subject of history. He is not merely driven by a blind fate. He can shape and create his own future. Hence, the central core of the messianic concept is the conviction that history is not blind. It has direction and a goal. And wherever there is a goal, the future is no longer something to be dreaded. The future is not what *will* be, but that which *should* be. It is a task entrusted to man, a command to shape his life and make the historic process the instrument of the realization of that which is good.

It is in these thoughts that the messianic ideal reveals its significance as the central feature of the image which Jews have of themselves and of the meaning of Jewish existence. Man's life on earth is not a blind groping in darkness. It is not a succession of unrelated accidents, devoid of point and purpose, "mere blind matter in senseless agitation," or, in Macbeth's words, "a tale told by an idiot, full of sound and fury, signifying nothing." Life has meaning. History has direction. There is purpose to man's endeavors. And this purpose can be fulfilled by the man who learns to listen to the voice that calls—*election;* who responds by saying *hinneni*—"Here I am"—*covenant;* and who, accepting his role in the messianic drama, becomes God's partner in the never-ending task of creation.

8. *Judaism as a Source of Personal Values*

MAURICE L. ZIGMOND

A Liberal View

THIS PAPER attempts no comprehensive treatment of the nature or content of Judaism but seeks to indicate certain values which I as an individual have found in my Jewish heritage. What aspects of Judaism have been important to me? What Jewish teachings do I cherish most? What elements in my philosophy of life do I attribute to my Jewishness?

Two frank admissions must be made at the outset. First, I do not claim that my "brand" of Judaism is the only kind. Quite apart from the "exotic" Jewish traditions of North Africa, Asia, and elsewhere, there is great diversity of thought and practice among Jews. For every "Jewish" idea which has been influential in my life, others may well find an alternate or a contrary idea. It may be possible tentatively to identify major as against minor themes; yet such a judgment can always be challenged. Whatever the concept, its opposite, too, is likely to exist somewhere in our tradition. Many Jews (including myself), for example, would insist that in Judaism there is an emphasis on this world as against a preoccupation with the world to come. Yet the statement of Rabbi Jacob may be quoted to the contrary: "This world is but a vestibule before the world to come; prepare yourself in the vestibule so that you may enter the banquet hall." Again, Jewish literature contains numerous passages exalting peace as the noblest ideal; but one can easily cite other references in which some types of war are not only condoned but commanded. In short, within the immense accumulation of Jewish writings, substantiation for almost any concept can be found.

Second, it must be freely admitted that many of the ideas which I trace to Judaism may be found in other traditions as well. The claim of "uniqueness" is usually as meaningless as it is erroneous. Who thought of it first? Who said it first? Charles Darwin in science and Thomas Mann in literature have painstakingly demonstrated that every "beginning" has its beginning and that the Ultimate Beginning is as elusive as are all ultimates.

It is, therefore, not my concern here whether Judaism expressed an idea first or better. I maintain simply that Judaism expressed it. In the vast congeries of traits of which cultures are composed, it would be odd indeed if there were not an appreciable amount of overlapping. Cultural exchange and diffusion are characteristic of all cultures. The anthropologist A. L. Kroeber estimated that more than half of the elements in any given culture originated outside it. Culture growth is impossible without culture contact.

What, then, are some of the concepts and values in the Jewish cultural tradition that have brought me personal satisfaction?

I

The first is one of Judaism's basic concepts—monotheism. In one sense, the numerical factor in the belief in one God is not its strongest feature. Much can be said for the more balanced notion of dualism in which both good and evil are real entities struggling for the world and the soul of man. Thus human goodness can conveniently be attributed to the influence of a benign deity and human perversity to that of a malevolent deity. The monotheist is in the more difficult theological position by having to explain the existence of evil in a world exclusively in the control of a righteous God. The issue troubled biblical writers and constituted the central theme of the Book of Job. Monotheism poses almost as many problems as it solves.

To me the sublimity of monotheism lies in its symbolic presumption of harmony in the world. If God, the Lord of the universe, is one, then the world is an integrated whole, and there is an essential congruity between all its parts. Oneness pervades all things—the physical universe, the relationship of man to nature, the relationship of man to man. Man is not to consider himself surrounded by hostile forces that threaten his existence, but by potentially beneficent elements out of which he can fashion his home, by the physical ingredients out of which the Good Life may be created. And his relationship with his fellows is to be governed by the stance implicit in the prophet's questions: "Have we not all one Father? Has not one God created us?" An affirmative reply is, from the Jewish point of view, inherent in both man and his world.

Hence, evil, for monotheism, is not an independent entity, a self-sustaining force which stands in opposition to good. Evil is the absence of good, the area into which good has not yet penetrated. Into it the expansion of the good is not only possible but necessary and, in the long run, inevitable. Just as the "evil" in nature (i.e., the physical phenomena that threaten human welfare) challenges man's constructive abilities, so the "evil" in man —antisocial behavior, war, crime—challenges man's moral sense. Monotheism presupposes that man has the potentiality, not yet fully realized, to establish ethical and moral oneness in the social order.

Judaism portrays man as a co-worker with God in perfecting creation, as His partner in completing His work. But does Jewish tradition not assert that the universe was "finished" on the sixth day? What, then, is left for man to do? Unlike other creatures, man was endowed with the power and intelligence to build an ideal life out of the resources of his world. In the sense that the ideal life has not yet been achieved, the "work of creation" is not completed. Divine harmony is a pattern which man must strive to reproduce on earth. Man, according to Jewish tradition, was, in fact, placed here for this purpose and possesses the gifts essential for its realization. "He who performs a righteous act is associated with God in creation." The Jewish concept of man's stature is perhaps best epitomized in Psalm 8: "Thou hast made man but little lower than the angels. Thou hast given him dominion over the works of Thy hands; Thou hast put all things under his feet."

The notion that the physical and the social worlds are a challenge to man and that man has the ability to meet this challenge has far-reaching consequences. Let us examine a few of its implications.

In the first place, the doctrine of original sin, according to which every descendant of Adam and Eve must automatically and inevitably bear the burden of their disobedience, has never become a major theme in Judaism. Although the story is an integral part of Jewish literature, Jewish tradition did not find in it a curse on mankind for all time. It always emphasized that the sin was Adam's and Eve's and that they had to accept the consequences of their own misconduct. According to the *Tanhuma,* Adam says to his descendants, "You die on your own account, not on mine." The Jewish sages generally conceived of man as born, not with a prenatal curse but with a "clean slate." "My God, the soul which Thou hast placed within me is pure," declares the Daily Morning Service. In a letter to a Jewish community in Egypt, Saadyah wrote (928 C.E.), "Remember that God has created you upright and that it is you who soil your souls with wickedness." The Hebrew word for "sin" (*het*) has as its primary meaning, "missing the intended mark or goal." Thus Proverbs 19:2 says, "He who makes haste with his feet misses his way [*hotay*]." The goal is human perfection. Man seems always to be missing the mark. But the possibility is ever present that his aim may improve. He may try again—indeed, he must try again. Who knows but one day he may hit the mark?

Thus—a second implication—there is scant basis in Judaism for a philosophy of life which finds that man is oppressed and overwhelmed by his own limitations, that he is but a worm, that one need not go back more than a few decades to witness the depths of bestiality to which humanity can plunge, that man is not capable of solving his social and moral problems, and that his best efforts to lift himself from the dust are doomed to failure.

Judaism has no place for a defeatist philosophy of life. "Thou hast made man but little lower than the angels, and hast crowned him with glory and honor." "Say not, 'From God is my transgression,'" Ben Sira warns, "For He does not make the things He hates." And the *Tanhuma* adds, "You yourselves pervert your goodness. When you are a child, you do not sin; when you grow up, you sin." Man cannot blame inborn limitations as an excuse for his failures. His failures are due to the misuse or nonuse of his abilities. His tragic past is not an inevitable precedent for his future. He may yet establish the divine on earth.

In this connection, it is interesting to note the dominant Jewish attitude toward miracles. The presence of miracles in the biblical text could not be denied. Yet if the problems of the world are man's to solve with his God-given talents, why should God disturb the arrangement by taking matters, so to speak, into His own hands? Some rationalist thinkers of the past seek to explain away many biblical miracles as allegories or dreams. Others insist that some of the wondrous events of the past only *seemed* miraculous, but that there was actually no interruption in the chain of cause and effect. And still another ingenious theory argues that the biblical miracles were neither random nor spontaneous, but an integral element in the divine plan of creation and, thus, foreordained, limited in number, and not designed to replace the orderly processes of nature. By implication, then, man is not to expect miracles to solve his problems. In a remarkable talmudic passage, two sages are debating a legal point. One is so certain of the validity of his position, that he calls upon God to support him by miraculous manifestations. The Holy One is inclined to cooperate with him until his opponent, quoting Deuteronomy 30:12, insists, "It is not in heaven!" Later Elijah, when asked about the divine reaction to this defiance, replies, "God smiled and said, 'My sons have defeated Me.'" Man has been given intelligence and understanding; with them he is to confront all the issues of life.

Third, the challenge of life has led Judaism, on the one hand, to concentrate its attention upon this world to the relative neglect of the world to come, and, on the other, to a frank acceptance of life's joys, which are regarded as neither sinful nor detrimental to the development of the spirit. If it is man's role to realize the divine pattern on earth, then to maintain that life's inequities and injustices will be adequately compensated for in the world beyond is to lack moral courage. Even though we may not be able to eliminate poverty, corruption, and war in our generation, we are committed to combating them. "It is not your duty to complete the work," said Rabbi Tarphon, "but neither are you free to desist from it." The world to come is a realm ultimately to be enjoyed, but life on this planet is a "thing in itself" with its own problems, its own standards of progress, its own rewards, and its own penalties.

As for the enjoyment of life, the sages advocated moderation in all things. While they condemned excesses, they also repudiated asceticism. One rabbi maintains that on the Day of Judgment men will have to answer for the joys they could have enjoyed but refused. The spirit of God, says another, does not rest upon men in a state of gloom. Judah Ha-Levi insisted that fasting on a fast day does not bring a man nearer to God than eating, drinking, and rejoicing on a feast day. The Jew does not conceive of his body as hostile to his soul. In general, the satisfactions of the one are regarded as conducive to the serenity of the other.

Finally, if "God created man in His own image" and man is "but little lower than God," then human life is sacred, the most sacred of all things on earth. "I have set before you life and death," declares the Deuteronomist, "therefore choose life." It is a religious duty to preserve life, and to this end all commandments may be transgressed save the three forbidding idolatry, murder, and incest. The verse in Leviticus, "You shall not stand idly by the blood of your neighbor," is used to formulate the principle that one is in duty bound to do everything possible to save one's own life as well as that of one's fellowman. One must satisfy the needs of a sick person even though his illness be superficial. A physician must minister to his patients even on the Sabbath and holidays. Furthermore, though cruelty to animals is expressly forbidden, the life and welfare of all creatures are subordinate to man's well-being.

The most basic relationship between men is expressed in the word "peace." According to a talmudic text, "the whole Torah exists only for the sake of peace," and Rabban Simeon, son of Gamaliel, says that the world stands on three things, "justice, truth, and peace." A special talmudic tractate, *Perek ha-Shalom,* is devoted to the extolment of peace. "Great is peace; other commands are conditional, but the command of peace is unconditional, as it is said, 'Seek peace, and pursue it' [Ps. 34:15]."

The biblical attitude toward war, as already indicated, is ambivalent. Later, when military action on the part of Jews had become largely a theoretical issue, some support for certain types of war could still be found in Jewish literature. Yet there is clearly discernible a persistent effort by the rabbis to "pacify" the biblical text. "There are no heroes," according to the *Avot de-Rabbi Natan,* "except heroes of Torah." Accordingly, Joshua and Othniel are transformed from warriors into scholars of the Law. Military leaders, such as Joab, Abishai, and Abner, are seen to be more at home in the realm of Torah than on the field of battle. Indeed, the verse of Isaiah, "the Lord of hosts will be . . . strength to those who turn back the battle at the gate," is said by the rabbis to refer "to those who distinguished themselves in the disputations of the Torah." Such weapons of war as sword, bow, and arrow are taken variously to mean the keenness of scholars who know the Law, prayers and supplications (in the case of Jacob), or the power of the good deeds of the righteous. And the Midrash goes so far as to maintain that "if the children of Israel were to practice idolatry, and, at the same time, peace prevailed among them, God would say, 'I cannot exercise authority against them in anger because peace is among them.' " God has appointed man His partner on earth and has stamped His image upon every human being. Thus, to take a human life is to desecrate the divine, whereas "he who saves a life is as one who saves the world."

Jewish monotheism lifts man to a unique place in the universe. If the challenge is great, so are man's endowments. If the work is hard, God is infinitely patient. Judaism breathes a spirit of optimism—not the naïve assumption that everything will take care of itself, but the confidence that man can meet the challenge of his times if he so wills.

II

If man is God's co-worker, he must properly equip himself for his sacred assignment. But how? By learning all that he can of his world—in short, by educating himself. Judaism not only places upon man a great responsibility; it provides him with the incentive to fit his talents to the job. Man will best prepare himself to meet the challenge of existence through the acquisition of knowledge. The search for wisdom becomes man's noblest activity, surpassing all other enterprises. *Talmud Torah keneged kulam*—"Learning takes precedence over all things."

The rabbis debate the question as to which is more sacred: a life devoted to prayer or a life devoted to study. While both are declared to be indispensable to the welfare of man, it is pointed out that praying itself requires the learning process. Study must, therefore, have priority. Hillel declared that "an ignorant man cannot be pious," and although views to the contrary exist in Jewish tradition, it can still be said that nothing is more characteristic of Judaism than its emphasis upon learning. Study is a holy activity. The very act of study is in itself a prayer to God. This idea is literally embodied in the Siddur. It contains "study paragraphs" extracted from talmudic literature. Such selections have no "prayer value" in the conventional sense, but symbolize the place of learning in worship and the high esteem in which the scholar is held. In fact, while Judaism has never been preoccupied with attempts to define the precise nature of the world to come, it has been quite specific about the kind of afterlife for which the scholar is destined. Tradition has it that he will sit eternally with his colleagues and study in a *yeshiva shel ma'alah,* a "college on high." While such a heaven might not appeal to the modern college student, the learned men of old could conceive of no greater bliss.

The paramount importance of education was never questioned. However, the *content* of Jewish learning changed from age to age. The sacred texts, at first of the Bible and subsequently of the Talmud, constituted the basic core of study, but the very nature of Jewish law demanded a wide range of information. The determination of the Sabbath, New Moons, and festivals required a familiarity with astronomy; the regulations governing diseased persons called for medical knowledge; and the rules of personal purification assumed an acquaintance with physiology. Of Rabbi Samuel it is said that he knew the stars of heaven as well as he knew the streets of his own town. The Bible amply testifies to a broad knowledge of neighboring lands and peoples. The universalism of the prophets is at least in part prompted by an acute awareness that different nations have different histories, gods, and customs. The words of Amos presuppose an international approach: "Did I not bring up Israel from the land of Egypt [says the Lord], and the Philistines from Caphtor, and the Syrians from Kir?" Multilingualism early became an integral part of Jewish culture, and the Bible itself reveals clear traces of the influence of alien thought and literatures. On the other hand, the rabbis warned of the grave consequences awaiting those whose insatiable curiosity led them to embark upon the uncharted seas of strange philosophies and ideologies.

Universal schooling was a Jewish goal perhaps from the time of the Babylonian Exile. The denial of the right to study was one of the issues behind the Maccabean and Bar Kokhba revolts. Joshua ben Gamala (first century C.E.) is gratefully remembered because he "came and arranged that teachers for elementary schools be on duty in every province and in every city, and that children enter at the age of six and seven." A few centuries later, a sage inquires, "Is it possible to find anyone without elementary school knowledge?" and the reply is, "Yes, it is possible in the case of a child who was taken captive among non-Jews." The supreme importance of education is reflected in the talmudic statement, "The Holy One is engaged part of each day teaching Torah to little children." And at the time of circumcision the traditional blessing includes the prayer: "May he [the newborn] enter [the study of] Torah."

The pursuit of knowledge has continued to be one of the most cogent pressures in Jewish life. The strong desire of Jewish parents to give their children the best possible education no matter what the sacrifice, the high percentage of Jews who attend college, the honor and respect still given the educated man, are modern expressions of an ancient tradition. Our ancestors would have been unhappy to know the extent to which the Jewish world today has strayed from sacred texts; but they would at least have understood the urge. If we are no longer, in a strict sense, the People of the Book, we are still the people of the books.

III

The monotheism of the Jew has had profound consequences in another direction. The belief in one God to whom one appeals in a direct approach without the need of intermediaries, either human or superhuman, provided poor soil for the flowering of elaborate theologies. "True it is that Thou art the first and Thou art the last, and beside Thee we have no King, Redeemer or Savior." It is as simple as that. This is not to deny that, largely under the influence of other religions and within certain Jewish movements, the nature and attributes of God were analyzed in great detail and with patient and loving care. But the dominant tendency in Judaism is to regard all such considerations as subordinate to the practical problem of establishing the proper relationship with God by doing His will upon earth.

Hence, it should not be surprising that Judaism has no official creed. Not that some of our rabbinic authorities did not attempt to encompass basic Jewish concepts in brief and concise form. Maimonides' Thirteen Articles of Faith constitute merely one of several compositions of this type. Indeed, the Maimonidean formulation was ultimately regarded so highly that it was included in the daily prayerbook. Yet the acceptance of this or any other "creed" was rarely used for the validation of membership in the Jewish group.

Viewed objectively, the lack of a simple method by which identity with Judaism may be easily determined is a very real handicap. It deprives Judaism of a convenient definition of itself. It leaves to the individual Jew the terms under which he participates. Who is a Jew? What is a Jew? It is frustrating not to be able to give clear and concise answers to these legitimate questions. Before many a Christian audience I have been forced to confess that, after more than three thousand years, we have no ultimate criteria by which we might delimit ourselves. The anthropologist Melville Herskovits, in an article on this subject, concludes that "a Jew is a person who calls himself a Jew or who is called Jewish by others."

This formlessness leads to an apparent impasse. The Jewish heritage, whose most persistent tradition is its monotheism, comes ultimately to a situation in which even those who deny the existence of God cannot be excluded. Numerous Jews reject religious belief as obsolete or meaningless for modern man. They may dedicate their lives to some phase of Jewish culture—to Yiddish, social service, the building of Israel; but they are allergic to rituals and rabbis. It is futile to insist that they have thereby placed themselves outside the realm of Judaism. If there is no acceptable way of defining the terms of Jewish identity, we must admit the right of the individual Jew to determine the areas of his affiliation.

This situation may be disturbing and even intolerable to some. I have found in it a great satisfaction. "Belongingness" in Judaism is not a matter of unquestioning acceptance of a pat set of doctrines. For a set of doctrines at best represents the definition of those who compose it and therefore fully understand the meaning of its terms. Belongingness in Judaism involves choice, judgment, and hence a measure of maturity. Only flexibility permits adaptation, development, and growth. Without the ability to absorb both internal and external change, there can be no life. Judaism lives because our ancestors discovered long ago that continuity rather than fixity is the secret of survival.

A modern Jew can hardly be satisfied with a definition of Judaism which might have been devised in the Patriarchal Age. The bald fact is that the sages of the Talmud were no less dissatisfied. They made their revisions and modifications in the name of "interpretation" and thus avoided a break in the chain of tradition. Every debate upon the Torah, every commentary and translation involved changes which reflected the social, moral, and intellectual background of the debater, comment. or, or translator. But they stubbornly clung to the uninterrupted line of tradition. The teachings of Jesus might have had an altogether different reception among the Jewish people had they been presented as an inevitable elaboration of *Halakhah* and not as a replacement.

Years ago, a biblical pageant of vast proportions called *The Eternal Road* was produced in New York City. I happened to attend a performance in the company of an Orthodox rabbi. As we left the hall, I asked him for his impression. He startled me by replying, "It wasn't Jewish." Wasn't Jewish? How could that be? The dramatizations were entirely from the Jewish Bible. There were scenes of the Exodus, of Moses on Mount Sinai, of the conquest of Canaan. Yet it wasn't Jewish. That is to say, it gave no hint of the post-biblical, rabbinic treatment of biblical stories and personalities. It failed to incorporate the midrashic enrichment which generations of Jewish minds and hearts had wrought upon them.

The fluidity of the Jewish tradition has enabled it to avoid the snare of being identified with theories or philosophies which, when invalidated, might have endangered Judaism itself. Jewish ideology suffered no embarrassment when the Ptolemaic astronomy was forced to give way to the Copernican. It lost no cardinal principle when scientists assailed the early chapters of Genesis. It was able to absorb the Platonic notions introduced by Philo and the Aristotelian ideas introduced by Maimonides. Thus I have some basis for my confidence that Judaism will not fall before the onslaughts of atomic physics or of the latest theories of psychiatry. Judaism encourages the unconditional quest for truth and trembles not at all at the possible consequences. It says, in the words of the New Testament (if John 8:32 may be taken out of context), "And you shall know the truth and the truth shall make you free."

IV

The paramount concern of Judaism for human needs, human values, and human life stems directly from its concept of monotheism. Here is the whole of the verse of which I have already quoted the first half: "Have we not all one father? Hath not one God created us? Why do we deal treacherously every man against his brother, profaning the covenant of our fathers?" (Malachi 2:10). If all of us have one Father, our relationship to one another ought to be characterized by brotherly love. In explaining how man may make atonement on Yom Kippur, the sages say: One must first become reconciled to one's neighbor whom one has wronged before one can become reconciled with God. It is our supreme duty to protect, preserve, and prolong human life, to enrich it, and to fashion a social and physical environment for man which will be conducive to creative living. Contrary to the frequently repeated charge that Judaism places outward form and the punctilious observance of the Law above human welfare, its prior concern is always with human needs and their fulfillment. While it is true that the Jewish sages put no emphasis on an abstract concept of "spirituality," then concretized the idea in such terms as charity, the saving of life, communal affairs, and education. Ethics takes precedence over philosophy and, in its sophisticated sense, theology.

V

These, then, are some of the aspects of my Jewish heritage which I cherish. Within the framework of Judaism I have found it possible to live a full and satisfying life. For me it has opened wide the door to unlimited inquiry, to precious human relationships, and to the acceptance of man and his works as "the center of all things." I have never found myself burdened or restricted by my Jewishness. It has been at once motivation and fulfillment, goad and goal. The "values" of Judaism are transmitted through institutions that have survived to our day—the family, the synagogue, the school, the cultural and social center, and now the State of Israel. That transformations will occur in the years to come can hardly be doubted. Yet the chances are that the Jews of the future are likely to exhibit in their thought and conduct at least some of the values that have relevance in our time.

NORMAN E. FRIMER

A Traditional View

JEWISH LEGEND HAS IT that when one of the sages
of the past century was nearing the end of his life, he offered the
following personal experience as his last will and testament: "In
my youth," he stated,

> when the call to God's service first came to me, I resolved not to
> rest until I had gathered all of my brethren throughout the world
> under the banner of the *shekhinah*. As I grew older and grasped
> the vastness of such a task, I reluctantly reduced the scope of my
> work to my own land. Later on I was satisfied to focus my influence
> upon the Jews of my city. With increasing age and experience I
> began to concentrate my efforts upon my family and a coterie of
> students and close friends. Now, as I survey the shambles of my
> ambition from the sobering perspective of my approaching end of
> days, I realize where I made my first and biggest mistake. I should
> have done much more with myself.

This statement of priority could hardly have been intended as
a disparagement of the vital role of social values. They are central
in our tradition. Moreover, in life itself, the personal can no more
be divorced from the social than the individual can be severed
from the group. They are inextricably related and, in the Jewish
context, live symbiotically one in the other.

Nevertheless, in the logistics of Jewish living, Judaism requires
the forging of a solid sytem of personal values in the individual
as the best guarantee for the cultivation of a vigorous and healthy

164

world-view in the community. For such is the law of life: *Adam karov etzel atzmo,* "man is closest to himself"—both physically and psychologically. What man holds to be true and applicable with regard to his own person, he will invariably project as the true and the applicable with regard to his fellowman. For inevitably he fashions him in his own image. In the understanding of this process lies the genius of Hillel's well-known maxim, *Im ain anee lee mee lee.* First he underscored the personal—"If I am not for myself, who will be for me?" Then he moved on to an enlarged social vision, *ukh-sh'anee l'atzmee mah anee*—"but when I am only for myself, what am I?"

Thus Jewish tradition strongly urges the development of mature and compelling personal values which can in turn serve as stepping-stones for man's and society's climb to the Good Life.

I

What are some of these values?

My first choice is the conviction that, for Judaism, all human values are religious. They find their source, validation, and ultimate purpose in a faith in God and His revealed will. This thesis appears self-evident from even a superficial examination of Jewish tradition.

The Ten Commandments are introduced with the statement, "And God spoke these words saying. . . ." The ethical teachings of the prophets bear the indelible imprimatur of divine directive: "It hath been told thee, O man, what is good, and what the Lord doth require of thee." Rabbinic literature generally presupposes obedience to the dictum, "A man ought not to say, 'I have no desire to eat the flesh of swine, or to commit adultery,' but rather let him say, 'I would eagerly do all of these things; yet what can I do? My Father who is in heaven has forbidden them.' "

In Judaism, the sanction for values, be they ethical, ritual, personal, or social, is not individual caprice but the injunction of a Creator and Legislator to whom we are finally and inescapably responsible.

II

From this position we can move to a second value. It is second only structurally; logically, it is antecedent. I refer to the assumption that the true essence of life, particularly human life, is not physical in quality but spiritual. In other words, the Jewish yardstick for good and evil, for the beautiful and the ugly, is not the satisfaction or attraction afforded, but the dimension of spirituality and of moral and ethical content.

The basic source of this concept is the Torah itself, which, at its very outset, portrays God as the Master Architect of all creation. He is, so to speak, personally involved in every successive act. It was He who "spoke and the world came into existence." It was He who breathed into man's nostrils (*nishmat hayim*) the soul (or breath) of life. No student, scholar, or saint has as yet deciphered the profundity of meaning contained in these and similar sweeping strokes of the divine quill. Yet life's and man's spiritual origin and purpose are writ irrefutably large in every line of every page of Scripture. It is by virtue of his spiritual eminence as the *tzelem elokim,* the image of God, that man is entitled to have dominion over the earth which mothered him. It is as a godlike creature that he merits the exultant tribute which the Psalmist utters in glowing answer to a rhetorical question:

> What is man, that Thou art mindful of him?
> And the son of man, that Thou takest account of him?
> Aye, Thou hast made him but little lower than the angels
> And hast crowned him with glory and honor.

This depiction of man in the Bible—amply reinforced throughout rabbinic and medieval Jewish sources—compels us to measure his stature by other than an earthly, material gauge. His life, actions, and thoughts, the very being of this child of God, who shares in elements of godliness, cannot be evaluated except by heavenly, spiritual standards. One does not honor and revere a synagogue for the exquisite ark it houses but for the holy Torah which rests therein. To do the former is, to rephrase Abraham

Heschel, not only spiritual vulgarity but a religious travesty border-
ing on the idolatrous. For idolatry is the confusion of means and
ends, imputing to the instrument the sanctity and reverence rightfully and uniquely due the Master Craftsman.

Too often, therefore, must we plead guilty to the sin of mis-
takenly judging a man's worth by the price his estate commands,
a man's leadership by the popularity he enjoys, a man's cause by
the persuasive glibness of his public relations. Too often are we
among those who in exclusive choice would prefer personality to
character, beauty to purity, wealth to wisdom. The *Mesillat
Yesharim,* the *Path of the Righteous,* though written in the eighteenth century, addresses our generation when its author complains
that "the learned lack saintliness because they do not give it
sufficient thought."

I am not glorifying the virtues of the hermit life. Jewish
tradition puts no premium on asceticism. And it has a strong and
healthy regard for the aesthetic. The aesthetic, however, is defined in and subordinated to the profounder criteria of the spiritual
rather than the superficial terms of the physical.

A simple Jewish folk tale illustrates this point. Its hero, a
recently arrived immigrant, Yossel, has just received a visit from
a *landsmann* who is inquiring about his own uncle, Fetter Moshe:

"Which Moshe are you referring to?" reacted Yossel. "I know
several people by that name."

"Moshe, the cross-eyed one," replied the visitor.

"Cross-eyed?" repeated Yossel questioningly. *"Kennst du mir
efsher geben noch a zeichen?* Perhaps you can give me another
clue?"

"Of course, my uncle has a bucktooth right in the front of his
mouth."

"Cross-eyed, bucktoothed," murmured Yossel. *"Gib mir noch a
simen."*

"Fetter Moshe had a *parch,* an open sore, on his forehead,"
continued the *landsmann.*

"Cross-eyed, buck-toothed, a *parch* on his forehead? *Noch ein
simen!* Just one hint," pleaded Yossel.

"Uncle Moshe," added the visitor, "was known for his bulbous
nose."

"Oh, him!" shouted Yossel. "Sure I know him, *aza scheiner Yid*—
he's such a beautiful Jew!"

Physically, Uncle Moshe was as unprepossessing as a ramshackle
house, but spiritually he was *aza scheiner Yid,* such a beautiful
Jew. And in the last analysis, this was the Jewish yardstick for
evaluating a fellow Jew.

Oscar Wilde's parable, *The Picture of Dorian Gray,* presents a
similar moral lesson that seems distinctly Jewish. The plot revolves
around a portrait of a man of extraordinary beauty. His features
are Grecian in their loveliness and blessed with unchanging youth-
fulness. Dorian Gray succumbs to vanity, and his youth and his
beauty become a snare and a delusion. With hedonism his new
philosophy and the senses his lustful master, the gratification of
his passions becomes his life's consuming ambition.

One day, as if by a miracle, the canvas springs to life. Subtly
and imperceptibly at first, then more noticeably, the painting
begins to mirror the inner corruption and concealed depravity of
Dorian Gray. Eyes, once depicted as clear and innocent, become
cunning and evil; a mouth, once delicate and refined, becomes
cruel and sensual; a forehead, once smooth and proud, is seared
with wrinkles; hands once soft and effeminate become coarse and
bloated. Each loathsome act adds to the disfigurement of the
portrait, until only his vicarious suicide gives it final release.

Beauty is not merely physical, and it is more than skin-deep.
Conversely, there is no ugliness greater than spiritual ugliness, for
it defaces and deforms the inner man, stamping him as hideous
and repulsive, despite the grace and the loveliness of the outer
form. Such spiritual criteria are the classic standards of Jewish
aesthetics.

III

My third value is humility.

Dorian Gray was the narcissistic victim of his own beauty. Yet
self-adoration can be corruptive on other levels as well—on the
intellectual, for example, and even on the spiritual. The pit of

vanity and smugness has claimed the self-styled saint as readily as the confessed scoundrel. As a safety precaution, therefore, the Rebbe of Kotzk used to counsel his disciples, "Let each of you always carry on your person two medallions. One should bear the talmudic inscription. 'For my sake [i.e., man's] was the world created,' the other, the words of our Torah, 'For I am but dust and ashes.'" In this seeming paradox lies the sane though delicate balance of Jewish thinking and living. The quality of humility is offered as an antidote to man's pride and pretensions, and his partnership with God as the uplifting and challenging vision to counteract his sluggish earthiness.

A comparable paradox is attributed to the Almighty Himself. Rabbi Yohanan said:

> Wherever you find mention of God's supreme majesty, there too shall you find evidence of His lowly humility. This is written in the Torah, repeated in the Prophets, and cited a third time in the Writings. It is written in the Torah, "For the Lord your God, is the God of gods and the Lord of lords, great and mighty and revered." Yet it is written thereafter, "He doth execute justice for the orphan and the widow, showing love to the stranger by giving him food and raiment." It is repeated in the Prophets, "For thus saith the high and exalted One that inhabiteth eternity and whose name is Holy." What is the sequel? "I dwell in the high and holy place with him also that is of a contrite and humble spirit, so that I may revive the spirit of the humble and revive the heart of the contrite." It is cited a third time in the Writings, "Sing unto God, sing praises unto His Name; extol ye Him that rideth upon the heavens whose name is the Lord." Yet what follows? "He is a father of the fatherless, and judge of the widows is God in His holy habitation."

What, then, is humility? Like all spiritual elements of life, it cannot be easily analyzed, only analogized. It cannot be taught; it can only be caught. Yet its manifestations can easily be observed. It is present in the sense of miracle a mother has when her first child is born. It accompanies the sense of wonder and amazement the astronomer must feel as he surveys the myriads of stars in their orderly courses in the sky. It suffuses the first gentle love experience of a young person and the gripping awe stirred by the fury of unleashed nature. Edison must have sensed just this when he said, "I am overcome with the realization of the enormous strength and potential dynamic power which spend themselves in the roar of the waves and in the lashing gale." It is part and parcel of the religious reverence and exaltation which the Psalmist expresses for all sensitive persons in the inspired words: "How manifold are Thy works, O Lord; in wisdom, hast Thou made them all."

How humbled must man therefore feel as he contrasts the infinite capacities of his divine endowments with the limited and all too often self-destructive realities of his human achievement. In the words of the biblical narrative, God told Adam and Eve to "be fruitful and multiply and replenish the earth and subdue it." Make nature your servant! Command its obedience! With his inventive genius, man went on to fulfill this God-given behest. He succeeded in outflying the bird in the air, in outswimming the fish in the sea, in outrunning the deer on land, but, alas, he failed miserably in learning to walk God's earth in dignity, as man. We shall not subdue nature without, according to Jewish tradition, until we shall learn to discipline our human nature within. Genuine mastery consists of self-mastery.

Some people mock such soulful sensitivity. Yet Jewish tradition focuses upon them the piercing searchlight of existential reality. It confronts the proverbial self-made man who "worships his own maker," with the challenge of the crushing words, "Surely man walketh as a mere phantom. For vanity are they in turmoil; he heapeth up riches, and knoweth not who shall gather them in."

It was the human predicament which motivated Hugh Walpole to write, "To the person who feels, life is a tragedy; to the person who thinks, life is a comedy." Time makes a mockery of man's driving ambitions. He bestrides the earth like a colossus, seeking to clutch vast continents in his greedy grasp and decreeing the fate of millions at a drunken whim. But he does so only momentarily. For "in the morning he bloometh and sprouteth afresh; but in the evening he is cut down and withereth."

The same notion is underscored in the rabbinic observation that when a child is born, his fists are clenched, betokening a firm determination to encompass the whole earth with his hands. When man dies, his palms are outstretched, as if in humble confession that one's glory does not descend after him; he shall carry nothing material away.

No wonder that the highest praise which the Torah could bestow upon Moses was humility. "The man Moses was most humble above all men on the face of the earth." Only these words are a fitting epitaph to be inscribed in the hearts of his people.

When we set this value into the context of American life and its "cult of successism," a plea for emulating humility tends to sound sermonic and misty eyed. You can't make a million dollars that way. It blueprints no sure-fire method for gaining admission to high society or rising to an executive position; it certainly offers no guarantee for attaining fame or prestige.

Nevertheless, if we set this value against the background of our deeper yearnings, against the image of our inner selves, against the picture we project of the society we would like to pass on to our own progeny and the kind of world we feel can actually and realistically be achieved, humility becomes preferable to a philosophy of pride and self-aggrandizement at any cost, and modesty becomes more desirable than aggressiveness and greed. Humility, like most other spiritual values, may in our society involve a sacrifice of material advantages. Yet they are the inexpendables in the larger and (for the Jew) nobler question of man's and society's ultimate destiny and fulfillment. Moreover, with the sands of time running out on man so quickly, every person's decision on this issue becomes literally a crucial determinant in the human race against peril and perdition.

Humility, however, should not be confused with meekness. In Judaism, Uriah-Heepism is hypocrisy, and "turn-your-other-cheekness" is self-degrading. Meekness smacks of destructive self-evaluation. It points to what man is not. Humility points to what man can be. Man is dust and ashes only when he addresses himself to his God. In the face of his fellowman, man is the son of Adam, and the Jew, the scion of Abraham, Isaac, and Jacob. Judaism asks us only to be equal and true to this lineage.

To tie these last two points together, one might say that man, in his spiritual capacity, is the creation of God, the crown and glory of the universe; in his physical capacity, he is "like the beasts that perish." In terms of his divine potentiality, man is "little lower than the angels." In terms of his human actuality, he is "like a fragile potsherd." High drama and nobility reside in the fact that these facets are parts of an indivisible though paradoxical unity. It is in the tension of this dialectical polarity that we tap the secret of man's grandeur and the wellspring, goal, and sense of adventure of his religious quest.

IV

My final personal value is the sanctity of the word. Our time can be characterized as the "age of the word." The word is supreme and all-pervading. Silence and serene contemplation, once considered by our ancestors as healing balm for body and soul, are noticeable by their absence. We are incessantly bombarded by the raucous chatter of the written and spoken word. The word literally encircles the globe.

But our capacity to communicate provides not only the power to communicate the truth but simultaneously the power to propagate the lie. Political conventions and campaigns are hardly designed to bring the central issues frankly to the people. Words are merely gimmicks, tools, highly polished and oiled, used in order to manipulate, not to educate; to exploit, not to explain; to confuse, not to enlighten.

The same is true in other areas of human interaction. Most of us would unhesitatingly state that people, in their personal relations with members of their family, maintain a high degree of integrity and loyalty. We would insist that people do not lie deliberately to their near and dear ones, nor indulge in outright deception, but are eager to establish a working rapport based on mutual trust and faith. I maintained such a position recently in a discussion with an attorney friend, only to have my suppositions dismissed as unfactual and my arguments demolished as rabbinic credulity and naïveté. The frightening array of case evidence he marshaled, involving sordid contests of family wills, dissolutions of family partnerships, suits of breach of promise and divorce, shook my defenses to their foundations and my faith in my thesis to its roots. My friend did not intend to demonstrate that our society has begun to approximate the corruption of ancient Sodom and Gomorrah. But we would be Pollyannas if we ignored the sociological studies that bear witness to the increasing threats to the stability and durability of family loyalty and relations, due in no small measure to the fact that the marriage pledge betokens less the sanctity of a vow of fidelity before God and man than a convenient and expedient verbal formula.

A similar attitude is reflected in the widespread cynicism observable on many campuses toward the question of honesty in exams. Recent studies confirming the existence of extensive cheating in college classrooms mirror statistically what is basically an underlying philosophy of life—an attitude reflected in the retort of a student to his professor, who, at the outset of the term, had announced his intention to build a spirit of teamwork in his class and who would, therefore, conduct all tests and examinations on the basis of the honor system: "O.K., Professor. You have the honor, and we'll have the system."

There was a time, however, when a Jewish community, less sophisticated and less formally educated than ours, took very seriously the biblical mandate, *motza sefateha tishmor veassita,* "that which goeth forth from thy lips, shalt thou observe and do." A Jew's word was sincerely considered his bond. In fact, our forefathers were naïve enough (!) to believe that the word was so sacred that God Himself employed it as His creative instrument. "By ten utterances," said the sages, "was the world brought into being," and the Ten Commandments, they added, "were given to correspond to these ten sayings of Creation." Speech was God's special gift to man. In interpreting Genesis 2:7, "And He [i.e., God] breathed into his nostrils the breath of life and man became a living being [*nefesh haya*]," Targum Onkelos, which is the authoritative Aramaic version, translates "And there was in man the power of speech [*leruah m-malloh*]." Rashi puts it somewhat more explicitly: "Cattle and beasts are also designated as *nefesh haya*, but the soul of man is the most highly developed of all of them because to him was granted understanding and speech." The same high regard for man's unique capability of communication is also reflected in medieval religious philosophy in which the species man is commonly designated as "the speaking one."

Scriptural and rabbinic writings are replete with mandates and injunctions regarding the sanctity of the word. "The lips of truth shall be established forever," states the Book of Proverbs, "but the lying tongue is but for a moment." "They bend their tongue, their bow of falsehood," the Prophet Jeremiah whips at his people, "and they are grown mighty in the land, but not for truth." "Let your yea be yea and your nay be nay. Let your yea and your nay both be righteous," admonish the rabbis. "Do not speak with your mouth what you do not have in your heart." Raba said, "Jerusalem was destroyed of old only because men of truth ceased to be in its midst." The public-relations cultists of Madison Avenue are challenged by the rabbis "It is prohibited to steal the minds of men, even the minds of heathens." Innocent gossipers who relish the tidbits and titillations of slander are warned by the Talmud, "The slanderer is considered as if he denied God. His sin is so great that . . . God says of him, 'He and I cannot live together in the same world.' " And for the self-righteous devotee of uncompromising candor, the person who insists that he is interested only in telling the truth—invariably about others—the commentators on the Torah point out that in the enumeration of God's Thirteen Attributes of Divine Mercy, God is spoken of first as *rav hesed,* "abounding in loving-kindness," and then as *ve'emet,* "abounding in truth." That is to say, let your motivation for truth be love and kindness, not hate or cruelty. A Hasidic rabbi put it another way: Frankness is a coveted virtue when it is impelled by the desire to help others, not yourself. It is characteristic of the respect of the Jewish tradition for the sanctity of the word that we are bidden to recite thrice daily the prayerful plea, "O my Lord! Guard my tongue from evil and my lips from speaking guile."

V

Every new child that is born, remarked a philosopher, is another of nature's continuous efforts to create the perfect man. This thought is related to the rabbinic concept that every Jewish child is potentially a Jewish Messiah. Similarly, every new generation of youth can represent history's recurrent opportunity to forge the perfect society. This is the vision of Judaism and its redemptive flame. We dare not be free from the obligation of feeding its fire. It is a responsibility which rests in the hands of every single Jew. According to a rabbinical saying, "Whoever preserves even one human soul among men is counted as if he had preserved a whole world." Every single individual incorporates in his very being the ultimate reason and purpose for the existence of the whole world. But the soul which we are bidden to preserve must be not only that of another but also our very own. For when a Jew has a profound, not a superficial, a genuine, not a specious, concern for the redemption and fulfillment of his own life, he cannot help but be vitally concerned with the redemption and fulfillment of the life of his fellowman.

"In my youth," said the sage of yesterday, "when the call to God's service came to me, I resolved not to rest until I had gathered all of my brethren throughout the world under the banner of God's presence. . . . Now, as I survey the shambles of my ambition from the sobering perspective of my approaching end of days, I realize where I made my first and biggest mistake. I should have done much more with myself."

9. Judaism as a Source of Social Values

ARTHUR J. LELYVELD

Transient Isms and Abiding Values

THE QUEST FOR an explanation of the cosmos, though somewhat abandoned in the first half of the twentieth century, has been one of the great human preoccupations throughout history. Emerging in early Greek philosophy, it spurred the pre-Socratics to look for an overarching substance or explanation. It led to the development of systematic thought such as that of Aristotle, dominated Spinoza's attempt to demonstrate geometrically a complete explanation of the universe that would account for the moral aspirations of man and the great phenomena of the universe itself, and motivated Kant's efforts to construct a comprehensive system founded upon his despair of proving the existence of God, yet finding his way back to eternal absolutes through systematic thought.

The emphasis of the second half of the nineteenth century seemed to shift from a drive to explain the total cosmos toward a drive to validate an ideal arrangement of society. This, too, has been a human preoccupation which can be traced through the whole heritage of philosophy, from Plato through the Marxian derivations from Hegelianism to twentieth-century instrumentalism.

But just as man has looked for completeness in his overarching explanations, so men have frequently distrusted the neat categories of systematic thought. Time and again throughout the history of the human quest, a mood has struggled for expression which found voice in Walt Whitman's cry, "I charge that there be no theory or school founded out of me!" [1]—a distrust of schools and theories, of systems and all "isms."

This distrust of the "ism," of the neat categorization, can, in its most developed form, be found in Jewish thought. For Walt Whitman's prescient statement of what was to develop into a twentieth-century despair of systems is deeply akin to the distrust of systems evident in Judaism.

I

Judaism has always stressed the "inner dialogue." Judaism has distrusted systemization because our heritage has always evidenced an awareness of the fullness and complexity of life. We have always agreed with the biblical statement that the *nistarot,* the secrets of the universe, are for God; only the revealed things are for man.[2]

The universe has a dynamic quality. According to the *Siddur,* God "reneweth daily the work of creation." Judaism testifies to the growth that is present in the life of mankind and declares not that "all is flux" but that "all is development." The very word "Juda*ism*" is artificial. It implies a systematic ordering that does not exist. *Yahadut,* an abstract term used to translate "Judaism" into Hebrew, is a late coinage. Judaism stresses not an "ism" but an inner dialogue conditioned by the group's historic experience. It offers us not a system of thought but an inherited code of conduct—a code of conduct that claims our commitment and embodies what may be called "values," the factors which determine our judgments of right and wrong.

But is it possible to speak of distinctive Jewish "values"? Can we say of certain concepts or value clusters that they are distinctly or uniquely "Jewish"? Or is the term "Jewish" to be applied with equal validity to any act performed or any thought expressed by a Jew? This is not an artificial question. It is debated with intensity among Jews everywhere, and especially in Israel today. Many Israelis feel that to speak of distinctive Jewish values is *narishkeit.*

Everything Jews do, whether good or bad, is distinctively Jewish. The excesses of the Maccabees, particularly in the time of Yannai, or the brutality of the incident at Kibya, too, were acts performed by Jews and must therefore be characterized as "Jewish." If one wants to determine what is Jewish, one has to look at what Jews do and think.

My thesis is that there are abounding significant and distinctive values in that complex which we call our Jewish heritage. In fact, one distinctiveness of Jewish history may be the fact that the formulation and expression of moral ideas and spiritual values have been the major business of the Jew.

We have neither built great physical structures nor excelled in the graphic arts. Our major instrument of cultural expression has been the *word*. Even our music has been geared to enhancing and decorating the word. Hayim Greenberg once said, "Upon vast expanses of time and apparently out of nothing more than memories, strivings and aspirations, our people created such grand structures as the Babylonian Talmud, the palaces of Kabbalah and Hassidism, the gardens of medieval philosophy and poetry, the self-discipline and inspirational ritualism of the Shulchan Aruch, the color and aroma of Sabbath and holidays." [3] Greenberg used the word "structures" to describe these creative expressions of the Jewish people. Yet when we look for the central instrument of Jewish self-expression, we look for the word. We look into Jewish literature.

Virtually all concerns and dimensions of Jewish life and experience have found expression in that literature. From the war song of Deborah in the fifth chapter of Judges, a violent expression of the primitive exaltation of force; from the horrible cry for vengeance concluding the beautiful 137th Psalm which begins with the touching lament, "By the waters of Babylon, there we sat and wept," but ends with a revolting anathema against those who despoiled Israel and carried the people of Israel into captivity; from the cynicism of Kohelet, abandoning the quest for meaning, and taking, as it were, an existentialist point of view, "whatever thy hand findeth to do, do it with all thy might," because everything is vanity and there is no way to find meaning behind the cosmos— from these rejected and unrepresentative ideas to the preservation of every minority viewpoint in talmudic literature, almost every variant of human thought and emotion can be found in Jewish literature.

Nevertheless, certain ideas emerge as central, approved by the folk and by tradition over the millennia. They are what can be called "normative" ideas—they are the mainstream of Jewish thought.

The values in the Jewish heritage which I would consider most important may differ significantly from those to which others would accord the highest position on their scale. Yet no one can in good faith and on the basis of adequate study claim that Jewish tradition contains antithetical or contradictory values which can be considered normative.

It is, for instance, a truism that Jewish thought exalts gentleness over brutality. Nevertheless, the 137th Psalm illustrates the fact that sentiments of vengeance and cruelty can be found in Jewish tradition, too. However, the 137th Psalm is an atypical expression of a natural longing, an infantile yet understandable straining by the writer of the psalm after the most brutal thing he could say. The brutalities in our tradition must be seen as human failure. They are there because of the fact that our tradition preserves the good and the bad. Despite these lapses, the approved and central ideas and values become clear as we study that tradition.

It should be added that more important than the value *terms* we possess are the value *judgments* in the tone of the words—the "feeling center" of meaning in the rich associations with which Jewish tradition surrounds these words.[4]

This dimension of language was seen by Suzanne Langer, for whom words are "charged symbols."[5] This is especially true of value terms and words which deal with relationship. Ludwig Lewisohn wrote,

> Words are purest incantation,
> Summoning forth the heart of things,
> As on the morning of creation
> The magic word both says and sings.[6]

Language not only "says," or points, it "sings," or expresses. This is why value terms are rarely translatable.

The "cluster words" of Jewish tradition belong in this category. *Kadosh* is not "holy." *Mitzvah* is not "command." *Derekh eretz* is not "good manners." Hayim Greenberg, in an address given before the World Zionist Congress and later reprinted in his posthumous collection, *The Inner Eye,* both distinguishes between designative and expressive language and correctly perceives the role of central value terms when he says: ". . . a Jew who can name all the plants in Israel in Hebrew, or call all the parts of a tractor . . . by their correct designations (in new Hebrew coinages) possesses one qualification for useful service in the State of Israel. . . . But if he does not know to their deepest soundings and in their context of spiritual tensions such Hebrew expressions as *mitzvah, averah, Geulah, tikkun . . . kiddush hashem . . . teshuvah,* he cannot carry a part in that choir that gives voice . . . to 'the Jewish melody.' " [7] These are the true cluster words: they are not simply emotive in expressing the feeling of the speaker or that which he seeks to induce in the listener; they are words which are charged with referents which fuse. They are, to use Wheelwright's terminology, "multisignitive." [8]

II

An immediate example of this distinction between the terms and their overtones is the first value I consider central to Jewish distinctiveness: *kedushah.* The term is untranslatable. It is not caught by the English words "holiness" or "sanctification." It is one of those magic words that can be understood only in the context of manifold associations with which Jewish thought surrounds it. *Kedushah,* a noun, is related to *kadosh,* a term which, in its earliest associations in Scripture, carries with it the aura of untouchability, the tabu idea, the kind of "sanctity" that threatens the person who comes near it with the power inherent in it. But from this primitive notion we rise to the great nineteenth chapter of Leviticus with its injunction, "Ye shall be *kadosh (kedoshim),* for I the Lord am *kadosh,*" [9] and to the remarkable verse where God is represented as saying, "And I shall become *kadosh* among the people of Israel." [10] What can we do or what can our situation produce that will make God *kadosh?* A unique notion seems to emerge at this point: in some way the reputation of God is in our hands! The ideas of *kiddush hashem* and its alternative, *hillul hashem,* tell us that we can make the reputation of the name of God *kadosh* or that we can destroy the reputation of God by our acts. *Kiddush hashem* is usually translated as "sanctification of the Name," but this rendition, like most translations, is inadequate. It means the protection of the *kedushah* of God. That quality which God seeks to find in us, *kedushah,* must by our acts be demonstrated to be part of God's nature. *We* must so live that God will be regarded as *kadosh* by mankind.

Jewish thought progresses from *kiddush hashem* to *kiddush hahayim,* from investing God's name with *kedushah,* to making the whole of life *kadosh.* To mistreat our fellowman, Jew or non-Jew, means not only to engage in an immoral act and to destroy our own reputation; in a deeper sense, it is a failure to testify truly to the nature of God. For this reason, the term *kiddush hashem*—protecting the reputation of the Divine—became the common term for martyrdom. The supreme example of a concern for the name of God is evidenced when a man is willing to give up his life for the ideals he associates with the *kedushah* of God.

A second value present throughout Jewish tradition is captured in the word *mitzvah. Mitzvah* refers to those injunctions of God that grow directly out of the concept of *kedushah.* Conduct becomes the most important method of exemplifying man's relationship to the Divine. Thus conduct becomes even more important than creed. The great prophetic emphasis on deed finds its full development in rabbinic thought. The first chapter of Isaiah asks the ringing question, "Who has required it of your hands to trample my courts? New moon and Sabbaths—I cannot abide iniquity along with the solemn assembly. Wash you, make you clean, put away the evil of your doing from before mine eyes; cease to do evil, learn to do good, seek justice, relieve the oppressed." [11] And Micah summarizes, "It has been told you, O man, what is good and what the Lord requires of you—only to do justly and to love mercy and to walk humbly with your God." [12]

The rabbinic elaboration of these ideas leads to the formulation of the principle that it is not the exposition of ideas which is mean-

ingful—*lo hamidrash ikkar ela ha-ma-asseh* [13]—but the performance of deeds. The development of a pattern of conduct which
preserves the group's values and which itself grows out of these
values is summed up in the concept of *mitzvah:* God Himself is
enjoining upon man a pattern of action founded on ideals which
are drawn from experience and a concept of the ultimate nature of
things.

This experience of the people through thirty centuries has conditioned a third value which has characterized Jewish life—a value
described not by a single word but by a phrase: the "slaves in
Egypt" motif in Jewish thought.

No one can read our liturgy or literature without discovering a
striking and almost disproportionate emphasis on the Exodus from
Egypt. We remember not only at the Seder but on every single
Sabbath that we came out of Egyptian servitude. We constantly
hark back to the time when our ancestors were persecuted bonds-
men, slaves in Egypt [14]—a stance that differs radically from the
normal human striving to find in one's background the *yihus* of
great scholars, warriors, or thinkers, or the pride associated with
the claim that one's ancestors came over on the Mayflower
or were the first to amass great fortunes or rise to high positions.

The Jew does not acclaim this kind of glory in his past. He says,
"My ancestors were humble slaves. And from this fact I am to
learn how to shape my conduct so as to be sensitive to the needs
of others. Precisely because they did it to me in Egypt, I must
learn not to do it to others."

In this insight lies the origin of the golden rule, which, though
widely quoted, is rarely understood in its fullness because many
people identify it solely with verse 17 of the nineteenth chapter of
Leviticus, "Thou shalt love thy neighbor as thyself," but fail to
read on to its completion in verse 34, "The stranger that so-
journeth with you shall be unto you as the home-born among you,
and thou shalt love him as thyself; for ye were strangers in the
land of Egypt."

This "slaves in Egypt" motif is integrally related to a fourth
facet of the Jewish value stance, those convictions about the ultimate nature of the universe at which the Jew had arrived. These
convictions are embodied and expressed in the Jewish insistence
that there is meaning in history, that within the experience of this

people the larger meaningfulness of Providence itself is reflected, and that history labors toward a far-off goal which man may perceive dimly but which must become the focus and pattern of his striving. The redemptive theme in history centers in Jewish thought in the notion of *aharit ha-yamim,* the end of days, the projection of perfection into the future. That this golden age of the future will be characterized by peace and by social justice is a distinctive Jewish notion. Man is to work for and look ahead to a time when men will beat their swords into plowshares and their spears into pruning hooks, when, as Micah puts it, "They shall sit every man under his own vine and under his fig tree; and none shall make them afraid." [15]

A fifth concept which must be ranked among the primary values that have shaped Jewish thought is the concept of *tzelem elohim,* the idea of the image of God in man. Ben Azzai may well have been right in choosing this concept as the *kelal gadol,* that verse in Scripture that is the all-inclusive principle of Jewish thought. For Ben Azzai found it in the first verse of the fifth chapter of Genesis, which begins, "This is the book of the generations of man,"—a verse that discloses its full significance in its concluding half— "when God created man, in the image of God created He him." [16]

The idea that God's image exists in every man must inevitably condition our attitude toward our fellowmen and society. All other values of the Jewish heritage—love, justice, truth, and everything else—can be said to be founded on this primary value.

The value tone of Jewish thought is captured, then, in this triple emphasis: the reputation, as it were, of God in the world, the sanctity of the individual, and the vision of the good society. Whoever sees God's image in man must inescapably be concerned about social justice. He must be concerned about the dispossessed, the stranger, and the weak. Whoever respects God's image in man cannot possibly become guilty of callousness toward the suffering of any being anywhere. This value tone can be expressed in a single word: *rahmanut,* tenderness—a response that lies at the heart of all Jewish tradition.

Miguel de Unamuno, the Spanish novelist, scholar, and philosopher, wrote in his book *The Tragic Sense of Life:* "A human soul is worth all the universe, someone—I know not who—has said, and has said magnificently." [17] The Jew who knows his tradition could tell him who had said this magnificently. For we are told in *Mishnah Sanhedrin* that mankind began with the creation of a single man in order to teach us that the preservation of a single human soul is equivalent to the preservation of the entire world. *Ha-mekayyem nefesh ahat keilu kiyyem olam moley,* a human soul is worth all the universe! [18]

This concern for the individual is not achieved at the expense of the group. Another distinctive quality of Jewish thought comes to modify our thinking at this point—the Jewish gift for paradox. The Jewish esteem for the individual did not lead Jewish tradition to embrace anarchy any more than Jewish respect for the community led to repression or neglect of the individual. Balanced respect for both ends of the scale is the product of this gift for paradox. Evidenced time and again in Jewish thought, the idea has been given contemporary expression by Martin Buber. According to Buber, the Jew sees reality as something about which it is not always possible to be logical. Logically, as Buber points out, one may say that *A* cannot coexist with non-*A*. Yet in life, *A* and non-*A* often exist side by side. Logic says that only one of two contraries can be true, yet in the reality of life, as man lives and experiences it, they are frequently inseparable. In the unity of the contraries is the heart of the mystery.

Buber illustrates this thought by his comment on the great paradox of Akiba which affirms both God's power to foreknow all that will happen and, at the same time, man's freedom to choose— *Hakol tzafui vehar'shut netunah.* "The person who makes the decision knows that his deciding is no self-delusion," Buber says. "But the person who has acted knows that he was and is in the hand of God, and there is no contradiction." [19]

It is characteristically Jewish to grasp both horns of the dilemma and force them together, to insist that all that is given us in structure and thought may be seen from many perspectives, and that the different facets presenting themselves to us at different times may be equally real. Thus, Hillel's paradox exalting both self-love ("If I am not for me, who will be for me?") and responsibility to the community ("But if I am for myself alone, what am I?") contradicts those who set up society as the antithesis of the individual and attempt to convince us that we cannot have both economic justice and individual freedom, and that, since we must choose, we must recognize that the search for self-realization is bourgeois and outmoded. It is an answer also to William White's call to swing the pendulum back to the individual as an antidote to the menacing characteristics of the organization man. It affirms that the aphorism, "In the place where there are no men, strive thou to be a man," is as valid as the aphorism, "Do not separate thyself from the community."

This tension or balance between the individual and the group can best be understood by pinning down the point at which, throughout Jewish history, the Jew rose in resistance to the power of the state.

Jews have been a compliant people in many respects. Shakespeare said of us, with a measure of justification, "Sufferance is the badge of all our tribe." At times we were willing to say *dina de-malkhuta dina*—in certain respects the law of the land becomes the guide of our lives. But there is a point at which the authority of the state must be resisted. Nathan accepts the authority of David until David uses it to bring about the death of Uriah so that he may satisfy his lust for Bathsheba. Elijah stands up to King Ahab after the power of the monarchy has been misused by Jezebel to slay Naboth and appropriate his vineyard. The Maccabees rebel against the Syrians when Antiochus seeks to force his paganism upon the Jews. The Jews are patient with Rome until they are denied the right to teach and hand down their tradition. Their resistance arises at the point at which they might have been forced into the shedding of blood, into abominable practices that desecrate the image of God in man, or into paganism and idolatry. The point of resistance is always the same: it is reached when the state threatens to defile the image of God in man or to infringe upon man's right to preserve his ideals and convictions.

III

These are some of the abiding values of the Jewish heritage. Are they relevant to our times, meaningful for our own lives in the world in which we live?

In the history of Jewish thought, many "isms" can be found—Pharisaism, Sadduceeism, Karaism, Zionism, Reconstructionism, Reformism. I would define "isms" as systems or movements devised to fit specific circumstances and proposed as answers to certain specific needs. The proponents and disciples of each of these "isms" have usually felt that it represented a permanent strand in the fabric of Jewish life. But times change, and most "isms" which arose in Jewish history have disappeared.

The "isms" outside the Jewish orbit have an equally transient character. Marxism, for instance, was attractive to many young Jews and especially to university students during the last generations because it seemed to incorporate some of the redemptive hopes found in Jewish tradition. It proclaimed a *Heilsgeschichte* in materialistic terms; it represented an attempt to explain human history as a history of redemption. Engels, in his *Anti-Dühring,* places great stress upon the interplay between matter and motion. Yet today the meaning of materialism itself has been radically changed by the advance of knowledge. The distinctions between matter and spirit, matter and energy, matter and motion have largely been obliterated by post-Einsteinian physics. Just as its philosophical underpinnings have been cut from under it, so Marxism's pretensions to an ideal society have been exposed in all their hollowness in the totalitarian systems of our day.[20]

The same can be said of another nineteenth-century "ism"—capitalism. There have been repeated attempts to prove that the economic system of the United States can no longer be described as "capitalism." This claim may be largely true. What we have is a developing new form to fit new conditions, which may in some respects be better described as "corporate" or "managerial" collectivism than as "private initiative." It is precisely for this reason that any attempt to find in Jewish thought an endorsement of any particular system of government or pattern of economics would be a futile endeavor.

Human situations and the complexities of human requirements shift from generation to generation. The simple tribal organization of the desert, for instance, which conditioned the growth of prophetic thought, may have been marked by values which could today be considered democratic. But the desert form of organization has little relevance to the needs of a multinational, industrialized, technological state of 200 million people. Moreover, it is just as possible to conceive of a monarchical, capitalistic, or socialistic form of government that would be marked by respect for the individual and his human freedom, as it is to conceive of the antithetical alternatives of capitalist or socialist states in which no respect for the image of God in man exists.

The forms change, but the values live. It is our task to make these values our own by studying the past, by reworking what we drew from it in the crucible of our own experience, and by applying it to the social issues and concerns of our own day.

The Book of Jonah, for example, contains a significant message of concern for the people of Nineveh. Jonah is not a story about a whale. The "great fish" is merely a *deus ex machina,* a device to make the story go on; but it is irrelevant to the essential meaning of the book. One of the reasons for reading the book on Yom Kippur afternoon is its dramatization of the universality of God's mercy. The people of Nineveh were the very people who had destroyed the ancient state of Israel; yet the children of Israel are instructed by the Book of Jonah that these very "enemies" are not beyond the range of God's justice and mercy.

What relation does such a notion have to our lives? Our newspapers contain daily reports of famine and suffering, of malnutrition and starvation—be it in Haiti, India, Biafra, or some other part of the world. What are these countries to us? What are we to them? What were the people of Israel to Nineveh? Suffering and malnutrition, the death by starvation of thousands upon thousands in some parts of the world should be as much my concern as the bloodshed on the borders of Israel or the suffering of my own family.

Or read one page in the *Talmud Masehta Arakhin,* dealing with *lashon hara*—slander, the evil tongue. And then consider the character assassinations which have become part and parcel of our political and sometimes of our personal lives, and attempt to understand what the Jewish ideal of respect for the image of God in man may have to say about insinuation and innuendo as being equivalent to bloodshed.

Or think of the great *Midrash* which contrasts God's creative power with the work of a human manufacturer of coins. A maker of human coinage uses one seal, one mold, to turn out coins each of which is essentially like every other coin. But God creates man in the image of God. He, too, uses just one seal, yet no two individuals are alike. Every human being has a distinctive personality or, in the phrase used in our Holy Day liturgy, *hotem yad kol adom bo,* the thumbprint, the distinctive individual seal of every man, is in God's book of life.[21] Hold this concept up against the trend toward mediocrity in contemporary society, its crowd culture, the menace of the faceless multitude, to understand how relevant Jewish tradition can be to contemporary issues.

IV

I have emphasized, among Jewish values, *kedushah, mitzvah,* the "slaves in Egypt" motif, insistence on meaning, and the *tzelem elohim* ideal producing respect for the sanctity of the individual and the rights of all men. Leaving all questions of psychology and epistemology aside, my credo is that as a Jew and as a human being, conditioned by my Jewish group belongingness and formed by my Jewish identity and experience, I prefer these values above all others. I prefer *kedushah* and the sanctification of life by righteous action to disdain for the holiness of life and the concern only to develop techniques and to meet the exigencies of the moment. I prefer the love of the stranger and the respect for God's image in all men to all the dehumanizing approaches that would deprive man of his individuality and thus depersonalize him and rob him of his dignity.

I prefer these values, and I know of no reliable sources for them other than the tradition in which they were born and which gave them to mankind. I know of no protection for variety and distinctiveness, no safeguard against faceless mediocrity, other than the cultivation, by each group, of that which is best in its tradition. And I know of no adequate means by which to preserve those values and to insure their presence in society so that man may attempt to live by them, other than the dedicated study of that tradition.

RICHARD J. ISRAEL
Jewish Tradition and Political Action

IN THE MORNING, if I can summon up the courage, I glance at the newspaper. I usually find it a deeply disturbing experience. First, I ask myself a question: Am I ever going to read another morning newspaper before the world goes up in smoke? Then I wonder whether there is anything I can do that may help forestall doomsday. But I don't know what makes sense. I suppose I can make gut-level decisions without any greater difficulty than anyone else; but I don't want to speak or act out of private feelings alone: I want some guidance. One of the areas I want some guidance from is my Jewish tradition. What kind of resources are available to me as, in the words of Maurice Pekarsky, "a human-being-born-Jew?" In what sense does my being a Jew give me help, direction, or purpose?

I

First of all, what kind of a resource is the Bible for me? Some people believe the Bible is full of solutions to the most contemporary kinds of problems. All we need to do is search the Book, and its words will tell us how to behave and what is right. But one can prove so much from the Bible, that one can prove very little. Is the Bible in favor of peace? Of course: "And they shall beat their swords into plowshares, and their spears into pruning hooks. Nation shall not lift up sword against nation, neither shall they

189

learn war any more" (Isa. 2:4). But what of the Bible on war? It is in favor of that, too. We read: "Prepare war . . . let the men of war draw near, let them come up. Beat your plowshares into swords, and your pruning hooks into spears! Let the weak say: 'I am strong' " (Joel 4:9–10).

I am not attempting to suggest that the Bible does not say anything at all, but only that it is a very difficult book to use today. There is a clear message in the Bible that God is near, that He cares, and that He reacts to reward or to punish when something He cares about happens. God cares that man fulfill his ritual and ethical obligations. These obligations are very specific. Thus, it is wrong to muzzle an ox when he is threshing. One must not eat shellfish. It is wrong to gather wood on the Sabbath. One must leave the corners of the fields for the poor to gather. One must return a lost ox to its owner.

Yet, if there is any overriding religious theme in our own age, it is that God is far and that God is silent. Moreover, because we have lost the feeling that we know what God wants, we have lost our sense of sin. The Bible thus is not a readily available source of social or religious values for us today. It contains many passages whose tremendous force we can still feel, but it cannot be easily used as if it were a contemporary document. Any book is great, among other reasons, because its words have resonances which reach far beyond themselves and their simple meaning. That does not give us the right, however, to make the Bible say whatever we want it to say. Its contemporary use is too often that of a literary flourish. We know what we are trying to prove, and handily quote a first-rate verse which works out beautifully in the last paragraph. The Bible, unless used with great caution, is not so much a source of values as it is a decoration to give apparent substance to values we already have.

II

There is another source of Jewish social values that ought to be more promising: the halakhah, the legal system of the rabbinic tradition which had to respond to the continuing needs of the community as it confronted day-to-day problems. Halakhah is supposed to embrace all the Jew's life, from the first moment of his waking when he washes his hands as an act of purification, until he says the *Shema* just before he goes to sleep. During the day, the halakhic Jew is reminded of his obligation to God and his fellowmen in countless ways. He has to recite at least a hundred blessings a day. There are foods which he may and may not eat. How he may conduct his business is clearly prescribed. His sexual relations with his wife and his conduct toward his children are designated.

People argue that religion should not deal with all these trivial details. But generalities are a very dangerous guide for anything. A well-known story tells of a preacher whose congregation, overwhelmed with the beauty of his sermon on the subject, "Thou shalt not steal," became angry and indignant the following week when he preached on the subject, "Thou shalt not steal chickens." I do not know what others may need; but I need sermons on not stealing chickens. To give an example of another sort: even though the United States Constitution is a splendid document, which I endorse with enthusiasm, it is only because the City of New Haven (where I live) has a law against parking in front of fire hydrants, that I manage with some reasonable degree of consistency to do what I know I ought to do. A law educates with a force that a publicity campaign or a general moral pronouncement alone does not possess.

I speak thus of the halakhah to describe some of the enormous appeal it has for me. I can take its authority seriously as far as it goes. The problem is that it does not go far enough. I do not think that it is adequate to deal with the really important problems of our day, the problems which may determine whether or not we are here tomorrow to *daven shacharit,* properly slaughter another chicken, or give to the United Jewish Appeal. For, while the halakhah is a comprehensive and sophisticated code of law that deals impressively with the interpersonal, aids in the development of the inner life of the individual, and promotes harmony in the Jewish community, its main concern with the world at large is, How we can minimize damage to the Jewish community from the non-Jewish community? It is almost totally apolitical in any sense in which we know modern politics.

The halakhah can tell me in great detail how I should conduct myself personally with fellow pacifists, vegetarians, or United States Marines. It cannot tell me which group, if any, I have an obligation to join, except perhaps to say, "Don't do anything dangerous for yourself or the Jews."

To extend my position even further: if the religious parties of Israel suddenly found themselves with an electoral majority and had to assume full responsibility for the direction of the government with all its modern problems, they would undoubtedly want to govern in a way which could assume that responsibility and, at the same time, would be consistent with Jewish law. Yet the body of law that would permit them to do so does not presently exist.

One of the most salient features of contemporary Jewish life is that this is the first time that large Jewish communities have existed without any form of legally recognized self-government. Though there were variations, the basic pattern until the breakup of the ghettos was that the Jewish community was responsible for its own tax collections, its own internal civil litigation, and its own criminal litigation aside from capital crimes and some crimes affecting the crown. The *individual* Jew had no *rights* in a given place. The *Jewish community* had a number of *privileges* that were generally granted directly by the reigning monarch and in which individual Jews participated. When rabbis throughout the Middle Ages cited the verse in *Pirkei Avot* that one should pray for the peace of the government, for without it men would swallow each other alive, they were describing their own situation accurately. They felt they were continually living on the verge of a disaster. Any sudden change in government or governor was likely to have serious implications for the Jew. Governments were viewed as frail, temporary structures which could not be relied upon. Not only were they empirically unstable; theologically they were trivial as well. No institution that was not divinely authorized in the Torah could make any truly serious claim upon the Jew. Furthermore, all governments would be overturned at the coming of the Messiah. The only important law was Jewish law, halakhah, which they could take with them wherever they fled. It was a law not attached to any land.

It strikes me as noteworthy that the discussion in the Shulhan Arukh concerning the fact that the Jew is obligated to pay taxes is part of the discussion of thievery. Its context is the question whether or not taxes are theft and, thus, whether or not we are obligated to pay them. If they are theft, we are not obligated. It is concluded that taxes are not theft if they are parceled out in non-discriminatory fashion. If a man's primary concern about the state is whether or not it is an honest and justifiable institution, he is certainly not going to pay much attention to its general welfare and still less to the problems between states. Within such a context it is not surprising that we have no theology of the state that would parallel the literature of the Roman Catholic church. Once, two thousand years ago, we began to develop such a theology; but since we have seldom been close to the sources of power, we have not continued to develop an adequate rationale for dealing with it.

Thus, if we want to find out what to do about communism, air pollution, or urban renewal, we are not going to find out from Jewish law. I am not saying that this material cannot be developed. I am making a plea that it should be. It should be developed quickly, too, before halakhah is relegated, even by those who care, to the realm of the unimaginably trivial. Whether or not swordfish have scales, whether marshmallows are kosher, and how high a *mehitzah* should be are not questions which will save either Judaism or the world. To relegate the totality of a glorious tradition to these kinds of questions, as most of the halakhic literature and intersynagogue warfare does, is to commit a very serious *hilul hashem,* a profanation of God's name.

III

Another source for Jewish values in addition to the biblical and the halakhic is the expediential, the Jewishly expediential. Its yardstick is a simple question: Is it good for the Jews? Let me give some examples. Even though the non-Jewish world, by and large, is quite certain that the Jewish community is monolithic and of one mind on almost every issue, we know that the real truth lies in Stephen Wise's old saw that the only thing two Jews can agree upon is what a third Jew should give to charity. How much more startling, then, when we come across an issue upon which Jews in the United States really were unified: namely, that there should not be prayers, denominational or otherwise, in the public schools, and that we really are not very enthusiastic about Christmas celebrations sponsored by public institutions. The Supreme Court seems to have agreed with the Jewish community. Of interest to me, however, is the nature of the Jewish community's argument: that we must maintain the wall of separation between church and state which alone permits a pluralistic American people to dwell together in harmony.

Where did we get this argument? Not from Jewish tradition, which would hold that the complete permeation of learning with religious values is the ideal. Jews never believed in the separation of religion and state. Traditionally, a state in which all the laws and lawgivers would be religious would be the best kind. If there is any idea that is remote from Judaism, it is that religion and law should be separate.

The real argument behind all the other arguments was very clear, though never explicitly stated. We did not want Christianity taught to Jewish children if we could possibly help it. This kind of sensitivity is a real source of Jewish values, values which may or may not be present in the Jewish tradition, but which are very much present in Jews. Why were Jews, in far greater numbers than any other religious group in the United States, against Senator Joseph McCarthy? He was no anti-Semite. He carefully covered himself by using Jewish assistants, Cohn and Schine, to make that point very clear. But most members of the Jewish community assumed that if full due process were not available to everyone all the time and if people were found guilty outside the courts, it would not be long before it would not be good for Jews. (I do not take this to be a cynical motivation, by the way. Enlightened self-interest is a motivation I can trust. I know how to deal with it—and cultivate it—in ways that are impossible with either altruism or avarice.)

I think a major factor motivating Jewish interest in the civil rights movement is related to this kind of enlightened self-interest. It is not the only motive, but it cannot be discounted. Not too long ago, I received a letter which cost me more than one night's sleep. It was a short letter which said, "Dear Rabbi Israel: Congratulations for your civil rights efforts. You have come to our town, marched on our streets, prayed on our court-house steps and been imprisoned in our jail. Now you have returned to New Haven from your mission of justice to the warmth of your home. It may interest you to know that thanks to you and your colleagues' splendid efforts, last evening our city hosted the largest Klan meeting in southwestern Georgia in the past twenty years. As a Jewish merchant whose customers have already expressed their warm interest in your prayers, I thought you would want to know how much peace and comfort your spiritual efforts produced for those of us who find in the South a home and not a place to make headlines. Sincerely. . . ." What do I answer a man like this? Here I was, a cheap hero, while he had to suffer for my conscience. One thing that I cannot do is write him off as a bigot and forget him.

My only answer to this man—and it is not a short-range answer and will be of no consolation if his customers stop coming or if someone puts a match to his stock—is to recall the words of the German Pastor Niemoeller: "When they arrested the labor leaders, I was not a labor leader. When they arrested the communists, I was not a communist. When they arrested the Jews, I was not a Jew. And when they arrested me, it was too late." Freedom is indivisible. If your freedom is in danger, then so is mine. When the Negroes in southwest Georgia are full participants in American democracy, then my correspondent will not have to live in fear for the welfare of his family and his business. Injustice never stops with someone else. When it is bad for others, the Jew will soon feel it, too. From our concern for Jewish self-preservation, we have come to care for the virtue of society as a whole.

IV

There is yet another source of our values: our marginal status, the fact that we live in two cultures at once. We are Jews because we have a unique law, a unique past, and a curious contemporary history. In short, we are a peculiar people. There is the story of the Hasid from a New York yeshiva who went to gather funds in a little Southern town. When he got off the train, the children of the town took one look at his beard and earlocks, his broad-brimmed hat, and his long, dark coat and began to follow him down the street with curiosity. The Hasid turned around in annoyance and said to them, "What's the matter? You've never seen a Yankee?"

Let us analyze this story. First of all, the Hasid really does feel like a Yankee. He is much more at home in his own New York environment than he is in the little town. If, like many Hasidim, he was born in this country, he is distinctly different from his fellow Hasidim, say, in Jerusalem, and they would look upon him in a sense as a Yankee, as affected by the American environment. But tell that to the children of the town and their response would surely be, "Man, you're the funniest Yankee we have ever seen."

Yet I am that Yankee. I feel like an American, and my Americanism is an important part of me. When I visit other countries, people look upon me primarily as an American; but, to my fellow Americans, I am a very special sort of American.

If anyone thinks that Jews in America are viewed just like everyone else, he ought to pause for a moment and consider the following question: What if the assassin of President John F. Kennedy had been a Jew? Would this have affected the Jewish community in exactly the same way Protestants were affected by the accusation of Lee Harvey Oswald? Perhaps I am an alarmist. I am sure we would all have survived. Nevertheless, the thought sends shivers down my spine.

I would assert that a unique aspect of Jewish community life outside Israel (and I am not altogether sure about Israel, either) is that we are marginal. We are almost, but not quite, full citizens of the countries in which we live. Though our legal rights are full, we still feel a sense of "we" and "they." Young people feel this less than their parents, and the parents less than their parents, but the feeling is there. From this feeling of marginality emerge many attitudes of the Jewish community.

Why does such a large percentage of Jews go to college as compared with non-Jews? There are two ways in this world to achieve status. One is to *be* someone important, the other is to *do* something important. Since we do not have the pedigree to be important, we have to do important things, and one of the best ways to do important things is to be a professional. Education is the quickest way up.

Do so many Jewish students go into medicine because of the Jewish insistence upon learning? What Jews used to study were traditional texts. If learning for its own sake were the goal, one might assume that as many Jewish students would study to be rabbis as doctors; but, as the old story goes, being a rabbi is no profession for a nice Jewish boy. Is it a question of healing and social welfare? Why, then, are Jewish girls as underrepresented in nursing as Jewish men are overrepresented in medicine? I would submit that medicine is viewed as offering quick social status, a good living with security, and the independence from the non-Jewish community which comes from self-employment. In short, Jewish marginality conditions our educational aspirations.

But it is not only Jewish doctors who are the products of Jewish marginality. The entire structure of the American Jewish community has, by and large, been created to provide uniquely American organizations to help us feel comfortable as Jews. The defense organizations, using the stated values of American democracy as a justification, that is, that all Americans should have an equal chance, have organized to protect the lot of the Jew in America.

Since all good Americans must belong to some kind of church, Jews who have very little concern for the religious values of Judaism join the synagogue, which then serves as their locus of secular Jewish identity. We have taken an American institution, the Protestant church, and utilized it so that we can feel at home in America and comfortable with our Jewishness. The synagogue is probably the oldest institution functioning continuously in western civilization. But to show that, for most of its members, it is still a continuation of that ancient religious institution, one would have to explain the discrepancy between the number of Jews who join the synagogue and the number who worship there.

Our Jewish marginality is a source of values for us, values that I view as positive, like our concern for education and our ability to criticize our culture because we are not quite of it. At the same time, there are less positive aspects of the same phenomenon, e.g., mandatory Sunday morning trips to the delicatessen, and Jewish golf and bridge as essential aspects of community life.

V

Thus far I have attempted to indicate a number of sources of Jewish values. I have tried to show some of the kinds of values we have derived from each of these sources as well as some of the problems each of them presents. I have suggested that I find that I can use none of them exclusively. Let me now say that the only resolution I have found to the problems I have posed is a resolution that creates as many problems as it solves. It is, however, the only one available to me—that of personal synthesis: facing the world and attempting to deal with it as best I can as a modern western man and as a concerned Jew. I use the tradition as a check on and a source of social values. It cannot present me with a rule book, much as my temperament tells me that I want one. If the tradition does not or cannot tell me explicitly whether I may endorse the use of atomic weapons or nerve gas, I might still find in it ideas that will give me help so that I am not left altogether to my own devices. One author put it rather well when he said that we could use the tradition in these areas of social concern as a goad, a guide, and a goal: a goad, in that it prods us into caring; a guide, in that it presents us with some limitations and suggested lines of action; a goal, in that it gives us a vision of the ideal future for which we are working.

I realize that I am proposing a very dangerous method. I run an enormous risk of tendentiousness, of being biased and deceitful, and of presenting my own vision of the truth as the tradition's vision. Moreover, to use such a method legitimately, I am obligated to be more Jewishly literate than I am ever likely to become.

In spite of all these qualifications, it must be this way for me. I have no alternative but to live a life of commitment plagued by great doubts. I must act without hesitancy out of information that is questionable. I know that I shall never have definite answers or even very good answers to most of the questions I am asking— not even to the important questions; but there is too much to do in the world to wait for all the answers to be in. All major decisions of my life—whether choosing a school, a wife, or an occupation—were made upon insufficient information. Yet since someone is going to be making the major decisions of my life, it might as well be me.

Let me detail some of my attempts at synthesis. I shall begin with some of the social attitudes I have derived from my tradition. I present them as truths and as traditional Jewish values, subject to the qualifications I have already stated.

I am a Jew and I am living in the twentieth century. I cannot deny either my modernity or my Jewishness. The form of government which I warmly support is western democracy. I am a liberal and a civil libertarian. I am strongly affected by the claims of my conscience, and I believe that others ought to have the right to respond to the claims of theirs. These attitudes do not make me a better Jew. They do not emerge from the Jewish tradition, yet they are part and parcel of me.

Democracy has never been a Jewish value. The messianic state was envisioned as a kind of constitutional monarchy. That people should vote regularly on important issues when the Messiah comes is unthinkable and silly. Not only in an ultimate messianic state but in the self-contained Jewish communities throughout history, democracy was the exception rather than the rule. There was voting within the governing bodies, but the representatives were rarely elected on a truly popular basis.

In the realm of civil liberties, due process and the rights of the accused are wonderfully protected by Jewish law, but freedom of speech or the press was unknown. The unconventional mind had difficulties in surviving within the community.

The appeal to conscience was irrelevant. If one is dealing with absolute truth, as the classical literature does, dissent has no place. There might be disagreement as to what the law should be or what ritual should be observed. But once the decision was made, one did exactly what the rest of the community did except within the narrowest of limitations. For example, the claim of a nonreligious person in Israel who says, "I do not believe in religious marriage, and I demand the freedom to be civilly married in accord with my own beliefs," would carry absolutely no weight in most religious circles. One should force a man to do the "right" thing even against his will.

I have grave difficulties in identifying with these aspects of my tradition because of those values of mine which I previously enumerated. But I am not only a twentieth-century American liberal. I am also a Jew, and that is also very much a part of the core of my being. So I engage myself seriously with the Jewish tradition, its texts and teachers, and in this engagement I find other positions, supplementing and challenging my western values.

It is true that Judaism is not greatly interested in democracy, but it is passionately concerned with justice. I can respond to that. The tradition does not care what kind of government there is. But it does care that people be treated fairly and equally. This forces me to pause before I try to export my form of government to another culture and another continent. It may be that two houses of Congress, a President, and a Supreme Court are the best way to govern my particular land justly, but it is by no means clear to me that it is the best or the only way to govern other lands.

I know that my own country is important to me, but I know, too, that no state is of ultimate value. The rules governing the relations between people are important, but no nation-state really is, except insofar as it promotes justice in the relationships between men. I am in favor of social legislation which will promote a more equitable distribution of the good things of this world for all men, because the welfare of the community is far more important than the right of private property. After all, the earth is the Lord's and the fullness thereof, the world and they that dwell therein (Psalm 24). It is not mine. It is the Lord's world, and He wants justice.

It is not only my life that belongs to the Lord, but the lives of all the other people in this world as well. They are not mine to take at will. The earth of my nation belongs to the Lord, and so does the earth of my nation's enemies. I find it difficult to believe that my tradition, which would not sanction the cutting down of an enemy's fruit trees at a time of siege, on the grounds that they are the Lord's, would allow the burning of wheat stores, the defoliation of jungles, or the bombing of irrigation dams; or that a tradition which insists that noncombatants be allowed to leave the scene of battle would countenance imprecise high-altitude bombing in civilian areas.

Given my tradition's reservations about nation-states, I find it hard to understand some attitudes about other nations that seem to be among my nation's patriotic requirements. Thirty years ago, all Japanese had buckteeth, wore heavy glasses, and were hideous, fanatical fiends. Now they arrange flowers, drink tea in charming rituals, and are the bulwark of democracy in Asia. The Nazis were murderers to a man. A good German did not exist.

Teutonic viciousness was a national trait. Suddenly I discover that all that Germans want to do in this world is to clink beer glasses, sing joyous songs, and hurry about, being efficient; indeed, they are the only efficient nation in Europe, and thus are responsible for the miraculous economic recovery of the continent. The Chinese, of course, have gone in the other direction, and the French should be forewarned that unless they begin to treat us with proper deference, we shall shortly begin to discover just how effete they are and that their grand manner is merely a cover-up for an inner core of rottenness.

Nowhere in this nonsense is there any assumption that the citizens of all countries are people. The common humanity that we share is the uniqueness of each man, each with his own particular combination of strengths and weaknesses which can lead him to do terrible things or lead him to do wondrously virtuous ones, regardless of whether his government and ours happen to be allies at this particular moment.

But though I do not believe that my government or nation necessarily finds more favor in God's eyes than does my neighbor's, neither do I believe that his finds more favor than mine. I have every right to defend myself. (I must be exceedingly cautious about how I utilize the notion of defense, for in the rhetoric of modern nations, both sides engaged in a war are somehow always defending themselves. No one is ever an aggressor.) If I am honestly defending myself, defense is a religious obligation. This means that I would not only be foolish but immoral to lay down my arms before an enemy. Thus I would hold that, as I understand the Jewish tradition, any kind of total unilateral disarmament without careful and tight inspection that would be enforceable is wrong. Not only would the Russians or the Chinese exploit me were I to disarm; I quite believe that we would exploit them were they to do so. The *yetzer hara,* the "evil inclination," is present in all of us. I am intrigued by the notion of peace initiatives, in which each side agrees to reduce its armaments by a significant but not all-important unit, waiting until the other side responds with a comparable act. This, I think, would be in accord with what I understand to be the Jewish view.

Again, I know that every man is created in the image of God

and that to despise my fellowman is to despise the living God. The Midrash tells me to cast myself in a fiery furnace before I consent to embarrass or humiliate my neighbor. I find that I am daily complying in the humiliation of our Negro neighbors by denying them access to the housing, education, and employment that people with white skins and the same ability are able to obtain. Thus, I must enter into the maelstrom of the demonstration with all its hazards, if it is the most effective means to gain speedy public recognition of critical issues. I know I am descended from slaves and can hardly afford to disparage others who are descended from slaves.

I am not stopped by a call for civil disobedience, for civil law has for me no metaphysical or ultimate status. Its only function is to promote peace in the land. Peace, however, is not the absence of tension but the presence of justice. If the law does not promote justice, it is not a law which I have an obligation to follow. But if I disobey, I must do so in such a way that I show my respect for what the law ought to represent. I must submit to its punishments in order to recall it to its own intentions, purposes, and obligations: the promotion of justice.

What I have attempted to suggest is that the biblical and halakhic traditions are no longer generating the kind of continuous guidance that we need for the world in which we live. The contemporary Jewish community is more likely to derive its answers to these kinds of questions from its own sociological status. We can, however, let the tradition challenge us, and we can try to respond to that challenge honestly and fully. Jewish tradition still possesses great vitality, even though it does not always provide us with complete answers. It gives us a chance to stand back from our totally contemporary perspective and view our problem through other eyes.

VI

These considerations represent a context within which one can act. What about the process of action itself? For those who are ready to act, general ground rules can be spelled out.

First of all, fight for things that matter. Second, choose areas in which you can be effective; that is, every problem can be reduced to a size that you can comprehend and do something about. I would hold that the structure can still be repaired and does not need to be thrown out. Occasionally, pick areas where you have some chance of success. They will support you through many long, lean periods. In 1950 I was with a group of students who picketed two segregated music schools in Cincinnati. After one week apiece of picketing, each of the schools capitulated, and Negro students were admitted. We were then ready to take on the world. For a starter, we went to the local amusement park to protest the fact that swimming privileges were segregated. We barely escaped with our lives. (I will always remember my indignation when they began calling the whites in the group "dirty Jews." After all, we didn't look Jewish. How did they know we all were? Later on, I became more sophisticated.) Without the earlier experience, I think the sheer physical fright induced by the second would have kept me away from the barricades for a very long time.

Next, understand your opponents. Recognize that each is a man like you with virtues and vices along with strengths and vanities. Try to imagine how you would behave if you owned his property, held his political office, or had his job. If you can do this, you stand a much better chance of being able to communicate effectively. If you treat a man as if he were a living personification of evil, the chances are that he is going to behave that way. If you treat him like a man, with motivations no less complex than your own, he may respond to you like a man. In Georgia, I found that it was much easier to be arrested than it was to confront face to face the people who opposed what I was trying to stand for. It was probably safer, too. I suspect that it was also less effective. But then I was there trying to fight the system. I now think that I should have been there trying to talk to people.

Your greatest opposition may come from your families. They are worried about the implications your actions may have for your future. They will be worried about your life and safety. Be gentle with them. Recognize that their concerns and worries are real and cannot be dismissed as trivial.

Even outside your family circle, you are not going to find sympathy in all quarters. Most infuriating of all will not be those who oppose you, but those who write you off as an immature idealist. I am personally very much in favor of clean-shaven demonstrations. But remember, whatever you do, you are going to be labeled. I was in jail with an Episcopal priest who had an ulcer and who, after twenty-four hours of fasting, just had to have Maalox and requested some from the jailer. One of the local papers reported the next day that among those arrested were junkies who couldn't live without their stuff.

To the timid I must say that though there will be those who will both fight you and ignore you, there will also be some marvelous people whom you will be very proud to know, who will support you. There will be many more who will think you are a bit extreme, but on the side of the angels anyway.

Remember that the people who express themselves have more power than the people who do not. The activists constantly worry the Establishment because it is always concerned about new trends and public opinion.

The biggest changes that will result from any action you take will take place within you. You will change your own life in ways which you may not expect. If you are not very careful, some of the changes may be for the worse. The demonstrator and direct-actionist is in grave danger of feeling like a hero with nothing but contempt for those who do not at once follow his one right way. Such a person does a rather poor job of sanctifying the name of the Lord among the multitudes. He becomes an ineffective leader and, worse, he serves as a very poor model for those who might be interested in his cause.

Rabbi Yitshak of Vorki once took his sons to see his teacher, Rabbi Bunam, who gave each of them a glass of bock beer and asked them what it was. The older boy said, "I don't know." Menahem Mendel, the younger, was asked and said, "It is bitter and good." Rabbi Bunam then turned to Menahem Mendel and said, "This one will become a great leader in Israel." If you have the stamina and the stomach, if you can take tradition and challenge it, if you can look at the world about you and force it to face up to the tradition, you will find the draught bitter and good.

Part Three

THE EXPERIENCE
OF TRADITION

ROBERT GORDIS

10. A Modern Approach to the Bible

NEARLY TWO HUNDRED years ago, the famous French philosopher Voltaire said, "The Bible is more celebrated than known." If this statement was true two hundred years ago, it is considerably truer today. The Bible is reputed to be the world's best-seller; but no one has ever claimed that it also is the world's best "reader." It is the kind of book one gives to a bar mitzvah boy, who has no choice but to accept it; and a copy is usually handed to a bride just before she walks down the aisle, but it is covered with lace so that she cannot open it. It is the kind of book everyone considers to be an ideal gift for someone else—it will do him a world of good.

I

The neglect of the Bible among Jews is largely due to the fact that its reader or student faces a number of problems as he seeks to read or understand the Bible. In the first place, there are technical difficulties. The Bible happens to be one of the world's worst-printed as well as most-printed books.

The average edition of the Bible is printed in two columns. The margin is covered with numbers, like a catalog. This arrangement may facilitate its use for reference purposes but is not likely to bring the reader closer to its contents. Prose and poetry, footnotes and genealogical material, exalted vision and the most prosaic legislation are printed in the same kind of type, cataloged chapter and verse. As a result, many sincere, devoted, and intelligent persons who may want to read the entire Bible start in the beginning but bog down somewhere in Chapter 11 of Genesis in the genealogy of Noah's children.

There is a second difficulty. The Bible is a sacred book. Yet the very fact that it is sacred to the two great religions of the western world creates a kind of aura about it: we approach it with the expectation of being edified rather than stimulated by its contents. We expect it will be good for us to read the Bible. But it rarely occurs to us that it may also be fascinating, challenging, revelatory of new facets, insights, or experiences.

Moreover, and this is fundamental, many people no longer know what attitude to adopt toward the Bible. The traditional point of view—or what passes for it—is no longer tenable for many modern Jews. Yet they have not been able to develop an approach that would be compatible with their outlook. It is of more than passing interest to define the difference between these two approaches to the Bible.

II

The first of these I call the "dogmatic" approach to the Bible. It continues to be shared by millions of devout men and women in the Jewish community as well as in the Christian world. They maintain that the Bible is literally the word of God. In every age, God selected certain men, and probably even some women, of great piety and sanctity and dictated to them His word representing His will. Therefore, the Bible is a record of God's revelation through the medium of the lawgivers, prophets, and sages whose writings have come down to us in the Bible.

The Talmud, for example, expresses this view clearly in an interesting passage dealing with the death of Moses as it is described at the end of the fifth book of the Pentateuch. The question arises immediately how Moses himself could possibly have written the story of his own death and burial. In one discussion, the Talmud attributes this passage to Joshua. However, in another, the Talmud declares that God was dictating while Moses wrote down the story of his death with a tear in his eye. From this point of view, the Bible is literally the will of God and, indeed, the very language of God. God Himself is speaking through the medium of chosen persons whose words become the record of God's plans and purposes for man.

Several important consequences follow from this dogmatic approach to the Bible.

One consequence is the belief that, if the Bible is literally the word and not merely the revelation of God, nothing in it can be unimportant. Maimonides draws this logical conclusion when he says that the description of the descendants of Esau in Genesis 37 is just as sacred as the Ten Commandments because both of them go back to the same source. There can be no difference in validity and importance between one part of the Bible and any other.

A second consequence is the belief that everything in the Bible is relevant and significant at all times and in all places. That which comes from God must apply always and everywhere. Everything is of equal and permanent importance.

This attitude toward the Bible has produced some valuable and significant fruits within Judaism. Our ancestors, convinced that the Bible was literally the word of God, found in it the instrument by which their growing religious and spiritual insights were continuously stimulated. If the Bible is the word of God, nothing outside the Bible can match or surpass what is in the Bible. Therefore, they turned to the biblical text as the source of their emerging ideas.

The Talmud, for example, is derived from the Bible through its interpretation by the rabbis. To illustrate the process of interpretation: the struggle for the emancipation of women is an important problem in the history of mankind. In ancient times, women had virtually no rights. In all ancient societies, a woman was under the power of her father, who had every right over her body and soul until she was married. From then on she was at the mercy of her husband. This was true among the Semitic peoples as well as among the Greeks and Romans. The Bible reflects this attitude to some extent. Various laws indicate that the father had power over his daughter, could marry her off and deal with her as he might choose.

But as we reach the talmudic period, the ethical sensitivity of the sages had grown beyond the idea that one human being could possibly be completely subservient to another. Therefore the rabbis decided to extend the scope of woman's rights. They achieved this goal by a simple process of interpretation. Whenever the Bible speaks of a woman in connection with her father, the word *na'arah*, "girl," is used. The rabbis defined *na'arah* as a technical term; they applied it to a girl between twelve and twelve and a half years old. Before the age of twelve, Jewish law considers her a minor, and she receives special consideration on that account. Above the age of twelve and a half, she has attained her majority. Now she is a mature person and, therefore, has certain rights and prerogatives.

Thus, by a process of interpretation of the biblical text, the words of Scripture did not confine the development of the Jewish ethical and religious tradition but, instead, stimulated its development. In the same way, a vast degree of ethical literature, called *Aggadah*, emerged in Judaism, based upon the text of the Bible.

The nature and meaning of *Aggadah* can be illustrated by a tradition based on a passage in Exodus which says that Moses was taking care of the sheep of his father-in-law, Jethro. This statement, the rabbis felt, could not have been intended to report the insignificant fact that Moses was a shepherd. It therefore became the basis for a beautiful tradition which describes how Moses was selected to become the great leader of Israel. One day, one of the sheep strayed from Moses' flock. Moses followed it over hill and dale, until it came to a brook. He noticed that the sheep was thirsty and therefore had gone there in search of water. He bent down tenderly, lifted up the sheep, and said, "Poor creature; I did not know that you were thirsty. You must be tired; let me carry you back to the flock." Whereupon a heavenly voice was heard: "Thou who art the keeper of sheep and hast shown them mercy, art worthy of being the shepherd of My people Israel." A vast ethical and religious literature grew up on the basis of the literal interpretation of the Bible as the word of God.

Other areas of Jewish culture, too, were decisively shaped by this literalistic attitude toward the Bible. Jewish philosophy, from Philo to Saadyah and Maimonides, cannot be adequately understood unless it is seen as an attempt on the part of these and other thinkers to interpret the science and philosophy of their times in terms of what they found in the text of the Bible. If the Bible is the word of God, everything we regard as true and valuable must be part of the divine revelation.

But the most significant advantage of this literal conception of the Bible is the fact that without it we would have had no Bible at all. The great books of practically every other culture have disappeared. The Bible was preserved because the Masoretes ("preservers of the text") counted the words of Scripture, used scrupulous care to copy the text as they found it, and prevented it from being subject to errors and changes. Generations of pious men and women did everything in their power, even at the risk of their lives, to preserve the Bible scrolls from destruction. Had it not been for their profound conviction that what they were saving was not just another book or manuscript but the word of God, the Bible might not have survived to the present day.

Even those of us who may not accept the "dogmatic" conception of the Bible must recognize the tremendous debt which the world and the Jewish people in particular owe to that conception for the preservation of the Bible and its development.

Nevertheless, one cannot disregard certain defects which are inherent in this approach to the Bible. It meant, for instance, that people read things into the Bible which the biblical text could hardly have been intended to imply. A manufacturer said during the Depression that he was opposed to the five-day week because it was a direct contradiction of the biblical dictum, "Six days shalt thou labor." People ought to work six days, not five. A Baptist minister once claimed that the Bible had ordained the segregation of the Negro—Noah had established it. The burning of the witches in Salem was possible only because the Puritans took the words of Scripture literally. Dangerous excesses of this kind have by no means been infrequent. They have been much less common in the Jewish tradition because for us the word of the Scripture always goes hand in hand with its interpretation.

The greatest defect of this approach is that the Bible became overlaid with a vast superstructure of exegesis and interpretation. Much of this superstructure was beautiful; all of it is worthy of being known; and a great deal of it deserves our reverence. But the Bible itself, its essential content and meaning, were lost sight of under mountains of commentaries and supercommentaries.

Therefore, a great voyage of rediscovery was required—a massive effort to clear away this vast growth and to get down to what the Bible itself said, once again to discover its authentic message.

As a result, another approach developed which, for lack of a better term, we may call the "modern" approach to the Bible.

III

Like everything that is modern and valuable, this approach was not born yesterday. Its roots are ancient. Its origins can, in fact, be found in the Talmud itself.

When the Talmud formulates the principle that the Torah speaks in the language of men, or that every passage must be understood in its simple and uncomplicated sense, it begins to lay the foundation of the modern approach to the Bible. It is an approach that wants to see what the Bible says. It wants to read the Bible, not read something into the Bible.

This voyage of rediscovery, which began with the Talmud, was continued by the great commentators of the Middle Ages. In medieval and modern times, Christian scholars contributed significantly to our understanding of the Bible, though their work has not always been free of bias—one of the penalties we pay for having our work done by others. Today, a vast amount of material is available which enables us to understand the Bible far better than the scholars of the Middle Ages did. That we are able to understand the Bible better than men like Rashi and Maimonides did, does not imply that we are greater than they were. They were intellectual giants, we are dwarfs. But even a dwarf who stands on the back of a giant will see farther than the giant himself.

One of the new disciplines that are available to us today is the science known by the ponderous name of *comparative philology*. Applied to biblical studies, comparative philology implies that Hebrew, the language in which the bulk of the Bible is written, is related to other languages. Just as we can study anatomy best when we compare the structure of a human being to that of related animals, we understand Hebrew best when we study it, not in isolation, but in comparison with Arabic, Aramaic, Akkadian, and other languages of the same group.

A second discipline of modern biblical research is archeology. Some people claim that important archeological discoveries in our time have proved the Bible to be "true." Archeology does not prove the Bible to be true. It does something much more significant; it sets the Bible into its context. It gives us the background which enables us to appreciate more fully what the Bible says.

Here are a few random examples of the contributions of archeology to our understanding of the biblical world. Near-eastern archeology began about a century and a quarter ago, when Napoleon made his ill-fated expedition to Egypt. He took with him on his expedition an archeologist, Champollion, who, in the course of his travels in Egypt, found the Rosetta stone. It contained a Greek inscription and a hieroglyphic and a demotic text, which ultimately enabled a group of scholars in Germany and France to decipher the language of Egypt. As a result, the entire civilization of ancient Egypt, which had not been known at all before, was opened up. At untold points, the Bible reveals familiarity with Egyptian customs and ideas.

Nobody, for example, had been able to prove the historicity of the Exodus from Egypt. Not very long ago, a well-known scholar declared that "Moses is the greatest man who never lived." Today, virtually all scholars are convinced that the biblical account of Moses is in all fundamentals validated by what we know of the political, social, and religious history in Egypt as revealed in the Book of the Dead, the literature emanating from the reformation of Ikhnaton, the Tel-El Amarna letters, and much more. This material has not "proved" that what the Bible tells us about the Exodus and the Conquest is true, but it has made Moses a credible figure who fits into that period to perfection.

Similarly, the story of the ten plagues has been regarded by many people as a kind of fairy tale. Yet the preponderant mass of critical opinion today sees in the story a description of a great physical upheaval in Egypt. Everything about the ten plagues fits into the geography, topography, and climatic conditions of Egypt. It is quite credible today to regard the reference to the ten plagues as a poetic description of authentic historical events—referring to a period of national chaos in Egypt which enabled the Israelites to escape (under the leadership of a man who, incidentally, had an Egyptian name).

Some facts of importance for almost every other period of Jewish history were unearthed in Egypt. Nobody, for example, knew seventy years ago that in the fifth century B.C.E., there existed a great settlement of Jewish soldiers on the southern boundary of the Egyptian empire, near the cataracts of the Nile. In 1902, a group of German scholars discovered a large collection of documents written in Aramaic, which revealed the existence of a Jewish military garrison in Elephantine in southern Egypt. It was a typical Jewish Diaspora community, in many respects like our own. Among these documents we have, for instance, lists of pledges the Jews made for the maintenance of their own house of worship as well as for the support of the temples of their non-Jewish neighbors (interfaith activities seemingly already existed in antiquity). These and other details are disclosed by the ancient documents of Elephantine.

In Babylonia, too, archeology does not prove the Bible to be true; but it places the Bible in its setting. No one, for example, has found an autographed letter from Abraham. Yet the name "Abraham" has turned up about twenty-odd times in documents which were unearthed in the city of Ur (Abraham's birthplace, according to the Bible), and which date back to just about the time when Abraham is assumed to have lived.

These documents corroborate the biblical tradition that there was a man named Abraham, and they fit him into the picture of the times. This conclusion is supported by a particularly remarkable discovery which was made in Ur and is related to the story of the sacrifice of Isaac and Abraham's ultimate sacrifice of a ram that was caught in a thicket. Among the religious objects which were found in Ur is a little figurine showing a ram caught in a thicket. The Babylonians did not possess the story of the sacrifice of Isaac; yet something which has a bearing on it was found in Ur, dating back to the time of Abraham.

Until about thirty years ago, very few discoveries were made in Palestine, in contrast to the rich discoveries that were made in Egypt and Babylonia. Scholars felt that the soil of Israel is too damp to preserve documents, and little was found initially in Palestine and Syria. After the First World War, however, a period of extraordinary and significant archeological discoveries began.

In 1929 a French scholar, Claude Schaeffer, came to an Arab village in Syria called Ras Shamra, where he discovered the remnants of a literature and of a language, the very existence of which had not been suspected. It is now called Ugaritic, because the old name of that village had been Ugarit. Ugaritic is a dialect of Hebrew. Biblical Hebrew and Ugaritic were two dialects of virtually the same language.

The Ras Shamra inscriptions are of a much earlier period than most parts of our Bible. They shed a tremendous amount of light on the mythological background and poetic form of biblical literature.

The separation of meat and dairy food in our dietary laws, for instance, is grounded in a biblical verse, "Thou shalt not seethe a kid in its mother's milk." The reason for this injunction is not given in the Bible. The law, itself, however, is mentioned three times.

Maimonides, who was eager to find a rational explanation for all biblical laws, felt that the injunction might have been issued in order to eliminate a pagan custom which the Torah wanted to prohibit because of its pagan origin. It was not until 1944, seven hundred years after Maimonides, that the Ugaritic documents revealed evidence showing that Maimonides' assumption had been correct. In Ugaritic worship, part of the fertility cult was the seething of the young kid in its mother's milk. The unremitting struggle of Judaism against idolatrous practices was at the heart of the biblical law. Literature, history, religion—all phases of our understanding of the Bible have been tremendously enriched by the material coming from Ugaritic sources.

In 1937, in the southern part of what is now Israel, another collection of documents was found, the so-called Lakhish letters. These letters date back to the early part of the sixth century B.C.E. Here we have a series of letters written by the Jewish military commanders in the field during the final, critical days when the Babylonian enemy was closing in on the country and town after town was falling to the invader. The documents are day-by-day dispatches from the battlefield—the desperate and unsuccessful battle for the preservation of Israel against the Babylonian conqueror.

Even more recently, in 1946, the world received the first word about what has been described as probably the most important archeological discovery ever to come out of Palestine, the Dead Sea Scrolls. A series of documents, manuscripts, and fragments discovered in the Dead Sea area provide an enormous amount of new material about the history of Judaism during the period of the Second Temple—the time when the Christian religion was born. Among them are some of the oldest biblical manuscripts we possess—for instance, a manuscript of the Book of Isaiah which is at least 900 years older than the oldest manuscript we had up to that time. In short, archeology reveals in a vivid and dramatic fashion the materials of the civilization which created the Bible.

Other sciences—anthropology, linguistics, comparative religion—are similarly helpful. The so-called higher criticism of the Bible seeks to clarify questions such as, When was each part of the Bible written? How is it to be understood? What were the motives of the author? What were the purposes that led to the compilation of the book in this particular form?

Textual criticism attempts to discover the form in which the original text was written. Correct as the Bible is in 999 out of 1000 passages, the constant copying of the text by scribes has inevitably led to certain errors in the text. Occasionally we can correct an error without much difficulty. The 29th Psalm, *mizmor le'David,* for example, depicts a thunderstorm and describes the voice of the Lord as it is heard over the landscape of Israel, in the north and in the east, over the desert and in the forests. It contains an interesting passage, which, in our usual Bible translations, reads, "The voice of the Lord maketh the hinds to calve." The thunderstorm causes the young deer to give birth. Some scholars argue that this verse means precisely what it says: that during a thunderstorm, a young deer that is pregnant is likely to give birth out of fear of the event. But the whole passage makes it quite clear that nothing is said about a young deer. For as soon as we change two vowels in the word *ayalot* ("hinds"), we get *eylot* ("oak trees"), enabling us to translate the passage, "The voice of the Lord makes the oak tree dance and strips the forest bare." Through textual criticism, a beautiful poetic image can be restored as the poet had intended it.

IV

The modern approach to the Bible has emerged from the findings of these sciences. What can the Bible be and mean for a modern person?

In the first place, the Bible is for us the great source of religion. It is not simply a book written by men. It is the revelation of God.

The concept of revelation requires definition. Revelation means the communication between God and man. Communication is always a double process. Someone is speaking, someone else is listening. The listener is as active a participant in the process of communication as is the speaker. It is noteworthy that the Hebrew word *shomea* means not only "to listen" but also "to understand." All communication requires a speaker and a hearer, one who is the source and one who is the recipient. God, who is eternal and unchanging, is the source of revelation; but the revelation of God comes to us mediated through men. In other words, at the other end of the process is man, and men differ among themselves—in their insights, in their capacity to grasp the word of God, in their understanding of the meaning of the message they receive.

The statement that the Bible is the revelation of God does not mean that it was dictated directly by God, but that it is something which has come to chosen spirits of the human race. By the will of God, most of them have been the prophets, lawgivers, and sages of Israel through whom He has revealed His will to men. Each of them has transmitted his understanding of that revelation on the basis of his own insight and profundity of outlook.

For this reason the Bible contains different levels—heights, valleys, and plains. The Bible is not uniform, for it is a reflection of all those to whom the revelation of God came. For us, the greatest revelation of God, the one that was most immediate, was the one that took place on Sinai. But every revelation thereafter, to our day, is part of this unending process of God's self-disclosure.

Similar to its insistence on the interrelationship of "speaker" and "listener" in the process of revelation is Judaism's regard for creation as well as redemption as processes that depend upon man as well as upon God. I call this relationship betwen God and man "cosmic symbiosis," a fundamental interrelationship of God and man. The process of revelation depends both upon the unchanging source, which is God, and the finite and imperfect recipient and mediator, who is man.

This concept of revelation, in which men play an active role with God, has its roots in the Jewish tradition. Hasidism, for example, says that just as a wise father who wants to play with his baby will talk baby talk to the youngster, so God adapts His message to the capacity of His children to understand in any given period. The Talmud, too, recognizes levels of inspiration when it says that there is a great difference between Moses, who looked upon the world with a clear telescope, and the other prophets who looked out upon the world with a blurred telescope, obviously seeing things not quite as clearly as Moses did. Incidentally, the Bible itself makes the same distinction. With Moses, God spoke *peh el peh,* "mouth to mouth," as two people may speak to each other, meeting him *panim el panim,* "face to face," while with the other prophets, God spoke only through visions and dreams.

Thus, the notion that revelation depends upon an unchanging source that is God, and a finite recipient who is man, is in consonance with the spirit of the tradition of Israel. It has its basis in Hasidism, the Talmud, and even in biblical thought itself. Once we accept this concept, we are not compelled to deny or reject the discoveries of the sciences. They reveal this process of revelation. They indicate the levels of insight that are involved, yet they are powerless to destroy our conviction that, when we read the Bible —read it with our hearts and our souls—we are not reading just another book. We are reading literally the word of God as mediated through His chosen servants. And we can play our part in this creative process by making His words manifest in the lives of men.

Second, the Bible is not only the great source of religion; it is also a great cultural monument in at least two basic ways. The Bible is the proudest cultural achievement of the Jewish people. The Bible indicates at the same time that the Jewish people never lived in isolation from the world. God could have given us a holy land in Greenland, Australia, or Tierra del Fuego. The fact that the land of Israel is at the very center of the Eastern Hemisphere, the heartland of Europe, Asia, and Africa, at the crossroads of the world, is an indication that the creative capacity of Israel was nourished and stimulated by the interaction of cultures, the constant clash of different ideologies and points of view.

Thus, the Bible is a product not of an isolated, hermetically sealed sect but of a people that was exposed to the varied currents of science, philosophy, and religion, to all the conflicting outlooks and world views which coexisted in the intellectual life of the Near East.

In another sense, too, the Bible is an important cultural monument. It teaches us something not only about the life of Israel but about the life of the human spirit. The Bible helps us document the stages of human progress. It shows, as I have already tried to indicate in the instance of the rights of women, how some of the noblest achievements of man emerged from the most ignoble beginnings.

Think of the Sabbath Day. The famous Canadian physician Sir William Osler said that the Sabbath is the greatest Jewish contribution to civilization, even greater than the idea of the one God. We know from our archeological discoveries that the Babylonian kinsmen of our ancestors had various kinds of observances which bore some resemblance to the Sabbath—for example, the festival of Sarpanit. The Babylonian calendar regarded the seventh, fourteenth, nineteenth, twenty-first, and twenty-eighth days of the month as days of ill omen. Physicians were not allowed to heal the sick; the king would not go on a trip; cooking was forbidden. Obviously, this festival is poles apart from the joy of the Jewish Sabbath and its elevation of the spirit. Yet, that there is some relationship between these two days is clear. Our Semitic ancestors, in primitive times, undoubtedly had a superstitious dread of certain days. However, the religious genius of Israel transformed such a day into that unique instrument for the ennoblement of human nature which is the Sabbath.

To add a final point. Over and above the significance of the Bible as a source of religious teaching and as a cultural monument, the Bible is a collection of literary masterpieces. There is practically no literary genre that is not represented in the Bible by works of surpassing beauty and value. If we are interested in narratives, not even Thomas Mann has written anything nobler than the story of Joseph, which Tolstoi termed the greatest narrative ever written. There is no more perfect short story than the Book of Ruth, no finer tale than the Book of Jonah. If we are drawn to religious poetry, we can turn to the Book of Psalms; if it is love or nature poetry, we have the God-speeches in the Book of Job and, of course, the Song of Songs. If our taste runs to history, we have the classic pages in Samuel and Kings, never surpassed and rarely equaled. If we prefer philosophic reflection, we can open that small book called Kohelet, the charming, wise philosopher who grappled with the fundamental problems of life. If we are troubled by religious doubts, we can find scattered in the words of the prophets, sages, and psalmists approaches to the same basic problems that are confronting us today. If we are interested in the development of human institutions and laws, we can study some of the great law codes of the world, the greatest of which is represented by the Ten Commandments. And if we have a love for that which borders upon the greatest achievements of the human spirit, we have, for example, that book which grapples with the problem of human suffering in God's world, the Book of Job, which, in Thomas Carlyle's words, is "one of the grandest things ever written with . . . pen." In my admittedly biased but considered opinion, it is worth twenty years of a person's life to learn enough Hebrew to be able to read the Book of Job in the original.

Whatever our interest in literature may be, whatever dedication we have for the human spirit, whatever concern we feel for deciding our place in a world into which we were placed by a power beyond ourselves—the Bible is a superb guidebook to life. This is why even those of us who are not able to accept the older, traditional attitude toward the Bible can and should approach it with an attitude of reverence and appreciation. Modern man can echo the words of the ancient sages who said of the Bible, "Turn it over and over, for everything is in it; and grow old and grey in it, but do not swerve from it, for there is no better portion."

11. The Way of the Law

ERNST SIMON

Law and Observance in Jewish Experience

SHLOMO ALKABETZ opens his famous Sabbath hymn, *lekhah dodi* (composed about 1540), with the words *shamor vezakhor bedibbur ehad,* "observe and remember the Sabbath Day—these commandments God caused us to hear in a single utterance." Alkabetz' phrase recapitulates a formulation of the Talmud [1] in which the rabbis seek to explain the discrepancy between the two versions of the fourth Commandment in the Torah—the one in Exodus 20:8 which says, *zakhor et yom hashabbat, "remember* the Sabbath day," the other in Deuteronomy 5:15 which reads, *shamor et yom hashabbat, "observe* the Sabbath day." The rabbis of the Talmud felt that both terms belong together. They are "a single utterance" and represent a unity which in turn reflects God's unity and indivisibility in space and time.

In the act of *zakhor*—by evoking the past and recapitulating it —we can also discover the rationale for *shamor,* our observance of halakhah.

I

Halakhah has several characteristic features which reflect Judaism's distinctive attitude toward life and the world. One of these distinctive features is that halakhah makes a plea for sobriety in religion. Philo, the first Jewish philosopher (ca. 25 B.C.E. to 50 C.E.), who wrote in Greek but is usually quoted in Latin, once

221

spoke of *sobria ebrietas,* "sober drunkenness." A modern scholar, Max Kadushin, refers to the same phenomenon by using the term "normal mysticism."

Both terms describe the spiritual and intellectual climate which halakhah seeks to create—sober drunkenness. We cannot help being drunk when we come near to God. Yet classical Judaism has always insisted that this intoxication be kept within the limits of sobriety.

But how can drunkenness be sober? Is drunkenness not a state in which I seek to gain myself by losing myself? Is mysticism not a posture in which man seeks what the philosophers have called a *unio mystica,* a union with God which can be achieved only by means of ecstatic contemplation and the complete abandonment of the self? In the ecstasy of the mystic experience, the distinction between God and man disappears, and the danger arises that in this experience God will lose His divinity, and man, his humility.

Precisely because the danger of a complete abandonment of self is always present when man seeks to approach God in prayer, Judaism has attempted to "normalize" mysticism. Halakhah is Judaism's means of maintaining the delicate balance between sobriety and God-intoxication. It tempers self-surrender with self-control and preserves the distinction between God and man: man's relationship to God is achieved not in a mystical union but in the fulfillment of God's commandments in the here and now. And unlike mysticism, which restricts the mysterious experience of a union with God to a select few, halakhah obliterates the distinction between the few select who can experience God, and the masses who cannot. Law and observance are a way to God which is open to all without distinction.

II

A second characteristic of halakhah is what I would like to call its nontotalitarian totality. Jewish law is all-embracing. It is total: it governs all aspects of man's life. No province in the kingdom of man and his life is beyond the reach and discipline of Jewish law. In this respect Judaism differs from the philosophy of the Stoics, who maintained that there are *adiaphora*—"things undecided" which are neither good nor bad, neither commanded nor forbidden. The *adiaphoron* represents an area of neutrality and hence of freedom in the moral realm. Classical Judaism hardly knows such a neutral sphere. No things or actions can ever be morally neutral. Halakhah regulates every area of life—eating, drinking, prayer, work, man's relationship to family and fellowman, even his love life, the most intimate sphere of human experience. It is a total system. It aims at the sanctification of every action and moment of man's life.

I find the meaning of halakhah expressed with particular poignancy in the order of worship which requires that the daily evening prayer is to be said immediately upon the conclusion of the Neilah service on Yom Kippur. The Jew has prayed and fasted throughout the entire day. Now the day is ended. Everyone is eager to go home and break the fast. People are rushing out. Yet there is always at least a small group of persons who remain behind to recite the regular daily evening prayer. Having just cleansed and purified themselves, they again pronounce the daily bid for forgiveness. The Jewish year—time—has no pauses. Halakhah governs the totality of man's life and time.

Nevertheless, this totality is nontotalitarian. Halakhah is demanding and commanding but not despotic. It could not become totalitarian because it leaves room for doubts, discussion, disagreement. Its principles and conclusions are not fixed or frozen into immutable finality. The Talmud is not a book but a record, in twenty volumes, of discussions which were going on in Babylonia and Palestine for a period of at least six or seven centuries. It does not mention the year or period when certain things were said. All the generations talked with one another. Every question may become an answer, and many answers turn out to pose new questions.

Yet the Talmud is not only a record of discussion. It can actually be studied only through discussion. A man can read or study every book in world literature by himself except the Talmud. The Talmud can be studied only by the same oral method—the method of discussion—in which it was developed. There are no commas, no question marks, and, only rarely, periods. Questions and answers or the ends of sentences must be indicated by the rise or fall of the speaker's voice. Rashi, the most famous of all Talmud commentators, gives us a clue to this almost hidden treasure. Whenever a sentence or phrase in the text should be read as a question, even though there is no question mark, he says *"bin-huta,"* an Aramaic term which means "in a lowered voice." Rashi uses an acoustic notation to describe a nonexisting but desired graphic or visual symbol. The melody of speech has become the melody of learning. Hence the Talmud is not a dry book. It has music. And it could never become totalitarian because it contains the music of discussion, the staccato arguments of debate, the counterpoint of disagreement, and the final harmonization of differing views.

There is a second reason for which this total system is not totalitarian. Since talmudic times, Judaism has had no central religious authorities, no ecclesiastic hierarchy. When I began my career as a high-school teacher in Germany before my *aliyah* to Israel, I asked my principal on the first day of school to permit me to take Shabbat off altogether or at least those morning hours which I needed to attend synagogue services. At first he denied my request. The regulations left him no choice. When I told him that I would neither write nor carry my books on Shabbat, he suggested that I consult my rabbi and ask him to give me permission to do both. There was only one answer I could give him. A rabbi who would give me permission to violate the Sabbath could not be a rabbi for me. Unlike the Roman Catholic church, Judaism makes no distinction between priesthood and laity. There is no special group of persons who are entitled to perform particular priestly or sacerdotal functions for others. The entire people is to become a "kingdom of priests"; every Jew, be he the Chief Rabbi of Israel or a simple unlearned Jew in the streets of New York City, is required to fulfill the *mitzvot*. Jews may and do differ in the degree of conscientiousness with which they fulfill the religious commandments. Traditional and liberal Jews and their various subdivisions and denominational groupings differ in the way they define the nature and implications of *mitzvah* and law in Judaism. These are legitimate differences of conviction. But to establish a difference in the standards of observance between rabbi and "layman" would be illegitimate. Jews have no ecclesiastical hierarchy or caste of priests ordained to do the job for them. One cannot be a Jew by proxy. Every single Jew bears full responsibility for his own observance of the law.

In talmudic times, the Jewish community had a central authority, the Beit Din Haggadol. It served as a sort of Supreme Court for the Jewish community, and its decisions, proclaimed in a certain place in the sanctuary, were law. Nevertheless, a scholar who disagreed with the pronouncements of the court was still permitted to question the law and to express his disagreement with it when he taught his students in the academy. He was not permitted to advocate that the law be violated, but he retained the freedom of intellectual dissent. The law was not totalitarian.

Still another factor assures the nontotalitarian character of halakhah: the relative freedom of teaching and opinion that exists in rabbinic Judaism. Near the beginning of his famous codification of the law, the *Mishneh Torah,* Maimonides makes the statement that anyone who believes that God has a body like a human being is a sectarian. He is not a good Jew. Maimonides was a rationalist, the leader of the enlightenment of his day. His philosophic training had convinced him that the anthropomorphisms of the Bible could not be taken literally. However, his views did not remain unchallenged. One of his contemporaries, Rabbi Avraham ben David (the RaBaD), dissented sharply: better and wiser men than this author believe that God has a body, yet they do not call the people sectarians. The people are entitled to their beliefs, even though they may be erroneous. They have derived their beliefs from the Aggadah and the Midrashim, Judaism's traditional sources. Maimonides' antagonist fought for the freedom of belief of people whose beliefs he himself did not share. Like Maimonides, Avraham ben David was antianthropomorphic and could not accept the belief that God has a body. Yet he insisted that one can be a good Jew and affirm this belief.[2] Judaism regulates man's acts but not his thoughts. No one has the right to read someone else out of Judaism or to consider him a less adequate Jew because their views of God's nature may differ. Judaism must be able to accommodate both views. Both are possible expressions of Jewish tradition and Jewish faith even though they may contradict each other. The unity of the Jewish people is based not on everyone's acceptance of the same dubious results of philosophical speculation but on every single Jew's faithful performance of the *mitzvot*. Man's notions or thoughts may well be mistaken or erroneous. God's nature is beyond our grasp, but His commandments are neither hidden nor far off.[3]

This relative freedom of thought and teaching is one of the characteristic features of rabbinic Judaism. Luther and Zwingli, two of the giants of the Protestant Reformation, were troubled by a question which was similar to that which had troubled Maimonides and Avraham ben David, when they discussed the question whether the host, the consecrated wafer, merely *symbolizes* God's body or actually *is* God's body. If God has a body, why could He not be in this holy bread? When Zwingli insisted that the bread was more than a symbol and that it actually was God's body, Luther broke off the discussion and said to his colleague, *Wir haben nicht denselben Geist*—"ours is not the same spirit." As a result of this disagreement, the Reformation movement was split into two parts—divided by a question which had been settled by Maimonides and the RaBaD through a single side-remark stating their disagreement but accepting both views as authentic. The controversy did not destroy the unity in Judaism, and every reader of the *Mishneh Torah* today can study both views and reach his own conclusions. Halakhah does not impose specific views upon the Jew. It is not a totalitarian system.

III

A third characteristic of rabbinic Judaism is its partial asceticism. In this respect it differs from the Greek world which, with some noteworthy exceptions, was nonascetic. According to the Greek view, man realizes his humanity by living out his life to the fullest, physically and intellectually, even though this course of action might involve indulgence and physical excess. This concept became a conspicuous ideal once again in the Renaissance which spoke of *uomo universale,* all-embracing, universal man. The universal man is the person who actualizes his potential of body and mind to the fullest. Man thus obliterates the distinction between virtues and vices; he is less interested in whether an act is good or bad than whether it is an authentic or inauthentic expression of the individual. The same criterion is correctly applied in the realm of aesthetics. Its highest value is authenticity of expression. Shakespeare's Richard III is an authentic person; Shakespeare could never have created him without a deep empathy for authentic evil. What matters is not whether a man's conduct and life are morally good or bad but whether they are an authentic expression of his personality. This is one approach to life. Its most recent form is existentialism.

Christianity advocates the opposite way of life, complete asceticism. Echoing a saying of ancient Greek mysticism that "the body is a tomb," Christianity, with important exceptions, considered the experiences of the senses sinful and insisted that the desires of the body corrupt and destroy the soul. The ideal Christian personality type was not universal man but the monk and the nun, the person who withdraws from family and the world to avoid temptation and to achieve purity from the desires of the body.

Judaism represents a third way. It posits partial asceticism. It rejects uncontrolled indulgence of desire just as vigorously as it objects to complete asceticism. The body is no less the work of God than is the soul, and it can therefore not be inherently evil. Self-negation is not necessarily a virtue. On the contrary, it may well be an evil by destroying man's ability to experience the fullness of life. According to a rabbinic interpretation, the biblical verse, "Thou shalt rejoice before the Lord thy God," [4] refers not only to the joys of the spirit—study, worship, and good deeds— but also to the joys of the body, "food and drink, raiment, and fellowship." [5]

According to the Talmud, man is not only not forbidden but actually bidden to enjoy food, drink, love. They are God's gifts. In the last analysis, the complete ascetic who rejects these gifts rejects God.

Jewish tradition posits partial asceticism—a way of life which is neither surrender to unbridled hedonism nor an ascetic withdrawal from the world. It is a way of life that enables the Jew to live in this world, to enjoy it fully and with all his senses. At the same time, it demands that he always remain in control of himself and invest everything he does with *kedushah,* with holiness, with intimations of the divine.

IV

A fourth element which characterizes rabbinic Judaism and is embodied in Jewish law is its nonutopian messianism. Messianism is a pointing to the future. How, then, can Jewish messianism, the Jewish drive for the millennium and its hope for a better future for Israel and mankind, be defined as nonutopian? "Utopia," a Greek term, was coined by Thomas More in 1516 when he wrote his *Utopia* as an answer to Machiavelli's *Principe.* "Utopia" literally means "no place," and More's book describes the ideal society, which exists in no place but which is to serve as a model for the earthly place and society of the man who envisions it. Distant in the realm of space, it is near in the realm of time. Hence all utopian thinking is pseudomessianic: it tries to hasten the end of historical time, to speed the coming of redemption.

Judaism represents a nonutopian messianism. Jews exist today and can continue to define themselves as Jews because their forefathers, in a decisive moment of Jewish history, said no to various utopias, whether it was the utopia of Christianity or that of communism.

In his last work, *Where Judaism Differs,* Abba Hillel Silver made the point that through the *nays* you can hear the *yeas* of the Jewish people. That which is rejected by Judaism often provides a clue to what Judaism affirms. Judaism rejected Christianity. Among the people who rejected Jesus as the Messiah and refused to accept Christianity were probably some of the best as well as some of the worst Jews. The worst were the cynics who rejected the new faith because they could not believe in the possibility of a better future. The best were the believing realists who rejected the promise of utopia in terms of redemption-in-the-making precisely because they saw the world as it was—still unchanged, still incomplete, still in need of fulfillment.

The Jewish attitude is compellingly illustrated by a story of a

Hasidic rabbi who had gone to Eretz Yisrael and had made his home near the Mount of Olives. One morning he heard the sound of the shofar, on a day on which the sounding of the shofar is not prescribed by Jewish law. He left his little hut wondering whether the Messiah had come, for, according to an ancient tradition, the arrival of the Messiah would be heralded by the sounding of the shofar. But as he looked around, he responded to what he saw in the streets in just a single sentence, "The world has not changed." The Messiah could not have arrived. And he returned home to pursue his life of study and piety.

The power to resist pseudomessianic movements and promises has made the Jews the people that carries with it the message of *geulah,* of final redemption. Had they fallen victim to one or the other type of utopian messianism, they would today be disappointed Christians or disappointed communists. Their nonutopian messianism has enabled them to remain hopeful, actively hopeful Jews.

V

A fifth and last characteristic of the Jewish posture is a critical identification with a religiously defined nation or people. Associated with this identification is what I consider to be this generation's main task, the building of Eretz Yisrael.

"Critical identification" is a dialectical combination of terms. How can identification be critical? And how can a critic be identified with the cause he criticizes? To paraphrase Pascal's distinction, criticism is a function of the mind, identification is an involvement of the heart. How can the heart become critical and the mind, identified?

The answer can be found in another, more familiar phrase. We sometimes speak of "critical love" in order to characterize a relationship in which love and criticism, attachment and detachment, are fused together indissolubly. Love should not be so blind as to silence criticism, criticism not so detached as to corrode and kill love.

It is possible to remain critical of the Jewish people from without—without love, without identification with our people and the country which once again has become our homeland. In this case, our criticism will remain external and ineffectual. Obversely, we can permit our glowing hearts to become identified with our people's life and work in Israel to such an extent and with such intensity that our love will silence even justified criticism of ourselves and our work. In this case we tend to become chauvinists, and everything we do today may ultimately lose its meaning because the Jewish people and the Jewish state will no longer be and represent what we hoped and worked for in order to stem the danger of collective assimilation in Israel—instead of individual assimilation in the Diaspora—and to make this land the setting for the fulfillment of an age-old dream.

Critical identification is a characteristic of the attitude of rabbinic Judaism and especially of the prophets. No prophet ever dreamed of leaving his people. No prophet ever claimed that everything Jews did was good because it was done by Jews. They criticized their people precisely because they loved them; and they suffered deeply because their concern for their people's welfare and destiny compelled them to silence their love and compassion in order to criticize. The Prophet Jeremiah personified this attitude.[6] Hananiah, who turned out to be a false prophet, stood up in besieged Jerusalem, whose capture and destruction by the Babylonians had been predicted by Jeremiah. Hananiah proclaimed that the yoke and stranglehold of Nebuchadnezzar on Jerusalem would be broken, that the city would be freed and the captives returned. Jeremiah was present when Hananiah spoke. He listened carefully. He wished from the bottom of his heart that Hananiah was right and that his own prophecies of doom were wrong. He loved his people. He did not want them to suffer. Thus he said "Amen" after Hananiah's oration. Yet he also knew that Nebuchadnezzar's yoke would not be broken and that the suffering that lay ahead was God's punishment for the moral corruption and decay of the people and their disobedience to God. He loved his people, yet he had to criticize them. He wanted to comfort them, yet he had to admonish them for the sake of their welfare and their responsibilities under their covenant with God. But he never parted company with them.

His commitment to his people was put to its most severe test when his prophecy came true and Jerusalem was conquered. The victorious king considered Jeremiah a sort of ally and gave him the choice either to accompany him to Babylonia and live there with the highest honors or to remain in the nearly destroyed city in order to help Gedaliah, son of Ahikam, resettle the remainder of the Jews. Jeremiah remained in Jerusalem. Even after Gedaliah's assassination by his rivals, Jeremiah continued to urge his people to remain in the country and to serve as the nucleus for its re-building. Only when they once again began to reject the divine truth that spoke through him, did he finally decide to join the pitiful remnants of his people that were led into exile in Egypt.[7]

This is critical identification. One can be the sharpest critic of one's people yet remain fully identified with it and wish to share its life and tasks. At the end of the volume which deals with the destruction of the Second Temple by the Romans in the year 70 C.E., Heinrich Graetz (1817–1891) asked why Jeremiah, who had predicted the destruction of the First Temple, had been accepted by the Jewish people as a true prophet, while Flavius Josephus, who quoted one of Jeremiah's speeches when he was standing among the Roman legions before the walls of Jerusalem that were besieged by Titus and Vespasian, was considered a traitor, despite the fact that his warnings, too, had come true. Graetz's answer was, "Jeremiah spoke from within; Josephus spoke from the tent of the Roman general." Where you stand when you speak—that makes all the difference. It makes either for identification or for lack of it.

VI

Law and observance provide the climate of Jewish life that safeguards and sustains its distinctive features: its emphasis on sobriety in religion, its nontotalitarian though all-embracing character, its partial asceticism, its nonutopian messianism, its demand for critical identification with the Jewish people. Nevertheless, law and observance may also involve certain dangers to the health of Jewish life.

One possible danger is petrification, arrested development. The term *halakhah* is derived from the verb *halokh,* "to walk." Halakhah is a way of life, not a standpoint of life. It involves movement, change, progression, not immobility and standing still. Yet many Jews use the Talmud or the Shulhan Arukh and our other codes as the Sadducees and the Karaites used the Bible. The Karaites rejected the rabbinic tradition and claimed to base their teachings solely on the text of the Bible, disregarding the outer and inner developments that had taken place between the time of the Bible and their own time. Many Jews have become Karaites of the most recent codification of the oral law. They act as if nothing had taken place since it was published. Thus, there exists what can be called an *evolutionary deficit* in halakhah. Orthodoxy does not reject the principle of change as such. But its method of change has become so ineffective and slow that the danger of petrification is very real.

A second danger lies in the *aesthetic deficit* that can be found in Jewish tradition. Visual art was largely neglected in Jewish life. One of the reasons might have been that the Jew met visual art only in the context of pagan worship and idolatrous practices which were often hideously immoral. The aesthetic realm had no autonomous existence in ancient times. Even in Greek civilization, art was intimately related to religious practice, worship, and cult. The Jew rejected visual art because he rejected the religious and moral aberrations of the idolatrous practices for which the artist's handiwork was used.

Whatever the reasons for the absence of a concern with visual art in Jewish life may be—the fact remains that there is an aesthetic deficit in Jewish tradition. It should be reduced. I do not propose that we place aesthetic values at the top of the pyramid of Jewish values or, for that matter, of human values in general. But we must place them higher than we have done in the past.

A third danger which threatens meaningful observance is excessive legalism, an *emotional deficit,* that can occasionally be found among strictly observant Jews. Some years ago, I wrote an article for a Hebrew journal in which I attempted to show that a religious experience encompasses peaks as well as valleys of intensity. We oscillate between moments of greater and lesser emotion in prayer and observance. In the same way, we respond with varying degrees of intensity to different parts of the Torah. There are some ideas and *mitzvot* which we stress more, which we can feel more deeply, and with which we can identify more adequately than with others. A very observant rabbi, in answer to my article, wrote that I was wrong: all parts of the Torah are of equal value and religious importance; we have no right to make a distinction between the *Shema Yisrael,* for instance, and a biblical sentence dealing with the status of a woman who was a concubine. In my answer, I pointed out that I had never heard or read that our martyrs, in the Spanish period or in our own time, went to their death proclaiming their faith in a sentence such as *vetimnah hayta pilegesh*—"and Timnah was a concubine";[8] the cry that rose from their lips at the moment of agony was quite another verse: the *Shema Yisrael.* Emotionally and existentially, there is a vast difference between these verses. Yet it is not easy to accept the validity of such a distinction from a purely legalistic, exclusively halakhic point of view.

There is a last danger. It is the danger of chauvinism. There are people, especially in the Diaspora, who claim that a true Jew must be a pacifist—as if Judaism had always identified itself with the unconditional quest for peace. The facts do not support this claim. According to its classical sources, Judaism is neither for peace nor for war. Jewish tradition—the Bible, rabbinic Judaism, even the Rambam and the prayer book—contain notions and events which support both positions. The opening prayer of the *Selihot* service contains a phrase in which the worshiper forgives his enemies and adversaries and asks that no man should suffer or be punished for his sins and the sins committed against him.[9] Yet only a few pages later, the entire congregation joins in a recitation of the *ashrei,* which says, *v'et hareshaim yashmid,* "and the wicked people God will destroy." Jewish sources are often inconsistent. The Jew today must have the courage to face the fact that his definition of the ideas and commitments of Judaism depends on the sources which he uses. Judaism frequently contains strange or contradictory notions, and the decision as to which element of the Jewish heritage to choose or stress depends on each individual's interests and concerns. Only a chauvinist can claim that everything which is recorded in Jewish tradition is good and above criticism and that nothing Jews ever said or did is wrong. Sometimes, when certain parts of the Torah are read in the Sabbath service, I have the fervent wish not to be called upon to recite the blessing over the Torah. I recite the *berakhah* when I am called to the Torah because I am a good soldier who is bound by discipline and, perhaps, do not have enough courage. But I do not always find it easy to reconcile a benediction with the content of the passages which are being read.

VII

Halakhic observance poses certain dangers; but it also possesses a capacity to create and strengthen the distinctive quality of Jewish life which far outweighs these dangers.

Only halakhah gives Jews the possibility of becoming a religious society and not merely remaining unrelated religious individuals. It is difficult to be a religious Jew as an isolated individual, divorced from the community. This is one of the significant differences between Judaism and Christianity. Both religions bear the mark of their native hours. Judaism was born in a collective experience, the experience of an entire people at Mount Sinai. Christianity was born in an individual experience, the experience of one person believed by his believers to be the son of God. Therefore, the believing individual is central to Christianity, while Judaism, be it traditional or Reform Judaism, has always stressed the community. Judaism and Christianity represent two different approaches to the life of faith, and each may conceivably have something to learn from the other. Jews can learn from Christians how to become believing individuals. Christians can try to learn from Jews how to become members of a religious society. One could write a history of Christianity as a sequence of experiments to achieve a religious society. When Christians tried to establish such a society, as Cromwell and other Puritans tried, they took their guiding principles from the Hebrew Bible. The New Testament does not contain those principles of communal life and organization which could serve as a foundation for the establishment of a Christian society. The Hebrew Bible and halakhah do contain these features. The achievement of a genuinely religious society remains an unfulfilled need.

Another aspect of halakhah which contributes to its efficacy is what both the Hebrew poet Bialik and the German rabbi Josef Carlebach called its "obligating prose." Even though Jewish tradition is characterized by an aesthetic deficit, modern Judaism still possesses too much poetry and not enough obligating prose. In religious life, prose is more important than poetry. Poetry addresses itself to the imagination. Prose addresses itself to the will. Poetry can make a claim for the beauty of expression alone. Prose makes a claim upon man. It demands action and sustained effort. Chaim Nachman Bialik, who succeeded in capturing the poetry of the Aggadah and made it accessible to a wide public in his *Sefer Ha'aggadah,* had the courage to say, in his essay "Halakhah v'aggadah," "We have too much *hibah,* too much loving-kindness, and not enough *hovah,* not enough obligation." If I were able to compose prayers, I would perhaps pray, "Give us *mitzvot;* give us obligations."

What "obligating prose" means can be illustrated by two examples from the recent Responsa literature. Jewish Responsa literature contains the answers to halakhic questions which rabbis are asked. Among the volumes recording the questions and answers of our people during the Holocaust is a Hebrew volume by Rabbi Oshri, formerly a Dayan of Kovno, entitled *Me'emek Habakhah.*[10] The book contains the answers which Rabbi Rubinstein and his colleagues of the rabbinic court, among them the author, gave to questions asked by Jews of Kovno during the time of the Nazi occupation and at the height of persecution (e.g., whether it was permissible to eat nonkosher food in order to maintain one's strength, or to break the Shabbat in order to escape death). The questioners were prepared to accept whatever answer the rabbis would give them. They sought guidance. Therefore, the answers were obligating prose, guidelines for conduct in the face of danger and the threat of imminent death. As far as I can remember, there were only two cases in which the rabbis did not grant permission to do what people had asked for. In response to the question whether a young man was permitted to kill himself in order to escape torture and death at the hands of the Nazis, the rabbi answered, "No, my son. We should never do their evil work for them. We have to live to our last moment." Suicide is the ultimate loss and abdication of faith. It means final despair, the conviction that God cannot help any more.

The second case concerned a young girl's question of whether she was permitted to register as a gentile and dress and act like one in order to save her life. Again the answer was in the negative, despite the fact that Maimonides, in his *Iggeret Hashemad,* had given a different answer. The rationale and motivation of the rabbinic court—as difficult as their acceptance may be for us— were based on the unshakable conviction that no person should desert the Jewish people, even under extreme stress. Halakhah is obligating prose, up to the last hour.

Still another feature of halakhah is its tenor of religious chastity. I do not mean the chastity of the body, an important concept in rabbinic thought. I mean the chastity of the soul. A person who studies the Talmud will discover that it says relatively little about God. He is rarely mentioned in the really important passages of the Talmud which are studied customarily and with regularity. Unlike the Billy Grahams of today, the rabbis rarely spoke of God, not because they lacked faith, but because their faith was so profound and secure that it did not require discussion or verbalization. God's presence was felt in all they thought and did. A man of tact and sensitivity does not discuss with others his love for his wife. In the same way, the rabbis of the Talmud rarely spoke of their deepest love, their love of God. The atmosphere of the legal parts of halakhic discussion is one of religious chastity.

VIII

Can a modern Jew still find a rationale for the observance of halakhah? Specifically, can a non-Orthodox Jew take a positive stand with regard to halakhah, and on what grounds can he affirm its validity and accept its claims for himself and his community?

I believe such a rationale can be formulated. Halakhah safeguards the identity of the Jewish faith and the Jewish people. Judaism is a religion that is practiced by Jews. Judaism accepts proselytes but does not seek them. Persons who profess a Christian faith cannot be Jews. A Jew who embraces another faith leaves the Jewish people. He may be a deeply moral person, yet his conversion terminates his membership in the Jewish people. There is a relative identity between the faith and the people, and this relative identity can be established and maintained only by a sanctified way of life. Halakhah is our only means to establish and maintain this sanctified way of life.

Above all, however, halakhah can have profound relevance for the modern Jew because it embodies and represents an attitude toward life which emphasizes the need for a restitution of the intellect in a partly anti-intellectual society, for discipline in a partly libertarian world, for orientation and a sense of direction in a chaos of over-information, and for a rational religion in the face of the inroads of mysticism and obscurantism.

Halakhah stresses the use of the intellect and its restitution in a partly anti-intellectual society by virtue of its uncompromising emphasis on study and the life of the intellect as a mode of worship and religious expression. Dr. Robert Hutchins, the former chancellor of the University of Chicago, concluded the fifth of a series of lectures which he delivered in Jerusalem by saying that the Jewish people had always had his unconditional support and admiration because it was the only people he knew which had made learning a religious duty. Hutchins was not wholly correct; the Chinese had a similar emphasis. Nevertheless, he was right in pointing out that halakhah has always and vigorously insisted on the primacy of intellectual activity and concerns over against emotionalism—an emphasis which can serve as a vitally needed antidote to the anti-intellectual trends in contemporary society.

Halakhah calls for the restoration of discipline in a partly libertarian world and for the recovery of a perspective and a sense of direction in the chaos of over-information. To use the title of a well-known book by Professor Wolfgang Koehler, it calls for a "place of values in the world of facts." Halakhah teaches the place of values in a world of facts. We live in a world that lacks equilibrium between too much and not enough information. We know too much, yet, at the same time, too little. We know too many details but do not have sufficient principles to organize them meaningfully. One function of revelation is to provide orientation and direction. When Jews pray, they turn East in order to face Jerusalem. They have a point of reference by which they orient themselves. It gives them direction and helps organize the data of their experiences. Halakhah provides such orientation, occasionally too much so. But it is easier to reduce a surplus than to fill a vacuum.

Lastly, halakhah represents the unceasing demand for relative rationality in religion, for a rational religious way of life in a world challenged, on the one side, by shallow secularism and, on the other side, by religious obscurantism. The concluding verse in the twenty-ninth chapter of Deuteronomy says, "The hidden things belong unto the Lord our God, but the revealed things belong to us and our children for all eternity, that we may fulfill all the words of His Torah." [11] When I spoke at an academic convocation honoring Professor Gershom Scholem, the foremost authority in the field of Jewish mysticism, on the occasion of his sixtieth birthday, I concluded my address with the words, "At a time when the hidden things are being revealed, the revealed things are being hidden."

Halakhah stands not for what is hidden but for what man can know and do. My plea is for the revealed things—to study them and to fulfill them.

JAKOB J. PETUCHOWSKI
Some Criteria for Modern Jewish Observance

JEWISH TRADITION speaks about the "613 Commandments" of the Torah. But Rabbi Simlai, having been first to
mention this number,[1] did not then proceed to enumerate them.
As a result, later scholars differed among themselves about the
best way to arrive at that number. For if only the commandments
of the written Torah were counted, the figure would be less than
613. If, however, the commandments of the oral Torah were to be
added to those of the Bible, the number would far exceed 613. A
whole branch of medieval rabbinic literature is devoted to the task
of "enumerating the Commandments." Various authors argued on
behalf of their own counts. However, gradually the enumeration of
Maimonides, in his *Sepher Hamitzvot* ("The Book of the Commandments"), achieved the greatest popularity; and it is generally
his enumeration to which modern writings refer in their discussion
of the 613 Commandments.

This discussion of the 613 Commandments continues vigorously,
even though no modern Jew—the most pious included—observes
all of them or could observe them even if he so desired. Numerous
commandments have application to the Jerusalem Temple and the
sacrificial cult. Others refer to the regulations governing the purity
of priests and Levites, a subject which, again, is related to the
Jerusalem Temple cult. Still others apply only to the reign of a
Jewish king. In other words, the 613 Commandments—whatever
they might be, and whatever enumeration of them we might choose
to follow—were never meant to be observed by every Jew. Never-

theless, the concept of the 613 Commandments has become a slogan in modern Jewish life. The claim is frequently made that Orthodox Jews observe the 613 Commandments, while Reform Jews reject them.

That this claim cannot possibly be true of any Orthodox Jew we have already seen. But it is also not true that the Reform Jew *rejects* the 613 Commandments as a whole. If a Reform Jew loves his neighbor, he is observing one of the commandments (by everybody's method of enumerating them). If he refrains from murder, adultery, or theft, he is observing a second, a third, and a fourth commandment. If he pays his employees on time, returns a lost article to its owner, and honors his father and mother, he is observing a fifth, sixth, and seventh traditional commandment. There is no need to keep count of all the commandments that a Reform Jew does observe. If he leads a reasonably moral and ethical life, his style of life will not be bereft of a goodly number of the 613 Commandments. For they are not limited to the so-called ritual and ceremonial observances. The love of one's neighbor is no less a part of the commandments than is the practice not to mix meat and milk dishes. Thus, neither the Orthodox nor the Reform Jew can be described as either totally observing or totally rejecting the 613 Commandments. Both are *partial* observers. It should be added that the observance of the ethical commandments is obviously not a monopoly of the Reform Jew. Nor can it be said that even the most radical Reform Jew has completely divested himself of all so-called ceremonial observances.

It is, however, true that in matters of ritual and ceremonial observance the Reform Jew maintains less of the traditional heritage than does the Orthodox Jew. In the nineteenth century, Reform Judaism gave up many traditional Jewish observances because, as was said at that time, they were "too Oriental" or no longer "spoke to modern man." There was also an attempt to side with the "prophets" against the "priests," to regard the moral law alone as "divine," and to view the "ceremonial law" as something of purely human origin, which could either be modified or totally abolished.

This was indeed a break with Jewish tradition—a tradition which knew only of *mitzvot,* divine commandments, without distinguishing between moral and ritual commandments, to the detriment of the latter. Ritual and ceremony are not authentic Jewish concepts. Moreover, recent biblical scholarship no longer takes it for granted that the prophets invariably and inevitably took an antagonistic position toward the cult. It is, therefore, easy to criticize much of the position of nineteenth-century Reform Judaism from the perspective of the twentieth century.

Nevertheless, the position adopted in the last century contained an important insight to which the twentieth century must not close its eyes. In its most radical form, this insight was expressed by Samuel Holdheim (1806–1860). The ancient rabbis had already made a distinction between the *mitzvot* which are obligatory only in the land of Israel and those which retain their validity beyond the borders of the land of Israel.[2] The Jew of the Diaspora is obligated to fulfil the latter only. Holdheim went one step further. The Torah, he argued, has a twofold content. It contains a strictly religious element, which is eternally valid. But it also contains the legal constitution of the ancient Israelite theocracy; and that constitution is time-conditioned. Since God Himself abolished the theocracy by permitting Temple and State to be destroyed in the year 70 C.E., the constitution of that theocracy has likewise been abolished.[3]

Holdheim drew several radical conclusions from this distinction. He asserted, for example, that, while the weekly day of rest was an eternally binding religious commandment, the particular day of the week on which it is to be observed was determined by the constitution of the state, not by religion. In ancient Israel it happened to be Saturday; in Prussia it was Sunday. Altogether, Holdheim had a tendency to make life easy for himself by relegating all the commandments he did not particularly care for to the constitution of the ancient Israelite theocracy, thus depriving them of their binding character.

Holdheim went too far. Nevertheless, he was right in his view of the Torah and its twofold content. The Jew who, in the period of the Emancipation, voluntarily accepted his Judaism, did so in terms of a commitment to *religion,* not to the legal constitution of an ancient state. The commandments he observed were indeed— to use Franz Rosenzweig's terminology—"commandments," not "legislation." Behind the "commandment" there is only God, not the constitution of a state.

In the final analysis, the decision of the individual Jew to observe many, few, or no "commandments" depends on the seriousness with which he tries to hear the word of God in the Jewish tradition, and on how many of the old "laws" address him personally as "commandments." This applies no less to the western type of Orthodoxy than it does to Reform Judaism. Orthodox Judaism in western Europe and America has tacitly managed to ignore quite a few paragraphs of the Shulhan Arukh, while a man like Franz Rosenzweig, on the basis of a liberal approach, was able to accept as "commandments" addressed to him a maximum number of traditional observances.

But Reform Judaism committed two serious errors in the nineteenth century. The nonobservance of the *mitzvot* was made to look like one of the demands of Reform Judaism. One of the "planks" of the famous Pittsburgh Platform of 1885 stated with regard to the Mosaic legislation that "we accept as binding only its moral laws, and maintain only such ceremonies as elevate and sanctify our lives, but reject all such as are not adapted to the views and habits of modern civilization." [4] This, of course, was quite in Holdheim's spirit. Only the moral commandments are binding. The individual is not given an opportunity to hear—as Franz Rosenzweig did—"commandments" also among the "ritual" laws.

Such a categorical rejection of a large body of the *mitzvot* contains no less dogmatism than does an uncritical acceptance of the totality of the Shulhan Arukh. If Reform Judaism is truly meant to be liberal, it must be left to the individual to decide which of the commandments he accepts as binding for himself. However, in order to be able to make his decision, the Reform Jew must know and understand the material from which the choice is to be made. This, in turn, necessitates an intensive study of the Jewish tradition. Only the educated Jew who is well acquainted with his tradition can come to terms with it and make his own selection from the plethora of traditional ordinances. Yet, in this respect, a second error was committed in the last century. Once it had been agreed that only the moral commandments were binding, it was no longer felt to be necessary to burden religious instruction with the study of the "ritual" *mitzvot*. Jewish education was largely reduced to talk about ethical monotheism and a few chapters of biblical history. While there was a stress on the Reform Jew's freedom of choice, he was not familiarized with the material from which that choice was to be made.

The student of Jewish history can understand the reasons and conditions that led to this state of affairs. He can, on occasion, even find excuses. Nevertheless, the problems of the twentieth century are of an altogether different kind. We no longer believe that the European Jew becomes a better European, or the American Jew a better American, by shedding his Jewish particularism. Moreover, our knowledge of psychology has also made us somewhat more circumspect in our evaluation of "ritual" and of the "nonrational." If it was the task of Judaism in the nineteenth century to "adapt" itself to "the views and habits of modern civilization," we are today more critical of that "modern civilization." If the nineteenth century felt it necessary to tell the Jew what he no longer had to observe in order to be like all other men, the twentieth century faces the task of leading the Jew back to the sources of Judaism in order to make him aware of the distinctiveness of his Jewish tradition and outlook.

These sources—Bible and Talmud, Midrash and philosophy, Kabbalah and Codes, poetry and the classics of the scientific study of Judaism—are the property of all Jews. In the obligation to study these sources there is no difference between the Orthodox and the Liberals, the Conservatives and the Reformers. It is a *mitzvah* which even the most radical of the Reformers cannot afford to ignore without calling into question his good faith and the seriousness of his conviction. That is why tradition said that "the study of the Torah surpasses the other commandments in importance." [5]

Only if the Reform Jew acts out of a full knowledge can there be talk of Reform Judaism at all. An ignoramus is only—an ignoramus. It is, of course, possible and even likely that, under certain circumstances, the Reform orientation might lead to the nonobservance of several traditional laws. It is possible but not inevitable. The example of Franz Rosenzweig again comes to mind. Nevertheless, even if the Reform orientation should lead, in a number of cases, to the nonobservance of *mitzvot,* it would be a nonobservance based on careful evaluation and not on ignorance. A true Reform Judaism, therefore, and one worthy of its name, would have to cultivate the study of the totality of our tradition, applying to it a set of criteria to guide the modern Jew in making his selections from it.

What, then, are those criteria?

I would suggest four criteria. First, *What has been the main thrust of the millennial Jewish tradition in a given case?* In examining the traditional material, we must not remain satisfied with first impressions, especially so because, in a tradition which spans four thousand years, the meaning of a given observance has not always been uniformly understood and interpreted.

A modern Jew might, for example, be under the impression that the prohibition of work on the Sabbath was simply directed against strenuous physical labor. He may assume that the Sabbath, throughout the centuries, has been a day of physical rest and relaxation. Moreover, we know that it was difficult in ancient days to make a fire by rubbing two sticks or stones together. Hence, the prohibition to cook or bake on the Sabbath was quite understandable. These activities involved hard work. But can this part of our tradition not be discarded today when it is no longer hard work to make a fire?

This conclusion is frequently drawn. Yet it is not warranted. A study of the Jewish sources will soon lead to the discovery that far more is involved in the Jewish Sabbath than the mere abstention from exhausting physical labor. The Sabbath is the day on which man, who works and creates throughout the week, shows himself to be but a creature. God alone is recognized as the Creator. On the Sabbath, the Jew refrains from interfering in the processes of nature. It is a day on which he is to leave nature unchanged, in recognition of the fact that his own powers over nature are limited. Consequently, if the purpose of the Sabbath is to express the notion that God, and not man, is the real Creator, the abstention from work, commanded in the Torah, aims at something over and above man's relaxation and physical recuperation.

The Sabbath law, with all its commandments and prohibitions, contains and implies far more than we have been able to hint at in connection with the prohibition of work. However, it illustrates what we mean by demanding, as one of the criteria for a modern Jewish observance, that, in any given case, an investigation be made into the main thrust of our millennial tradition. This examination is, of course, an objective and detached process. It does not yet commit us to anything.

What we are to do with the findings of our investigation is determined by our second criterion: *the manner in which I can best realize the traditional teaching in my life and in the situation in which I find myself.*

If the first criterion was purely scientific and objective, this second criterion already contains a conscious application of the Reform principle. Orthodox Judaism is, for example, objectively quite correct in deducing the prohibition of the use of cars and electricity on the Sabbath from the biblical prohibition of work—with "work" defined according to rabbinic categories. Tradition may indeed be so construed.

But as a Reform Jew, I must go beyond these considerations. I live in the here and now, and it is in this context that I must ask myself in which way I can observe the Sabbath best. Do I observe the Sabbath better if, on account of the distances involved, I refrain from going to the synagogue on the Sabbath, or from visiting friends, the bereaved, or the sick? Or is it not just the use of my car which helps me in my observance of the Sabbath in my particular situation? Does the true observance of the Sabbath compel me to keep my house cold and dark? Or is it not just the use of electricity which helps me to make the Sabbath the "day of light and joy" it was meant to be?

In other words, the Reform Jew is far more concerned with the Sabbath itself than with the letter of the Sabbath legislation, which testifies to the reality of the Sabbath as experienced by *past* generations. He wants to observe the Sabbath in the here and now. That is why factors come into play with which the legalists of earlier generations did not have to reckon.

A third criterion is *the voice of my own conscience.* This criterion, even more than the second one, reveals the liberalism of the Reform Jew and the influence of the Emancipation. The Reform

Jew, in the words of Leo Baeck, is characterized by the "piety of the individual," and not, as was the Jew of the ghetto, by the "piety of the environment." As an individual, he is no longer subject to religious compulsion or the dictates of any ecclesiastical authority. As an individual, he is free to participate or not to participate in religious observance. Even if others believe that they have found the key to the proper observance of the law in the here and now, his conscience still has to assent.

Consider, for example, the law which states, in connection with Passover, that "there shall be no leaven seen with thee in all thy borders seven days" (Deut. 16:4). The main thrust of the tradition with regard to this law seems clear. Anything remotely subject to the suspicion that it may contain "leaven" ingredients not only must not be "seen" in the Jew's home during Passover, it must not even be in his possession. The application of this law, as interpreted by the rabbis, could thus lead to the wholesale destruction of food in the Jew's house just before Passover, were it not for the fact that the same rabbis who elaborated the stringencies of that law also evolved a legal fiction by means of which the full force of the law could be evaded. By "selling" the food to a non-Jew, with a minimum down payment and with the understanding that the Jew can buy it back after the festival, the food not only need not be destroyed but can remain on the Jew's premises, provided it is suitably locked up.

There is nothing wrong with legal fictions as such. No legal system can function without them. Indeed, one can appreciate the inventiveness of the ancient rabbis which enabled them to keep their legal system within humane dimensions. But it is one thing to appreciate the phenomenon historically, and quite another to accept it for myself, especially if I do not view my relation to God primarily in terms of a legal system. Thus, while it would be quite possible for the Reform Jew to solve his "leaven" problem along the lines indicated by the rabbis, possible even with his own "here and now," it is quite conceivable that he might also say, "Yes, it is possible to do it this way; *but my conscience speaks against it!* I shall refrain from eating leaven during Passover. I shall keep all leaven out of sight in my home. But I feel no need for the legal fiction of 'selling' my leaven. This would add nothing to my Passover observance. On the contrary, I would not feel intellectually honest were I to engage in this legal fiction. My conscience rebels against it."

In terms of the criterion we have outlined here, the Reform Jew would be justified in using such an argument. But he would also have to add that his fellow Jew has an equal right to listen to the voice of *his* conscience—even if his conscience makes him "sell" his leaven for Passover. Both are "Reform Jews," and the one cannot resent the other's selling of the leaven any more than the latter is able to regard the former's noncompliance with this practice as a sin.

The last-named criterion may well carry within itself the seeds of religious anarchy. The fourth criterion helps to maintain the balance. It is *the feeling of responsibility toward the covenant community.*

Judaism cannot be abstracted from the faith-community within which Judaism is lived—the faith-community with which God made a covenant at Sinai and which remained loyal to Him throughout the millennia. This covenant people, Israel, not only has a historical significance; its significance extends to the realm of redemptive history. Everything, therefore, that contributes to the survival and to the unity of the covenant community of Israel must be regarded as a religious commandment. On the other hand, everything that hurts the covenant community must be avoided.

In accordance with this perspective, the Reform Jew will observe a number of *mitzvot* toward which he might feel no personal obligation if his religion were a matter of the individual only, and not also of the community as a whole. Into this category belong the specific seventh day on which the Jewish Sabbath is to be kept, and all Jewish festivals, which have to be observed according to the Jewish calendar. In theory, it is conceivable that one could celebrate the ideal of freedom on some evening other than the eve of the fifteenth of Nisan. But the Seder, as the *Jewish* festival of freedom, can only be celebrated then. The same consideration governs the use of Hebrew in the Jewish worship service. Important as it is to find room for the vernacular in the synagogue, it is nevertheless true that the worshiping community of Israel knows itself as such particularly during moments of Hebrew prayer.

These illustrations do not reflect purely theoretical issues. They are based on questions which, at one time or another, were raised within Reform Judaism, and to which some radical answers were proposed in the last century. The twentieth century has largely turned away from radical solutions. And the feeling of responsibility toward the covenant community has played a not insignificant role in the change of orientation which has taken place in Reform Judaism.

It may not often occur that the four criteria that we have mentioned will be in complete accord. They are more likely to be in a constant state of tension. Moreover, one Jew may rate one criterion higher than does another Jew. Yet all will have to reckon with all the criteria all the time.

The four criteria, in their aggregate, represent the yardstick that the modern Jew must apply to his inherited tradition. Yet a yardstick is only—a yardstick. It cannot be the total content of one's religious faith and life. The latter requires more than a yardstick. It needs the material itself, the material of the millennial tradition. There are no shortcuts to the acquisition of that material. Two thousand years ago, when the tradition was still in its youth, Hillel stated that "the ignorant man cannot be truly religious." [6] What was true then is all the more true today. Only an intensified Jewish education—of child, youth, and adult—can make the application of the criteria meaningful. But only an application of the criteria can make tradition itself live.

IRA EISENSTEIN

Jewish Law and the Ways of Judaism in Our Time

I LOOK UPON JUDAISM not as an "ism," nor as a movement with a creed or set of propositions to which one subscribes and gives assent intellectually, but as an evolving religious civilization.

I know, of course, that throughout Jewish history people have attempted to formulate the basic ideas, the kernel and essence of Judaism, as they saw them at their particular time. If we were to make a survey of these formulations, we would find a series of different and frequently contradictory concepts. Judaism, therefore, is not so much a creed as it is the total historical experience of the Jewish people. This experience has either been recorded and preserved in our social institutions (our laws, customs, traditions, literature, art, and music) or embodied in our sancta, the sacred objects, places, or events engaging the minds and hearts of our people. All these elements are part of the civilization of the Jewish people.

The term "religion" did not appear in the vocabulary of Judaism until quite recently. The Hebrew language has no word for religion. The only concept we have is Torah. What makes Judaism a total civilization is Torah, that is to say, that body of laws, customs, practices, and literature which, at any given time, represents the highest expression of that civilization. When we speak of Judaism as a "religious" civilization, we are merely making a concession to the limitations of the English language in order to stress the fact that our civilization has had a particular quality. It is not a civilization whose chief expression can be found in the arena of political theory or action. We honor the writings and activities of the prophets much more than we honor the kings in whose reigns they lived. Nor has our civilization excelled or sought primary expression on the battlefield. Joshua, the Maccabees, and Bar Kochba were minor characters in Jewish consciousness practically until the rise of modern Zionism. Nor does our civilization have an essentially scientific orientation. There are few Jewish scientists in the whole range of Jewish history. We did not develop scientists until modern times.

Jewish civilization has expressed itself most characteristically in that which we call religion—in an effort to define the good life, to find the way which would be closest to what man was intended to be and to do, to discover man's *summum bonum,* his highest good. The vocabulary of our tradition defines this conduct and attitude as "living in accordance with the will of God." When our forefathers talked about the will of God, they were in essence saying, "This is the right way; this is the true way; this is the way man was intended to live." Jewish life has been a constant search for this true way.

Rabbi Jacob Agus expresses the same thought succinctly in his book *The Evolution of Jewish Thought:*

> We do not and cannot claim to know all about God nor all about man's need for salvation. As Jews, we do not strike the pose of all-knowing prophets, but rather "sons of prophets," determined seekers of truth. The Jews are heirs of hundreds of generations of deeply earnest men and women who sought God by the feeble lights in their possession. They denied themselves many things for the sake of their faith, forswearing the luxuries of life and even life itself when the test came, but they never denied the God of their heart. The history of the Jewish faith is the magnificent tale of an endless quest by a world-wide community, a community of people remaining true to its search in spite of many temptations and refusing to compromise with its conscience.[1]

In this paragraph, Dr. Agus summarizes what is meant by a religious civilization: one that is predominantly concerned with salvation. Judaism has been concerned with the fulfillment of the individual and of the people as a people. It has been concerned with their relationship to the rest of the peoples of the world. In other words, it has been concerned with defining this people's life and role in time and space.

The third term in my definition is "evolving," a term needed to emphasize, perhaps gratuitously, that this civilization has always been changing, that it has grown and developed and never remained static. Although there were long periods when changes were hardly perceptible, there has been a constant adaptation to new situations, always for the purpose of defining or refining our understanding of the good way of life.

I

My definition of Judaism as the evolving religious civilization of the Jewish people has several implications with regard to Jewish law and the numerous concepts and practices associated with it.

My definition implies, for instance, that the constant element in Judaism is the Jewish people. There is an uninterrupted chain of generations which makes it possible for us to regard ourselves as having descended from Abraham, Isaac, and Jacob. We may question this statement biologically; nevertheless, they were our ancestors to all intents and purposes. We are members of one *mishpahah,* even though our cosmology, our conceptions of the universe, our way of living, our whole hierarchy of values, may differ radically from theirs. Our relationship to our earliest childhood as a people is analogous to the relationship we have to our own childhood. We think and live differently from the way we did when we were children. Yet, when we think of our childhood, we maintain that we are the same persons we were before, even though there may not be a single cell in our body that has remained unchanged since we were children; but there is a continuity of personality which consists of memories, associations, and habits.

As we mature, we go through a series of changes in our relationships to our parents. Three stages in the growth of the child can illustrate the various stages in our changing relationship to the past of our people.

In stage one, when the child is very small, the parent is infallible. Papa knows everything. When the child comes and asks, "Daddy, what is this?" the father is the best and most wonderful person in the world. He knows everything and he can do everything. This stage may be called the Garden of Eden period.

The second stage sets in when the child reaches adolescence. The parent is cast out of the Garden of Eden. He knows nothing. He can do nothing right. Everything he says is wrong or even unprincipled simply because he is a parent. It is during this period that the child achieves the pinnacle of his own infallibility.

Beginning with the age of 17 or 18, however, the third period starts in which a father and mother somehow begin to show increasing signs of intelligence. The sophomore at college begins to descend from his Olympian heights of omniscience. He is no longer so sure that he has all the answers, and as he gets older, he begins to become even less sure of himself. He grows. He matures. He begins to develop ideas and convictions of his own, values that differ from those of his parents. He does not stop loving his parents. But now he sees them as they really are, as human beings with their own strengths and weaknesses, aspirations and difficulties. As the child matures, he finally reaches the point where he is willing to listen to the views of his parents even though he may not agree with them.

An analogous development takes place in our relationship to our tradition. In our relationship to the history of our people we recapitulate, in a sense, the stages of our personal development. In the beginning, as we look at the past, every word ever written, every law ever promulgated, every notion ever conceived, seems perfect. But there follows the second stage at which we reject everything. This is the time when the past does not make sense precisely because it is the past. However, as we mature, we finally reach the point when we realize that our ancestors were people, ordinary men and women who were trying their best to make their way in this world with the limited knowledge they had and in the face of their limited opportunities for contact with other cultures and civilizations. They were literally trying to pull themselves up by their own bootstraps intellectually, morally, and spiritually. They were trying very hard. Sometimes they succeeded; at other times they failed.

II

If we study the Torah in the light of this approach, we can begin to understand why it shows tremendous heights in one chapter and deep valleys in the next. One chapter may attempt to justify genocide, while the next chapter and sometimes even the very next verse set forth the loftiest notions concerning human relationships. You will find a law which condones slavery, and then you will come across a verse in which slavery is denounced in the most vigorous terms. You will find a statement according to which a woman is practically without legal rights: she cannot testify in court, and her intelligence is not relied upon. Yet in the written and oral traditions of our people you will also find the deep respect for womankind that made Jewish family life the envy of other cultures.

These contrasts and contradictions exist because our ancestors were people like us, men and women who were searching, probing, trying to understand the mystery of the world, attempting to formulate a way of living and to create institutions that would translate their best insights into reality.

It is on the basis of this approach that we can love the past, revere and consult it, but also disagree with it. We can live with it without tension or guilt because we see it as a great reservoir from which we select that which is useful, needed, and relevant, while we do not feel compelled to use what we may have outgrown or what life itself has rendered obsolete.

The same considerations apply to our rituals. We are neither destructive nor irreverent when we recognize that our Sabbath observance is the product of a long process of evolution, and that its rituals represent the symbolization and dramatization of certain ideals. We feel that some of these ideals should still be cherished, whereas others may no longer be relevant in our time. We try to salvage what is still applicable.

Three principles are involved in the way in which we approach Jewish law as exemplified, for instance, by the Sabbath. First, we give precedence to tradition. We study what our ancestors had to say about the role of the seventh day in living the good life. It would be cultural and spiritual vandalism if we were to wipe out tradition merely because we do not happen to be in the mood to observe it. Second, before we eliminate anything which appears to be obsolescent we make every attempt to modify or readjust it. Third, in making our selection we weigh our decision on a scale of values which fuses the values and insights of tradition with the dictates of our own reason. Modern life, for instance, will frequently compel us to make a choice between observing the tradition of not riding on the Sabbath and observing the tradition of worshiping together with our fellow Jews. Yet many Jews live too far from a synagogue to be able to observe both traditions. If we take the halakhic point of view, we may not ride on the Sabbath. Hence, if we want to say our prayers, we shall have to say them by ourselves.

Yet Jewish worship is public worship, and we must ask ourselves whether it should be the norm and standard of Jewish conduct in our time that each of us pray alone at home, or whether it is preferable that each join his fellow Jews in public worship. Can I achieve spiritual growth by not riding, or do I discharge my responsibility as a Jew better and achieve greater spiritual growth by going to the synagogue? My own answer is to attend public worship. Riding is merely a means to an end. On my scale of values, the end outweighs the prohibition against riding.

The question of *kashrut* in one's home confronts us with a similar choice. Should we or should we not maintain *kashrut* at home? The arguments against *kashrut* seem formidable. Kosher food is more expensive. *Kashrut* involves a good deal of trouble and inconvenience. Moreover, it requires the observance of certain rituals and forms which may no longer speak to us at all and seem to make little or no sense. Yet, if our home is not kosher, we are in fact putting up a sign at our front door: "Only nonobservant Jews are welcome here." Observant Jews will unhappily have to eat elsewhere. In weighing the value of *kashrut* in their homes, many Jews find that, in their hierarchy of values, their ability to welcome any and every Jew into their home is more important for them than the assertion of their independence from the kosher butcher. In my scale of values, more is to be gained by offering unlimited hospitality to parents, relatives, friends, and colleagues than by excluding them from my table by yielding to my doubts about the relevance and meaningfulness of these laws.

By acting this way I am obviously not affirming the validity of the halakhic regulations for me. I am approaching the observance of *kashrut* from the point of view of a culture and civilization that are concerned with ethical and spiritual values such as loyalty, identification, hospitality, public worship. I feel free to engage in this process of evaluation as long as my evaluations are based upon knowledge and conscientious research and are not merely the whim of the moment or the caprice of a particular type of temperament.

Hence, I do not consider it inconsistent to keep a kosher home yet to ride on the Sabbath. I am prepared to recognize the fact that a man might have to go to his office or store on a Sabbath morning and therefore use Friday night or Saturday afternoon for his Sabbath observance. This, too, does not involve an inconsistency. It merely takes cognizance of the realism of the situation which imposes upon us the need for selection, for choosing the most and the best of the Sabbath that we can possibly achieve and preserve for ourselves. To take an attitude of "all or nothing" is to encourage hypocrisy. To do the things you have to do, but to do them with a sense of sin, or to conceal the fact that you are doing them, or to pretend that you are not doing them, is the kind of hypocrisy that makes a man drive his car to the synagogue on Sabbath but park it two blocks away. It is the kind of hypocrisy that made a man once say to me, when we were getting ready to go to the synagogue on a rainy Friday night, "All right, we'll drive over. But we are going to walk the last two blocks. The one thing we have got to be sure of is that our umbrellas are wet when we come in." What kind of spiritual life are we building if these are the standards by which the Sabbath is honored?

I believe it is not an inconsistency to ride on Sabbath when larger values are at stake. I know, of course, that some people consider my approach dangerous. They fear that as soon as I permit the use of a car on the Sabbath, people will use it to drive not only to the synagogue but also to the beach or the ball game. This risk exists. It is a very real hazard. But it is the hazard of democracy, the hazard of one's belief in people. If we believe that Jews regard the Sabbath and our ritual and observances as a kind of strait jacket and that they are merely waiting for someone to permit them, or show them a way, to escape from it, we had better stop talking about Sabbath, religion, and spirituality. When people are treated like children who have to be watched, checked, and disciplined, we should not be surprised if they rebel against the discipline and disregard it completely. I believe it is possible in a mature Jewish society to explain and interpret to people what acts we consider appropriate and why so that they will maintain and safeguard the spirit of Sabbath. I believe it is possible to communicate to them something of the spirit of the Sabbath so that they will not go beyond the limits of propriety. Those who are prepared to go beyond these limits will not consult us in the first place. Those, however, who are looking for guidance may find our approach meaningful as a rationale for Jewish living in our time.

III

These examples illustrate my approach to the problem of an evolving religious civilization. If we want to retain the basic values of Jewish laws, we must come to terms with the changes in our mores that have occurred over the centuries, and we must reckon with basic human needs through a process of weighing those values that are affirmed as well as those that are rejected in each decision we make. One may disagree with the one or other particular decision we make and arrive at an entirely different conclusion. What is important is not so much each particular act or decision, but the method, the philosophy, and spirit that govern our approach. Our great need is for a guide that is non-halakhic yet does not lead to total anarchy. It must attempt to maintain the continuity of tradition and Jewish experience, yet at the same time accept change in an orderly process. In doing so it will establish new precedents that another generation in turn may want to reevaluate and either accept or reject, or perhaps modify in accordance with their views and needs. This is the spirit in which I approach the ways of Judaism in our time from the point of view of the Reconstructionist movement.

NORMAN E. FRIMER

Law as Living Discipline: The Sabbath as Paradigm

MAN, HISTORICALLY, is not only a thinking and feeling being, but a "doing" being. His life is expressed in activity and relationship, in habit and structured productivity. When a thought or emotion moves him, he will not rest until he has converted it into objective form. Thus, man's life, like the product of genius, is one percent creativity and ninety-nine percent routine. Routine remains bearable only because of the nurture of creativity.

The same holds true for a community. In Milton Steinberg's words, "The ideas and ideals of a people may give it significance, but its group habits give it life." Whatever truths a group possesses must, therefore, be transmuted from abstractions and universals into group habits, the "stuff of life," which is particular and situational. Otherwise, they would remain lofty but ethereal, inspirational but nonoperative. Man can live neither by bread nor by principle alone.

Every social entity faces this problem. It was, however, central for the Jew. The presuppositions of his birth, existence, and destiny were unique and had to be uniquely embodied in the very bone and marrow of his daily activity. For this purpose, an all-embracing instrument was needed which could transform a slave rabble into a nation, inspire and direct the formation of a social order, withstand the shock of Israel's dispersion and, by hurdling barriers of language and culture, serve as the great unifier of a people across time and space.

The force which undergirded the truths of Israel's life-view and translated them into daily routine—of home and marketplace, field and factory, school and sanctuary—was the dynamic folk conviction regarding Torah and *mitzvot*. Torah was the divine teaching and tradition out of which scholars and teachers in every generation were to forge whatever forms, practices, and institutions were needed for their own time. These were then to be built, as bricks and girders, into the very structure of life's demands and challenges and thereby be converted into repositories of Israel's heritage of truth. The *mitzvah* was to be the diurnal, but existentially crucial, act of life prescribed in the divine teaching by means of which the universal "ought" can be transformed for the individual, as member of the community, into a personal "I must," "I can," "I will." In a conjoined relationship, means and ends are fused into an indissoluble unity.

I

This process is illustrated, for example, by the way in which our forefathers sought to meet the challenge to fashion man's life in accordance with Judaism's faith-premise, viewing God as Creator and man as His creature.[1]

The stark fact is that for six-sevenths of every week man struggles to master his natural environment, to draw sustenance from its resources, and to bend it to his will for his enjoyment or advantage. This is good, for creative labor is good. It is a *mitzvah* commanded by God Himself.[2]

Yet several dangers lurk in the shadows of human productivity. First, man paradoxically tends to become dependent upon the very instruments he has fashioned to free and serve him. Gilbert Murray emphasizes this point in his analysis of *Five Stages of Greek Religion:* "On us the power of the material world has, through our very mastery of it, and the dependence which results from the mastery, both inwardly and outwardly increased its hold. *Capta ferit victorem cepit.* We have taken possession of it and now we cannot move without it." [3] Second, the danger is very real in modern industrial society that man, as worker, becomes depersonalized and functions merely as a human cog in a vast assembly line.

Above all, however, there is the opposite danger—the danger that man, aware of his power and success in dominating nature, will begin to regard himself as the measure of what is right and the yardstick of the good. "Beware," warned Moses thirty centuries ago, ". . . lest when thou hast eaten and art satisfied, and hast built goodly houses, [probably split-level ones] and dwelt therein and thy silver and thy gold is multiplied . . . [when thine industrial plants and commercial enterprises have multiplied] then thy heart be lifted up, and thou forget the Lord thy God . . . and thou say in thy heart: My power and the might of my hand hath gotten me this wealth." [4] Men are singularly susceptible to these spiritual foibles.

To balance this impulse, Judaism felt the need for a powerful reverse thrust. Only a counteracting spiritual force, operating radically and publicly in the social fabric of the community, might shake man out of his propensity for self-enslavement and self-deification. He must be impelled to stretch his spirit or shrink his ego so that he can begin to assume his authentic stature as man.

Consequently, Jewish law stepped in with boldness and an uncompromising demand. "Six days shalt thou labor, and do all thy work; but the seventh day is a sabbath unto the Lord thy God, in it thou shalt not do any manner of work, thou nor thy son, nor thy daughter, nor thy man-servant, nor thy maid-servant, nor thy cattle, nor thy stranger that is within thy gates." [5] Make the whole machine-community come to a dead stop. Let inner man take over. Only the safety, security and survival of an individual or the group can justify an exception.

Our oral tradition went beyond this generalization and spelled out the implications of labor in comprehensive detail.[6] Thirty-nine categories of productive and purposeful work were delineated and prohibited, each directed at breaking man's dependence or hold on nature and releasing his shackling grip on his fellowman. If you are a farmer, commands the Law, you must not plough, sow, reap, bind, thresh, winnow, grind, knead, or bake. Go and prepare your food in advance. If you are a sheepherder or artisan, you must not shear, bleach, comb, dye, spin, weave, sew, tear. Prepare your clothing ahead of time. If you are a builder or craftsman, you must not construct or demolish, kindle fire or extinguish it, manufacture or ship your product. Close down the assembly line. This is Shabbat! Even if you represent management, you too must cease and desist. For on this day there are no employers and no employees. There are to be no exploiters and no exploited, no manipulators and no manipulated, no freemen and no slaves, no citizens and no strangers. On the Shabbat all are to stand equal in one human family before their one divine parent.

Yet even these specific details were considered inadequate. The sages of the Talmud developed additional categories enjoining any similar, related, or conducive task.[7] Moreover, Isaiah had long ago provided the rabbis with the scriptural grounds for outlawing any activity patently identified with the weekday world.[8] For him, even talking about commerce was desecration, let alone negotiating oral agreements and binding contracts.[9]

The extremes to which the rabbis went in building their halakhic "fences" and defenses reflect a twofold insight. One is their awareness of the gripping hold which work as job, career, or profession has on the life-pattern of every human being. A job or profession is more than a means to one's material livelihood. In the moving words of the High Holy Day liturgy, *benafsho yavi lahmo,* man literally invests part of his very being in his task.[10] Craft and craftsman unite in a common partnership. In addition, however, the sages intuited the mortal struggle within every man between the twin forces of the creative and the acquisitive. God had intended man to use the acquisitive creatively; man persists in exploiting the creative acquisitively. Consequently, Jewish tradition pitted against this pair another set of twins, the affirming *zakhor* (remember) and restraining *shamor* (observe) of Sabbath power.[11] By arresting the acquisitive—through the negative *shamor*—Judaism aimed at releasing the creative, allowing it to come into its own. By encouraging the creative—through the positive *zakhor*—it redirected the flow toward the divine end for which it was originally intended.

Even a small measure of self-discipline and affirmative action can help man return to the deeper sources of his being—to his family, to his community, to himself, and to his God. For the problems of western society are essentially no longer material.

They are psychological and spiritual. As Lewis Mumford perceptively predicted in his *Condition of Man,* "At the very moment that mankind as a whole is clothed, fed, sheltered adequately, relieved from want and anxiety, there will arise new conditions calling equally for struggle, internal if not external conditions, derived precisely from the goods that have been achieved." [12] And it is regarding the alleviation of these crucial problems that the Shabbat has much to say to contemporary man.

II

An entire community, however, in order to live by its faith and to retain the vitality of its seminal ideals, requires more than merely a formal knowledge of their origin and nature or a mechanical obedience to observances embodied in its tradition. A time may come when the hand of tradition begins to weigh too heavily upon us. If the past is to work dynamically through us, if its events and their derivative lessons are not to remain merely facts and statistics in the musty files of our intellectual archives, memory must become motive power, the experiential must become existential, "the past must become contemporary."

This is more than suggested by the biblical claim that the covenant with Israel at Sinai was not concluded with our ancestors alone. "Neither with you only do I make this *berit* and this oath, but with him that standeth here with us this day before the Lord our God, and also with him that is not here with us this day." [13] In some inexplicable way we, too, were involved.[14] For this *berit* to be alive and compelling, the voice of Sinai must also address us, this very day.[15] We must be with Abraham at Mount Moriah, with our Hebrew brethren in the lime pits of Egypt, by their side in their majestic procession of freedom toward Horeb, as well as with Elijah on Mount Carmel in his dramatic confrontation with the priests of Baal.

What was to be the power which would enable the Jew to acquire that sense of the eternal presentness of Sinai? According to an ancient tradition, revelation took place on the Sabbath Day.[16] Thus, when a Jew of piety and faith sits in the synagogue on

Shabbat, wrapped in his prayer shawl, and listens to the voice of the reader reciting from the Torah, *Vayomer Ha-shem el Moshe,* "And the Lord spoke unto Moses, saying: 'Speak unto the children of Israel, and bid them,' " [17] he must somehow transcend time and space and be conscious that the biblical yesterday has become his today, and that Moses spoke not to his ancestors alone, but speaks to him. It is in this spirit that he is expected to listen to the reading of the Law and to proclaim aloud upon its termination: "This is the Torah which Moses placed before the children of Israel." [18]

This is no role-playing, no make-believe. It is a personal act of will, a personal leap of commitment, a personal identity of soul. The synagogue has been transmuted into an old–new Sinai, and the Shabbat into a hallowed interlude in infinite experience. For the fraction of a second, there is no time–space dimension. There is only *am Yisrael hai,* the reality of a living Israel in a living relationship with its living God.

III

Unfortunately, this kind of ecstasy and union of souls is the gift of the rare man who stands at the peak of the mountain of the Lord. The rest of us stand only at its base or are, at most, on the ascent. Are we to be robbed of having any part in the experience of Shabbat? Was Judaism made only for the angelic, the saintly, the sage and the mystic?

Eliezer Berkowitz, in his exposition of *God, Man and History,*[19] has underscored the fact that Judaism is more than just a "spiritual" or "intellectual" religion. It does not direct its call only to the soul or mind of man. For when man stands over against God in a one-to-one relationship (as all of us must ultimately do in our existential aloneness), the relationship is not partial, but total; not fragmentary, but full—involving the whole person. In this linkage the body, too, is partner with divinity. God created it. It is not profane unless man deliberately makes it so. Like the ark housing the Torah, the body enshrines the soul in an inextricable life-union. Neither can meet its maker without the other. The soul remains mute and helpless without the body; the body is cold and cloddish without the soul. As a divinely joined composite, however, they can aspire to fulfill the liturgical task enunciated in the *nishmat* hymn of the Sabbath, "All my limbs do declare, O Lord, who is like unto Thee!" [20]

To implement this union, the Sabbath ordinances applied and explicated Isaiah's words, "Thou shalt proclaim the Sabbath joy." [21] How? By good food and good drink. [22] "And shalt honor it." [23] How? Through attractive clothing and decorous garments. [24] The whole personality of man stands before his King on the Sabbath Day. Clothed in the apparel of inner and outer dignity, every man, woman, and child may be received in audience before their God.

Can anything be too good in order to help celebrate this unique privilege? For God not only receives us but allows the Shekhinah, His Divine Presence, to come into our home as our special guest. For three full meals, gathered as a family in joyous repast, we are both His companions and His children. Consequently, the table must be bedecked with special linens. Flowers are to adorn the setting, wreathing the radiance and beauty that stream from the flickering Sabbath candles. The choicest wine is served, as are two loaves of white bread tastily baked. A leisurely meal of several courses is eaten, accompanied by joyous song. Moreover, on this day a Jew must not kindle any fire, especially not the fire of anger or personal controversy.

This Sabbath delight was never meant to be the monopoly of the affluent. Every Jew had the right and was to have the opportunity to share in its blessing. In order to celebrate the Sabbath, the Jew was required to give concrete evidence of a sensitivity and a responsiveness to the deprivation of others. He was admonished to contribute private *tzedakah* before kindling the Sabbath candles and to invite indigent or lonely guests for the Sabbath meal. In addition, Jewish law required every community to establish a welfare program for its needy citizens. No man must be reduced to the degradation of begging. Moreover, the allotment of food or funds adequate for an entire week was, by talmudic practice, to be distributed on *Erev Shabbat*. In this way, the poor family, too, would be able to honor and celebrate the hallowed day with joy, secure in the knowledge that the morrow was provided for as well. Otherwise it would have been folly to chant on the Sabbath afternoon, "Let my soul leap up in blessing unto the Lord," [25] having neglected the body which provides the springboard and the momentum for that winged leap. The popular mind might consider the stomach a good way to a man's heart. Jewish thought recommends it, along with learning and faith, as a conduit to the Jew's soul. Through this sacramental experience, he can literally "taste and see that the Lord is good." [26] In the concise words of Judah Ha-Levi, "the joyous observance of the Sabbath rites brings one closer to God than asceticism or monasticism." [27]

IV

Yet a complex problem remains. What can serve as a conveyor belt for such principles? Aristotle was more than theorizing when he insisted that "people do not become good by listening to lectures on moral philosophy." How then can ideals be transmitted from person to person and from one generation to the next?

"Ritual" has become a word of disdain for many young people, and "ceremonial" is often merely a synonym for distasteful pomp and circumstance. Yet, when used with integrity and earnestness, both are the indispensable tools of which every society must avail itself in order to hurdle the chasm of time. Existential appropriation is a gift for which few are ready, a capacity too private to make it socially operative. Yet ritual and ceremonial provide us with a nonverbal language whose idiomatic meaning can, by dint of repetition, become universally communicable and applicable to all ages. Jewish law has consequently availed itself of its usefulness and richly endowed the Sabbath with its eloquent beauty.

The Sabbath is basically a family celebration. Therefore, "he who is privileged to rejoice on the Sabbath, surrounded by sons and daughters, finds great favor in the eyes of the Almighty." [28] For, as the generations gather about the Sabbath table, they are not only bound by this expressive though silent symbolism one unto the other, but with all past generations of Israel.

In this setting, the flicker of the Sabbath candles, the words and chant of the *kiddush* are the dramatic script and lighting effects for the depiction of the miracles of Creation and Exodus. The two *hallot* speak of God's providence and sustenance. The traditional washing of the hands links us with the High Priest in the ancient Temple, with the table as our altar and the food as the *mat'nat kehunah,* the portion of priestliness. Moreover, through the special medieval *zemirot* (Sabbath melodies), which even the smallest children may learn lispingly, tradition weaves its gossamer threads, which, with increasing strength, tie our children to the souls of such mystics as Rabbi Isaac Luria [29] and Rabbi Israel Al Najara.[30] Subtly and unknowingly, their hearts too may be filled with a heavenly yearning, which some day may spring forth as an unabashed love song unto God.

Similarly, the words of Torah—and no Shabbat table should be without them—form timeless linkages with patriarchs and prophets, sages and scholars, with the heroes and heralds who in every age pioneer and preserve our sacred way. More than that, Sabbath study is an *imitatio Dei,* an emulation of the ways of God who, after six days, rested only from His physical creation, but whose intellectual and spiritual essence remained undiminished. Therefore we are bidden, especially on this day, to immerse ourselves in the life-giving waters of Torah.[31]

V

Any treatment of the Shabbat would, however, be incomplete if it limited itself to a description and interpretation of the parts alone. The parts are integrated into the wholeness of a living entity by that divine attribute which is the end purpose of its creation and the ultimate meaning of its observance—*kedushah,* freely translated as "holiness" or "sanctity." *Zachor et yom ha-Shabbat,* "Make the Sabbath a day of remembrance," commands Exodus, *lekadsho,* "to make it *kadosh.*" [32] *Shamor et yom ha-Shabbat,*

"Safeguard the Sabbath Day from all desecrations," enjoins Deuteronomy, again, *lekadsho,* "to make it *kadosh.*" [33] *Kedushah* constitutes both a religious striving and a fulfillment.

It seems peculiar that the Jew is bidden to make the Sabbath *kadosh* when, according to the biblical record, the day already was *kedosh ha'Shem,* "the *kadosh* of God." [34] For when, at the very end of the beginning, the divine artisan had completed His physical task and found it to His satisfaction, He Himself bestowed upon the Sabbath His blessing, *vay'kadesh oto,* "and designated it *kadosh.*" [35] Must man repeat this act?

It is Judaism's unique claim that everything in the course of history is shared by the effort of man. Man, for example, is God's partner—only a junior one, to be sure, but still a partner—in the completion of the work of creation.[36] Sinai, too, would not have seen the consummation of the covenant without Israel's assent [37] of *na'asseh v'nishma.*[38] The same, according to tradition, holds true for redemption. Unless the world is faced with utter annihilation necessitating an apocalyptic intervention, redemption, too, will be the accrued dividend of the divine–human investment.[39] Similarly, therefore, though God Himself designated the cosmic Sabbath of creation as *kadosh,* man, too, must carry his share of responsibility and make the human Sabbath of history worthy of being stamped with the seal of *kadosh.* This is why the Sabbath is proclaimed as an *ot,* "a binding sign" between God and Israel.[40] For just as God rested on the Sabbath *vayinafash,* "and ensouled the world," so must Israel, in celebrating its own Sabbath, never lose sight of its destiny and *raison d'être* to "ensoul" all of history.

It is a high calling, and one for which there are few volunteers. Yet Jewish tradition insists that divinity has conspired to conscript us, and history has unerringly demonstrated time and again that there is no Tarshish to which a contemporary Jonah may escape. Ours, it seems, is not to reason why; ours is but to appropriate this sacred mission and to live in its fulfillment.

Nevertheless, it seems inevitable that even the best of us will grow weary in the fight against darkness and despair. Battle fatigue is the inevitable concomitant of long combat. Our exhaustion is not solely physical. It stems from a numbness of the soul, as we lose sight of our purpose. Our morale wanes quickly when the sources of our faith in our destiny begin to dry up. What healing and therapy can be provided for the fireless soul?

By its laws, Jewish tradition attempts to set up and place us in a temporary and temporal refuge to which the Jewish body and soul can move for haven and healing. It is not an escape from reality, for we act with full awareness of life about us. It is even less a flight from time, for we are to utilize it in full measure. Yet temporally and spatially we are to live on a new level, in a new dimension. It is thus not withdrawal but an uplifting, a kind of second-story existence. We remain actively in history and time, but try to reshape our entire social environment and refashion the stuff of its being into a new experience of living. For at least one complete day we strive to live according to an ideal vision of life as it can and ought to be, for both the individual and the community. It is the vision of a life in which man can have, not rest and peace *from*—which so often constitutes our own Sabbath— but *for,* "the peace for self-perfection that Thou dost desire," "the rest for love and generosity," "the rest for peace and serenity, quietude and trust." No man can derive this quality of Shabbat from any other human being or from life without, "for from Thee alone cometh that brand of peace and rest." [41]

Thus, by making God sovereign over every segment of our life on Shabbat, we invest our individual lives with the *kadosh*. By joining together as a community and bearing witness to the glory of His mighty acts, we also renew our group vision of the messianic redemption and collectively move all of Israel (since we are one of its parts) one step closer to its destined task of becoming a *mamlekhet kohanim,* "a kingdom of priests" (or, in Nachmanides' translation, *meshortai,* "My servants"), *vegoy kadosh* (in parallel translation), a people of Him who alone merits the transcending designation of *kadosh, kadosh, kadosh.*[42]

Israel yearns to prolong this divine–human relationship beyond this single and singular day. It has always been man's yearning to extend ideal into real society. Yet man seems far from ready or willing to act out in reality what he is abundantly able to do in potentiality. Israel must, therefore, bide its time in patience and faith and prepare at the end of each Shabbat realistically but sadly for its return to the reality which is sundered and split. For in it there still is a separation of the sacred from the profane, of light from darkness, of Israel from the nations, of Sabbath from the workday week.

The Jew bids a plaintive farewell to this great day, but with zeal replenished and faith renewed. For his eyes are now lifted to a new Sabbath, a distant yet beckoning Sabbath, when life will be holy and one, humanity whole and one, and God's name perfect and one. He sees from afar the day of the *mizmor shir leyom ha'Shabbat, mizmor shir leatid lavo,* the day when the Sabbath will in and of itself be a psalm of song, a hymn to the future that can be. What kind of future? A *yom she'kuloh Shabbat umenuhah lehayei haolamim,* a "day which is totally Sabbath and tranquillity unto all eternity." [43]

VI

This is the manner in which Jewish law performs its Sabbath tasks. It helps objectify the truths and principles of Judaism and wed them actively to the lived concrete. It holds captive the experiences of yesterday until man releases them into a situation of existential relationship that is contemporaneous and self-involving. The Sabbath laws join body and soul together, bind heart and spirit as one, so that in total union they encounter God in the wholeness of human personality. And, finally, the law marks out a chunk in life and hews out of its stuff an ideal living experience which is both memory and vision of man's potential and God's intention for personal and social achievement. By the strength of this renewed and renewing glimpse of the perfectible in expectation, Israel emerges from the Shabbat, refired and restored to stand as faithful and exemplary sentinels in vigil over those truths which alone can make Israel free and prove redemptive for all mankind.

This, of course, is the Shabbat *in potentia.* As for the rest of the objective, we have not yet ceased to be the human partners of the divine, and thus continue to be charged with its actualization.

ERNST SIMON

12. On the Meaning of Prayer

AN EXAMINATION of the meaning of prayer and worship in Jewish experience involves the analysis of several major questions. What is the nature of prayer, and what are its presuppositions? What specific features characterize Jewish prayer? What is the efficacy of prayer, and what dangers does it involve? To what extent and in what ways can prayer be relevant for the modern Jew?

I

Genuine prayer is based on three presuppositions. They are not psychological but logical or, to be precise, theological presuppositions. The first is a belief in a personal God as the peak of a hierarchically ordered universe. There is a hierarchical order of being in the universe. We can distinguish different levels of being. In the mineral world, terms such as "character" or "personality" are meaningless and inapplicable. Nevertheless, individual stones or mountains do exist, and they would lose their specific character if further divided. Hence they can truly be considered *in-dividuals*. The same is true in the world of plants. Here, too, we find entities which cannot be subdivided without loss of identity.

On the animal level of being, however, we also find "character," if character is defined as the sum total of specific dominant qualities which possess a certain constancy. To ascribe character to an

269

animal or a human being is not a value judgment but a statement of fact: we simply mean to say not only that it or he is an individual but that his or its reactions possess a degree of constancy and can be predicted with reasonable accuracy.

On the level of human existence, we speak not only of individuality and character but also of personality. Only human beings can be personalities. The word "personality" is derived from the Latin noun *persona,* the mask which an actor put on for his performance in the amphitheater. This mask had two functions. It served as a sort of loudspeaker in the great arena, and, at the same time, it helped the audience visualize the character played by the man whose voice it amplified—the role to which his voice gave sound. We speak of personality when we feel that a person gives voice to something that lies beneath the visible surface or, more accurately, that is above it and is sounding through him—a meaning which the Latin verb *per-sonare* indicates even more distinctively than the noun.

As personality, man represents the highest peak in the hierarchical order of being within the world. To become a personality is his highest possibility. God cannot possibly be less than the highest peak which human beings may attain. If He exists, and I believe He does, He must be at least as much as I am—He must be a personality. I do not know what kind of a personality God might be, but I believe He is the source of the possibility that human beings have to become personalities. He is sounding the voice that is sounding through the human personality.

A second presupposition of prayer is man's faith that this personal God cares for His children. Everything that happens on earth is important to Him. The chapter of the Bible which tells the story of the Flood that covered the earth in Noah's time contains a significant sentence, "and it grieved Him in His heart." God was sad that He was compelled to bring the flood upon the earth. God cares.

There is a third presupposition. It embodies man's conviction that he has the capacity to turn to God with his praises and thanks without wishing to flatter or bribe Him, and to approach Him with his supplications without wishing to force Him to do man's bidding. Prayer defined as supplication implies that man requests something of God. But man cannot know whether his request will be granted. This point differentiates prayer from magic. In magic man tries to force God to act in accordance with man's wishes— and he may score a visible success. But by trying to force God to do his will, man transforms Him into an idol. A god who can be forced to do man's will is an idol. The danger of magic lies in its seeming success. The successful man pays a heavy price for his achievement: he loses God. An idol can be defined as a man-made object of adoration in which the worshiper adores his own product, be it the product of his hands or the product of his mind. Idolatry is the duplication of the ego—be it the individual ego or the collective ego, as in racialism or chauvinism. Hermann Cohen once pointed out that it is no less anthropomorphic to speak of God's spirit than it is to speak of God's hands. We may commit idolatry even by speaking of God's spirit if this term denotes a concept that originates in man's mind. Authentic prayer addresses itself not to a god we make but to the God who made us. A prayer of supplication is legitimate only if man turns to God with full awareness of God's freedom of decision, prepared to accept the decision— gratefully, should it be positive, but also to accept it, though perhaps with anguish, should it be negative. God may say *yes,* but He can say *no,* too.

Yet the question remains: Why should we praise God? And why should we thank Him? Is He not above our thanks and praises? Aristotle, in a passage which probably refers to Plato, said that "everybody may criticize him; but who is permitted to praise him?" And Goethe expressed the same concern when he said, *Wer einen lobt, stellt sich ihm gleich,* "He who praises another person places himself on the other's level." If there are valid doubts about our moral right to praise other human beings, must our doubts not be much more severe in our relationship with God? Why then do we praise or thank Him?

We praise God because our hearts need to praise Him. Once, when my son was four years old, he happened to see some beautiful flowers and said to me: "Abba, I am happy with these flowers. What is the proper benediction for them?" Though a small child, he expressed a universal human sentiment. Children can love and enjoy flowers just as deeply as adults can, perhaps even more so.

But this child was a little Jew who had already learned in his parents' home that nothing is eaten or experienced without a *berakhah,* a benediction. Hence it was natural for him to seek a specific Jewish religious formulation to express a general human emotion.

Prayer and religious observance must, of course, be more than merely the products of a conditioning process in the home of one's parents. They must be rooted in a deeply felt and affirmed conviction—a conviction expressed, for instance, in a beautiful saying of the Talmud, "He who enjoys anything of this world without a benediction is likened to a man who robs the sanctuary." The Talmud Yerushalmi makes the point even more strongly when it says that a *berakhah* is the price we pay for being permitted to enjoy this world. To thank God and to praise Him is our acknowledgment that God is our Creator and the Creator of the universe.

II

Prayers and benedictions acknowledge God as man's Creator; supplications address themselves to God as man's judge. These definitions apply not merely to Jewish prayer; they characterize prayer in general. However, Jewish prayer possesses additional aspects and features which give it its specific and distinctive character.

First, Jewish prayer is communal prayer. Friedrich Heiler, in his monumental work, *Das Gebet,*[1] emphasizes that the Jews were the first people to introduce communal prayer. Jews can and do pray in solitude, but if they do, they are expected to recite their prayers at the same time at which the community worships. We require the presence of a *minyan,* of at least ten adult males, for many of our prayers, and every *minyan,* in turn, is representative of the entire Jewish people standing before God in prayer. The element of peoplehood occupies a legitimate place in the framework of our faith.

Second, communal prayer must be formulated prayer. Judaism recognizes that there is a tension between individual and group prayer, between spontaneous and fixed prayer. Prayer can and should be *avodah she-balev,* service of the heart. Judaism knows individual, spontaneous prayer, for prayer must be able to express what is in *your* heart, not in somebody else's. According to Jewish tradition, a Jew may speak or listen to God as his heart may dictate.

But man is not only an individual. He is a participant in his community. He is a member of the Jewish people. Hence, as Milton Steinberg put it, it is not enough that he address God in his solitariness.[2] Prayer, for the Jew, is also *kiyyum mitzvah,* the fulfillment of an essential commandment, which requires him to pray at specified times and in accordance with the specific order of a preestablished text. Communal prayer is formulated prayer.

The third distinctive quality of Jewish prayer can be found in the way in which it employs a multitude of external symbols for internal meanings—the *talit,* the phylacteries, the *shofar,* the *succah, lulav* and *etrog,* Sabbath candles, the spice box for *havdalah.* Other religions use symbols, too; but only in Judaism has "ritual" become a way of life, designed to sanctify every act and stage of man's life, to evoke a constant awareness of God's presence, to discipline man's thoughts, acts, and emotions, and to relate the Jew to his people's past as an ever-renewed contemporary experience.

The fourth quality which characterizes Jewish prayer is its equation of study and worship. Jewish prayer has an intellectual dimension: the study of Torah is a regular and integral part of Jewish worship even on weekdays. If we turn to the *God of creation* in our prayers of gratitude and praise, and if, in our supplications, we address ourselves to the *God of justice,* to God as our judge, in the study of Torah, we invite the *God of revelation* to speak to us through His words and their explanations. In all other forms of prayer we speak to Him; by studying Torah we listen to what He says to us.

III

Prayer opens up new dimensions of experience to the worshiper. However, it also involves dangers. One danger can be described in the words of Isaiah:

> And the Lord said: Forasmuch as this people draw near,
> And with their mouth and with their lips do honour Me,
> But have removed their heart far from Me,
> And their fear of Me is a commandment of men learned by
>   rote;
> Therefore, behold, I will again do a marvellous work among
>   this people,
> Even a marvellous work and a wonder;
> And the wisdom of their wise men shall perish,
> And the prudence of their prudent men shall be hid.[3]

Isaiah raises the fundamental question of *kavvanah,* man's spiritual intent and concentration in the act of prayer. Its lack can seriously threaten the meaningfulness of prayer. Even a deeply pious Jew will rarely be able to say all his prayers with real *kavvanah.* All of us, and the most pious persons perhaps even more than others, occasionally succumb to the danger of praying by rote. Martin Buber, in criticizing the way in which the Torah is frequently read in some synagogues, once spoke of the *Aussatz der Gelaeufigkeit,* "the leprosy of fluency." This leprosy of fluency threatens organized prayer, too. Prayer must be alive, not the mechanical mumbling of words. Routine destroys *kavvanah* and transforms prayer from a dialogue with God into the mechanical fulfillment of a routine assignment.

There is a second danger. The worshiper may be so smugly satisfied with the fact that he is praying that he forgets before whom he should be standing in prayer. He does not speak or listen to God while he prays. He listens to himself. His prayer becomes a performance in which he himself is the audience. This attitude may lead to a third danger, the danger of competitiveness and exhibitionism in prayer. The worshiper begins to compete with his neighbor. What counts is not a person's *kavvanah* but whether he prays more, louder, longer, or in a more conspicuously intense fashion than his neighbor. This exhibitionism destroys prayer: you think neither of God nor of your own feelings in the presence of God; you think of your neighbor.

These dangers are very real, but they do not vitiate the efficacy of prayer and its capacity to open up a new dimension of experience. We may not be able to meet God in prayer. But prayer makes it possible for us to reach the meeting point between God and man, the moment—that point in time—when the I encounters the great Thou. We cannot reach more, but this point we can reach. And in the rare moments in which we are able to reach this meeting point, we reach beyond ourselves.

One can train oneself to pray and to avoid the dangers of rote and exhibitionism. A young man, now a strictly observant Jew, for many years felt unable to attend a *minyan* even on Shabbat. When I asked him one day to accompany me to the synagogue, he refused and said, "How can I pray in the synagogue? I have not yet learned to pray by myself." He has learned it since then. Prayer is one of man's greatest but also most difficult arts. Nobody forces man to pray. But if he wishes to pray, he must learn the art of praying. And one of the ways to learn it is to direct our *kavvanah,* our spiritual concentration, toward a specific theme or thought among the many themes that are embodied in our prayers. I cannot think of any benediction or prayer which, although formulated and fixed by past generations, could not become topical for me or a fellow Jew in a moment of personal or historic import.

More than a hundred years ago, the leaders of Reform Judaism in Germany eliminated the prayers for Zion and Jerusalem from their prayer books. They felt these prayers had become outdated and irrelevant. One rabbi is reported to have gone so far as to transform *Tisha be-Av* into a day of rejoicing. According to Jewish tradition, the Messiah was born on the day the Temple was destroyed—*Tisha be-Av*. The civic emancipation of the Jews was proof to this rabbi that the Messiah had arrived or was about to arrive. Hence, he felt there was no longer any need to pray for his coming or to mourn the destruction of Jerusalem. *Tisha be-Av* could become a day of rejoicing. The notions and emotions of the past had become meaningless to him and his followers. They felt the forms and formulations of the past contained nothing that had topical relevance to their own lives and experiences.

Yet there were other Jews, often simple people, far less educated or sophisticated than the leaders of Reform Jewry, who prayed three times a day, "May our eyes behold Your return to Zion." Some of these men may also have doubted the validity of some traditional beliefs. Others may have recited their prayers by rote. Yet these men were among the people who reclaimed Eretz Yisrael and rebuilt it and saved it for the Jewish people. These men may have lacked the capacity to analyze the text and composition of the prayer book critically and in accordance with the principles of historical scholarship. But they had a feeling for the historical reality of the Jewish people. The text spoke to their hearts, if not to their minds. It was related to their understanding of themselves and their experiences as Jews. It continued to speak to them. It affected their thinking, their actions, their orientation to life.

Many prayers can have a similar relevance to our lives. Therefore I would be extremely careful before I would change the formulations of our prayers. But every Jew should be sufficiently trained to be able to concentrate his *kavvanah* on that theme within the established prayers that is closest to his heart and concerns. He may want to omit other themes, yet the time may still come when some of them return to him so that he may return to them.

An outstanding example of the way in which a formulation or phrase of the past can be made to speak to the concerns of the present is a sermon which Rabbi Nehemiah Nobel, of Frankfurt am Main and one of the great spiritual leaders of German Jewry at the beginning of the century, delivered after he had returned from the Zionist Congress in Karlsbad in 1921. The Congress was torn by a bitter conflict between religious and labor Zionists. Chaim Weizmann had tried in vain to restore unity. Rabbi Nobel, himself a member of the Mizrachi delegation, succeeded in resolving his own inner tension when, preaching at the first Shabbat service after the end of the Congress on the words of the prayer book, "Who healest the sick of Thy people Israel," he transformed the traditional text into a moving and compelling prayer for Weizmann who "was sick with the sickness of the Jewish people." The text was traditional, but in Dr. Nobel's skillful and inspired approach, it revealed a new depth of meaning and relevance. Nobody who heard the sermon will ever forget it. We are not Nobels, but we can probe the text and seek to discover its meaning and applicability in the same way. Our prayers, though formulated by previous generations, have the potency to illumine the predicaments of later generations and to speak anew to the needs of each successive generation. More than is written in them can be found in them.

Personal prayer can also be strengthened by praying with a *minyan*. The impact of a *minyan* upon the depth and meaningfulness of personal prayer was brought home to me by the *minyan* I was permitted to organize in the sickroom of Franz Rosenzweig nearly thirty years ago. Rosenzweig was already too ill to leave his room. He could no longer move around and was immobilized in his chair. Several days before Rosh Hashanah I asked him whether he wanted a small group of friends to conduct a holiday service for him in his home. He eagerly consented. We conducted services on both days of Rosh Hashanah in Rosenzweig's room. The next day he asked, in the only way in which he could still communicate —by pointing his finger in the direction of certain letters on the typewriter while his wife attempted to guess what he meant— "What about Shabbat Shuvah?" We continued our *minyan,* first on Shabbat Shuvah, then on Yom Kippur, and from then on every Shabbat and holiday until his death. It was a good *minyan*. It taught us how to pray. The *minyan* had not been organized for this purpose, yet one of its by-products was that it taught many of us to pray. Rosenzweig was too ill to pronounce the *berakhah* over the Torah audibly. Nevertheless, we often called him to the Torah and then brought the Torah over to him. Rarely can a benediction have been said with such power, vigor, and *kavvanah* as was the silent benediction which Rosenzweig pronounced while bending his noble head.

Prayer fulfills still another function. It can best be described in the words of the prayer book, "Purify our hearts to serve Thee in truth." Every Jewish prayer is a small Yom Kippur. It challenges us to examine our hearts and thoughts. It demands that we ques-

tion ourselves—whether we have been silent when we should have
spoken out; whether we have been selfish when we should have
been responsive to the needs of others; whether we have been
thoughtless when we should have been sensitive; whether we have
pursued the hollow when we should have reached for that which
can hallow our life. In this kind of prayer, we do not ask God to
do our will. We accept God's challenge to fulfill His will. We
confess our guilt and ask Him for strength to purify ourselves.

IV

Can prayer still be meaningful and relevant to the modern Jew?
Prayer is the bridge between God and man, but it can also be the
bridge between Jew and Jew. *Vetaher libenu*—these words are
known to most Jews, if not from the prayer book, then as the text
of a *horah*. Even at the time of the greatest estrangement between
the *halutzim* and the traditionalists, the *halutzim* could still express
in the language of dance what the pious Jews expressed in the
language of prayer. From the Torah to *halutziut,* there is a continuous stream of religious consciousness which has bound together
all our habitations and generations. Prayer can create a unity of
experience which transcends the boundaries of time and space and
bridges the diversity of conviction.

Our definition and understanding of what is or should be true
service to God have changed through the generations and will continue to change. Nevertheless, many formulations of our prayer
book have demonstrated their elasticity to encompass a variety of
definitions and convictions. Indeed, some of our prayers, especially
those which have been central to Jewish self-understanding, have
never changed. Think of the *Shema*. Neither its formulation nor
its role as a formula giving voice to the deepest loyalties of Jewish
consciousness through the ages has ever changed.

The meaning and implications of the *Shema* once were the subject of a discussion between Franz Rosenzweig and his teacher,
Hermann Cohen, at a time when Cohen, who was an anti-Zionist,
was involved in a bitter controversy with Martin Buber, a committed Zionist. To Cohen's disappointment, Rosenzweig, though

not a Zionist, sided with Buber rather than with Cohen. When Rosenzweig visited Cohen one day, his host asked him, "What do you find in Buber that you do not find in me?" Rosenzweig answered, "You have only *Adonai ehad*—'our God is one and a unique God.' In Buber I also find the *Shema Yisrael,* the call to the people." For a moment, Cohen was silent. Then he rose, opened his file cabinet and took out the manuscript of what was to be his last book, *Religion of Reason from the Sources of Judaism* (published posthumously), and read a passage to Rosenzweig which revealed that Cohen, too, had finally discovered, in the *Shema Yisrael,* the call to a particular people, Israel, as the bearer of the belief in the one and universal God.

Both aspects are unified in Judaism. The particular and the universal are fused together. The *Shema* speaks to both, to the traditional Jew and to the liberal Jew, to the religionist and to the secularist; and it unites them in the experience of a common past and the commitment to a common destiny. *Shema Yisrael:* we are the people that is to listen. God is *our* God, the God of our people. But this God is at the same time the God of the universe.

The proclamation of God's dominion over the world is not a statement of fact but of trust and hope. We conclude every worship service with the *Aleynu,* and every *Aleynu* in turn ends with the words of the prophet, *bayom hahu,* "on that day God will be One." He is not yet altogether One; He still bears various names. Therefore, the prayer continues with the prophet's words, *ushemo ehad,* "His name will be One." The end of the prayer which we recite at the conclusion of our worship points to the end of time, when mankind's destiny will be fulfilled—the days of the Messiah.

To pray is to turn to God as our creator whom we praise and thank. To pray is to stand before Him as our judge to whom we address our supplications. To pray is to acknowledge Him as the giver of Torah which we are to study. Ultimately, however, every Jewish prayer ends with the *Aleynu* in which we turn to Him as the God of the future which will see mankind's redemption. Thus, prayer is a gate to our living past. As we probe its enduring meaning, it can become a source of power that points to the ultimate goal of man's existence.

Part Four

OF AMERICAN JEWS
AND WORLD JEWRY

MAURICE B. PEKARSKY

13. The American Jewish Community— What Lies Ahead?

EVEN THOUGH it is my assignment to discuss the future of the American Jewish community, I must reject the implication that I or anyone else can prophesy or predict the future. Predictions must be based on scholarly research, and prophecy should be buttressed or validated by some superscription such as "Thus said the Lord, the God of Israel," as is done in the Bible.

I am not equipped to make predictions on the basis of scientific studies supported by statistical graphs and tables. And even if Jeremiah himself were to appear in the American Jewish community today and say, "Thus said the Lord, the God of Israel," I am not sure he would be believed. People did not believe him in his own time either, although for different reasons, and they claimed that his words were not God's words. The predicament of the Jew today lies in his uncertainty as to who can speak in the name of God, or even whether there is a God. Having said this, I have almost stated the fundamental problem facing Jewish community life.

However, even though I have no graphs or statistics about Jews, I have a great deal of contact with Jews. More specifically, I have contact with many Jews whom one rarely meets in the Jewish community. I meet them in the universities—students and graduate students, scholars, librarians, and professors. They rarely belong to our community, and if they do belong, they seldom attend meetings. They are influencing the life of the American Jewish community in many ways. Yet even when they join a synagogue or communal institution, they hardly ever employ their knowledge and intelligence to help us improve the Jewish community. Occasionally, they attend religious services. Quite often they send their children to Hebrew school because they want them to become *bar mitzvah* or confirmed. But in the world of their ideas and intellectual concerns, in the lectures they deliver or the books they write, Judaism is either peripheral or not discernible.

Their distance from Jewish life is essentially due to their feeling that the Jewish community has little or no room for them. Their intellectual interests are out of place at men's clubs and sisterhood meetings, in the *bar mitzvah*-centered worship of the synagogue, and in the numerous activities of our communal organizations. Although some have established a relationship with the Jewish community or achieved a sense of at-homeness in it, they frequently echo the sentiments expressed by Evelyn Rossman in *Commentary* some time ago:

> I go to Temple and don't pray. I light candles on Friday night but don't observe the Sabbath. I contribute to Israel but I do not share the faith of my Israeli friend that only superior people live in Israel. I support a Jewish Youth Center, but I'm opposed to Jewish boy scouts and Jewish basketball teams. . . . I teach my own children the prayers and blessings that my father taught to me, though I haven't said them since my own childhood. . . . Perhaps I shall some day be able to say "No" to the voice on the telephone that pleads, "Could you help us out just this time? I've called dozens of people. I can't find anyone else. . . ." But when it's time to say *No,* I lack the courage. . . . I do not want, even now, to separate myself from the community, but cannot find a way to feel at home in it; or a way to live a Jewish life that is not submerged in trivialities. I know, however, that many people depend upon the activities that I can't bear, and that they fulfill some need I don't have.[1]

Mrs. Rossman expresses her predicaments more vigorously and emphatically than do many other Jews who accept their membership in Jewish organizations quite naturally, in fact so naturally that they tend to become indifferent to the meaning and implications of that membership. Nevertheless, neither the mushrooming membership lists of our synagogues nor the enormous increase in Jewish school enrollment and attendance nor the multiplicity of projects of Jewish organizations that constitute the texture of American Jewish life can conceal the fact that there are numerous people who share Mrs. Rossman's feelings.

One does not need to be a university teacher or student to sense the emptiness and hollowness, the superficiality and more than occasional vulgarity that dominate much of Jewish communal life. American Jews have settled down to a kind of Judaism that demands little and offers little in return. The middle-class character of the American Jewish community has emerged clearly. The forms and patterns of Jewish existence are now deeply rooted in modern American experience. Although some Israelis still may wonder whether American Jews will survive as Jews, I think we can take for granted that we will survive for a long time. We have developed a formula for our integration into American society. We define ourselves as a faith group, as a religion. We may be religious more in sentiment than in content. Nevertheless, this self-definition is in harmony with the dominant American attitude which accepts the validity of religious pluralism and supports America's traditional affirmation of freedom of religion. This formula has made Jewish identity in America acceptable. It is respectable. It is secure. It is an authentic ingredient of American society.

Moreover, our sense of at-homeness in America is fortified by the security that springs from a sense of achievement. Ours is a significant record of achievement. The image of generosity which the Jewish community has created—its dynamic organizational structure, its response to human needs here and abroad, its phenomenal rise from immigrant beginnings to a position of economic, political, and intellectual prominence in American society and world Jewry—all of this rightfully merits respect and admiration.

Nevertheless, the individual frequently seems lost and overlooked in the organizational activities and projects of our community. We attend numerous meetings in which we discuss the problems and needs of our community, yet somehow we fail to ask the questions which are fundamental to these discussions: What is the character of Jewish group life and what significance does it have for the life of human-beings-born-Jews? What is the place of a Jewish person in the Jewish community? What should a Jew derive from his membership in the Jewish community besides the satisfaction from activities in which he engages? What does he do with his solitude when he does not attend a meeting or solicit support for some Jewish cause? Must he always *do* something in order to be Jewish?

The machinery of Jewish community life is running at full speed. We are constantly "busy," engaged in a variety of community projects. We support distinctive Jewish projects and institutions because we feel they are needed to help us maintain our distinctive identity as Jews in the modern world. Yet we have not really begun to face the fundamental question that has confronted Jews and Judaism ever since their entry into the modern world: What is the ultimate meaning of Jewish difference?

This question was not asked by the Jews of the ghetto. They knew precisely why they were different and what the nature of the difference was. Their self-image was clear. It was shaped by their faith in a God whose plan called for one nation, His chosen people who, though dispersed throughout the world, would worship Him everywhere. The Jews' dispersion among the nations and their distinctive ways of thinking and doing were part of a divine plan that would ultimately lead to their personal and collective salvation. This plan gave meaning and direction to their lives. Above all, it gave them a sense of purpose and of role in the world. Their community structure and the way of life they managed to create within the confines of the ghetto reflected their awareness of this role. Often they found God's way quite difficult, but they also found it to be good. Their way of life was structured by the Ten Commandments and was woven together by the fellowship of like-minded Jews, a community-wide system of education, and the shared beauty of holidays and festivals. They found purpose and joy in their identity. And they knew what they were. Their speech and gestures, their ways of eating and drinking, the way they dressed and worked, prayed and rested—all reflected and expressed the fact of their Jewish being.

Spatially the ghetto was separated from its neighbors. It had a boundary line that kept Jews and non-Jews apart. In addition to the boundary line, however, there also was what I like to call a "gatekeeper," who enforced the separation. If a city has a boundary line but no gatekeeper, you have freedom of mobility—you can move whenever you want to. The ghetto had both a boundary line and a gatekeeper, the gatekeeper being the various forces—pressures of the non-Jewish majority, governmental edicts, municipal laws, and similar factors—which prevented the Jews from moving into the non-Jewish world.

However, even though the Jews of the ghetto could not move in space, they were able to move in time. Everything the Jew did related him to time—it related him to Sinai; it related him to creation; it related him to Abraham, Moses, and Jacob. He got up in the morning, washed his hands, and recited the appropriate benediction. The benediction was a link in time to the source of all life. On his way to the synagogue, he met another Jew, and walking together they became involved in a discussion of some talmudic passage. Rabbi Akiva, who had lived around 130 C.E., became a contemporary. They talked as if they knew him personally. They quoted him and argued about him. He was one of them. Tradition was a contemporary experience. The two men entered the synagogue and began to pray in that particular intonation which had been handed down from generation to generation—from time immemorial, as far as they were concerned.

Whether on weekday, Sabbath, or holiday, the language and music of prayer made the past contemporaneous and reminded them of time—of patriarchs, prophets, and scholars. On Passover, Elijah would come and visit them. In their *succot,* during the harvest festival, they had a special way of welcoming Abraham, Isaac, and Jacob to their table and observance. They went beyond space into time. They had a means of locomotion in time because their way of life linked past and present. The difficult and often tragic life of the ghetto became transmuted by an association with the great spokesmen of Jewish tradition. This extension in time gave Jews a sense of at-homeness in a much wider world and provided them with resources of life and thought which enabled them to survive. But they were concerned with more than mere physical survival. They were living for something that was heaven-bound, for a way of life that gave meaning and purpose to their existence as Jews and provided an answer to their predicament and concerns as human-beings-born-Jews.

We do not possess the same sense of purpose and meaning. Many Jewish discussions today still tend to end with the question, What is a Jew? One can, of course, define what a Jew is. Yet no study can answer what I consider to be the essential question: Will it be satisfying to be a Jew? Does being Jewish give us a sense of the parochial and the limited, or does it link us with forces, personalities, and ideas that can change us—that will not merely help us survive but will provide an answer to our problems as human beings? The major predicament of Jewish life in our time arises precisely from the fact that it is earthbound. It is no longer limited in space. In fact, ever since the Emancipation, Jews have conquered the world of space. Yet in the process they have lost their sense of time, their connection with the roots of their life and thought. As a result, they no longer have an understanding of their history. Occasionally they even want to reject it.

Some years ago, for example, a well-known Jewish musician endorsed the aims of the Free Land Movement, which sought to establish a Jewish homeland not in Israel, but in Australia. He felt it would be good for the Jews to start afresh, without the burdens of the past.

To some Jews, the nature of Jewish experience in the past constitutes a genuine burden. To many others, the past is not even a burden. We do not possess it. It is not ours, for we know little or nothing about it. Not knowing our history, we really have no history.

Therefore our Jewishness is limited. It possesses a space dimension, but no time dimension. As a result, we have no adequate answer to the question, What is a Jew? For if you have no time dimension, you do not have the fundamental Jewish orientation which is implicit in Jewish history—that sense of purpose and of role which motivated Jews in the past. They knew why they were living in this world.

Having lost this sense of role as well as the mechanism for its discovery, Jews today are limited in time. Yet we cannot be saved by space alone. We cannot be saved by walls or gatekeepers. Nor shall we find an answer to our problems by relating ourselves to the Jews of Israel, as some of our leaders advocate. The State of Israel still provides what is largely a spatial solution. It has not, or not yet, been able to resolve the conflict between space and time and to integrate the past with the present. Many young Israelis reject time and want to begin history anew—with a new nation and a new tradition divorced from two thousand years of history. They feel the past merely signifies martyrdom, cowardice, a failure of the national will. Therefore they, too, reject time and thus confront the problem of having to discover an answer to the question, What is a Jew?

Our difficulty is that we have tried to answer this question only in the present tense and in terms of spatial relationships. Such an approach, however, can clarify the meaning of our Jewish identity as little as it can clarify my identity as a person. If, in answer to the question, What am I? you were to define me solely in terms of what I am at this very moment, you could never really define me. A person is a continuum which begins on the day of his birth and, indeed, antedates his birth. Similarly, a Jew cannot be defined except in terms of a historical context, that is, in a time dimension. When I speak of "time dimension," I am not referring to a detached, academic investigation. I do not suggest you read a number of history books and distill what you have read into a definition. Time dimension is experience. You begin to sense your own link with the past—with Abraham, Isaac, and Jacob, with Moses, Jeremiah, and Spinoza, with good and bad Jews, with lowly and wealthy Jews, with saints and sinners. They all are part of our history, and a meaning for Jewish life and Jewish experience in our time can emerge only as we develop a relationship with them.

A conclusion seems inescapable. If our Jewish community wants to rediscover its primary purpose; if it wants to begin to sense that it is not merely a speck on the sands of time but has a beginning, roots, and a future, the program of Jewish education must be reshaped. Jewish education once again must help us discover the means of traveling in time.

American secular education does this for American children. When we study Lincoln or the Civil War, when we read Jefferson or the Federalists, when we delve into American literature and read about the heroes of American folklore, we have a means of locomotion in time. As we think about these men, read about them, or see a flag, we are reminded of the past and we sense a relationship to it. It is linked with our life. It becomes part of our life.

For several reasons, Jewish education does not do the same for us. All too often, it is flimsy and shallow. We do not give it enough time to discover time. A recent national study of Jewish education has shown how little Jewish education our children really get, even though the great majority may attend some Jewish school at one time or another.

Insufficient time for Jewish education is one problem. A second problem is that the purpose of Jewish education in the United States is often a kind of group therapy. You send your youngsters to a Jewish school because it will facilitate their adjustment in a hostile world. Jewish education is preventive therapy so that they will know who they are in case they encounter prejudice or are exposed to other manifestations of group hatred. Many community leaders, including religious leaders, advocate as rationale for Jewish education that it will ensure group survival. We are troubled by the fear of intermarriage. This fear is what makes many parents send their children to Hebrew or religious school. They feel we must create pleasant Jewish experiences for our children so that they will remember that it is pleasant to be Jews and will not break away from the group and its institutions.

Thus, the education we offer in our schools is largely therapy education, survival education, education in pleasantness. Such emphases may do until a child reaches the age of twelve or thirteen. But pleasantness is not enough to answer his questions when he leaves school and enters college. As he studies philosophy, anthropology, or sociology, he begins to encounter some of man's most persistent and profound questions—his questions about God and man and the relationship between man and man. He begins to discover the answers of some of the other great traditions of the world. What does Judaism have to say to him about these questions? Is Judaism designed to answer the questions of man as man? Other traditions seem to offer an answer; the Judaism he knows does not.

We must go beyond group survival as the chief purpose of Jewish education. Indeed, we must transform Jewish education into something which extends beyond the walls of the school and challenges the entire community.

The Hillel Foundation at the University of Chicago annually conducts a Maccabean festival in the beautiful university chapel. It is a major event on campus. The chapel carillon plays Hanukkah music. Jews from all over the city attend the program. Yet every year we face a dilemma as we begin to plan the program. What should be its nature? For instance, what musical selections should we use? I am familiar with Israeli folk dances and songs. I like many of them. But they are hardly great music. And I often ask myself what the Jewish community has done to stimulate the creation of something of which intelligent and sensitive Jews can say, "This is mine, and I enjoy it. This is something that links me in time." Has any Jewish community, for instance, commissioned a great musician to compose a new Hanukkah oratorio so that we shall have something besides Handel's *Judas Maccabaeus?* As it plans a mass event in conjunction with an annual United Jewish Appeal or Bonds for Israel campaign to which artists from all over the world may be invited, has any of our large communities ever given thought to the possibility of sponsoring an equally impressive Passover festival for which it would commission a Passover cantata or oratorio—something that would enhance Jewish culture, enrich the culture of the United States and the musical world, and give us something in our solitude—a tune I can retain and carry with me as I walk home from the concert or as I travel on a plane or train somewhere far away?

The Jewish community must begin to think of Jewish education not as education for parochialism or survival, but as education for life, for answering the problems of human beings who were born Jews and who, as human beings, are not different from their neighbors. We must bring Jewish tradition out into the open as one of the great traditions of the western world. We must express it spiritually and aesthetically in the various dimensions possible in our time so that its answers and commitments will become implicit in the lives we lead, the things we do, the institutions we establish, the community we create.

Membership in the community I have described would be more than an act of membership in the present or in a particular synagogue or particular organization at a particular time. It would be membership in a community which reflects an affirmation and experience of relationships, no matter how tenuous, beyond this place and beyond this time to other times and other places, to the historic experience and creative expression which we designate as Jewish tradition.

Thus conceived, the community is more than the sum of concrete, living, visible persons labeled Jews at any given time. It includes the invisible Moses and Akiva, Hillel and Shammai, Judah Ha-Levi and A. D. Gordon, Louis Brandeis and Stephen S. Wise. It includes a host of others like them and unlike them, as objects of emulation or as subjects of dissent. They all are members of the Jewish community that I am describing, as symbols, ideas, and unconscious influences. As such they have a voice in our community's life and form.

But we must be able to hear and see them. Therefore it is for us to create the instruments that will enable us to make their voices heard and their faces seen. Linking the past with the present, we may be able to establish the linkage which will assure the future.

ALFRED JOSPE

14. The Three-fold Rebellion: Some Reflections on Israel Today

THERE IS A Hebrew term that describes what I feel is the spirit of Israel and its people: *hutzpah.*

When I speak of *hutzpah* I mean a spirit of creative defiance. I mean the spirit of the story of Abraham arguing with God that God has no business destroying Sodom and Gomorrah and disregarding the merits of the righteous, few though they may be in number. I mean the spirit expressed in the famous "Kaddish" of Rabbi Yitzchak Levi of Berditchev, shaking his fist at God and taking Him to task for neglecting His people Israel and for delivering His firstborn into the hands of God's enemies. Erich Fromm, in the discussion of the Sabbath ritual in his *Forgotten Language,*[1] defines "work" as interference by man, be it constructive or destructive, with the physical world, while "rest" (for instance, on the Sabbath) is a state of peace between man and nature. Man must leave nature untouched; he must not change it in any way, either by building or by destroying anything.

Hutzpah, as I conceive it, is the opposite. It is the rejection of peace between man and nature. It is the drive to touch, to build, to transform, to change the physical world as well as man's inner world. It is the spirit of rebellion that is unable to make its peace with that which is for the sake of that which ought to be. It is the spirit of defiance which refuses to acquiesce in the status quo and is ready to defy the forces of man, of nature, of history, yes, even of God, in order to reach out for something better, more complete, closer to the realization of hope and ideal.

This defiance is perhaps the dominant characteristic of the spirit that has brought Israel into being and sustains it today.

I

Israeli life is, first of all, characterized by what I would call a *defiance of nature*.

Imagine traveling through the Negev. The facts about the Negev are well known; you can pick them up from books and newspaper stories. Before 1948, this area was almost completely uninhabited by Jews and only sparsely populated by Arabs. The Jews held some strategic outposts, but for the most part these vast spaces were empty wasteland abandoned to the occasional Bedouin and the roving jackal.

Israel has transformed the south into an area alive with self-confidence and vibrating with the expectation of growth. There are new cities. Beersheba now has a population of 60,000 and continues to grow rapidly. Ashkelon has 40,000, Kiryat Gat 10,000, Dimona, Ashdod Yam, and Sh'deroth, each about 5,000. Except for Beersheba and Ashkelon, whose origins go back to biblical times, all of them exist where there was no human life whatsoever ten or twenty years ago.

You must travel through the Negev, you must see it, smell it, sweat in it, and breathe its hot, sand-blown air to understand the *hutzpah* with which the Jews are defying nature there. Two hundred and eighty kilometers of utterly depressing desolation, traversed only by a superbly engineered narrow blacktop road. All you see is sand, rocks, sky, loneliness, erosion which has bitten deeply into the rocky ground. There are just a few inches of rain during the entire year. Sandstorms blind and choke you. The unrelieved lifelessness is only slightly tempered by the fascination of the strange rock formations and their luminous colors. As my wife and I were driving through the Negev, I told her I had the feeling that the Jews have a streak of perversion in them. They are trying to do the impossible. They are moving in where even God seemingly had been unable to cope with the barrenness of this piece of land which He had created but then left to rot away in the simmering desert heat. But the Jews won't let Him get away with it. They are going to show Him—and thus they are building where even God had failed, and they labor and sweat to improve the virtually unimprovable.

This attitude is exemplified, for instance, by a young couple in Beersheba, both Americans and former students of mine who have lived in Israel for about twenty-five years. After a period in a kibbutz the husband studied soil chemistry, and today he is among Israel's leading experts in his field. We had a long talk with them. They see the same forbidding desolation which we see in the Negev, but they also see something else. Where I see nothing, he sees the possibility of agricultural development with the water that his co-workers are bringing down in pipelines from the Jordan or that they are going to develop through the desalination of sea water. He sees a booming potash and bromide industry; today it exports less than 100,000 tons a year, but he is certain that in another three or five years they will export 200,000 tons annually. He sees a tremendous population increase—new cities and houses where only rocks and sand exist today. He sees new highways and railroads. He sees oil flow north through the recently completed pipeline from Elath. He sees refineries being erected, attracting thousands of people by excellent wages. He sees the development of the Negev in response to the exigencies of military defense and settlement. Where I see lifelessness, he sees life, growth, a living future filled with tremendous possibilities.

Of course, there is much more to Israel than the Negev. There are large, fertile sections carefully nursed and beautifully developed. But the spirit is everywhere the same. There is a vision to whose realization people inch closer day by day through every day's hard work: the desert and many other parts of the country are a rich potential, bursting with minerals or the promise of fruit waiting to be brought forth, lacking nothing but water to yield unheard-of crops. And water they will bring, tomorrow, the day after, in five or ten or twenty years, but bring it they will. They defy nature in order to conquer it.

This vision is nourished by a vigorous sense of purpose which pervades Israel. Today you can probably find such a sense of purpose only in a young country. I suspect many of us in the western world no longer possess it. When I speak about a "sense of purpose" in Israel, I am not romanticizing. It is something which is almost tangible; it is in the air; you sense it everywhere. Even our son, then a boy of thirteen, felt it. When my family and I were on our return trip and attempted to define some of the things which had impressed or affected us most deeply, our boy told us that he wanted to return to Israel when he was older because "you have a sense of purpose there—you see what you are doing." In his adolescent way he put into words one of the most striking impressions you receive from Israel: you see what you are doing. You know the country is small, the people are few. Every person counts. You are not anonymous, a nameless entity disappearing in the mass, an unknown cog in some depersonalized machinery doing some piece of work yet never seeing the completed whole. There you can see the results of your efforts. You get the feeling that what you do counts and matters. And you know not only that you are building for yourself and your family but that every man's efforts have a larger significance—that, whatever your place may be, you participate in the task of redeeming a people from the ravages of history by redeeming a land from the erosions of nature.

II

Israel's defiance of nature is accompanied by what I would like to call its *rebellion against history*. Israel does one thing to you: it smashes your stereotypes to pieces. The longer you stay, the more you begin to discard your preconceived notions about the Jewish people. Many of us who have long been Zionists had always accepted and affirmed Herzl's felicitous dictum that the Jews are a people, one people. Even so, in Israel you discover that we are not one people but countless peoples, with countless different racial strains; with radically different cultural patterns; with different philosophies of life and attitudes toward work, religion, family, and society—and that there are Jews who look and behave unlike anything you may have thought a Jew could ever be or look like.

Israel's Jewish population is composed of two major elements. About half came from the middle-eastern countries, the other half from Europe, in the main from eastern and central Europe. Two thousand years ago, these groups had a common home, but history separated and isolated them from it. They were dispersed on different continents and became acculturated to the people among whom they lived. And when they arrived in Israel, the cultural and emotional baggage they brought along contained many items that had been shaped by or taken over from the cultures of their non-Jewish environment.

During the period from 1882 to 1948—the period of pre-state development—the overwhelming majority of the immigrants came from eastern and central Europe. The culture they developed in their new home was essentially just a Hebraized version of whatever their European culture had been. The German Jews, who arrived in large numbers after 1933, imported the culture of the German middle class—its books and love for art, its social patterns and intellectual ambitions, the culture, skill, and managerial competence of the "Herr Doktor." The Jew from Russia or Poland had brought along the *shtetl;* he imported Yiddish and the religious values and habit patterns of the ghetto; or he brought along the secularized messianism of the Russian socialist which he sought to translate into reality in the communal settlements of Palestine. His culture was largely the culture of the *shtetl* translated into Hebrew.

And then came the North Africans and the Orientals—and I use these terms without derogatory intent or implication. Hundreds of thousands of them came after the State had been established. They came from the coastal plains of North Africa, the rocky remoteness of the Atlas mountains, or the vast emptiness of the Sahara. They came from what had once been the crowded mellahs of Morocco and Algeria. They came from Egypt, Syria, Iraq, Yemen—Arab or Arabized Jews who were endangered by the hatred of the Moslem world and had to be evacuated.

The differences between East and West are enormous. There is a striking difference in outward appearance. Some newcomers look as if they had come straight from the pages of the Bible. Others look like Ali Baba and the forty thieves, with their baggy pants and dilapidated but colorful Oriental clothing. Elsewhere you would be afraid to meet them alone at night. In Israel you aren't.

You know that despite their fierce looks they are incredibly gentle, though often endowed with gratingly loud, harsh voices which they use with gleeful abandon and a predilection for violent gesture.

There is a difference in color. On the one end of the color scale you have the astonishing flaxen hair, blue eyes, and peaches-and-cream complexion of many little sabras of European parentage. And starting from there, you have every conceivable color, from the light brown of some immigrant from Casablanca or Agadir, to the near-black of the Falasha or Indian Jew from Cochin China.

They are different even in the way they speak. Long after they have learned to use Hebrew, and after Hebrew has, at least in public contacts, replaced their original Yiddish or Arabic or Polish or German or North-African French, you can still hear their former vernacular in the inflections of their voices and their intonations of the new language.

But the differences between East and West go far deeper. A major difference exists with regard to what students of the Arab world have called "familism." In the Middle East, the family plays a very important role. The individual is deeply attached to his family and, in fact, subordinated to it to a degree that is inconceivable in the western world. Specifically, as Raphael Patai has shown in his study of *Cultures in Conflict,*[2] the middle-eastern family has several distinct features. It is patrilineal: every person is regarded as belonging only to the family of his father. It is patrilocal: the newly married couple takes up residence in the house, tent, or compound where the husband's father and his family live. It is patriarchal: the father has all the authority over the family, and all other members of the family must subordinate themselves to his authority. And it is endogamous: the preferred marriage is within a very close circle of blood relatives.

This eastern familism and the European or western concept of family life represent two entirely different worlds. For us the home and the family are a point of departure for the children; in the East they are a point of steady return. Our basic aim in education is to make the children gradually independent of the family; to train and equip them to become persons in their own right; to have them strike out for themselves, establish their own families, and live their own life potentials to the fullest. In the East the basic aim of education is to retain the individual as an obedient member of the family or tribal unit.

Again, the groups differ radically in their approach to education. In the western world we seek to provide education for all youngsters. We offer it free and make it compulsory. Orientals are accustomed to consider education voluntary and restricted to boys. The primary purpose of education is to prepare the boys for participation in the life of the community. Girls do not receive any education, and even after many of these families arrived in Israel, there remained a strong emotional block on the part of the parents against having their daughters go to school and sit together with boys in one classroom.

The "ingathered," as the *olim hadashim,* the newcomers, are called, present still other problems of cultural and social integration. Among them are people of whom you have probably never heard—Jewish cave dwellers from the Atlas Mountains of North Africa. They had never slept in a bed and had to be taught how to sleep in one. They had never used a toilet in their lives and had to be patiently shown what the toilet was for and how it had to be used.

Among them, too, were the Yemenites who had been airlifted to Israel in the famous "Operation Magic Carpet." Some Yemenites had, of course, been living in the country long before statehood. We were told that among them, especially among the older ones, it was a custom to rush into the streets as soon as it started raining. Unprotected against the rain, they walked or stood in it for hours. When we asked for an explanation of this strange custom, we were told that to walk in the rain was for many Yemenites an intoxicating proof of their freedom. For centuries the rulers of Yemen had forbidden the Jews to be out in the rain lest the holy drops of the scarce liquid would be contaminated by falling upon a Jew. For centuries they had been denied the experience of feeling the coolness of a raindrop on their parched skins, and walking in the rain in the Old City of Jerusalem became the symbol of their redemption and return.

I could multiply these illustrations, yet all of them would merely point up the same fact. What we have in Israel today is, in Horace

Kallen's words, "a pluralistic society whose togetherness is postulated on a common past which isn't common, on a simple faith which isn't simple, and on an ethnic unity which is conspicuously multiple." [3] The ethnic diversity and cultural multiplicity are symptoms of the ravages which history has wrought on the body and soul of the Jewish people, and Israel today represents a rebellion against these ravages of history. What Israel must do is nothing less than to mold a people out of these diverse elements which have been separated not only by thousands of miles but also by thousands of years. They occupy the same space today, but culturally they still are centuries apart. Israel must discover a way to bridge the gap that separates the groups. It must fuse them together into one people trained and equipped for their tasks as citizens; and it must do this in one or at most two generations of desperate effort.

The difficulties are great. Even language, communication, still presents a problem despite the rapid Hebraization of most newcomers. A school nurse tells that she once went to an urban school in one of Jerusalem's suburbs populated by new immigrants and saw a child in the first grade standing outside the room. She asked why he was not in class. The child answered that he did not know; the teacher had said something to him, repeated it, and then sent him out of the room. The nurse asked the teacher what had happened. The boy's nose had been dirty, and the teacher had requested him twice to wipe it with his handkerchief. When the child did not obey, she expelled him from the class. What had never occurred to the teacher, but what the nurse soon discovered, was that the child just did not know the Hebrew words for "wipe" and "handkerchief" and did not understand the teacher.

This kind of problem is bound to disappear. Other problems are more deep-seated. It was probably inevitable that Jews, coming from countless different countries and social settings, imported not only the good habits but also some of the cultural and racial prejudices they had picked up in the countries of their origin. Hence, even Israel—much as we would want to have it otherwise—is not wholly free from various manifestations of xenophobia, the fear of the stranger, the dislike of the unlike. In one of the small-holders' settlements (*moshav shitufi*) which had taken in a number of dark-complexioned new families from Iraq, we were told that a youngster who had recently arrived with his parents from South Africa refused to attend school together with what he thought were "black" children. Similar tensions exist elsewhere. The newcomers, in turn, frequently feel unwelcome, unwanted, and hence insecure and inadequate. No matter how successful and well integrated they have become, they continue to feel that they are not fully accepted, but are looked down upon—second-class citizens when they are compared with the "white" Ashkenazim, who settled and built the country till statehood and who now occupy and control all decisive positions in the government, the *Histadrut,* the economy as a whole. People tell the story of a little Moroccan girl who is reported to have said, "When I grow up I shall be an Ashkenazi." I don't know whether the story is true, but the very fact that it is being told reflects one of the tensions that still divide East and West.

These tensions will continue for some time because of the fertility of the "Easterners" who will soon outnumber the people from the West. Orientals in general have an extraordinary birthrate, by western standards. In the suburb of Jerusalem in which we lived, it seemed that two out of every three women on the street were pregnant. The streets teem with youngsters of all ages, and families of ten or even fifteen are no rarity. Even if the natural increase of the Ashkenazi population were to be augmented by an annual immigration of 10,000 Jews from America, the Oriental population would still grow faster by natural reproduction. And the question that troubles many people is whether the country will remain western—not only in its political orientation but in its mores, in its religious notions and practices, in its social habits and cultural stance—or, as many fear, it will slowly but inevitably become orientalized.

Today, the West—that is, Europe—is still the dominant factor. It sets the standards to which to aspire. It tries its utmost to speed the process of absorption, acculturation, and integration—all different terms for the same overriding objective: the westernization of the newcomers.

Various factors nourish the growth of social cohesion. Adversity pulls people together. When a common danger must be faced, most people rally as one man. And the threats to Israel's security and survival have never ceased. During one of our visits, we were in Israel at the time of heightened tensions between Israel and the Arabs, when the newspapers were full of reports of Egyptian troops massing along Israel's borders; when the radio, no matter to which Arab station right across the border you listened, would blare at you Nasser's impassioned appeals to the Arabs to extirpate Israel; and when the howling of the inflamed masses would remind you like nothing else you had heard in recent years of Hitler's virulent and hoarse harangues and the outbursts of mass hysteria of his followers. Our friends in America were worried and wrote us to ask whether it was safe to stay, since another war seemed imminent. It may have been imminent, but the Israelis reacted differently. Here is how my wife described the situation in our diary:

> In the press, there was no trace of hysteria or excitement. There was no editorial rhetoric. On the contrary. Occasionally, you could read in the papers that the situation was considered "grave but not serious." People on the street were calm. They did discuss the news, but with the shrug of the shoulder that is typical of an attitude of resigned and even somewhat amused acceptance of the inevitable. You obviously get used to crises when you live with them for decades. You don't belittle the inherent dangers. You know and remember only too bitterly what is at stake. The beautiful cemetery on Mount Herzl is witness enough of the unspeakable heartbreak of boys and girls killed in war. The grief of mourning, the remembrance of stark, simple hunger, the very realities of war experienced by every man, woman, and child in their very homes, day and night, are an integral part of Israeli life. No one remains untouched in a country so small and vulnerable. Yet why talk about it? You know, and that's enough. You hope with all your heart that it won't happen again. But if it does, you'll accept it as inevitable and do what you have done before: stand, or fall, at the place assigned to you.

This attitude is shared by East and West alike. The stark demands of reality solder them together. They stand side by side, no matter what their country of origin.

Western influences go to work on the "ingathered" in various other ways. The reshaping process begins in the school. Education in Israel is compulsory; boys and girls have to be sent to school, where they are Hebraized and absorb not only the customary subjects but also the un-Oriental habits of discipline, cleanliness, and punctuality. Punctuality in particular is a real problem. Few newcomers can initially afford clocks or watches. And above all, Oriental culture has a concept of time that differs from ours—the smallest unit of time is either the morning or the afternoon, as we ourselves found out to our occasional dismay when our little twelve-year-old Moroccan *ozeret,* whom we had inherited with our apartment, had faithfully promised to come in the late morning and simply walked in at five in the afternoon, with a friendly smile and no idea that she had kept us waiting for six hours.

Another unifying influence is the army. Every young man and woman goes to the army upon reaching eighteen, the boys for three, the girls for two years. The army is probably the single most potent factor in teaching them discipline, cleanliness, and Hebrew, and in breaking down the barriers between the different elements of the population.

There also is a process of westernization by legislation. For example, the government, not long ago, passed a law setting the minimum age for marriage for girls at seventeen. By act of legislation, the government actually broke a Jewish tradition which permits a girl to marry at twelve plus one day. At the same time, however, the law breaks with Oriental tradition generally.

An attempt is also being made to create a new nation—or people—even in the biological sense of the word. Intermarriage between East and West is encouraged in every possible way. Israel's 1960 beauty queen was the daughter of a German immigrant and a Yemenite woman. On *Lag ba-Omer,* 130 weddings took place in Tel Aviv, among them about twenty between Ashkenazim and Sephardim, and each of these twenty couples received a wedding present of one hundred Israeli pounds from the municipality.

Whether these and similar factors will ultimately assure Israel's westernization keeps some of Israel's keenest minds guessing. The general trend is toward westernization. Yet I believe that pronounced ethnic and genetic differences will continue to exist, and that Israel's culture will probably develop a permanent distinctive Oriental coloration—especially in the fields of decorative art, folk music, and religious custom. In all other areas, however, I share the hope of many others that the West will emerge dominant, for Israel's political, social, and scientific westernization is probably our only assurance that Israel's rebellion against history will succeed and that Israel will not be separated from the West by a culture gap that proves unbridgeable.

III

There is a third rebellion which must be mentioned. Some people, especially the strictly Orthodox elements, define it as the *rebellion of the godless* against God. It is a convenient designation for the problem, but I think the problem itself goes far deeper. In many places you are quite likely to find a rebellion against God— a denial of the validity of a religious faith. But what is happening in Israel is largely not so much the denial of the validity of faith as it is a rebellion against what many people consider the mentality of the ghetto, fortified by an outraged reaction to what these people feel are the coercive claims of the clerical custodians of institutionalized religion in Israel.

The ghetto and institutionalized Judaism are the inheritance of the Jewish past with which the Israeli, and especially the young Israeli, has to come to terms—and often is utterly unable to.

Actually, the conflict is rooted in the very origin and nature of our people. Historical Judaism is the fusion of two motifs: Egypt and Sinai, the one constituting Israel as a separate people, the other defining the purpose of this people's existence. In the traditional view, both belong together. The Torah needs the people for its fulfillment in time and space; the people need the Torah as its guide toward the realization of its national destiny. Jewish tradition hopefully claims that *Yisrael ve'oraita had hu,* Israel and the Torah are indivisible.[4]

However, that Israel and the Torah are one is a statement of faith, not of fact. Jewish life has always been characterized by the tension of these two elements—the tension between Egypt and Sinai, between *am* and *kadosh,* between body and soul, between the struggle for physical survival and the claims of the spirit, between life for its own sake and life "for the sake of heaven."

Our conflicts and debates today are merely a symptom of this persistent tension. Are we to be a people like all other peoples, or are we an *am segulah,* unlike any other people, carrying the burden of a special divine vocation whose obligations set us apart from all other peoples?

In Israel the battle lines are clearly drawn. Tremendous emotional forces are involved in this clash. On the one side, there are the traditionalists—of numerous shadings—who insist, often vehemently, that Jewish identity can be defined only in religious categories and that religion, in turn, can be defined solely in terms of *Torah mi'Sinai* and the *tar'yag mitzvot.* There can and must be no separation of church and state in Israel, no matter how much Israel might pattern herself after the western democracies in all other respects. In a Jewish state, the law of the state must be Jewish—God's immutable and irrevocable law as revealed to Moses and interpreted by the rabbinic authorities. The creed and code of *Medinat Yisrael* must be grounded in the Torah, and the state must use its power of legislation and enforcement to safeguard and compel public obedience to the ritual and sacerdotal practices of a timeless faith. The unyielding acceptance and continuation of the patterns of the past are the only guarantee that Israel's society will be a Jewish society and *Medinat Yisrael* a Jewish state.

On the other side, there are the men and women, often equally unyielding, who reject the patterns of the past precisely because they feel that in order to survive they must build a future that is different from the past.

The young Israeli finds it difficult to understand his forefathers, the junk dealers, tailors, peddlers, *melamdim,* the whole gamut of *Luftmenschen* of eastern Europe. He cannot understand how, during the nineteen hundred years of the Diaspora, his forefathers let themselves be passively massacred on the rack and in gas chambers. The young man or woman who, with machine gun in hand, smuggled the pitiful survivors of concentration camps ashore in the darkness of the night under the eyes of the hostile British patrols, or who is standing guard against the murderous invasions of the Arab commandos, cannot see any heroism in martyrdom. He fires back if he is attacked. This determines his attitude toward the last nineteen centuries of Jewish history. Whatever may have happened culturally and intellectually during these nineteen hundred years, to him they are primarily a record of cowardice and weakness. He knows little if anything about the successive flowering of Jewish centers in Babylonia, in Spain, Poland, Germany. Their philosophies and theologies, their halakhah and way of life are to him merely compensatory ideologies, an ersatz for the lost national status of the past, an escape from the miseries of an emasculated and degenerate pariah existence into the promises of an otherworldly salvation developed by a people in response to its persistent failure to achieve once again the dignity of national security and independence on earth.

For this reason, many Israelis reject the men who represent exactly what they rebel against—the bearded Orthodox Jew, his Yiddish, his habits, his mentality, his customs, his observances—they are the language and mores, the mentality and religion, of the ghetto. They vehemently resist any attempt to incarcerate them in the strait jacket of a narrow ecclesiastical definition of Jewishness. They insist that Jewishness encompasses more than religion—that what makes them Jewish is not an assent to some obscure metaphysical notions or the observance of some outdated rites, but the same factors which, for instance, make England Anglo-Saxon: the country they live in, the language they speak, the literature and art they produce, the way they eat and drink and work and rest and procreate and deal with the fundamental facts of birth and death and define the nature and meaning of their particular society.

Hence, they demand that in Israel, too, a man's religion should be his personal affair, that the basic guaranteed individual freedom of thought and belief should be inviolate, that the invasion of the civil code by the ritual code should be stopped, and that the complete separation of state and church should be enforced.

A second factor adds fuel to this rebellion. It is the fact that many young people consider the Israeli rabbinate obscurantist. They resent the intervention in politics by the so-called religious parties. They see religious groups, admittedly small yet vociferous and influential far beyond their actual numbers, which decry the very existence of the State as an unwarranted invasion by secular man of God's plan for Israel's messianic redemption. They see a rabbinate which seems to concern itself primarily with banning the pig, rioting over Sabbath observance, and demonstrating against mixed bathing in the Jerusalem swimming pools; and they feel the ecclesiastical authorities live in a world that is out of touch with modern realities. Joseph Badi, in his book *Religion in Israel Today,* concludes that "The synagogue today stands apart from the world. The rabbis are city or town employees and . . . they busy themselves only with ritual matters. Neither the synagogues nor the rabbinate as a whole has anything to do with youth work or education." [5] And the *Jerusalem Post* says, "When most of the young people come into contact with the rabbinate (e.g., at family ceremonies), their attitude tends to be one of more or less amused tolerance. It would be difficult for any rabbinate in the modern world to reach many of the young people; but with its present mentality, the Israel rabbinate is in danger of being regarded as little more than a museum piece."

This is strong language. But one can understand why the tempers flare. I remember that on the same day on which the radio and newspapers reported the Khrushchev explosion in Paris which shattered hopes for a summit conference, the Knesset spent its time discussing a motion introduced by the Agudat Yisrael to express lack of confidence in Ben-Gurion and his government because, in connection with his weekly Bible-study group, he had publicly stated his doubts that the number of Jews led by Moses from Egypt could have been 600,000, as the Bible claims. He felt it could have been about 600 because the biblical term *elef* probably was meant to designate "families" and not "thousands" in view of the fact that the desert could not possibly have supported that many people.

Here is another illustration, from an issue of the *Jerusalem Post* some time ago:

> Mayor Ish Shalom was under fire today. Deputy Mayor Moshe Porush, Agudat Yisrael, asked that a by-law be passed banning mixed bathing in the German Colony swimming pool.
> Mr. Arest, Achdut Avodah, asked whether steps were being taken to prevent the recurrence of a disgraceful incident in a synagogue in the Zikhron Moshe quarter where a rabbi called for fasting and mourning on Israel's Independence Day to bewail the establishment of the state.
> Rabbi Sh'ar Yashuv Cohen, National Religious Party, asked why the city was allowing cinemas to sell tickets before the end of the Sabbath.

To give a final illustration: "the case of Billy Rose's sculpture garden," now part of the area of the Israel National Museum. Billy Rose had allowed himself to be persuaded to present his entire collection of modern art, mainly sculptures, valued at about a million dollars, to the city of Jerusalem. In addition, he volunteered to donate a suitable tract of land in Jerusalem where the sculptures could be permanently exhibited. Hardly had he and his personal architect arrived in Jerusalem to select the land and design the sculpture garden, when a violent public controversy erupted. The biblical injunction against graven images is taken very seriously by the religious groups. There was a storm of arguments and protests against the placing of statues in Jerusalem. Finally, someone suggested that Billy Rose's nonobjective art might conceivably be exhibited in the open while those statues that have recognizable shapes or are likenesses of men or beasts would have to be placed inside, in a hall.

Multiply these day-by-day occurrences and you will begin to understand the emotional chemistry of this so-called rebellion against God.

Does this rebellion mean that the young Israeli has ceased to be a Jew? This assertion is often made. His way of being a Jew is undoubtedly different from that of the Jew of the Diaspora. The answer depends on what your definition of a Jew is. If Jewish identity can be expressed solely in terms of prayer, in visits to the synagogue, in the observance of the dietary laws and all other halakhic precepts, many young Israelis have in fact ceased being Jews even though they still require the services of a rabbi at their wedding since there is no civil marriage in Israel.

But have they really stopped being Jewish? Whatever your definition of Jewish identity may be, you cannot write off the vibrant Jewishness you find there: the Jewish consciousness of the people, their love of their land, their sense of kinship with Jews everywhere, their sacrificial concern for their fellow Jews, which is far stronger than, and probably unmatched by, what you find anywhere else.

You cannot write off the fact that the young Israeli usually knows his Bible better than the Orthodox Jew of the Diaspora, and that, as someone once said, a boy in an Israeli grade school can recite by heart more passages from the prophets than a professor of theology in Europe. And the Bible does mean something to him, though it may be something different from what it means to us. It is not dead, a document of a forgotten past. It is *his* history book, the history book of his people.

You cannot write off the fact that the young Israeli speaks Hebrew, which is not merely the living language of a living people today but just as much the language of our tradition. Every word is freighted with overtones that echo the emotions and experiences of thousands of years of Jewish life. Every word reverberates something of the spirit that fought for expression in the Bible, inspired our prayers, formed our traditions, and molded the attitudes of our people. The Hebrew-speaking Jew possesses an instrument of communication with his fellow Jews as well as with the past of his people whose spirit and concepts resound in his language and whose purposes confront him in every word he speaks.

Above all, I am not prepared to write off the young Israeli as no longer being a Jew in religious terms. I grant that there are genuine secularists in Israel. I grant that a young writer, Yitzhar, is right when he characterizes some segments of the youth population as the "espresso generation." I grant that there is no all-pervasive quest for religious values. Yet, after half a dozen visits to Israel and numerous discussions with young people, I think one can often sense a deeper quest underneath this so-called rebellion of the godless. I am not prepared to write off, for instance, the spirit of religious quest and affirmation which surges out of Hannah Szenes' poem, *Eli Eli:*

> My God,
> May there never be an end
> To the sand and the sea,
> To the whispering of the water,
> To the glistening of the skies,
> To the prayer of man.

This is religion, too, an outcry and outreach springing from the same depths of the human heart which may have motivated the Psalmist three thousand years earlier. It may not be continuous with the formalized expressions and canons of the Jewish past, but this is exactly the question which Israel poses: Can a Jew be defined only in terms of the standards and criteria of the past, or is there room for new expression? Are Jews today supposed to be merely custodians, the curators of a past which they did not create but which nevertheless makes a claim upon them, or may they also be creators, seeking to give expression to man's deepest impulses, aspirations, and commitments in a new language and in new forms? Can Jewishness express itself only in patterns sanctified by the past, or can it seek new forms and ways of life?

IV

What I have said here is merely an analysis of some of the tensions, not a solution. No one knows whether this kind of problem has a solution. Some efforts toward reconciliation have been made on both sides, notably that of Rav Kuk, the Ashkenazic chief rabbi of Jerusalem and later of the entire *yishuv,* until his death in 1935. Though a strict traditionalist, he won the love and respect of the supposedly godless *halutzim* because, in his scale of Jewish values, they too were engaged in a holy task—the redemption of the Holy Land. Others, less highly placed, experiment with various new approaches designed to re-create, at least in their small circles, the historic synthesis between *am* and *kadosh* either in traditional or in liberal terms. But I doubt that a full reconciliation of the opposing views can be achieved. No culture is ever wholly free of conflicts and tensions. In the pluralistic society of Israel, these conflicts will probably continue to exist both as creative tensions and as one of the dissonances in the emerging culture of a people which, though pledged to safeguard its civil code from the intrusion and domination of the ritual code, will nevertheless ultimately have to come to grips with the spirit of its own past that defines the purposes of its national existence.

AVRAHAM HARMAN

15. Challenges to the Jewish People in Our Time

I WAS A university student nearly forty years ago and attended my first Jewish student conference in the winter of 1933, at the beginning of what was to become one of the most decisive periods in the course of Jewish history. Some aspects of that period can shed light on some of the problems we confront today.

Nineteen hundred thirty-three was the year in which Hitler came to power and in which the forces began to emerge that ultimately led to World War II. About 400,000 Jews lived in England in those days, 250,000 of them in the metropolitan area of London—a tiny fraction of its total population, which even then was about eight or nine million people.

The number of Jewish students and the percentage they constituted of the general student population were far smaller than today. The number of Jewish students who were concerned with Jewish life was smaller still. Only a tiny minority was sufficiently interested in Jewish affairs to draw personal conclusions from their observations of Jewish life. In this respect, Jewish students did not differ from the rest of the students. In the general student community in which I lived, only a few young people were prepared to respond to their observations of society by committing themselves to a quest for new solutions to the problems of society. The general trend, even in those years of unusual tension and danger, was to jog along.

The small Jewish student group that was seeking a personal

solution to the problems of Jewish life in our time contained two distinct sub-groups. One group felt that the conditions of Jewish life were inextricably bound up with the conditions of society in general. Jewish problems, Jewish suffering, the persecution of Jews and discrimination against them—these were minor problems. They were parochial, marginal concerns which would disappear with the emergence of the new egalitarian society. The primary and most urgent task was to change the social structure and organization of mankind. By changing it you would also improve Jewish life and solve the Jewish problem.

The thinking of this group was based essentially on two assumptions. One assumption was that it was reactionary to concern yourself with Jewish problems. To concern yourself with the liberation of India was progressive; to concern yourself with Jewish liberation was parochial. The second assumption—not always stated explicitly but basic to the philosophy of this group—was the conviction that Judaism, Jewish culture, the accumulated experience and creativity of the Jewish people throughout the centuries, was equally marginal and parochial. Your involvement in Jewish affairs meant in effect that you were trying to withdraw from the mainstream of humanity's cultural and spiritual concerns.

Those of us who belonged to the second group rejected these notions. We felt we had to start from opposite premises. We were convinced that there was nothing parochial in our concern with Jewish problems. On the contrary, we felt our concern for our national heritage was the only approach that was truly compatible with human dignity and genuine internationalism. The establishment of a truly international world order required not the disappearance of national differences but the liberation of the creativity of each national group. We felt that we did not have to apologize to anyone for concerning ourselves with Jewish affairs. And we went further and said that it would be escapism not to concern ourselves with Jewish affairs in the world in which we lived.

I

What was the condition of the Jewish world in 1933?

At that time, more than nine million Jews lived in the Soviet Union, in eastern Europe, and in central Europe. Their conditions differed vastly. The Jews of Germany had just come under Nazi control, which was later to engulf most parts of Europe. The conditions of the Jews in eastern Europe—in Poland with its three and a half million Jews, in Rumania with nearly one million Jews, in Hungary with almost 900,000 Jews—were intolerable even before their communities were devoured in the Nazi Holocaust. Professor Oscar Janowsky characterized their situation effectively in his book *People at Bay*. Published in 1938, this book described the various ways in which Jews were driven out of the economy of eastern Europe in those years—how they were pauperized, proletarianized, removed from gainful participation in the national economy. Long before Hitler, the Jews in eastern Europe had been trying to escape from this cold pogrom, which every now and then flared up into physical violence. They tried to free themselves by emigration. These were the people who, to a large extent, created the Jewish community of America and many of its institutions. They created our community in Israel. They laid the foundations for the development of the Jewish communities of South Africa, Canada, and Latin America. The flow of migration was cut off with the outbreak of World War I in 1914. Restored to a small extent in 1919, it was halted again in 1921, and when Hitler came to power in 1933, the roads to freedom had been virtually sealed off.

Soviet Jewry, the largest group of all, had been shut away from the rest of Jewry since about 1923. In the early years of the Russian Revolution, the policy of the Soviet authorities with regard to the Jewish population had still shifted occasionally. Some Jews were able to leave from time to time. But after 1923, Russian Jewry was completely isolated. Communication was no longer possible. Nevertheless, even the claims of communist propaganda could not completely hide the fact that the Russian government was engaged in a campaign aimed at the dejudaization and denationalization of the Jewish group. By 1933 all of us had begun to realize what the Jewish people had lost in that critical period since 1923, when Soviet Jewry had been closed off from the rest of the Jewish world. From the 1870's until the Russian Revolution and the years immediately following it, Russian Jewry had been the great center of every revolutionary movement and idea in Jewish life. The concept of Jewish self-defense had first emerged in Russia, in response to the pogroms in the early part of the twentieth century. Russian Jewry had been the center for the renaissance of the Hebrew language and literature. Yiddish literature had been revived and flowered there. The concept of Jewish occupational transformation, later called *hakhsharah,* training in the basic economic processes of society, had been born among Russian Jewry, and the first steps toward its implementation had been taken by Russian Jews. Both the Zionist movement and the Jewish Socialist movement in their modern forms had originated and matured there. Russian Jewry, together with Polish Jewry, had been the great fermenting center of what Pinsker had called the idea of auto-emancipation, the self-liberation of the Jewish people. This center of creative Jewish thought and life was now cut off from the rest of the Jewish world.

II

This was the Jewish situation as some of us in the British student movement saw it in 1933. As Jewish students in England, we knew that we owed our freedom—and our right to think and to organize and express ourselves freely—to the fact that our parents had possessed the courage to reject the conditions of Jewish life in Russia and Poland and to seek out a place where their children could grow up in freedom. Therefore, we felt we had no right to close our eyes to the condition of the Jewish people in the world. We wanted to know it. We wanted to understand it. Above all, we wanted to do something about it.

Our approach was based on two fundamental convictions. One was our rejection of the cultural imperialism then dominant in our society. Few people consciously articulate the notion of cultural imperialism, but many live by it. It equates the value and significance of a thing or movement with its size. According to this notion, a language that is spoken by half a billion people is, by virtue of this fact alone, a superior and culturally more advanced vehicle for the expression of human creativity than is a language spoken by merely five or ten million people. But the value of a painting cannot be determined by the size of its canvas. We rejected the notion that bigness can be a yardstick of what is culturally meaningful, creative, and worth preserving.

Second, we insisted that not only individuals but peoples and nations had a right to exist and to be themselves. The basis of democracy in an individual society is the affirmation that every single human being is of value in himself and equal in rights and status to every other human being. They may and do differ in physical size and features, in their skills and talents, in the jobs they are competent to handle. But democracy assures each of them an equal right to exist and to be what he is or can become as a human being.

We felt the same principle had to be applied to international society. Nations differ—in the size of their populations and territories, in their economic development, political structure, cultural standards, and productivity—yet each has an equal right to exist and be itself. I would go further and say that each has an equal responsibility to exist. In the 1930's, this notion was considered reactionary. Today it is, fortunately, being propounded as a primary road toward international order and harmony. In his last address to the General Assembly of the United Nations, the late President Kennedy summarized the importance of this doctrine in a single sentence when he said that it was the task of the United Nations to make the world safe for diversity.

These were the issues for which we fought in the Jewish context of the 1930's. We felt and said that ours was an ancient civilization—the fabric woven out of the rich and varied experiences of our people across the centuries—which had been preserved under the most difficult circumstances. It had a right to exist. Its existence had meaning. It had a claim upon us to help safeguard and assure its continuity as one of the rich cultural strands in the tapestry of human civilization. And—perhaps more important than all the other reasons—we felt that we could not be ourselves, true to ourselves, express ourselves fully, except through identification with this heritage and commitment to its continuity.

III

These views were not very popular among the Jewish student population of Great Britain at that time. Only a small group supported us. Yet only a few years later, the physical persecution of the Jews in Germany, and later throughout Europe, reinforced the validity of our analysis. Those of us who had arrived at their views before Hitler's rise to power rejected this tragic endorsement of our position. Jews do not have to be killed in a pogrom in order to prove to anyone that they are entitled to live as free men. Jews are entitled to some place under the sun where they can be free and masters of their own destiny and civilization.

I know it is difficult to define the term "Jewish civilization." Jews see themselves and, in different periods of their history, have seen themselves, in different ways. Different circumstances and conditions of life produced different self-definitions. Is Judaism a religion? Of course it is. But Judaism is a religion which is peculiar to Jewish persons. Nobody else practices it. And Jews have observed and practiced it in different ways at different stages of their history, and may observe it in still different ways in times to come. The important point is not the way we define ourselves, but the fact that we need, and are entitled to, a place in which we can preserve our Jewish civilization—this accumulated body of our historic experience, regardless of how we define it—preserve it not in the sense of barren conservation but in a dynamic process that will stimulate and nourish its organic growth and natural development.

IV

Thus, the question with which we were desperately concerned long before the appearance of Hitler was where the Jewish people could find this freedom from physical pressure along with a place to develop its civilization creatively. Europe did not provide this opportunity, even though some people continued to insist that we had diagnosed the situation incorrectly and prescribed the wrong remedy. They felt we had no business to complain about the intolerable conditions under which three and a half million Polish Jews had to exist. After all, were the conditions much different for many non-Jews? The basic enemy, they said, was not anti-Semitism but Fascism. Once Fascism was destroyed, Jews would gain their freedom, too.

These people may have been well intentioned, but they failed to realize that the Jewish problem in eastern Europe at that time was unique and had to be treated in a unique way. The Jews were a national minority subjected to relentless pressures. The process of elimination from the economy had been going on for decades.

Somebody once said that people vote with their feet. Our people voted with their feet when, from 1880 to 1921, they moved from eastern Europe across western Europe to the world overseas and the western hemisphere in what became the greatest mass migration in Jewish history. People usually do not migrate for the sake of adventure. Some young people may set out for unknown continents for the sake of excitement; family groups rarely do. They move because they are attracted by a vision of greater opportunities and freedom than they possess where they are, or they move into the unknown because existing conditions are intolerable. In this, as in most instances, mass migration was motivated by both factors. Conditions in eastern Europe were intolerable; and the United States and Canada were great lands of opportunity, freedom, and promise.

However, even before the turn of the last century, some far-sighted people had warned that the western world· would not permit mass immigration to continue indefinitely. They anticipated the possibility of restrictions and felt that the Jews needed a country which would be under Jewish control in order to provide the ultimate answer to the problem of Jewish migration. The validity of their analysis was confirmed when immigration restrictions were imposed in western countries before and after World War I, choking off immigration from abroad except for a thin trickle. The situation became desperate after 1933. Israel was not yet established. There was Palestine; but there, too, immigration was severely restricted by the mandatory power. There was no place, no country which we ourselves controlled and which therefore would have been prepared to take in the remnants of European Jewry who desperately searched for a refuge but were denied admission everywhere. Yet we had to find an answer to Hitler. Thus we adopted a strategy which had been pioneered in Israel in the early part of this century but which had received its clearest political and philosophical articulation by Chaim Weizmann. This strategy postulates that, if I want to be free, I have to live today as though I were already free, even though I am not. I must never cease demanding my rights; yet, until my claims are satisfied, I must not stand still, wait, or be inactive. I must move forward, step by step, from one finite objective to another, in order to establish my freedom of action in ever wider areas and to underpin my protest by facts which will demonstrate that I am free and independent. To put it differently: if I want to save the world, I may find that among my first tasks might well be the need to do something about an orphan boy who lives next door. Resolutions proclaiming the right of orphans to receive proper care will not help this youngster unless and until some individual or agency takes some concrete action on his behalf. Where idealism limits itself to the formulation of programs that remain on paper, or to the proclamation of resolutions that remain words and do not lead to concrete step-by-step action, education is directed not toward progress but toward cynicism.

The building of Israel required not only political action but also this kind of practical action—concrete steps. Not all of us could go there. But there were alternatives. Some of our young people established and worked on *hakhsharah* farms and training centers in England and elsewhere in the late 1930's. Some people thought them absurd; yet they created institutions that functioned effectively during World War II, and their existence made it possible for us to save from Nazi Germany hundreds of Jewish students who were permitted to enter England in order to join these training centers. These young people were trained for farm work, and fought Nazism during the war. And in 1946 they began to go to Palestine. Hundreds of them, in close cooperation with the members of the British Jewish student movement, participated in the transformation of mandated Palestine into independent Israel.

V

In the two decades that have passed since then, the State of Israel has been established. We have overcome enormous difficulties. But it is probably inevitable that we continue to face dramatic challenges.

One challenge is the security problem of our country. It is a problem on which we shall have to work patiently year after year and, if need be, generation after generation, until our neighbors will be ready to acknowledge the fact and legitimacy of our existence. The situation requires strong nerves. All of us, whether in Israel or in the countries of the West, live in a world in which we have neither peace nor war. The great practical and moral problem of our generation is to preserve patience. There are no hard and fast solutions to the complex problems of our world. Hence, we must find or devise an approach that will enable us to keep pushing back the moment of ultimate confrontation in which the tensions might once again explode into open conflict— not because such a strategy guarantees peace, but because it pushes the moment of danger back farther and farther and thus gains time and enables us to go on living and working toward peace and the elimination of open conflict.

Israel has been exposed to the pressures of this tension ever since it came into being. Yet our response to the hatred of our neighbors against us has been neither hate nor the growth of a militaristic spirit. Our hearts and minds have remained open to peace, even though we know that it may not come for a long time and that we shall long continue to be exposed to grave dangers.

There are other challenges. We must rebuild a people out of diverse elements that represent vast cultural differences. About one half of our school population is of European origin; the other half is of non-European origin. Our aim is not the integration but the fusion of these diverse elements. To achieve this fusion is the supreme moral challenge confronting Israel today. It calls for forces and resources which we do not yet fully possess. We continue to start every new school term with a shortage of hundreds of teachers in our elementary schools. Our school population has increased by thousands. While all children will go to school, their education will remain far from adequate as long as the critical shortage of teachers continues. The rebuilding of a people is an enormous and sometimes nerve-racking challenge. We are making progress, but it is slower than we want it to be.

The task of rebuilding the country is our third challenge. We have done well in the northern 40 percent of the country; but the Negev, which contains 60 percent of our land area and has a population of 100,000 today, is still largely desert and remains to be brought back to life. The Negev sustained some human life and civilization in ancient times. We believe we can make it sustain human life once again by using, for its development, the technical and scientific resources that are now at our command. But the road will be long and difficult.

The fourth challenge which confronts us is the challenge of Judaism. Israeli, like American Jewry, is characterized by an enormous diversity of definitions of Judaism. But the religious situation in Israel differs decisively from that in the United States. The Hasidic Jew from Williamsburg in Brooklyn rarely, if ever, meets the Jew from Manhattan's Temple Emanu-El, located on Fifth Avenue. The extremes do not meet in America. In Israel they do. In the apartment house in which I live in Jerusalem I have to be aware of the fact—and I am aware of it—that some of my neighbors will be offended if they hear my radio being played on Shabbat. This fact poses a problem for me. Should I give consideration to their sensibilities, or should I disregard them? How should I conduct myself under these circumstances? One can generally avoid this kind of problem in the United States. It cannot be avoided in Israel. It is a symptom of the clash of forces and convictions that we experience in our daily activities and that are part of the larger problem of the relationship between religion and state in Israel. The problem is being discussed with great passion. It has created profound tensions. Yet I believe that these tensions, though they are great and threaten to split the community, are ultimately more challenging than an atmosphere of complete indifference would be. They are an indication that people care. Years may pass before these tensions can be resolved. It is conceivable that they will always exist. But they represent a fundamental challenge pressing us for a clarification of the image we have of ourselves and of the nature and meaning of our identity in the modern world.

VI

The challenges which Israel must face obviously do not exhaust the issues which affect the Jewish people in our time. Two great and historic challenges confront the Jewish world outside Israel.

One concerns those parts of the world in which Jews are still not free, in which they either live on the edge of physical danger or do not possess the freedom to live as Jews.

The second great challenge to Jewish existence outside Israel is the effort to ensure that Judaism will not merely survive but will flourish under conditions of freedom. American Jewry and the Jewish community of Israel both face this challenge, though in different ways. The danger confronting us in Israel is collective assimilation—the possibility that the entire community might surrender its historic Jewish values and ethical stance to the values and standards of the surrounding world. The danger confronting American Jewry is individual assimilation—the corrosion of Jewish vitality through the disappearance of Jewish identity, involving ever larger numbers of American Jews. These dangers are very real. Nevertheless, I for one do not believe it is inevitable that assimilation will undermine the Jewish communities of the free world. Decay and erosion are not inevitable in human affairs. The history of human experience is basically the story of man's efforts to resist and counteract the processes of erosion and decay that threaten society. While there is nothing inevitable about the durability of man or his works, he can overcome obstacles and move forward creatively by being alert to the dangers and challenges of his condition, by taking effective action to offset the dangers and, above all, by exploiting the opportunities for human, national, and international self-development which his freedom offers him.

I reject the view that Jewish life in the western world today is dead or dying. It is not. It is full of problems and dangers. But it is also full of challenges and opportunities. Many Jews will continue to see only the problems and difficulties. But there will be many others who are prepared to relate themselves to the challenges of Jewish life in our time, who will find it a profoundly meaningful and rewarding experience to express their human and Jewish convictions in the service of the tasks confronting the Jewish people, and who will thereby make a vitally needed and significant personal contribution toward the achievement of the human and international order to which all of us aspire.

Part Five

THE JEWISH INTELLECTUAL AND THE JEWISH COMMUNITY

MILTON HIMMELFARB

16. Jewish Tradition and the Educated Jew

TRADITION IS complicated, difficult, ambiguous. People speak, for instance, of the great tradition of English poetry. In that tradition Donne is a central figure for us. It is difficult for us to think of English poetry without Donne as one of the great names. Yet Donne was rediscovered only about the time of the First World War, when a scholar succeeded in reviving interest in his work. The discovery modified the tradition. Of course, there had been a Donne before then, but the working, actual tradition of English poetry had been a Donne-less tradition. After 1920, the tradition was transformed.

Tradition is not something fixed and given. We tend to think of tradition as something belonging to the past and therefore unchangeable, but it changes. That ambiguity is our first difficulty when we speak about tradition. Tradition is fixed, yet can at the same time be labile.

There is a second difficulty, the mention of which lays one perilously open to an accusation of male chauvinism. Tradition is feminine. Tradition is a feminine noun: in Hebrew, *masorah, masoret, kabbalah,* or *yerushat avot*—all feminine; in Latin, *traditio,* in other languages, *paradosis, Ueberlieferung*—again, all feminine. Tradition is feminine, and the one thing on which all masculines seem to agree with regard to feminines is that you can't live with them and you can't live without them. That applies to tradition, too. You can't live with it, and you can't live without it.

Modern people are ambivalent about tradition. "Modern" is not merely a chronological or calendrical term; it refers to a certain set of attitudes and feelings. The beginning of modernity in this sense can be dated to the eighteenth or even the seventeenth century. The modern outlook grows out of the Enlightenment of the eighteenth century.

What is characteristic of the modern attitude is that it is anti-traditional. When we say we are modern, we mean we are dependent upon modernity and not upon the past for our spiritual needs. To the degree to which the past is at all useful to us, it is historically useful. We may, for instance, want to study some aspect of the past out of intellectual curiosity, or in order to understand its influence on modern times. The decisive point is that we have moved beyond the past.

At any given time in the past, the people who were then living felt that what they did and what was being done around them was new. It is the preference for the new that is modern. Formerly, people took it generally for granted that the old (or ancient) was better than the new. A famous battle between the ancients and moderns took place just about three hundred years ago—the controversy in French literature whether Racine, Molière, and Corneille possessed sufficient worth to be spoken of in the same breath with the classical authors. A presumption had to be overcome: since they were modern, they had to be inferior. The dominant note of the premodern attitude is that tradition is better than modernity and that modernity is inferior to the past and to tradition.

The characteristic attitude of modern man is precisely the opposite. He is negative toward tradition. That is true not only for modern man but, above all, for us Jews. In a sense, we Jews are perhaps the most modern people of all. Who, for instance, is the symbol of modernity in James Joyce's *Ulysses?* The culture hero, James Joyce himself, is Stephen Daedalus. He rejects his actual father, has contempt for him. He will not gratify his dying mother even to the extent of pretending to mumble a traditional formula to comfort her in her last moments. He has to break away in order to preserve his integrity. He must assert himself, be modern, oppose tradition, even at the cost of cruelty to his parents and what they stand for.

Stephen, however, finds for himself a surrogate, spiritual father, who symbolizes Stephen's breakthrough into modernity. The story takes place in Dublin, capital of one of the most homogeneous countries in the western world. Stephen cannot find himself a native and indigenous Irish spiritual father to represent modernity for him; he is compelled to look for an outsider—a Jew, Leopold Bloom. That is no accident. We modern Jews have a greater interest and a greater stake in modernity than almost anybody else has.

Two quotations will show how characteristically Jewish the negation of tradition is—the feeling that I am more comfortable with the future than with the past. Both relate to Moses Mendelssohn, a father of Jewish modernity.

About two hundred years ago, Moses Mendelssohn was trying to secure the right of residence in the city of Berlin, where Jews were not allowed to live. The Marquis d'Argens, Frederick the Great's cultural advisor, asked the king to grant Mendelssohn the right of residence in the following words: "Un philosophe mauvais catholique supplie un philosophe mauvais protestant de donner le privilège à un philosophe mauvais juif. Il y à trop de philosophie dans tout ceci pour que la raison ne soit pas du côté de la demande." ("An intellectual who is a bad Catholic begs an intellectual who is a bad Protestant to grant the privilege [of residence in Berlin] to an intellectual who is a bad Jew. There is too much intellectualism in all this for reason not to be on the side of the request.")

Reason, of course, is opposed to tradition; it is the enemy of tradition. We are on the side of reason because it is on our side.

According to a nineteenth-century biographer of Mendelssohn, Salomo Ludwig Steinheim, "Mendelssohn despised apostasy [i.e., refused to be converted to Christianity] as dishonorable, though he would gladly have followed his friend Lessing in creating a society in which there were neither Christians nor Jews." Mendelssohn was too proud to convert to Christianity, but what he really would have wanted was an untraditional society of ex-Christians and ex-Jews. He expressed what I consider to be a significant view: The only honorable way for me to be a gentile's equal, the only society where I can be truly his equal, is the future society in which all tradition, and especially all religious tradition, has been discarded. Tradition, in this opinion, stands in the way of true human brotherhood.

No wonder that modern Jews have had a futuristic passion, a passion toward antitraditionalism. On the campus, Jewish students usually are the least traditional, the most future-oriented. The Jews have been in the liberal camp ever since Mendelssohn. The slogan of the nineteenth century was *juif donc libéral*—"Jew, therefore liberal." This is not just a political statement. It is a cultural phenomenon. It has something to do with our basic attitude toward the past, the present, and the future.

Another illustration. Who are the people who buy the Frank Lloyd Wright-influenced houses in the suburbs of our great cities? Of course, not only Jews; but a significant proportion of them are Jews. Or consider the furniture in those houses. Many Jewish women collect American antiques, but it is my impression that far fewer Jewish women collect American antiques than one might expect a priori, considering their wealth and general cultural level. On the contrary, Jewish women of this class are characteristically future- or at least modern-oriented in their furniture and interior decoration. The reason for this attitude is probably quite simple. We do not like to kid ourselves that our furniture really represents family heirlooms. If you have an Anglo-Saxon name, even though you yourself may not be a direct descendant of a Mayflower family or at least of an American Revolutionary soldier, you can nevertheless consider yourself to be a member of a group of people who are among their descendants. There is an easy psychological identification. It is psychologically comfortable, natural, and honorable for you to buy Early American.

But as a Jew I know that my grandfather was not Early American. Of course, there are exceptions. I happen to know a Jew who is a Son of the American Revolution. He once told me quite seriously that he was still annoyed with an ancestor of his who in 1785 had been given the choice between a parcel of land on Canal Street in New York City or one in White Plains, in Westchester County, and had chosen White Plains. That man has not yet forgiven his ancestor. There are American Jews whose families have been here for generations. Most of ours, however, have not. In school we used to sing, "Land where my fathers died." But that was only one more of the adult absurdities that we were expected to mouth. I *knew* my ancestors had not died here. I feel more comfortable in a Frank Lloyd Wright society than in a Colonial-revival or a Georgian society.

Yet our problem is precisely the fact that though we can't live with tradition, we can't live without it, either. We need tradition. All men need tradition. An extreme expression of antitraditionalism is to be found in an extreme expression of the Enlightenment, Marxism. There is a most significant line in the "Internationale," the popular anthem of Marxism, to express its vigorous rejection of all tradition: "No more tradition's chains shall bind us." Or, as the French original has it, "Let us wipe clean the slate of the past." Marxism rejects tradition. Yet Marxism itself has developed a tradition. Today a Marxist appeals to Marxist tradition.

The same is true in literature. James Joyce fits into a tradition now; he has become part of a tradition. The avant-garde either gets fitted into a tradition (and by getting fitted alters the contours of that tradition), or it deliberately attaches itself to a tradition, be it avant-garde, revolutionary, or antitraditional. It becomes absorbed into a tradition. To try to be something new can also become a tradition, as illustrated by the title of a book on that subject, *The Tradition of the New.*

We go so far as to invent tradition where none exists. A peculiar development is taking place among the emerging new nations in Africa. African intellectuals or their European friends are busy either discovering or inventing an African past. They insist that the notion that Africa has no past, or that the African past is empty, is not true, but is an expression of white colonial contempt for the Africans, or a white colonial attempt to demoralize the Africans. Actually, they insist, Africa has a glorious past.

The issue here is not whether or not Africa has a glorious past, but an entirely different question: Why should these people feel it necessary to assert that Africa has a glorious past? They are interested in the future. Yet there is something that makes them feel that that future becomes uncertain unless the African can be made to feel that he has a glorious past to which he can relate himself in some way. In principle, the humanity and humaneness of the

African are enough to qualify him for full and equal membership in the human race and the society of nations. In practice, the Africans and their friends are driven to discover an African past, or to invent it where it may not exist. Their very concern with the present and the future makes them turn to the past. We like tradition. We need tradition.

To give a personal illustration: recently I attended the liberal Friday night and the traditional Sabbath morning services at a Hillel Institute. I was not certain whether I should attend a traditional or a liberal service; there was no compelling ideological reason for me to attend the traditional Sabbath morning service in preference to the liberal service. I went to it because I felt a need for it. Yet though I went to the traditional service, I kept a certain distance from it. The traditional prayer book includes prayers for the restoration of the ancient sacrificial cult. I am not a very literal person when I pray. I do not take every prayer literally. I can say some things to which I cannot assent literally but which I feel free to interpret. Yet when everybody was chanting a prayer for the restoration of the sacrificial cult, I remained silent. That is a prayer which I cannot recite. I must maintain my distance from it. Similarly, I was not made very happy by some of the commandments concerning the destruction of the Hittites and Jebusites in the *parasha* that was read during the service. I have a distance from tradition, yet I attended the traditional service. I would not have liked the liberal Sabbath morning service. I like to worship in Hebrew and not in English, though I cannot assent intellectually to all that the Hebrew text says. Intellectually, the English version of the liberal service strikes me as more honest—though in some ways also as more blurred. Yet I find the English in the liberal Sabbath eve service gauche, graceless. That is no criticism of the compilers of the text. It is the best there is, but I preferred the Hebrew service. Why? It had an unfair advantage. It had the advantage of being traditional.

The story is told of a man who, while visiting one of the stately homes of England, asked the caretaker how he had been able to produce such a beautiful lawn. "It is very easy, sir," said the caretaker, "you merely sweep it every morning for three hundred years." The English of the Friday night service was a new lawn.

The Hebrew of the Sabbath morning was a lawn that had been swept every morning for much longer than three hundred years. It had that unfair advantage—an advantage even in the eyes of one who is modern. That is the other side of our ambivalence: we are modern, but we also like tradition. There is something about us that likes tradition, even though as a group we modern Jews are antitraditional.

For well-known and, I think, well-understood historical reasons, the distance between us and our Jewish tradition is in many ways greater than that between Christians and their tradition. Many of us feel more uncomfortable with our tradition than Christians do with theirs. The Christian tradition had a chance to develop step by step and could parry the thrust of modernity at each point. There was a Pascal to counter a Descartes, a Schleiermacher to counter a Voltaire. At each point Christianity was able to adjust itself to modernity.

In contrast, the Jews emerged suddenly into the light of the eighteenth century. One minute we were living, intellectually, not even in the thirteenth century—for instance, with Maimonides at the height of philosophical Judaism. Intellectually we were still living in pre-Saadyah Gaon days, in a prephilosophical Judaism. The next minute we had emerged into modernity. The yeshiva *bahurim* were dazzled by the light of modernity, by science, literature, and philosophy. The transition from the dim light of the ghetto to the glaring light of the summer sun at noon was so rapid and abrupt that we have not yet had time to complete our adjustment fully. That is one major reason why Jews are negative toward their tradition.

At the same time, however—and this is our paradox—we Jews have much more reason to be comfortable with our tradition than Christians have to be comfortable with theirs. I am not talking about the history of ideas but about Christendom, the life of Christian society as it has been molded and affected by Christianity. The thoughtful Christian contemplating the record of that Christian society has more reason to be critical of it and even to reject it than the thoughtful Jew, contemplating the Jewish tradition as it is embodied in life, has reason to reject *his* tradition.

Take the Torah reading containing the famous passage that

speaks of the retributive principle—eye for eye. That verse is still being held against us. People still say that Jews and Judaism are vindictive and that our God is a God of vengeance, in contrast to Christianity, the religion of love with a God of love. Yet when I follow this Torah reading, I tend to remember Samuel Johnson. He lived two hundred years ago and was a pious Christian— something of an exception in the eighteenth century, which some have called a century of infidelity. There is a famous passage in which Boswell recalls a statement Johnson once made about damnation. It goes something like this:

Johnson: "I am afraid of damnation."
Interlocutor: "What, Sir, do you mean by damnation?"
Johnson: "Going to hell, Sir, and burning for eternity."

He was a pious Christian, and I am sure he really meant what he said: for Johnson, Christianity was the religion of love; yet God condemns most human beings to burn eternally in hell.

Or consider another story, also reported by Boswell, about a former parson who had been defrocked and who was ill advised enough to forge a check or note. The punishment for forgery at that time was hanging. Johnson wanted to visit him in prison, but Boswell thought the prisoner would be too distracted. Johnson said, "Depend upon it, Sir, when a man is to be hanged in a fortnight, it concentrates his mind wonderfully."

Here is a pious Christian who despises "eye for eye" and for whom the Jewish God is the God of vengeance; yet it never occurs to him that it might be wrong and horrible to hang a man for forgery. Not once did it occur to him to ask why England—a society which claimed to be a Christian society, in which the king was the head of the Church of England and its bishops sat in the House of Lords—found it compatible with Christian love to hang a man for forgery, while among the Jews, with their eye for eye, forgery had never been a hanging crime.

To give still another illustration to show why Jews have less reason to be uncomfortable with their tradition than others— well into the nineteenth century the punishment for attempted desertion in the British Navy was a thousand lashes. The sailor so punished was probably dead after five hundred, yet they would keep on flogging the corpse. The Torah, which supposedly reveals our Jewish vindictiveness, imposes a maximum punishment of forty lashes. This maximum was set in order to preserve the honor and dignity of the human being, and the rabbis went so far as to reduce the maximum to thirty-nine, out of fear that the man executing the punishment might make a mistake and miscount, and thus become subject to punishment himself as having been excessively cruel and having violated the law.

I know, of course, that our own record is not entirely clean. There have been abuses and distortions. Nevertheless, there is a vital difference. In the last century, a Christian nation, a nation supposedly governed by the religion of love, was meting out a thousand lashes, while our so-called primitive Torah, with its retribution, had set a maximum of forty. Or, again, the man who made an attempt on the life of Louis XV of France was punished by having his body pulled apart by horses before he was drawn and quartered. The title of that king was "His Most Christian Majesty."

In Christendom, the change and reform that had to come were brought about not by the faithful but against the resistance of the faithful, by the heretics or the schismatics. It was not the Church of England that pressed for a more humane criminal legislation, but the Utilitarians, the Unitarians, and the Quakers—the outsiders, not the insiders.

Contrast Judaism, and the simple but arresting story told in *Life Is With People.* It is the story of a Jewish orphan boy who is badly in need of a pair of shoes but cannot get them from the heads of the Jewish community whose ward he is. One day he sees a pair of shoes in the marketplace and steals them. A hue and cry is raised, and a gentile policeman nabs the boy. A collection is taken up immediately among the women who are at the market to sell their wares, the money is slipped into the policeman's hand, and he lets the boy get away.

One may consider this an act of in-group solidarity, but I believe it expresses something more significant. It shows how deeply incorporated into daily life the Jewish value system was. In the lives of these women—uneducated, coarse, uncouth—the Jewish value system was so internalized that their reaction to need had become almost instinctive. The first protest was not against the boy. They did not beat or scold him. They did not even protest against the policeman. Their protest was against the leaders of the community who had permitted a condition to arise which would compel a Jewish orphan to steal! These women did not act on the basis of a thought-out or developed theory of social welfare. No one had told them that delinquency may arise out of slum conditions. They acted out of a deeply internalized system of Jewish values that interpenetrated their everyday life. The Jewish value system had been so built into them that they did not even have to think about it.

From this point of view, the Jewish value system has been a success. We Jews look upon Jewish society, have less reason to be critical of the Jewish tradition, which has molded that society, than Christians have to be critical of the Christian tradition, which has molded Christian society. In this sense Judaism has been more successful.

We should, of course, admit in all fairness that our disadvantage may have been our advantage. That we were an oppressed minority meant that we could be comfortable with "brother" ethics. Had we not always been a minority, had we been faced with the need to be serious about "other" ethics, the warmth and human closeness among us might have been dissipated. It is easy to criticize others, until you face the problems they have. We have no integration problem in our synagogues, whereas Christians face that problem daily in their churches. We have no right to assume a posture of moral superiority. We would probably not be terribly much better than the Christians if we had an integration problem in our synagogues. In other words, a disadvantage may work to one's advantage. Nevertheless, to the degree to which there has been a Jewish society, we have reason to affirm the tradition which formed and informed that society and to consider it as good and valuable.

We have a tradition that is good and valuable. Our difficulty is —my original thesis—that we can't live with it and can't live without it. But that too is not altogether new; it, too, is part of the Jewish tradition. Judaism not only affirms tradition, but also has a tradition of breaking away from tradition. Think of Reb Zishe's famous aphorism: "When I get to heaven, they will not ask me, 'Zishe, Zishe, why weren't you Moses?' They will ask me, 'Zishe, why weren't you Zishe?' " And we are wrong if we think the Jewish tradition to be a relatively straightforward glorification of our glorious ancestors. The Bible explicitly tells us that when our glorious ancestors left Egypt, they included large numbers of *erev rav* and *asafsuf,* rabble and riffraff. *Ka'avotekhem* means "like your ancestors." In the Bible that word occurs three times: twice in "do not be like your ancestors" and once in "do not be stiff-necked like your ancestors."

Goethe said, "Was du ererbt von deinen Vaetern hast, erwirb es, um es zu besitzen"—"What you have inherited from your fathers, you must earn in order to possess it." You must work at it. That is the task all of us share with regard to the Jewish tradition.

The Jewish community has enormous weaknesses. Yet we must love this Jewish community. We must love it not because of what it is but perhaps in spite of what it is. We must not approach it with the question, "What can it do for me? What has it done for me lately?" Seeing it with all its faults, we must nevertheless say, "This is mine. I will get right in and fight to change it." If that is not my temperament, if I am not much of a fighter or community activist, I will stay on the outskirts, but I will be defined by my being on the outskirts of the Jewish community rather than on the outskirts of something else. We have inherited tradition and community. We must strive to earn them in order to possess them.

MILTON R. KONVITZ

17. The Jewish Intellectual, the University, and the Jewish Community

I

NAPOLEON IS quoted as saying, "I hear we have no poets in France. What is the Minister of the Interior doing about it?" The Minister of the Interior could not, of course, beget poets —or scientists, or mathematicians, or engineers, or teachers—yet, in a sense, he did beget them, and others, too, and poets as well. Who can say how many poets have been stimulated and supported in France by such national institutions as the Opéra, the Opéra Comique and the Comédie Française; or in Italy by the Scala Opera of Milan, which receives generous support from the government; or in Austria, where the government supports the Vienna State Opera; or in the Netherlands, where the government maintains one of the world's great orchestras, as well as theaters, opera companies, and a national festival of arts?

Except for the four-arts projects in the days of the W.P.A., American history fails to disclose a governmental concern with poetry, the drama, music, or any other of the arts.

In 1962 we celebrated the centenary of the Morrill Act, by which Congress granted public lands for the establishment of agricultural and mechanical colleges. Under its provisions, twenty-six state universities and forty-two other institutions were founded or benefited. It was a tremendous contribution, which I in no way mean to belittle when I call attention to the fact that no statesman

336

thought of proposing to Congress recognition of the importance of the humanities for American life.

But fortunately we now see promise of a better day. Perhaps as we see the results of science, technology, and business prosperity —results which may be either a blessing or a curse, or something of each—we have begun to think of man's concern for human conduct and man's need for beauty and sublimity and holiness; and our spiritual and moral wants and aspirations have compelled even our governments to recognize the importance of cultural interests and activities for the future of the nation.

There are some events that look like stirrings of the spirit. Let me summarize them briefly:

In 1965 Congress established a National Foundation on the Arts and Humanities and declared that the encouragement and support of these fields, while primarily a matter for private and local initiative, is also a matter of concern for the federal government, and that "a high civilization must not limit its efforts to science and technology alone but must give full value and support to the other great branches of man's scholarly and cultural activity."

Congress has authorized a National Cultural Center in Washington that will house a theater, a symphony hall, and a hall for opera, ballet, and musicals; and it has authorized the conversion of a government building into an art museum.

The recognition given to Robert Frost by President Kennedy and Congress was unprecedented and may be taken as symbolic of the new status of literature and the arts on the national scene.

Lincoln Center for the Performing Arts has been built with funds supplied by the federal, state, and city governments.

Some states and cities have also awakened to the importance of cultural activities. Louisville, Philadelphia, and San Francisco have provided help for their orchestras. New York City has allocated funds for a free Shakespeare Festival in Central Park and in the schools. North Carolina supports its state symphony orchestra. Rhode Island's taxpayers share the cost of local ballet and concerts. In 1960, New York established the State Council on the Arts, which supports touring theater productions, concerts, and ballet and opera performances. It is making a survey of architecture worth saving, and it is entering upon a long-range art-loan program for regional museums from the Metropolitan Museum of Art and other major collections, and a broadening of exhibits and performances in the public schools throughout the state.

All these developments represent only a small coin dropped into the cultural charity box when compared with the billions of dollars that the federal government spends on scientific research and development; but when contrasted with the past, they represent a revolutionary change in our national system of values. We no longer think, as did the Puritans, that cultural and artistic activities are manifestations of the devil, or, at best, are wasteful and frivolous. The change from the past can perhaps be most succinctly noted when we read in the *Report of the President's Commission on National Goals,* and in the statement on "The State of the Performing Arts" made by Arthur Goldberg when he was Secretary of Labor, that cultivation of the arts must become one of the national goals, along with health, welfare, and similar aims, that are permanently on our national agenda.

Each of the developments I have mentioned would be, standing alone, too insignificant to occupy our time, but when taken together I see in their totality the beginning of a movement the end of which none of us can foresee. For we know what America's resources and know-how have accomplished when massively applied to industry, business, commerce, transportation, communication, and other tangible aspects of our technological civilization. Who can imagine what may yet be accomplished when American enterprise applies itself to the cultural aspects of human and social existence? We shall not soon see the great consummation of the spirit of America in a new world in which all things, all acts and events, will sing the poetry of life—a world in which Plato's lovers of wisdom will be, if not the rulers, at least the equal partners of the lovers of honor and the lovers of gain. The strivings of a new spirit, however, cannot be denied, and this is a fact in which we should find glory and joy.

II

When we, as Americans who are at the same time Jews, consider this awakening of the sense of public responsibility for American culture, we cannot help but feel profoundly grateful, *for it is only by reason of things spiritual and cultural that we are Jews.* In all other matters we are undifferentiated from other Americans. We must, therefore, not only as Americans *but peculiarly as Jews,* be vitally interested in all that moves men toward things of the spirit: toward the good, toward beauty, toward the sublime and the holy, toward everything that tends to awaken and stimulate the thoughts and emotions of human beings as they respond to life, to the world, to pain and joy, to despair and ecstasy, to whatever relates to the work of the human spirit that is within existence, and beneath the surface of existence, and that beckons to existence from afar and above—work of the human spirit that is expressed in religion, philosophy, criticism, poetry, drama, music, dancing, in all the infinite ways in which the spirit seeks to express itself in excitement, contemplation, and worship.

But it is just at this point that *as Jews* we also sense a grave danger. For we see that assimilation has already taken a great toll among us. If now the cultural wants and aspirations of Americans should be served by the great resources of our nation, what future may there be for the distinctive Jewish way of life and thought and feeling? Americans may become one *spirit* in freedom, even as America already is one *body* in freedom. Cultural cannibalism is a practice not unknown in the history of civilization; and it is a practice which can be more easily pursued in a free than in an autocratic society, for the latter may lead to the voluntary or coerced erection of ghetto walls; but in a free society ghettos sooner or later give way. In a free society, no man is an island. Yet, as Jews, we can exist only if, with apologies to John Donne, we insist that spiritually and culturally a man *can* be an island; and especially is this insistence necessary in a society in which all men are free and equal.

Thus, we see that, although we are quite accustomed to dangers and challenges, new and greater perils and challenges await us as American Jews.

I think that we may be better able to see our situation if we look at it in a historical perspective.

III

Our parents and our grandparents, when they came to these shores, applied themselves to making new homes for their families. They worked hard at their jobs and in their businesses, and they sought to give their children as good an education as they could afford or as they could get for them within the limits imposed by discriminatory practices. There were considerable odds against the Jewish immigrants and their children, but there were also circumstances that favored them: the country's need of talent, ability, and ambition; the limitless natural resources that waited for exploitation; the country's need of manpower that far exceeded the capacity of the western European countries to satisfy, so that America had to hold out a hand of welcome to the immigrants from other parts of the world; and, not least by any means, the great ideals of the Declaration of Independence and of the Bill of Rights of the United States Constitution. The Jewish immigrants built and supported the communal religious institutions—the synagogues, the Talmud Torahs; and they transported to their American ghettos the free-loan societies, the Passover relief societies, the orphan asylums, the homes for the aged, the burial societies, and their other religious and welfare agencies. In this way they made a new yet familiar home for themselves in a strange land.

For many, their religious beliefs and practices, coupled with their continued use of Yiddish, provided them with a transplanted Jewish culture that nourished their spiritual and cultural needs. Especially for the masses who settled in New York, Chicago, Boston, Philadelphia, and a few other large cities, there was satisfaction in their own Yiddish newspapers, their own theaters, their own cantorial concerts, their *Landsmannschaften,* their Yiddish-speaking trade unions; in their secular schools, like those of the Farband or the Arbeiter Ring; their ideological disputes, like those of the Bundists, the territorialists, the Zionists, with all their major and minor splinterings. They lived a life of their own on a Jewish island within the American ocean. It was in some significant ways a richer cultural and spiritual life than that of the non-Jewish masses—one may make this judgment, I think, not on the basis of partiality or sentiment, but on the basis of objective fact.

But while the immigrants had their own style of life, at the very same time their children or grandchildren were moving along through elementary and high schools, and a considerable number were entering the city colleges and the metropolitan and state universities, and some were even venturing on into the more exclusive institutions of higher learning that were gradually moving away from the churches that had established, supported, and dominated them. As America was becoming secularized, it was becoming more libertarian, and the young men and young women from the Jewish ghettos took their places in the business and professional world as undifferentiated Americans.

In their world, unfortunately, they found no place for anything Jewish except for a synagogue or temple, which they could rationalize and accept. But without any clear rationalization, except the need to meet the situation created by anti-Semitism, they proceeded to build Jewish hospitals, Jewish country clubs, Jewish downtown clubs, and similar institutions that were more of an answer to anti-Semitism than an expression of a positive Judaism or Jewish cultural needs. And in time the lives of the children reacted upon the parents, who saw in their offspring—their sons the doctors, the dentists, the lawyers, the businessmen—a freer and better life; and so the parents tried to forget their Yiddish, they tried to move "uptown," and to cut themselves off from Jewish culture and its values and institutions, and looked with parental pride on the way their children prospered. From the Jewish point of view, however, their lives—those of the parents and those of the children—were spiritually and culturally inauthentic and sterile.

The only exceptions were the obstinate Orthodox Jews and the perhaps even more obstinate secular, humanist Yiddishists who continued, under almost insurmountable obstacles, to sustain a Jewish cultural life and its manifold institutions.

The greatest cultural loss was among Jewish intellectuals. Perhaps the responsibility for this must be placed less on the Jewish community than on the American college and universities. Within the notorious quota system, some Jewish students did manage to be graduated and to join the ranks of the professions, where they found support from Jewish and non-Jewish patients and clients. Physicians needed, of course, hospitals, and when they found themselves discriminated against, or even excluded, they managed to get sufficient support for the establishment of their own or Jewish hospitals. But the young Jew who wanted to pursue secular scholarship could not look to patients or clients to support him. He had to have an offer from a college or a university to join its faculty. And here the Jew found a high and impregnable wall of exclusion.

From the standpoint of secular Jewish studies, the felony was compounded either by the total exclusion of such studies from the curriculum, or, if some of them were included—as, for example, biblical Hebrew, Old Testament studies—the subjects could be taught only by non-Jewish scholars. The appointment, in 1925, of Professor Harry A. Wolfson to the newly established Nathan Littauer Chair of Hebrew Literature and Philosophy at Harvard was an exception to the rule. Colleges and universities still acted on the assumption that the Hebrew Scriptures were important only as the Old Testament, i.e., as a part of the Christian Bible. And as for postbiblical Jewish thought and history, they acted on the silent assumption—which Arnold Toynbee and Christian theologians made explicit—that the Jews are a "fossil" people or "an anachronistic survival." If they are to be studied at all, they should be studied by anthropologists.

The rule of exclusion worked in such a way that few Jews were trained to teach English literature, American history, comparative government, or any other subject conventionally taught in American colleges or universities, as long as there was no marketplace where they could sell their services; and practically no Jews at all dared to make some phase of Jewish learning their specialty, for the door that kept them out of the academic marketplace had double locks: one against Jewish professors and one against Jewish professors of Jewish studies.

In the face of this cultural and spiritual catastrophe—that is not, I submit, too strong a word—the American Jewish community remained indifferent, seemingly unaware of what was happening. Jewish culture in the United States lived largely on memories, on remnants of Yiddish, and on what we could borrow from the Soncino translators of England and from our own translations from German or modern Hebrew.

In hearings held by the House Education and Labor Committee in 1961 on the economic plight of musicians, George London testified that when, in 1949, he became convinced that he would not be engaged by the Metropolitan Opera, he sailed for Europe, where within a week he was hired by the Vienna State Opera. Since then, he added, close to two hundred American singers had been engaged in European opera houses. "They were forced to go abroad," he said, "because they lacked opportunities in their own country." How many George Londons has the American Jewish community lost because there was no future for them in Jewish scholarship, in Jewish culture? Over the years the toll of our tragic loss must be in the many thousands.

IV

As we look at American college and university campuses today, it is clear that a radical change has come about. Today, thousands of Jewish intellectuals teach in the sciences, in mathematics, and in the humanities and social studies, equal as to rank and tenure with their non-Jewish colleagues. Most of them, however, are Jews only in the sense that they had Jewish parents. They have evaded or escaped from the Jewish community and have only slight Jewish ties or loyalties.

But among the Jews who are professors there are a minority who are deeply involved, sincerely committed, and well-informed Jewish intellectuals. Though few in number, and though a new phenomenon on the American campus, their role is not to be underestimated; for they offer, by their example, a vision to thousands of Jewish students, showing that it is not necessary for the Jew to drift with the mainstream in the world of opportunism, and to become rootless, trivial, and alienated; that it is still possible for the Jew to assert himself in his Jewishness through an autonomous decision and a free act. The National Hillel Faculty Program is a commendable attempt to recognize this fact and to give it community significance and direction.

With respect to the study of Jewish subjects taught by Jewish scholars, a notable and wholesome change has quietly come about. Although it has taken years, American colleges and universities have at last shown a willingness to follow the example set by Harvard with the appointment of Professor Wolfson. Supported by the B'nai B'rith Hillel Foundations, the Hebrew Culture Foundation, the National Foundation for Jewish Culture, and private resources, chairs in Jewish studies have been opening up all over the United States. A great many more such chairs, or even departments, could be established if there were sufficient support from the Jewish community.

There is now widespread recognition that the Hebrew Scriptures ought to be studied, not only as a preface to the New Testament, but also on its own terms, within its own complex and extensive provenance. It is also now widely believed that the New Testament cannot be understood unless weight is given to the fact that, except for Luke, all its writers were Jews who had been brought up with Jewish ways of thinking, feeling, and hoping; and so the conclusion is inescapable that the New Testament reflects solid blocks of Hebraic thought, the key to which must be found in the Hebrew Scriptures, the Hebrew language, and Jewish history. Now, for these studies the Jewish scholar may be at least as well qualified as his Christian colleague, for the Jewish scholar will be unencumbered by the demands of Christian assumptions and dogmas. These new approaches to biblical studies represent nothing short of a revolution, for which we have been waiting for many centuries. And this new attitude to Jewish scholarship must flow over from biblical studies to all other aspects of Jewish culture, which thus assume an interest and a dignity they never before had.

But the Jewish cultural scene in the United States has been so tragically neglected that we are hardly prepared to take advantage of the academic breakthrough. We have already lost much time and many of our best minds and talents. Even in what we might assume to be our own vineyard, the Hebrew Scriptures, we find that responsible Christian scholarship has outdistanced Jewish scholarship; and a considerable body of Christian work on the Old Testament and its thought has been done in such a spirit that it might have been done by Jewish scholars and thinkers. Our own vineyard we have not kept. From the standpoint of Jewish learning and culture, we have, I am afraid, witnessed a wind, and an earthquake, and a fire.

But after the fire, we know there came "a still, small voice," and this is all we need, if we would only do and listen.

The American Jewish community spends large sums of money on philanthropic causes. A study conducted by the Survey Research Center at the University of Michigan shows that Jews give substantially more to religious and charitable causes than does any other group, even after one adjusts for their higher income. In 1962 the Federation of Jewish Philanthropies of New York City raised over $20 million for the maintenance of its 116 local medical and social-service agencies. The Federation in three months raised $67 million toward its building fund. Among the contributions to this fund were ten gifts of one million dollars or more. It is estimated that American Jews contribute approximately $250 million annually to Jewish causes. Now, one million dollars can be a *permanent* endowment of three chairs in Jewish studies. A fund of ten million dollars could support *permanently* some thirty such chairs. I am sure that the money being spent on the building of new synagogues and temples, new Jewish homes for the aged, new Jewish hospitals and other institutions, is all for good causes. But what is the point if the Jews of the next generation will be like most of the Jewish intellectuals one finds today on our campuses —men who no longer have the remotest connection with any aspect of Jewish life or institutions?

In 1960, a single agency, the America-Israel Cultural Foundation, raised $1.2 million in the United States for the support of music, theater, dance, art, and literature in Israel. The Foundation is certainly worthy of this—and even greater—support. But how much did we, as a community, spend on the support of Jewish music, theater, dance, art, and literature in the United States?

Although Jews are only about three percent of the population, Jewish students are probably seven percent of the college population. Some eighty per cent of the Jews of college age are college students, and, at the rate we have been moving in education, we may expect that in a few years almost every adult Jew will be a college graduate. Jews may be educated citizens but ignorant *as Jews*. We must spend much more than we do on our Jewish community and congregational schools; we must give much more ample support to all Jewish cultural agencies. But we must make a major attack on the problem of Jewish education on the American university level. "It is too late," said Thoreau, "to be studying Hebrew; it is more important to understand even the slang of today." Thoreau could afford to say this, for he was not a Jew. But, for American Jews, the only thing that it is too late to do is to delay making provision for the study of Hebrew and Hebrew literature, Yiddish, and Jewish thought, history, and life. To this end, we must support every aspect of traditional and creative Jewish culture. We must give increased support to the Hillel Foundations so that they may attract and be able to serve the spiritual and cultural interests of the Jewish students and the thousands of faculty members of our colleges and universities. The organized American Jewish community must act as a Johnny Appleseed and go up and down the land to plant the seeds of Jewish learning. For the land is, at long last, receptive of the seed, and we have the seed in providential abundance, and we wait only for the sower and the sowing.

V

We must admit to ourselves that we have no alternative. Assimilated Jewish intellectuals will undoubtedly say that we talk nonsense, but we can answer them with words from Dostoevski's *Crime and Punishment:* "Talk nonsense but talk your own nonsense. . . . To go wrong in one's way is better than to go right in someone else's."

We must apply to ourselves as American Jews what John Stuart Mill wrote in 1859 about culture and individuality in a democratic society:

The circumstances which surround different classes and individuals, and shape their characters, are daily becoming more assimilated. Formerly, different ranks, different neighbourhoods, different trades and professions, lived in what might be called different worlds; at present to a great degree in the same. Comparatively speaking, they now read the same things, listen to the same things, see the same things, go to the same places, have their hopes and fears directed to the same objects, have the same rights and liberties, and the same means of asserting them. Great as are the differences of position which remain, they are nothing to those which have ceased. And the assimilation is still proceeding. . . . Every extension of education promotes it because education brings people under common influences, and gives them access to the general stock of facts and sentiments. Improvement in the means of communication promotes it, by bringing the inhabitants of distant places into personal contact, and keeping up a rapid flow of changes of residence between one place and another. The increase of commerce and manufactures promotes it, by diffusing more widely the advantages of easy circumstances, and by opening all objects of ambition, even the highest, to general competition, whereby the desire of rising becomes no longer the character of a particular class, but of all classes. A more powerful agency than even all these, in bringing about a general similarity among mankind, is the complete establishment, in this and other free countries, of the ascendancy of public opinion in the State. . . .

The combination of all these causes forms so great a mass of influences hostile to Individuality, that it is not easy to see how it can stand its ground. It will do so with increasing difficulty, unless the intelligent part of the public can be made to feel its value. If the claims of Individuality are ever to be asserted, the time is now while much is wanting to complete the enforced assimilation.

The time is *now,* not 1859. With the American community interested in furthering American culture, Jewish assimilation can go incalculably farther and faster. We cannot undo our past neglect and mistakes, nor can we hope to complete the work before us, but we know from our tradition that *we are not free to neglect our task.* By devoting our energies to the work before us, we shall not love America less, but shall love God more, for God's mandate to man was to live in such a way that "human development in its richest variety" shall take place. This is the American promise—and the opportunity for American Jews.

BENJAMIN M. KAHN

18. Leadership and the Jewish Community

ACCORDING TO THE Talmud, Rabbi Joshua ben Per-
ahyah, head of the *Bet Din,* said, "At first, that is, before I was
elected to head the Court, I would have thrown to the lions anyone who had advised me to assume such a position of leadership.
Now that I occupy it, however, I would throw into boiling water
anyone who would suggest that I resign." [1]

I

What are the qualities of leadership? What is the alchemy that
makes a man a leader of his generation? Is election to high office
automatically a sign of leadership, or is leadership a consequence
of inborn talent, of "charisma," a gift of nature or of grace? Does
the leader create the climate of his age, or is he merely its product?

Thomas Carlyle, in his famous definition of the hero (that is,
the leader), expressed his conviction that the work of the world is
accomplished through the heroes, or natural leaders. "Universal
history, the history of what man has accomplished in this world, is
at bottom the history of the great men who have worked here.
They were the modellers, patterns, creators of whatsoever the
general mass of men continued to do or attain." [2] For Carlyle,
heroes are sent to us, and we have to follow them without question
—a doctrine uncomfortably reminiscent of the cult of the *Fuehrer*.

The noted sociologist Max Weber advances a similar theory,

though in modified form. He maintains that the charismatic leader derives his mandate from the will of the people whose duty it is to recognize his exceptional powers and qualifications and to follow him. Yet Weber qualifies this definition by adding that charismatic leadership has to be balanced with "rational routinization": ideas have to be adaptable to the mechanics of institutions and material interests. These serve as a system of checks and balances to limit and control the power and authority of the leader.[3]

Still another theory of leadership is developed in a special issue of the journal *Daedalus,* which is devoted to an analysis of the ideals of leadership. According to this theory, the leader arises as a major innovator in a counterplay of social and historical circumstances. Leadership must be studied and understood in its interaction with the social and political organization which the leader founds or transforms, with special attention to the psychological appeals and political sanctions that give leader and organization a hold on their mass following.[4] The leader must therefore possess three significant charismatic qualifications: extraordinary powers of vision and the ability to communicate it; exceptional powers of practical leadership and mechanics of organization; and a sense of mission, a conviction of the rightness of his cause and of his having been chosen to lead it.[5]

II

Can the nature and function of leadership in the Jewish community be captured in the same categories? How has leadership been conceived and viewed by the Jewish people? Are there any distinctive qualities which the Jewish people sought to find in its leadership in the past?

One of the qualifications of leadership may indeed be a leader's conviction that he was chosen for his task. Yet Moses and the prophets continually questioned their own qualifications and eligibility for leadership. They felt unworthy of the call, unequipped to fulfill the role assigned to them. They tried to draw back from a divinely proffered role or power because they sensed that the power inherent in leadership harbors the seeds of corruption—by tempting them to compete with the One who alone can be sovereign and is to lead men.

Nor did the prophets demonstrate significant organizing skills or powers of practical leadership. They did not act as if they knew that the fastest way to lose a friend is to tell him what you really think of him. Not only were they not popular—they were masters of unpopularity. Yet, generations later, their ideas were, in Weber's phrase, routinized in the thought-patterns and institutions of rabbinic Judaism.

Here we can discover a significant and characteristic facet of the biblical view of leadership. True leadership does not depend on the success or failure of the leader's mission. In one of his essays, Buber points out that biblical leadership differs significantly from the conventional ways in which leadership is defined.[6] In the Bible, the leader is usually weak and humble. He need not possess power and authority, because the ideas he represents carry their own power and authority. In biblical terms, says Buber, the leader usually is a failure rather than a success. Yet failure does not matter to him. What matters is his goal, his conviction that he is fulfilling God's purpose which will ultimately win out, regardless of whether he himself is successful in his own day.

> When we consider the history of Moses, . . . we see that his life consists of one failure after another. . . . True, Moses brought the people out of Egypt; but each stage of this leadership is a failure. Whenever he comes to deal with this people, he is defeated by them, let God ever so often interfere and punish them. And the real history of this leadership is . . . the history of the wandering in the desert. The personal history of Moses' own life, too, does not point back to his youth and to what grew out of it; it points beyond, to death, to the death of the unsuccessful man, whose work, it is true, survives him, but only in new defeats, new disappointments, and continual new failures—and yet his work survives also in a hope which is beyond all these failures.[7]

Jewish tradition has also shown a healthy skepticism about the qualifications on which a claim for leadership could be based. Its spokesmen were keenly aware of the relativity of such claims. A Hasid once asked Rabbi Bunam, the great Hasidic leader: "The

Talmud states that God showed Adam each generation and then its leaders. Why didn't He do it in reverse order?" Rabbi Bunam answered, "Had God shown Adam the leaders first, Adam would have said, 'Should such a man as Bunam be a leader?' But when Adam saw the generations first, he said that 'in such a generation even Bunam is worthy to be a leader.' " [8]

The same awareness of the relativity of leadership standards is also illustrated by the talmudic interpretation of the biblical verse, "Noah was a righteous man in his generation." [9] Why does the phrase not simply describe Noah as a righteous man instead of adding the qualifying phrase, "in his generation"? The Talmud says that Noah, had he lived in the days of Abraham, would not have been recognized as a righteous man in comparison with the patriarch. In his own generation, however—a time of violence and corruption, bereft of men of integrity and distinction—even Noah could be considered a *tzaddik*. "As the leader, so the generation"— and, one may add, vice versa.

III

What, then, has leadership meant in Jewish history? How has it functioned in the past? In what ways can the experience of our people enlarge our view of the problem of leadership in the Jewish community of today?

When the Jewish people returned to Palestine after the Babylonian exile, its leadership was transferred from priest to king until the scholar, called the *nasi* ("prince"), who functioned as the presiding officer of the *Bet Din,* emerged as the recognized spiritual and legal authority. By the end of the first century B.C.E., the institution of the *Bet Din* had control over internal Jewish affairs. The *nasi* appointed judges, enforced decisions of the Court, and supervised the schools and all other institutions of the Jewish community.

When the center of Jewish life was shifted to Babylonia, two types of leadership emerged. The secular leader of the Jewish community of Babylonia was the *Resh Galuta,* the exilarch, usually appointed by the king. He possessed all the trappings of royalty; an escort of horsemen accompanied him, heralds proclaimed his approach through the streets, he appointed judges and collected taxes; and to all intents and purposes he was ruler of a Jewish *imperium in imperio*.[10]

Coexisting with him was the *gaon* ("the exalted one"), the head of the academy, the spiritual leader of the Jews. His hegemony was recognized not only in Babylonia but in all parts of the Jewish world, with which he kept in touch by a voluminous correspondence.

Divided leadership, however, is usually a seedbed of conflict. The two leaders frequently clashed because each felt that the other was infringing upon his domain. The conflict between the two offices reached a peak in the eighth-century quarrel between Saadyah Gaon and the exilarch, David ben Zakkai.[11] Their bitter struggle for supremacy split the Jewish community and became a public scandal. Saadyah was exiled for eight years before peace was restored.

This conflict marked the beginning of the end of the great Babylonian Jewish community. As it began to decline in importance, the center of Jewish life was shifting westward to Spain. Initially, secular and spiritual leadership in the Spanish Jewish community was not bifurcated. During the reign of Caliph Abd Ar-Rahman III, the functions of the exilarch and the gaon were reunited in the person of Hasdai ibn Shaprut (917–970), with whom Jewish life in Europe emerged from obscurity. Hasdai was a court physician, confidant of the Caliph, and his advisor. He served as minister of foreign affairs and represented the Caliph in negotiations with foreign kings and ambassadors. State visitors from other countries were first received by Hasdai, who interrogated them about the state of the Jews in their countries. Hasdai corresponded with the Khazars, the eighth-century Black Sea converts to Judaism. He helped ameliorate the condition of the Jews in southern France and made representations to the court of Constantine to avert a pogrom in the Byzantine Empire. And withal, he was a distinguished patron of learning who brought scholars to his country, supported them, founded an academy, and reestablished Jewish studies in the West. Under his aegis, scholarship became the hallmark of the Jewish community of Spain.

A generation later, we encounter another fascinating personality, Samuel ibn Nagdela (993-1056), affectionately known in Jewish tradition as Shmuel Ha-Nagid, "Samuel the Prince." Like Hasdai, he combined political and spiritual leadership. As vizier to King Habbus of Granada and subsequently to his son, King Badis, he managed virtually all the affairs of state and on occasion led the army in the field. He is reported to have written poetry in the midst of military action on the eve of a battle, and he produced and published Hebrew verses to celebrate victory. At the same time, he was the author of a dictionary of biblical Hebrew and a distinguished talmudist who himself presided over the academy. He set up a magnificent library, imported sets of the Talmud from Babylonia, employed scribes to copy texts, and supported needy scholars.

Both Hasdai and Samuel represented the ideal of Jewish leadership. They were civil and political leaders of the Jewish community, yet were integrated into the wider community. Successful leaders in public affairs, they were at the same time steeped in Jewish learning and tradition and dedicated to Jewish values and scholarship.

Few leaders in Jewish history have followed in their tradition. We have had important secular leadership. We have had great spiritual leadership. But both roles, with very few significant exceptions, were not combined again in one person.

One such exception was a fascinating personality of the sixteenth century whose name is virtually unknown despite the fact that he was an outstanding Jew of his time. His name was Joseph of Rosheim, a town in Alsace. To his people, he was familiarly known as Josel, "Commander of the Jews." [12]

Josel was first appointed by the communities of lower Alsace as their civil representative; eventually he became the spokesman for all of German Jewry, from whose affection and confidence he derived his authority. For forty years he traveled throughout the country, pleading the cause of his people before emperors, kings, princes, and bishops. He fought against trials for trumped-up charges of ritual murder, obtained freedom for Jews condemned to death, brought about the recall of expulsion orders, and secured privileges for his brethren as well as relief from economic restrictions.

At the same time, he did not have to turn to the rabbis and spiritual leaders for guidance when Judaism had to be defended against slander and attack. He himself was conversant with the whole range of Jewish literature. When Martin Luther called on Christians to avenge the blood of Christ by destroying the synagogues and Jewish homes, when he asked them to forbid religious instruction, deny Jews the right to travel, and eventually to expel them, Josel himself refuted and rebutted Luther's diatribes against the Jews.[13] He successfully presented to the government the case for the Jewish people and their right to remain in Germany and to live without interference.

Another exception is a man in our own time who represented the ideal of Jewish leadership, Rabbi Leo Baeck (1873–1956). He was a modern rabbi, a teacher, an outstanding scholar who produced a number of significant works. Yet, at the same time, he was the leading spokesman for Judaism and the Jewish community in pre-Hitler Germany. When the Nazis came to power in 1933 and Jewish life and survival began to be in jeopardy, the Jewish community called him to the presidency of the *Reichsvertretung der deutschen Juden,* the Representative Council of German Jews, foisted upon the Jewish community by the Nazis in order to speed Jewish emigration, organize relief, and supervise Jewish education. He persistently refused offers of refuge in other countries. As late as 1939 he escorted a group of Jewish children to England, and though they implored him to remain, he returned to Germany where he continued to lead his people until he himself was deported to Theresienstadt. There he lectured to his fellow prisoners, who crowded into his barracks to listen to him in the secret hours of the night. "They would listen and they ceased being numbers and once again became human beings." [14]

Baeck combined in himself the quintessential qualities of leadership: statesmanship in practical affairs and political prowess, but also—and even more important—scholarship, commitment, creativity, dedication.

IV

Notwithstanding these significant exceptions, however, the leadership of the Jewish people since the Middle Ages has generally been bifurcated. The rabbi–scholar inherited the role of the religious–spiritual leader; the role of the secular–political leader was taken over by the *Hofjude* in Germany and the *shtadlan* in eastern Europe. The latter was usually a man of wealth and influence; he functioned as a spokesman of the people before the rulers but was not necessarily Jewishly informed or endowed with the qualifications for intellectual or spiritual leadership. And yet it seems significant that the names we remember from European Jewish history are not those of *Hofjuden* and *shtadlanim,* but the names of the spiritual leaders—the Besht, the Vilna Gaon, Leo Baeck.

V

What relevance do these historical data have for the leadership of the Jewish community in our country and time?

Qualifications for leadership today rarely resemble or approximate the standards exemplified by the way in which the great leaders of the past combined exceptional skills in practical affairs with informed and committed leadership in matters of the spirit. A few rabbis occupy positions of leadership in Jewish organizations, but their number is small and their influence is circumscribed. Vice versa, some lay leaders can speak with authority of both the Jewish tradition and the Jewish people; they qualify as heirs of Hasdai, Samuel, and Josel of Rosheim.

Numerous leaders of the Jewish community today, however, are among those who, in Solomon Goldman's words, "plead for causes but do not incarnate them." [15] They have risen to leadership on the basis of civic achievement, social status, or wealth, rather than by virtue of their knowledge of Torah, their love for Judaism, their concern for the whole of the Jewish people, their devotion to the task of safeguarding the creative continuity and growth of the Jewish value heritage.

The Jewish community has been preoccupied with fund-raising for communal and overseas needs to such an extent, that the presidencies of fund-raising agencies have frequently become the key positions for leadership in the Jewish community. To be sure, fund-raising for the defense of Jewish life and rights throughout the world, for relief and reconstruction, for the support of Israel, was and continues to be a crucial priority in Jewish life. To meet these needs, Jewish federations and welfare funds in the United States have raised more than three and a half billion dollars in the past 25 years—a brilliant record unparalleled in the history of humanitarian endeavor. Yet, in all these years, only pittances have been provided by our communities for the support of Jewish education and cultural concerns. More specifically, numerous congregations throughout the country have erected magnificent edifices for themselves and their young, but have rarely increased their school budgets sufficiently to improve the quality of Jewish education provided in these new facilities. The fact that until recently no school of Jewish social work has existed in this country is a further example. A person who wanted to be trained for this form of service to the Jewish community had no institution in which he could not only learn social-work techniques and principles but also study the history, the tradition, and the life-patterns of the very people whom he wanted to serve. The creative survival of Judaism in America requires a leadership that will call our community to the task of building a *s'yag la'Torah,* the institution that can stimulate the Jew to seek greater self-knowledge and deeper commitment.

I am further concerned that many community leaders are not committed to *k'lal Yisrael,* the concept of the unity of the Jewish community and of the Jewish people. The history of American Jewry is a record of the failure of repeated efforts to unite it— witness the Board of Delegates of American Israelites in the second half of the nineteenth century, or the American Jewish Conference which, organized in 1943, had hardly more than a "shadowy existence" [16] until it was dissolved in 1949. Granted that there are several relatively effective endeavors to unify and coordinate the efforts of a few agencies in areas of common interest—the Synagogue Council of America, the Council of Jewish

Federations and Welfare Funds, the National Jewish Community Relations Advisory Council, the Conference of Presidents of Major Jewish Organizations—granted, too, that American Jews have been able to unite in the face of emergencies, as they did in May and June of 1967. The question is still, Can we not come together, not motivated by crises and emergencies, but in order to strengthen Judaism? We desperately need leaders who possess a vision of Jewish unity and of pluralism within that unity—men who can lead American Jewry in the direction of a democratically constituted, organic Jewish community that will negate and overcome the rivalries, headline-hunting and self-seeking power thrusts of organizations and agencies. We need leaders who will help construct a representative instrumentality that can take action and speak in one voice on matters of common Jewish concern on behalf of the American Jewish community as a whole—on the relations of the Jewish community to the non-Jewish community, on overseas problems and needs of the Jewish people, on Soviet Jewry, on the State of Israel. Above all, we require a leadership that is committed to the development and guardianship of standards for Jewish organizational life based upon a hierarchy of values that can capture the idealism and retain the loyalty of coming generations.

VI

Is the role of the Jewish student leader on campus and in the Hillel Foundation different from the role of the leaders of the Jewish community off campus? Is it not equally vital that the student leader, too, be knowledgeable in Jewish matters, that he know the life- and thought-patterns of the Jewish people—its experiences, its history, its language, and its faith? Can there be any significant leadership on the student level unless it is committed to Jewish survival—survival not as an end in itself, but as a vehicle for the transmission, to other Jews and the wider academic community, of an understanding of the value-heritage and stance which the leader himself should exemplify? Can a Jewish student truly be a leader unless he is convinced of the rightness of his cause, the validity of his tradition, the significance of its ideas, the survival values of the group he has chosen to lead? And can he be a leader unless he follows the example set by the officers of the Israeli Army during the Six-Day War? Twenty-five per cent of the casualties occurred among the officers because they had no word for "advance." The order was *Aharai!*—"After me!"

According to the Midrash,[17] the ancient Hebrews, on their way to Palestine after generations of slavery in Egypt, cut cedar trees in order to obtain the lumber they needed to build the Sanctuary in the wilderness. The rabbis asked, "Where did they find full-grown trees in the desert?" Their answer was that when Jacob traversed the wilderness on his way to Egypt many generations before that time, he planted little cedar saplings, so that his descendants on their return to their own land would find full-grown trees with which to build the Sanctuary.

This is the enduring task of leadership in the Jewish community and the Hillel Foundation: to plant the seeds for the sanctuary of the spirit that must symbolize the Jewish community of tomorrow.

Notes

The transliteration of Hebrew names and terms follows *The Standard Jewish Encyclopedia,* ed. by Cecil Roth (New York, 1962). Biblical sources were quoted in accordance with the translation published by the Jewish Publication Society of America, except where the authors preferred their own translation.

1. FREEDOM AND IDENTITY: THE CHALLENGE OF MODERNITY

1. Israel Friedlaender, *Past and Present* (New York, 1961), p. 144.
2. Erich Fromm, *Escape From Freedom* (New York, 1941).
3. Allen Wheelis, *The Quest for Identity* (New York, 1958), p. 19.
4. John Dewey, *Freedom and Culture* (New York, 1939), p. 5.
5. Edmond Cahn, *The Moral Decision* (Bloomington, Ind., 1955), pp. 9–10.
6. Ahad Ha'am, *Selected Essays* (Philadelphia, 1936), pp. 171–194.
7. Bernard Berenson, *Rumor and Reflection* (New York, 1952). Cf. pp. 115 ff., 145 ff., 309 ff.
8. Sol Liptzin, ed. and trans., *Peretz* (New York, 1947), pp. 266–275.
9. Karl Shapiro, *Poems of a Jew* (New York, 1958), p. 4.
10. David Frishman (1863–1922). The poem is published in an English translation by Maurice Samuel in Leo W. Schwarz, *A Golden Treasury of Jewish Literature* (New York, 1937), pp. 600–603.

3. ON THE MEANING OF JEWISH CULTURE IN OUR TIME

In the preparation of this paper, I have drawn on a number of sources, among them especially Solomon Goldman's *The Book of Books,* Leo Baeck's *Wege im Judentum,* and several essays by Trude Weiss-Rosmarin in *Jewish Survival.* Special indebtedness to these authors is expressed even where the influence of their material is not identified in direct quotation.

1. Trude Weiss-Rosmarin, *Jewish Survival* (New York, 1949), p. 107.

2. See Karl Schwarz, "The Hebrew Impact on Western Art," *The Hebrew Impact on Western Civilization,* ed. by Dagobert Runes (New York, 1951), pp. 405–504.

3. Friedrich Delitzsch, *Babel und Bibel* (Leipzig, 1902); see also *Die grosse Taeuschung* (Stuttgart, 1920).

4. Richard Wagner, *Ueber das Judentum in der Musik* (Leipzig, 1869).

5. Quoted in Herbert Howarth, "Jewish Art and the Fear of the Image," *Commentary,* February 1950, p. 143.

6. I Kings 5:6.

7. Martin Buber, *Juedische Kuenstler,* quoted by Herbert Howarth, *loc. cit.*

8. Ernst Simon, "Notes on Jewish Wit," *Jewish Frontier,* 15, October 1948.

9. Hans Kohn, *The Idea of Nationalism* (New York, 1944), pp. 30–33.

10. See Hans Jonas, "Heidegger and Theology," *The Phenomenon of Life* (New York, 1966), pp. 236–238.

11. Solomon Goldman, *The Book of Books* (Philadelphia, 1948), p. 15.

12. *Ibid.,* p. 16.

13. Hayim N. Bialik, "Revealment and Concealment in Language," trans. by Jacob Sloan, *Commentary,* February 1950, p. 171.

14. "Always we are chasing words, and always words recede. . . . The greatest experiences are those for which we have no expression. . . . To become aware of the ineffable is to part company with words. The essence . . . of human experience lies beyond the limits of language." Abraham J. Heschel, *Man Is Not Alone* (Philadelphia, 1951), pp. 15–16.

Cf. also Joseph Conrad, *Lord Jim* (New York, 1900): "Are not our

lives too short for that full utterance which through all our stammer-
ings is, of course, our only and abiding intention? I have given up
expecting those last words whose rings, if they could only be pronounced, would shake both heaven and earth. There is never time to
say our last word—the last words of our love, of our desire, faith,
remorse, submission, revolt."

15. Bialik, *op. cit.*, p. 175.

16. Several factors may account for this fact: the Oriental emphasis
on singing, on the man-made rather than machine-made music; the
fact that all music, in its beginnings, is associated with prayer, that is,
with words; the injunction against the use of musical instruments after
the destruction of the Temple; the lack of opportunity for instrumental
training for the medieval Jew; the development of the "oral" tradition
and its transmission through word and voice, etc.

17. See below, Ernst Simon, chap. 11, p. 232.

18. Ludwig Lewisohn, *The American Jew* (New York, 1950), pp.
25–26.

19. Quoted in T. W.-Rosmarin, *op. cit.*, p. 126.

20. Solomon Goldman, *op. cit.*, p. 23. Cf. also Goethe's *Faust*
(I, 1):

> Dass ich erkenne, was die Welt
> Im Innersten zusammenhaelt.

21. Solomon Goldman, *op. cit.*, pp. 22–23.

22. I.e., Exod. 20:3–4; Deut. 4:25–31; 27:15.

23. Ps. 115. It is interesting to note that the production of images
was prohibited even if they were to be symbolic representations of the
true God. Otherwise, the biblical injunctions seem to prohibit only the
creation of idols, the symbolic representation of false gods. This seems
indicated by the fact that the use of other imagery was permitted: the
Cherubim at the Ark, in the carpets of the Tent, the animal figures
supporting the Molten Sea (I Kings 7:44). During the Second Jewish
Commonwealth, the prohibition of imagery was extended to include
every kind of pictorial representation (Josephus, *Antiquities*, 17, 6 ff.).
Not even architectural ornaments were permitted.

This prohibition was modified in talmudic times, probably because
there was less danger of a relapse into idolatry. Rosh Hashanah 24A
(later codified in *Yoreh Deah* 141) lists three major regulations:

(a) Pictures of any kind can be made and used for scientific
purposes.

(b) Pictorial representations of animals and plants are always permissible.

(c) Other pictures are prohibited only if they are done in relief work [*haut relief*]. They are permitted (with the exception of sun, moon, stars, and planets) if they are drawn, painted, or done in embroidery or tapestry work. [However, even under these conditions, reproductions of the Temple, any of its parts, or its sacred vessels remained forbidden.]

Synagogues, in which no danger of idolatry existed, could contain pictures of all kinds except those of people, bas-reliefs, and "columnary" statues. In the home, even painted or drawn pictures of human beings were permitted.

24. Solomon Goldman, *op. cit.,* pp. 19–20.

25. T. W.-Rosmarin, *op. cit.,* p. 104.

26. Leo Baeck, "Two World Views Compared," *The Pharisees and Other Essays* (New York, 1947), pp. 129–130.

27. Isa. 57:14.

28. T. W.-Rosmarin, *op. cit.,* p. 104.

29. Leo Baeck, *The Essence of Judaism* (New York, 1948), pp. 23–24.

30. *Avot* V, 25.

31. See below, chap. 9, Note 10.

32. T. W. Huxley, "Romanes Lectures," reprinted by Julian Huxley in *Touchstones for Ethics.* Quoted by George G. Simpson, *The Meaning of Evolution* (New Haven, 1950), pp. 298–299.

33. Maurice Samuel, *The Gentleman and the Jew* (New York, 1950), pp. 30–31.

4. A FAITH FOR MODERNS: THE MEANING OF
GOD FOR THE CONTEMPORARY JEW

1. F. S. C. Northrop, *The Taming of the Nations* (New York, 1952), p. 216.

2. Ludwig Feuerbach, *The Essence of Christianity* (New York, 1967), p. xxxix.

3. William E. Hocking, *Living Religions and a World Faith* (New York, 1940), p. 104.

4. Henry Nelson Wieman, *Methods of Private Religious Living* (New York, 1929), p. 53.

5. BETWEEN GOD AND MAN: THE MEANING OF
REVELATION FOR THE CONTEMPORARY JEW

1. Claude J. G. Montefiore, *A Rabbinic Anthology* (Philadelphia, 1960), p. xxvii.

2. *Mekhilta,* Bahodesh 4, ed. Lauterbach, II, 221.

3. Max Kadushin, *The Rabbinic Mind* (New York, 1952), p. 312.

4. *Midrash Tehillim* 1,1; Buber 3a.

5. *Guide of the Perplexed,* II, xxxiii.

6. Gershom Sholem, *Major Trends in Jewish Mysticism* (New York, 1954), p. 9.

7. Quoted in David Philipson, *The Reform Movement in Judaism* (New York, 1931), pp. 355–356.

8. Robert Gordis, *Judaism for the Modern Age* (New York, 1955), pp. 159–161.

9. Jakob Petuchowski, *Hibbert Journal,* July 1959, p. 359.

10. Gordis, *ibid.*

11. Gen. 12:1 and 4; quoted from *The Torah: A New Translation* (Philadelphia, 1962).

12. Gen. 28:13.

13. Exod. 3:3 and 6.

14. Franz Rosenzweig, *Judah ha-Levi, Hymnen und Gedichte,* 2d ed. (Berlin, 1927), p. 196.

7. THE JEWISH IMAGE OF THE JEW: ON THE MEANING OF
JEWISH DISTINCTIVENESS

1. Nahum N. Glatzer, *Franz Rosenzweig: His Life and Thought* (New York, 1953), pp. 18–19.

2. "Reflections on the Jewish Question," *Mid-Century,* ed. Harold Ribalow (New York, 1955), p. 398.

3. "Who Are the Jews?", *The Jews: Their History, Culture, and Religion,* ed. Louis Finkelstein (New York, 1949), p. 1158.

4. Kurt Lewin, *Resolving Social Conflicts* (New York, 1948), p. 180.

5. *Ibid.,* p. 183.

6. *Kuzari,* Part I, pp. 27 ff.

7. *Das Judentum und seine Geschichte* (Breslau, 1910), chap. 3.

8. *Dialogues of A. N. Whitehead* (New York, 1954), p. 137.

9. Morris Adler, "What Is a Jew?", *Harper's Magazine,* January 1964 (reprinted in *May I Have a Word With You?,* by Rabbi Morris Adler, compiled by Goldie Adler and Lily Edelman [New York, 1967], p. 85).

Cf. also, "The peculiar genius of Judaism is expressed not in creeds, like the Nicene or the Chalcedonian, but in a lawbook, the *Mishnah.*" W. D. Davies, "Torah and Dogma," *Harvard Theological Review,* 61, April 1968, p. 93.

10. Arthur J. Lelyveld, "The Application of Jewish Values to Creative Living for the American Jew" (mimeographed), Jewish Welfare Board Biennial Convention, Washington, D.C., April 1958.

11. Leo Baeck, *The Essence of Judaism,* ed. J. Kauffman Verlag (Frankfurt am Main, 1936), p. 54.

12. Plato, "Crito," *Dialogues of Plato,* Pocket Library No. 7 (New York, 1955), pp. 55–62.

13. Cf. Hayim Greenberg, "The Universalism of the Chosen People," *The Inner Eye* (New York, 1953), pp. 3–56.

14. Mordecai M. Kaplan, *The Future of the American Jew* (New York, 1948), p. 219.

15. Moses Mendelssohn, *Jerusalem and Other Jewish Writings,* trans. and ed. by Alfred Jospe (New York, 1969), pp. 65–66.

16. Hayim Greenberg, *op. cit.*

17. *Guide of the Perplexed,* II, 25; see also University of Chicago Press edition (1963), ed. and trans. by Strauss and Pines, p. 329.

18. *Midrash Rabbah,* Num. 14:10.

19. *Tanna d'be Eliahu,* p. 162.

20. Will Herberg, *Judaism for Modern Man* (Philadelphia, 1951), p. 271.

21. Emil L. Fackenheim, "Can We Believe in Judaism Religiously?", *Commentary,* December 1948.

22. *Midrash Tehillim,* Ps. 9:17.

23. *Tanna d'be Eliahu,* p. 162.

24. Morris Joseph, *Judaism as Creed and Life* (London, 1925), p. 154.

25. Leo Baeck, *op. cit.,* pp. 55–57.

26. Nahum N. Glatzer, *op. cit.,* p. 243.

27. Quoted by Nahum N. Glatzer, *Faith and Knowledge: The Jew in the Medieval World* (Boston, 1963), p. xiv.

9. JUDAISM AS A SOURCE OF SOCIAL VALUES:
TRANSIENT ISMS AND ABIDING VALUES

1. Walt Whitman, *Leaves of Grass,* ed. E. Halloway (New York, 1942), p. 202.
2. Deut. 29:28.
3. Hayim Greenberg, *The Inner Eye* (New York, 1953), p. 78.
4. Cf. Arthur J. Lelyveld, "Values and Value-Stances," *Congress Bi-Weekly,* vol. 34, no. 7 (April 3, 1967), p. 5.
5. Susanne Langer, *Philosophy in a New Key* (Cambridge, Mass., 1942), p. 285: "The fact that very few of our words are purely technical and few of our images purely utilitarian, gives our lives a background of closely woven multiple meanings against which all conscious experiences and interpretations are measured."
6. Ludwig Lewisohn, *The Magic Word* (New York, 1950), p. 5: "The names of basic concepts in the kindred tongues of neighboring peoples . . . contain in their subtle but unmistakable shadings the whole character and the whole culture of the folk who have created and use them." See Arthur J. Lelyveld, *Atheism Is Dead* (Cleveland and New York, 1968), pp. 79 ff.
7. Greenberg, *op. cit.,* p. 85.
8. Philip Wheelwright, *The Burning Fountain* (Bloomington, Ind., 1959), pp. 25–29. Wheelwright makes a distinction between "expressive" or "depth" language and "steno-language" and defends "the ontological status of radical metaphor. That is to say, metaphor is a medium of riper, fuller knowing; not merely a prettification of the already given."
9. Lev. 19:2.
10. Lev. 22:32.
11. Isa. 1:12–14.
12. Micah 6:8.
13. *Avot* I:17.
14. E.g., Exod. 23:9.
15. Micah 4:4.
16. Cf. Ben Azzai's comment on Gen. 5:1 and the Midrash Bereshit R. 24:7 (see Theodor's note *ad loc.*): "See that thou do not say, inasmuch as I have been despised, my fellow shall be despised with me; inasmuch as I have been cursed, my fellow shall be cursed with me. R. Tanhuma said, If thou doest this, reflect whom thou doest despise: 'In the image of God, He made him.'" This radical reversal

of the psychological mechanism of projection is found in the distinctive Jewish concept of *kedushah* and constitutes itself one of the primary distinctivenesses of Judaism. "You know the very being of the stranger, for you were strangers in the land of Egypt," *therefore* "the stranger you shall not oppress" (Exod. 23:9).

17. Miguel de Unamuno, *The Tragic Sense of Life* (New York, 1954), p. 12.

18. *Mishnah Sanhedrin* 4:5. Some texts include the words *mi-yisrael*, "of Israel." However, this perverts the meaning of the total passage, which is concerned with man and the unique individuality of every human being. Cf. *Avot de-Rabbi Natan*, beginning of chap. 31.

19. Martin Buber, *Israel and the World* (New York, 1948), p. 17.

20. For a fuller discussion of the contention that Marx's worldview is obsolete, see Arthur J. Lelyveld, *Atheism Is Dead*, chap. 6, pp. 85 ff.

21. Cf. *High Holiday Prayer Book* (Hartford, 1950), p. 147.

11. THE WAY OF THE LAW:
LAW AND OBSERVANCE IN JEWISH EXPERIENCE

1. *Rosh Hashanah* 27a; cf. *Y. Nedarim* III 5; 37d.
2. *Mishneh Torah*, Hilkhot Teshuvah 3:7, and RaBaD there.
3. Deut. 30:11.
4. Deut. 12:18; 16:11; 27:7; cf. Lev. 23:40.
5. Milton Steinberg, *Basic Judaism* (New York, 1947), p. 72.
6. Jer., chaps. 27 and 28.
7. *Ibid.*, chaps. 40–43.
8. Gen. 36:12.
9. *Selihot*, The Rabbinical Assembly of America (New York, 1964).
10. Efraim Oshri, *Divrei Efraim: Hidushei Halakhot Ubiurei Sugyoth Beshas* (with appendix, *Me'emek Habakhah;* New York, 1949).
11. Deut. 29:28.

11. THE WAY OF THE LAW:
SOME CRITERIA FOR MODERN JEWISH OBSERVANCE

A German version of the main contents of this essay appeared in the Swiss journal *Tradition und Erneuerung,* November 1967. The essay will also be included, in a somewhat different form, in the author's forthcoming book, *Heirs of the Pharisees.*

1. *B. Makkot,* 23b.
2. *Mishnah Kiddushin,* 1:9; Sifre R'eh, para. 59 (ed. Friedman, p. 87a).
3. Cf. Samuel Holdheim, *Ueber die Autonomie der Rabbinen* (Schwerin, 1843), pp. 15–17.
4. Cf. David Philipson, *The Reform Movement in Judaism* (New York, 1907), p. 491.
5. *Shabbat* 127a.
6. *Avot* 2:5.

11. THE WAY OF THE LAW:
JEWISH LAW AND THE WAYS OF JUDAISM IN OUR TIME

1. Jacob B. Agus, *The Evolution of Jewish Thought From Biblical Times to the Opening of the Modern Era* (London and New York, 1959), p. 416.

11. THE WAY OF THE LAW:
LAW AS LIVING DISCIPLINE—THE SABBATH AS PARADIGM

1. Cf. Samuel Belkin, *In His Image* (New York, 1960), pp. 20 ff.
2. M. M. Kasher, *Torah Shleymah,* vol. 16, p. 69, sect. 240. Cf. also note 240 and addendum, pp. 242 ff.
3. P. 114.
4. Deut. 8:11 ff.
5. Exod. 20:9–10.
6. *Shabbat* 73a.
7. I. Grunfeld, *The Sabbath: A Guide to Its Understanding and Observance* (London, 1954), p. 33.
8. Isa. 58:13.
9. *Shabbat* 113a–b.
10. P. Birnbaum, *High Holyday Prayer Book,* p. 363.
11. Found in the two versions of the Ten Commandments (Exod. 20:8 and Deut. 5:12, respectively). According to tradition, they are an inseparable unit. See Rashi, *ad loc.;* also *Y. Nedarim,* chap. 3, sect. 2.
12. P. 337.

13. Deut. 29:13–14.

14. *Shabbat* 146a, Shebuot 39b.

15. Rashi (Rabbi Solomon ben Isaac, 1040–1105), commentary on Deut. 26:16 and 27:9.

16. *Shabbat* 86b.

17. Num. 15:37.

18. David De Sola Pool, *The Traditional Prayer Book*, p. 251.

19. Chap. 12, "The Holy Deed."

20. Pool, *op. cit.*, p. 175.

21. Isa. 58:13.

22. *Shabbat* 118b–119a.

23. Isa. 58:13.

24. *Shabbat* 113a.

25. Ps. 104:1.

26. Ps. 34:9.

27. *Kuzari*, part 2, ch. 50.

28. Pool, *op. cit.*, p. 713.

29. Founder of Lurianic Kabalah (1534–1572).

30. Prolific poet and liturgist (b. 1560).

31. *Y. Shabbat,* chap. 15, sect. 3. Cf. also Philo, *Moses*, II, 3a.

32. Exod. 20:8.

33. Deut. 5:12.

34. Isa. 58:12.

35. Gen. 2:3.

36. Gen. 1:28, S. R. Hirsch, *Horeb* (ed. I. Grunfeld), vol. 1, p. 62, sect. 139.

37. *Shabbat* 88a.

38. Exod. 24:7.

39. *San.* 88a.

40. Exod. 31:16.

41. Pool, *op. cit.*, p. 385.

42. Exod. 19:6. See commentary of Moses Nachmanides (1195–1270), *ad loc.*

43. Pool, *op. cit.*, p. 329; selection taken from end of *Tamid* 37b.

12. ON THE MEANING OF PRAYER

1. Published in English as *Prayer: A Study in the History and Psychology of Religion,* trans. by S. McComb (New York, 1958).

2. Milton Steinberg, *Basic Judaism* (New York, 1947), p. 117.

3. Isa. 29:13–14.

13. THE AMERICAN JEWISH COMMUNITY—WHAT LIES AHEAD?

1. Evelyn Rossman, "Judaism in Northrup," *Commentary,* November 1957, pp. 390–391.

14. THE THREEFOLD REBELLION: SOME
    REFLECTIONS ON ISRAEL TODAY

1. Erich Fromm, *The Forgotten Language* (New York, 1951), p. 243.

2. Raphael Patai, *Cultures in Conflict,* Herzl Institute, Pamphlets, I (New York, 1958), p. 6.

3. Horace M. Kallen, *Utopians at Bay* (New York, 1958), p. 103.

4. Zohar Lev. 73a.

5. Joseph Badi, *Religion in Israel Today* (New York, 1959), p. 37.

18. LEADERSHIP AND THE JEWISH COMMUNITY

1. B. Talmud, *Menahot,* 109b.

2. Thomas Carlyle, *Heroes, Hero Worship, and the Heroic in History* (New York, 1910).

3. H. H. Gerth and C. Wright Mills, *Max Weber: Essays in Sociology* (New York, 1958), pp. 245–252.

4. *Daedalus: Journal of the American Academy of Arts and Sciences,* Summer 1968, p. 689.

5. *Ibid.,* p. 748.

6. Martin Buber, "Biblical Leadership," *Israel and the World, Essays in a Time of Crisis* (New York, 1963), pp. 119–133.

7. *Ibid.,* p. 125.

8. Quoted in L. I. Newman, *Hasidic Anthology* (New York, 1944), p. 217.

9. Gen. 6:9.

10. Cf. Cecil Roth, *Short History of the Jewish People* (London, 1948), pp. 151 ff.

11. Cf. Solomon Grayzel, *A History of the Jews* (Philadelphia, 1957), pp. 275 ff.

12. Cf. Selma Stern, *Josel of Rosheim, Commander of Jewry in the Holy Roman Empire of the German Nation* (Philadelphia, 1965).

13. *Ibid.*, pp. 190 ff.

14. Leo Baeck, *This People Israel: The Meaning of Jewish Existence* (Philadelphia, 1965), p. xiv.

15. Solomon Goldman, "American Jewish Leadership," *Crisis and Decision* (New York, 1938), p. 69.

16. Solomon Grayzel, *A History of Contemporary Jews* (Philadelphia, 1960), p. 149.

17. Louis Ginzberg, *Legends of the Jews* (Philadelphia, 1910–1911), vol. 2, p. 119; vol. 3, p. 164.

Contributors

IRA EISENSTEIN, Rabbi, Ph.D.; Chairman, Editorial Board, *Reconstructionist;* President, Jewish Reconstructionist Foundation; President, Reconstructionist Rabbinical College

HENRY A. FISCHEL, Rabbi, Ph.D., D.H.L.; Professor of Near Eastern Studies, Indiana University

NORMAN E. FRIMER, Rabbi, D.H.L.; National Coordinator, B'nai B'rith Hillel Foundations, New York Metropolitan Area; Director, B'nai B'rith Hillel Foundation at Brooklyn College

ROBERT GORDIS, Rabbi, Ph.D., D.D.; after serving as Rabbi of Temple Beth-El, Rockaway Park, N.Y., for many years, Dr. Gordis is now Professor of Religion, Temple University, Philadelphia, and Professor of Bible, The Jewish Theological Seminary of America

AVRAHAM HARMAN, B.A., D.H.L.; President, The Hebrew University, Jerusalem; former Ambassador of the State of Israel, Washington, D.C.

WILL HERBERG, Ph.D.; Professor of Philosophy, Drew University

MILTON HIMMELFARB, Editor, *American Jewish Yearbook,* and Contributing Editor, *Commentary*

RICHARD J. ISRAEL, Rabbi; Director, B'nai B'rith Hillel Foundation at Yale University

ALFRED JOSPE, Rabbi, Ph.D.; Director of Program and Resources, B'nai B'rith Hillel Foundations; Editor

BENJAMIN M. KAHN, Rabbi, D.H.L., L.H.D.; National Director, B'nai B'rith Hillel Foundations

MORDECAI M. KAPLAN, Rabbi, D.H.L.; Professor Emeritus, The Jewish Theological Seminary of America; Founder, Jewish Reconstructionist Movement; Author

MILTON R. KONVITZ, Ph.D.; Professor of Industrial and Labor Relations and Professor of Law, Cornell University

ARTHUR J. LELYVELD, Rabbi, D.D.; Rabbi, Fairmount Temple, Cleveland, Ohio; President, American Jewish Congress; formerly National Director, B'nai B'rith Hillel Foundations

MAURICE B. PEKARSKY (1905–1962), Rabbi, D.D.; Director, Department of Leadership Training, B'nai B'rith Hillel Foundations, and Director, B'nai B'rith Hillel Foundation at the University of Chicago

JAKOB J. PETUCHOWSKI, Rabbi, Ph.D.; Professor of Rabbinics and Gustave A. and Mamie W. Efroymson Professor of Theology, Hebrew Union College–Jewish Institute of Religion, Cincinnati

LOU H. SILBERMAN, Rabbi, D.H.L.; Hillel Professor of Jewish Thought and Literature, Vanderbilt University

ERNST SIMON, Ph.D.; Professor Emeritus of Education, The Hebrew University, Jerusalem

MANFRED VOGEL, Rabbi, Ph.D.; Associate Professor in the History and Literature of Religion, Northwestern University

MAURICE L. ZIGMOND, Rabbi, Ph.D., D.D.; New England Regional Hillel Director; Director, B'nai B'rith Hillel Foundation at Harvard University